JOURNAL FOR THE STUDY OF THE NEW TESTAMENT
SUPPLEMENT SERIES

50

Executive Editor, Supplement Series
David Hill

Publishing Editor
David E Orton

JSOT Press
Sheffield

George A. Kennedy

PERSUASIVE ARTISTRY

Studies in New Testament
Rhetoric in Honor of
George A. Kennedy

Edited by
Duane F. Watson

Journal for the Study of the New Testament
Supplement Series 50

Copyright © 1991 Sheffield Academic Press

Published by JSOT Press
JSOT Press is an imprint of
Sheffield Academic Press Ltd
The University of Sheffield
343 Fulwood Road
Sheffield S10 3BP
England

Printed on acid-free paper in Great Britain
by Billing & Sons Ltd
Worcester

British Library Cataloguing in Publication Data

Persuasive Artistry
 1. Christianity. Scriptures
 I. Watson, Duane F.   II. Kennedy, George A. (George
Alexander) *1928–*   III. Series
 225.6

ISSN 0143-5108
ISBN 1-85075-284-2

CONTENTS

PREFACE

It is well known in horticulture that crossing diverse strains of plants often yields a hybrid more vibrant than the parent strains. The same can be said of crossing diverse branches of knowledge. The integration of biblical and rhetorical studies has yielded the new hybrid of interpretation—rhetorical criticism. This integration is in significant measure due to the creative efforts of George A. Kennedy.

In the current explosion of knowledge it is often daring to venture into an area even closely related to our own speciality. How much more daring to venture into another field entirely! Dr Kennedy has bravely and successfully traversed the domain of biblical studies to chart new territory. He has provided many careful studies of ancient and Western rhetoric, and shown the place of that rhetoric in the formulation of the Bible and its earliest interpretations. As a part of his prolific literary output, to his *The Art of Persuasion in Greece* (Princeton, 1963), *Quintilian* (Twayne, 1969), and *The Art of Rhetoric in the Roman World: 300 BC–AD 300* (Princeton, 1972), he added three more significant works which touch more specifically upon biblical studies: *Classical Rhetoric and its Christian and Secular Tradition from Ancient to Modern Times* (Chapel Hill, 1980), *Greek Rhetoric under Christian Emperors* (Princeton, 1983), and *New Testament Interpretation through Rhetorical Criticism* (Chapel Hill, 1984).

Biblical studies is now awash in a flood of creativity in which rhetoric is a major part, thanks in part to the catalyst of the aforementioned works. The implications of rhetoric for the composition, structure, intent, purpose, situation, and message of biblical books are being investigated with fervor. Rhetoric is being successfully used in conjunction with literary criticism, linguistics, semantics, hermeneutics, sociology, psychology, structuralism, women's studies, and many more fields of knowledge.

The contributors to this volume have had the privilege either of studying with Dr Kennedy or of finding his work in rhetorical criticism and his classical studies challenging and useful for their own work. The volume is both a note of gratitude and a visible demonstration of the strength of the catalyst provided by Dr Kennedy. The range of topics covered is indicative of the viability and applicability of his work. The challenges posed by these essays foreshadow the role of his efforts in fomenting future rhetorical investigation.

Duane F. Watson

ABBREVIATIONS

Ancient Rhetorical Works

Brut.	Cicero, *Brutus*
De Doct. Chr.	Augustine, *De Doctrina Christiana*
De Or.	Cicero, *De Oratore*
Eloc.	Demetrius, *Elocutione*
Her.	*Rhetorica ad Herennium*
Inv.	Cicero, *De Inventione*
Opt. Gen.	Cicero, *De Optimo Genere*
Or.	Cicero, *Orator*
Part. Or.	Cicero, *De Partitione Oratoriae*
Phdr.	Plato, *Phaedrus*
Poet.	Aristotle, *Poetica*
Quint.	Quintilian, *Institutio Oratoria*
Rhet. ad Alex.	*Rhetorica ad Alexandrum*
Rhet.	Aristotle, *Rhetorica*
Subl.	Longinus, *De Sublime*
Top.	Aristotle, *Topica*
Top.	Cicero, *Oratorum Topica*

Modern Works

AB	Anchor Bible
AnBib	Analecta Biblica
ATR	*Anglican Theological Review*
BAGD	W. Bauer, W.F. Arndt, F.W. Gingrich, and F.W. Danker, *A Greek-English Lexicon of the New Testament*
BDF	F. Blass, A. Debrunner, and R.W. Funk, *A Greek Grammar of the New Testament*
BETL	Bibliotheca ephemeridum theologicarum lovaniensium
BEvT	Beiträge zur evangelischen Theologie
Bib	*Biblica*
BibB	Biblische Beiträge
BJRL	*Bulletin of the John Rylands University Library of Manchester*
BJS	Brown Judaic Studies

BZAW	Beihefte zur *ZAW*
CBQ	*Catholic Biblical Quarterly*
ConBNT	Coniectanea Biblica, New Testament
CP	*Classical Philology*
EBib	Etudes bibliques
EKKNT	Evangelisch-katholischer Kommentar zum Neuen Testament
EncJud	*Encyclopaedia Judaica* (1971)
ExpTim	*Expository Times*
FFNT	Foundations and Facets: New Testament
FRLANT	Forschungen zur Religion und Literatur des Alten und Neuen Testaments
GNC	Good News Commentary
HBC	J.L. Mays, *et al.* (eds.), *Harper's Bible Commentary*
HBD	P.J. Achtemeier, *et al.* (eds.), *Harper's Bible Dictionary*
HSC	Harvard Studies in Classical Philology
HTKNT	Herders theologischer Kommentar zum Neuen Testament
HTR	*Harvard Theological Review*
HUT	Hermeneutische Untersuchungen zur Theologie
ICC	International Critical Commentary
IDB	G.A. Buttrick (ed.), *Interpreter's Dictionary of the Bible*
IDBSup	Supplementary volume to *IDB*
Int	*Interpretation*
ISBE	G.W. Bromiley (ed.), *International Standard Bible Encyclopedia*
JAAR	*Journal of the American Academy of Religion*
JBL	*Journal of Biblical Literature*
JETS	*Journal of the Evangelical Theological Society*
JR	*Journal of Religion*
JSNT	*Journal for the Study of the New Testament*
JSNTSup	*Journal for the Study of the New Testament* Supplement Series
JTS	*Journal of Theological Studies*
KBANT	Kommentare und Beiträge zum Alten und Neuen Testament
LCL	Loeb Classical Library
LD	Lectio divina
LSJ	Liddell–Scott–Jones, *Greek–English Lexicon*
MeyerK	H.A.W. Meyer, Kritisch-exegetischer Kommentar über das Neue Testament
Neot	*Neotestamentica*
NovT	*Novum Testamentum*
NRT	*La nouvelle revue théologique*
NTAbh	Neutestamentliche Abhandlungen
NTL	New Testament Library
NTS	*New Testament Studies*
OGIS	W. Dittenberger (ed.), *Orientis Graeci Inscriptiones Selectae*
PhilR	*Philosophy and Rhetoric*
PMLA	*Proceedings of the Modern Language Association of America*

PW	Pauly–Wissowa, *Real-Encyclopädie der classischen Altertumswissenschaft*
QJS	*Quarterly Journal of Speech*
RAC	*Reallexikon für Antike und Christentum*
RE	*Realencyklopädie für protestantische Theologie und Kirche*
RevExp	*Review and Expositor*
RSQ	*Rhetoric Society Quarterly*
RSV	Revised Standard Version
SANT	Studien zum Alten und Neuen Testament
SBLDS	SBL Dissertation Studies
SBLSBS	SBL Sources for Biblical Study
SBLSS	SBL Semeia Studies
SBS	Stuttgarter Bibelstudien
SIG	W. Dittenberger (ed.), *Sylloge Inscriptionum Graecarum*
SJLA	Studies in Judaism in Late Antiquity
ST	*Studia theologica*
TLZ	*Theologische Literaturzeitung*
TDNT	G. Kittel and G. Friedrich (eds.), *Theological Dictionary of the New Testament*
TNTC	Tyndale New Testament Commentary
TSFBul	*Theological Students' Fellowship Bulletin*
TSK	*Theologische Studien und Kritiken*
TZ	*Theologische Zeitschrift*
UTB	Uni-Taschenbücher
VT	*Vetus Testamentum*
VTSup	*Vetus Testamentum*, Supplements
WBC	Word Biblical Commentary
WUNT	Wissenschaftliche Untersuchungen zum Neuen Testament
WW	*Word and World*
ZNW	*Zeitschrift für die neutestamentliche Wissenschaft*
ZTK	*Zeitschrift für Theologie und Kirche*

RHETORICAL CRITICISM AND THE PROPHETIC DISCOURSE*

Yehoshua Gitay

I

I imagine that the first reaction of biblical critics to the combination of rhetorical criticism and the prophetic discourse is to expect that I intend to discuss stylistic phenomena such as figurative language, metaphor or simile, and sound repetition as ends in themselves. Traditionally, biblical scholarship assigns to rhetorical criticism the art of the final product; with this one can concentrate on the aesthetic evaluation of the text. On the other hand, classical biblical scholarship deals with the original text, seeking to discover its first meaning. The implication is that biblical prophetic scholarship works on two, parallel levels. Each level has its own task, and each is legitimate in so far as each confines itself to its defined area.[1]

The question is whether the distinction between aesthetic evaluation and the study of content is justified. In order to pursue this matter we have to look at the function and goals of literary criticism. Literary criticism has three functions: the study of semantics, the study of structure, and the study of pragmatics, that is, the reader's orientation. A literary piece is a product of words and sentences structured together in order to provide meaning. There is, however, a reader who is to respond to the text, and the writers design their pieces to communicate effectively with their readers. Thus, the writers select the appropriate form, choose the correct words and construct their

---

* The article is published honoring Professor George A. Kennedy. I spent the entire academic year of 1978–1979 at the University of North Carolina at Chapel Hill, enriching my study of rhetoric under Professor Kennedy's guidance. I discovered a knowledgeable scholar, a dedicated teacher, and a respectful humanist who left his mark on my scholarship.
    1. Consult E. Greenstein's systematic evaluation of the current trends of biblical scholarship in 'The State of Biblical Scholarship, or Biblical Studies in a State', *Essays in Biblical Method and Translation* (Atlanta: Scholars Press, 1989), pp. 3-27.

sentences in a way which will appeal to their readers. In other words, the selection of form and structure as well as words is a function of the reader's response.

The selection of the literary medium is up to the writers. They may choose according to their skills but also in light of their rhetorical goals. Thus, we may distinguish between prose and poetry in terms of their effect. Poetry appeals in its entire form, acting emotionally as a whole. Prose may appeal emotionally as well, but not on the basis of the form itself as a whole, for the reader's focus is on the subject-matter, the theme.

At this point one may raise a fundamental question. The reader's orientation, which determines the selection of form and words (this entire mechanism which we call creativity) characterizes, we generally assume, the modern period but not the ancient one, the oral culture. Thus, the Greeks did not have a distinctive word for artistic creation. An artist makes things according to natural rules and imitates nature. There was, however, one exception: poetry. Aristotle (*Poet.* 1451a-b), for instance, distinguished history-writing as imitation from poetry as the true world which is beyond the world of reality. Greek poets assigned their art to divine inspiration, not to the power of memory or the skill of imitation. Apollo, we should recall, was the god of poetry and oracles.

Nevertheless, it would be a mistake to consider the poets of antiquity as creators in the modern sense. The oral performance reinforced the employment of specific themes expressed in fixed forms or formulae. But still there was enough room for literary creativity, and the task of the rhetorical critic of the ancient literature is to discover the tension between tradition and creativity. In other words, the goal of sound rhetorical criticism is to study the conditions which make an effective communication possible. The major principle of effective communication is the reader's expectations. There is, in advance, a certain mental or linguistic agreement between the addresser and the addressee. The danger is, however, the routine, the cliché. The poets' goal (in the modern period as well as in the ancient) is to raise the readers' expectations beyond the routine, to encourage the addressees to respond by stimulating their curiosity.

There is another problem to be considered: the question of the collection of material, a process which in the ancient world can be described as the transition between oral literature and written litera-

ture.[1] When considering, for instance, a certain mixture of style and
motifs in the book of Jeremiah, prophetic scholarship seeks to distinguish between different literary strata and to discover the original
Jeremiah.[2] Literarily this is a peculiar goal, because the addition
together with the old creates an entirely new discourse. Since the point
of departure, the rhetorical situation of the new text, is changed, the
isolation of various literary strata in one specific unit is meaningless in
terms of the question of why, i.e. *context*, which determines the question of what, i.e. *content*, which determines the question of how, i.e.
style. The linguistic operation will, therefore, produce only separated
literary fragments, wandering texts.

This point leads me to another observation about a sacred cow of
prophetic criticism. Critics assume that any stylistic change, say poetry
versus prose, indicates different authorship, as, for example, in the
case of Jeremiah's authentic words versus the additions of his editors,
the Deuteronomistic school. The fact is that many literary creations
are constructed by phraseology which is not unified. Each style represents a different voice, or point of view, or another mood or temper,
or point of stress. There are cases in which the entire work is constructed by representing different voices, or views, each of which
speaks in its specific phraseology. It may be that character A describes
character B from A's point of view, then A speaks in person, B speaks
about A and so on. The phraseology of each character is peculiar to
that character. In such cases the unity of the entire work depends on its
common theme, not on its style.[3]

II

I would like now to invite readers to follow with me the context of the
drought poem of Jeremiah 14, read in light of the above remarks.

The text of 14.2–15.9 presents one theme.[4] The catastrophe, the
drought (vv. 2-6), is followed by a prayer (vv. 7-9), while v. 10 is

1. For the creation of the new text consult J. Goody, *The Domestication of the
Savaged Mind* (Cambridge: Cambridge University Press, 1977), pp. 74-111.

2. See S. Mowinckel, *Zur Komposition des Buches Jeremia* (Kristiania: Dybwad,
1914).

3. Consult B. Uspensky, *A Poetics of Composition* (Berkeley: University of California Press, 1973).

4. For this division (14.2–15.9) see also I. Meyer, *Jeremia und die falschen
Propheten* (Göttingen: Vandenhoeck & Ruprecht, 1977), pp. 48-65; H. Graf

God's negative response. Verses 11-12 refer directly to the prophet who intervened on behalf of the people, while v. 13 is the prophet's response providing the motivation for his plea. Consequently, vv. 14-16 refer to the cause, the false prophets, followed by another description of the people's disaster (vv. 17-18), which is challenged again by the people in vv. 19-22. Jer. 15.1-9 is God's final word, a detailed description of his judgment divided into two parts: God's revelation of his judgment to Jeremiah and God's final address to the people.

The tension between the judgment and the efforts to cancel it takes place on two, parallel stages as in a theatre.[1] On the first stage the actors are God and the people, while God and Jeremiah are the characters who appear on the second stage. Even though the stages are separated, their events are mutually related and dependent on each other. The people's prayer in 14.7-9 is supported separately by Jeremiah in his dialogue with God on the second stage (vv. 11-16). Jeremiah argues that in fact the false prophets assured the people, in contrast to God's judgment, of a peaceful time. Thus the second stage reacts against the first, since in light of the false prophets' argument, the people could interpret the drought as a disaster, which might be remedied by conventional religious practice such as prayer, fasting, and sacrifice (v. 12). The second stage, the dialogue between God and Jeremiah, functions, therefore, as a tool which informs the audience that the drought is a very severe matter; it is God's punishment, a fact which is strengthened by God's word against the false prophets (v. 14). The subject matter now turns directly to the audience and announces their destiny, a catastrophe (v. 16). Then we are taken back to the second stage, which now reflects the people's panic: 'where shall we go?' (15.2). God informs Jeremiah of his final judgment, which is told in detail to the audience on the first stage (15.5-9): 'So I have stretched out my hand against you and destroyed you. . .' (15.6).

Reventlow, *Liturgie und prophetisches Ich bei Jeremia* (Gütersloh: Gütersloher Verlagshaus, 1963), pp. 375-91; W.L. Holladay, *Jeremiah* (2 vols.; Hermeneia; Philadelphia: Fortress, 1986), I, pp. 418-44; W.A.M. Beuken and H.W.M. van Grol, 'Jeremiah 14.1–15.9: A Situation of Distress and its Hermeneutics, Unity and Diversity of Form—Dramatic Development', *Le livre de Jérémie, le prophète et son milieu, les oracles et leur transmission* (ed. Pierre-Maurice Bogaert; BETL 54; Leuven: Leuven University Press, 1981), pp. 297-342.

1. R.P. Carroll (*Jeremiah* [Philadelphia: Westminster, 1986], p. 312) considers the switch of the אמר in vv. 10-11 as a dialogue which takes place between deity and speaker.

Since the events on the two stages are played by different pairs of characters, though they act in the same thematic framework, the difference between the stages is marked by a specific stylistic usage. Stylistically, the reader/listener is faced with three modes of verbal expression: poetry, prose, and rhythmical prose or semi-poetry. Poetry and semi-poetry are the language of the first stage, which directly confronts the audience, while prose and rhythmical prose characterize the second stage, the dialogues between God and Jeremiah. That is to say, the two stages confront each other with a vivid and lively language on the one hand, and plain language on the other.

The difference in style is not just an external means of distinguishing between the two stages; it has a functional purpose as well. Rhetorically, the two stages are not equally related. In contrast to the people, Jeremiah does not have to be persuaded in this context. The people, however, require persuasion since Jeremiah points out that they have been assured by their prophets that they will face a period of peace and prosperity. Hence, style and form are adjusted to the subject-matter, or the rhetorical situation.

Rhetorically, I ask, what is the nature of the present text? It is not a political speech, not a court speech, but a religious discourse: an address which seeks to alter the opinion of an audience already persuaded to accept a view opposite to that of the narrator. The narrator did not choose to confront such a dispute by reason, which can be answered by another argument. His choice was to affect his audience by emotional and ethical appeals. Form and language provide the emotional atmosphere, while the dialogue that takes place between God and Jeremiah seeks to appeal ethically as well.

The drought poem, 14.2-6, attracts attention. In order to realize its impact it is advisable to compare this poem with Joel's treatment of the disaster. Joel, mainly in chs. 1–2, not only deals with the danger of drought and the people's plea, but also points out how the animals suffer:

> What mourning from the beast! The herds of cattle wander bewildered because they have no pasture. Even the flocks of sheep must bear their punishment. . . (1.18-20).

But what a difference in comparison with Jeremiah's description! Stylistically, this is the difference between rhythmical prose and poetry—a distinction made already by Aristotle, who insisted that

Herodotus 'could be put into verse and yet would still be a kind of history, whether written in meter or not' (*Poet.* 1451b). Samuel Taylor Coleridge wrote similarly about poetry:

> The poet, described in ideal perfection, brings the whole soul of man into activity with the subordination of its faculties to each other, according to their relative worth and dignity. He diffuses a tone and a spirit of unity, that blends, and (as it were) fuses, each into which, by that stylistic and magical power, to which we have exclusively appropriated the nature of imagination. This power, first put in action by the will and understanding, and retained under their irremissive, though gentle and unnoticed control, reveals itself in the balance or reconciliation of opposite or discordant qualities: of sameness, with difference; of the general with the concrete; the idea, with the image; the individual with the representative; the sense of novelty and refreshness, with old and familiar objects; a more than usual state of emotion, with more than usual order; judgment ever awake and steady self-possession, with enthusiasm and feeling profound.[1]

This is what Jeremiah is doing here in contrast to Joel. He picks a familiar motif, almost routine in this area of Judah on the border of the desert. But by dwelling on the subject, by depicting the pain and despair of human being and animal, by portraying concrete images, individual episodes with which the audience is able to identify, by creating an entire world picture, Jeremiah acts on his audience's emotions.

But not just the form as a whole makes this poem unique. A close analysis, which can be done only in a second reading following the first impression, reveals a specific order of words, syllables, and sound arrangements, which together shape the entire poem.

The poem starts with the people and ends with the animals. The animals are the climax; the deer's fawn dies but not the people's children. Poetry prefers to relate to the similarity either in metaphor or in images. The image illustrates the concrete more strongly than the direct reference. In this case a straight description of humanity's death could be overwhelming and too deterring. Furthermore, effect in any artistic form is achieved by raising curiosity, which can be done through the tension between the expected and unexpected, through contrasts. The contrast between the people's high expectations and the deep disappointment creates a dramatic effect:

---

1. Samuel Taylor Coleridge, *Biographia Literaria* (ed. J. Shawcross; London: Oxford University Press, 1907), II, pp. 1-13.

ואדריהם שלחו צעוריהם למים . . .
¹לא מצאו מים . . .
בשו והכלמו וחפו ראשם.

Her nobles sent their servants for water. . .
they find no water. . .
they are ashamed and confounded and cover their heads (v. 3).

Already the design of the first verse (v. 2) raises curiosity. The pair
'Judah' and 'Jerusalem' is expected, but unexpectedly Jerusalem does
not appear in the parallel line. The gap is filled by further description,
and meanwhile, the expectation to the parallel pair creates tension
which focuses attention on the entire verse. Furthermore, the combination קדרו לארץ ('dark to the ground') which portrays the mourners
turning their heads down (cf. Ps. 35.14) is contrasted with the mount-
ing scream: וצוחת ירושלם עלחה ('the outcry of Jerusalem rises').² Verse
2a is characterized by a series of long vowels. It creates an atmosphere
of slow motion and passivism, as well as continuation. Verse 2b is different. The stress is not on the end of the word, the long vowel, but on
the sound of a series of sound consonants: קדרו לארץ וצוחת ירושלם
עלחה. This combination creates a feeling of action: the people react.
Again notice the contrasting relation between the connotation of קדרו
לארץ and its strong sounds. The end of v. 2b, עלחה, is tied by assonance with the beginning of the verse, אבלה, but in this case the tone is
active. The long, open syllables of עלחה, which independently create a
feeling of slowness, are contrasted with the combination of צוחת.

The remainder of the poem is distinguished by the series of short
descriptions: the facts speak for themselves. The sharpness of the language is seen in the reference to the doe (v. 5). In contrast to the servant's description (v. 3) which expresses the messenger's feelings
('. . . ashamed and confounded and covering their heads'), the present
text is made up of mere verbs: no adjectives are employed. The doe
gives birth and 'forsakes'. The animal's behavior mirrors its despair.
Note the use of the verbs concerning the doe's behavior. Two verbs
are employed. The first is in the perfect tense (ילדה, 'gave birth'),

---

1. For אדריהם cf. Judg. 5.13. צעיריהם read with the *qere*. There is a tendency to
correlate the nobles with servants. However, the adjective צעירים refers as well to
young people who can run quickly (to the cisterns). The LXX omits the end of the
verse; nonetheless, the ending may refer to the nobles rather than to the young people
(note the verb הכלמו in the *hophal*).

2. Cf. Holladay, *Jeremiah*, I, p. 429.

whereas the second is in the infinitive absolute (עזוב, 'forsakes'). 'The infinitive *usually* emphasizes. . . the force of the verb in context. . . [T]he notion of certainty is reinforced. . .'[1] The conclusion, 'because there is no grass', is also distinguished. The statement 'no rain' or 'no grass' is repeated three times as a refrain. However, there is a difference: גשם, דשא and עשב create variety, and the conclusion כי־אין עשב (v. 6) this time is not in the past tense, and so perpetuates the situation: there is no solution.

The transition in v. 7 from the third person to the first person plural (עונינו) distinguishes between the drought poem and the people's prayer. We listen to two voices: the narrator's and the audience's. Structurally, the exchange of voices enables the author to give voice to the limited number of characters from different perspectives, a structure which assists a dramatic development. This technique enables Jeremiah not to appear in his personal voice, that is, as an outsider. Thus he can function as a negotiator or the one who tries to bridge the gap between the people and God. In this way he does not adjust his point of view time and again, and his concluding word, God's final judgment, sounds more authentic and hence persuasive.

In light of this structure the drought poem functions as an invitation to the audience to listen. The form as well as the internal structure intend to act emotionally as, indeed, the immediate plea reflects.

In v. 10 God's response is in the third person and does not address the audience directly ('Thus says the Lord concerning this people'). The switch to the third person requires attention. God does not announce his judgment directly; the debate is still between the narrator and God, a situation which leaves room for Jeremiah to intervene on behalf of the people. It is important to notice the stylistic conflict between the two parts of v. 10. Verse 10a is a graphic response:

כן אהבו לנוע	They have loved to wander thus,
רגליהם לא חשכו	they have not restrained their feet.

It responds directly to the people's plea in v. 8b. On the other hand, v. 10b is a conventional phrase (see Hos. 8.13; cf. 9.9):

Therefore the Lord does not accept them;
Now he will remember their iniquity and punish their sins.

1. See B.K. Waltke and M. O'Connor, *An Introduction to Biblical Hebrew Syntax* (Winona Lake: Eisenbrauns, 1990), p. 584.

On an emotional level, it is a spontaneous reaction contrasting with a controlled, quieter conclusion.

The dialogue, in direct speech, between Jeremiah and God functions first to establish the prophet's credibility, and second to refute a common belief shared by the audience. Jeremiah will announce God's judgment, which, as we have already noticed, contrasts with that of the official diviners and contradicts the people's belief in the power of the standard religious practice (v. 12). Rhetorically, this is a very difficult task, especially since Jeremiah, as the structure of the present text indicates, does not limit himself to the role of a mere messenger, but seeks to persuade.

Revealing his argument with God and his concern for the people, Jeremiah appears as one of the people, one who shows his understanding and sympathy for his audience's situation. In such a way Jeremiah decreases the potential for a hostile attitude towards his public appearance. Studies of the rhetoric of public address insist that the personal credibility of the speakers and their attitude towards their audience as it is reflected in their addresses are crucial factors for the effectiveness of the speech. Jeremiah's intimate conversation with God (cf. Amos 3.7), conducted in direct speech, establishes his authority as a prophet and as one who does not rush to announce a message of destruction. Such an approach intends to invite the audience to listen to the speaker without rejection.

In light of this careful structure the switch in v. 17 to direct speech (ואמרת אליהם) is significant. Hitherto, God has not addressed the audience directly. Judgment in v. 16 as well as in v. 10 is announced to the audience indirectly through the speech against the false prophets. Thus the command to announce to the people 'this matter' (v. 17) focuses attention on the new voice that is concerned with the people: God, who approaches them directly. But the tone is that of a lament, a sadness, and not a harsh statement of judgment. God's voice sounds personal and sympathetic:

> Let my eyes run down with tears,
> Night and day and let them not cease (vv. 17-18).[1]

This appeals ethically; that is, God does not appear as a demon. This enables Jeremiah rhetorically to continue to appeal on behalf of the people in vv. 19-22. Notice that there is no line of introduction

---

1. For תדמינה (דמה), cf. Lam. 3.49.

between v. 18 and v. 19. The first person singular is followed by the plural: באתי, יצאתי (God) versus הכיתנו (the people). The sympathetic tone of God's voice invites an immediate prayer. The plea is rejected in 15.1, which is also a prosaic section displaying, as we have already seen, the second stage, God's conference with Jeremiah. This section functions to increase Jeremiah's authority before his last direct confrontation with his audience, the announcement of God's final judgment.

A word should be said here about the prosaic phraseology of 15.3-4, which states:

> I will appoint over them four kinds of destroyers, says the Lord: the sword to slay. . . and I will make them a horror to all the kingdoms of the earth because of what Manasseh, the son of Hezekiah, king of Judah, did in Jerusalem.

The deuteronomistic color of these sentences (cf. Deut. 28.25-26)[1] may function as a formula, that is, in the language of explicit and brief communication. This is, indeed, the nature of God's communication with Jeremiah, which is not the language of illustration or persuasion. The reason given for the punishment, Manasseh (cf. 2 Kgs 21.10-15; 23.26; 24.3), is curious. It is strange, at least at first glance, that the sin, the cause of this severe punishment, depends on the past and not on a concrete present deed. Curiously, this phenomenon is not characteristic of Jeremiah. Thus, for instance, Isaiah in 1.4-9 employs rich, vivid language describing the disaster. However, when he refers to the people's sins he avoids specifics:

> Wash yourself; make yourself clean; remove the evil of your doings. . . seek justice; correct oppression; defend the fatherless; plead for the widow (1.16-17).

Similarly, when in a detailed address concerning the idea of God's punishment, Amos outlines the sins, the cause, all he says is:

> See the great tumults within her, and the oppressions in her midst. . . those who store up violence and robbery in their strongholds (3.9-10).

This is a schematic, almost uncommitted accusation. The same phenomenon occurs in Jer. 15.4. Thus we are not dealing here with a

---

1. See E.W. Nicholson, *Preaching to the Exiles* (Oxford: Blackwell, 1970), pp. 87, 100-102. But see H. Weippert's critique (*Die Prosareden des Jeremiabuches* [BZAW 132; Berlin/New York: de Gruyter, 1973], pp. 148-91) of the stylistic presupposition associating the prosaic material with the Deuteronomist.

specific phenomenon characteristic of the deuteronomistic circle. Stylistically the prophetic speech distinguishes between the cause and the effect. The effect is described in colorful language, while the cause is told briefly in plain language, even in formulaic style. This situation suggests that the prophet's rhetorical focus was on the punishment, the effect, an idea which the people refused to accept. So it required persuasion. The cause, the sin, was familiar. Yet why Manasseh? Manasseh symbolizes, like a myth,[1] the sin of unfaithfulness, which is a major theme in Jeremiah's prophecy. It is a motif which, in fact, was mentioned before by God as the people's sin (14.10).

Returning to our discourse, 15.5-9 concludes the address. This is the first time God points out explicitly, in direct confrontation with the audience, that he himself will execute his judgment. The structure of the discourse indicates that there is no room for further prayers; God's final judgment is definite. God's speech repeats thematically as well as metaphorically certain previous references to the people. Again he refers to the sin of unfaithfulness, employing the language of walking wrongly (cf. v. 10), and revives the tragic image portrayed already in the poem of labor and death.

And this is, indeed, the function of an effective epilogue: to dwell on major points but not to repeat them exactly, and thus to continue to attract attention and to strengthen as well the core of the speech.

III

In summary, Jer. 14.2–15.9, is, rhetorically speaking, one unit.[2] The address is structured as follows:

14.2-6	The catastrophe
7-9	The people's prayer
10	God's response to the people
11-12	God addresses Jeremiah
13	Jeremiah's response
14-16	God's response to Jeremiah
17-18	God's response to the people
19-22	The people's plea

---

1. For the myth as a convention of the common tradition, see N. Frye, *The Great Code: The Bible and Literature* (San Diego: Harcourt, Brace, Jovanovich, 1981), pp. 31-52.

2. Attention should be given to Beuken's and van Grol's illuminating rhetorical analysis ('Jeremiah 14.1–15.9').

15.1-4   God's judgment revealed to Jeremiah
  5-9   God's final address to the people

Changes in style (poetry versus prose) are not by themselves indications of different authors, but must be evaluated in light of the entire structure and the language of the time.

The prophetic speech, at least this one by Jeremiah, may be seen and heard as a full speech and not a brief communication. The prophet seeks to persuade. His major interest is the concept of disaster as God's punishment. The rhetorical analysis, the study of the mutual relationship between the text and its audience, sheds light on the structure and the language as a function of the pragmatic goal of reaching the audience.

DID THE SPIRIT INSPIRE RHETORIC?
AN EXPLORATION OF GEORGE KENNEDY'S DEFINITION
OF EARLY CHRISTIAN RHETORIC

John R. Levison

From 1980 to 1984, during which period George Kennedy published two significant books dealing with Christian rhetoric,[1] one aspect of his thought remained largely unchanged: his definition of early Christian rhetoric. In this brief essay I hope to explore, and even to challenge, Dr Kennedy's definition. I can contemplate no more suitable means by which to honor a person as curious and as capable as George Kennedy.

This essay naturally will begin with a summary of Kennedy's definition based upon his books on the topic published in 1980 and 1984. It will continue by surveying relevant aspects of the Jewish world that gave birth to early Christianity and its rhetoric. The purpose of the third section is to evaluate, in the light of early Jewish texts, Kennedy's interpretation of the two New Testament texts that form the basis for his definition of early Christian rhetoric, Mk 13.9-13 and 1 Cor. 1.22–2.13. The essay will conclude with an undramatic peroration.

I

In his *Classical Rhetoric and its Christian and Secular Tradition from Ancient to Modern Times* (1980), Kennedy draws a disjuncture between early Christian and classical rhetoric: 'Christian preaching is thus not persuasion, but proclamation, and is based on authority and

---

1. *Classical Rhetoric and its Christian and Secular Tradition from Ancient to Modern Times* (Chapel Hill, NC: University of North Carolina Press, 1980); *New Testament Interpretation through Rhetorical Criticism* (Chapel Hill, NC: University of North Carolina Press, 1984).

grace, not on proof'.[1] This definition hinges on two New Testament passages.[2] Of the first, Mk 13.9-13, Kennedy writes:

> Among the points to be noted in this passage are the importance of testimony up to and including the example of martyrdom; the fact that no special eloquence is required, for as in Exodus God will provide the words; and an apparent assumption that the disciples cannot expect to persuade their judges of the righteousness of their cause: that is God's work, and as with Pharaoh, he seems to intend to harden their hearts. All of this is completely contrary to the situation of the classical orator, who uses his eloquence to overcome enormous opposition in defense of himself and his clients.[3]

Kennedy continues to bifurcate classical and early Christian rhetoric by quoting extensively from 1 Corinthians 1–2, concluding with these comments on 2.6-13:

> This passage may be said to reject the whole of classical philosophy and rhetoric. For rhetoric the Christian can rely only on God, both to supply words and to accomplish persuasion if it is God's will. In place of worldly philosophy there exists a higher philosophy, only dimly apprehended by man.[4]

On the basis of these brief commentaries, we can say with some certainty that the three factors of early Christian rhetoric are grace, authority, and proclamation rather than the modes of persuasion of Aristotelian rhetoric known as *ethos, pathos,* and *logos*.[5]

In his later book, *New Testament Interpretation through Rhetorical Criticism* (1984), Kennedy includes a similar definition of early Christian rhetoric. He again utilizes the story of Moses and Pharaoh to argue that God's action, not Aaron's and Moses' persuasive abilities, convince Pharaoh to let God's people go. On the basis of references to the Holy Spirit in Mk 13.11 and 1 Cor. 2.13, Kennedy then makes a connection between this idea and the Holy Spirit as the source of early Christian rhetoric. Apart from this explicit connection, his definition is similar to his earlier one:

---

1. *Classical Rhetoric*, p. 127.
2. The story of Moses in Exodus, to which Dr Kennedy appeals for his definition, while illustrative of the Judeo-Christian perception of rhetoric, cannot be utilized as a primary source for understanding early *Christian* rhetoric, for a vast gulf separates the *Sitz im Leben* of the Moses cycle of stories and the *Sitz im Leben* of Mark's Gospel and Paul's correspondence.
3. *Classical Rhetoric*, p. 127.
4. *Classical Rhetoric*, pp. 131-32.
5. *Classical Rhetoric*, p. 123.

The Christian orator, like his Jewish predecessor, is a vehicle of God's will to whom God will supply the necessary words, and his audience will be persuaded, or not persuaded, not because of the capacities of their minds to understand the message, but because of God's love for them which allows their hearts to be moved or withholds that grace.[1]

Kennedy's later book contains, however, one refinement—though I would not say modification—of his earlier definition. Here he limits his definition to texts which he designates 'radical Christian rhetoric'.[2] These radical texts, which originate with the Holy Spirit, are different from New Testament texts which utilize classical modes of persuasion. There exist, then, three categories, one more than his earlier book suggested: (1) classical rhetorical persuasion, (2) early Christian rhetoric that utilizes classical rhetorical persuasion, and (3) radical Christian rhetoric. To the final category belongs, not the totality of early Christian rhetoric, as his prior book suggests, but only some of it, such as the Gospel of Mark.[3]

This refinement solves a dilemma that existed in Kennedy's earlier book. In 1980 he suggested that classical rhetoric and early Christian rhetoric were different phenomena. Such a definition rendered the enterprise of interpreting New Testament texts through rhetorical criticism superfluous. How could one apply rhetorical criticism to texts which utilized proclamation rather than Aristotelian modes of persuasion? This would be a contradiction in terms. In 1984 he limited his definition to *radical* Christian rhetoric. In this way he allowed that *most* New Testament texts—all but radical Christian rhetoric—could be analyzed through rhetorical criticism.

Nevertheless, two difficulties plague this refinement. First, Kennedy does not provide a complete set of criteria for distinguishing the two types of early Christian rhetoric. The basic criterion for discerning radical Christian rhetoric seems to be merely the absence of enthymemes.[4]

---

1. *New Testament Interpretation*, p. 8.
2. *New Testament Interpretation*, p. 7.
3. *New Testament Interpretation*, p. 104.
4. *New Testament Interpretation*, p. 7. Kennedy (p. 16) defines enthymemes as follows: 'Deductive proof in rhetoric is called the *enthymeme*. An enthymeme commonly takes the form of a statement and supporting reason, as in "Blessed are the poor in spirit, for theirs is the kingdom of heaven" (Matt. 5:3). The word "for" in English, *gar* or *hoti* in Greek, is commonly the indication of an enthymeme. Behind any enthymeme stands a logical syllogism. "Those who receive the kingdom of heaven are blessed" would be the major premise, universal and positive, acceptable

The second difficulty becomes apparent when Kennedy subjects the Gospel of Mark to rhetorical analysis. On the one hand, he regards it as an exposé of radical Christian rhetoric; on the other hand, he discovers enthymemes in it. Kennedy attempts to mitigate this problem by observing that these enthymemes 'are usually of a very simple sort'.[1] The fact remains, though, that even radical Christian rhetoric contains modes of persuasion from Aristotelian rhetoric.[2] *Proclamation* is, to some degree at least, *persuasion* in the Gospel of Mark.[3]

We are left, then, with a question: Was (radical) early Christian rhetoric really so free from persuasion as Kennedy's definition suggests? In other words, is Kennedy's most recent bifurcation of classically based early Christian rhetoric and radical early Christian rhetoric itself too radical? The following two sections of this essay present a tentative answer to this question.

II

Kennedy, while appreciating the contribution of Amos Wilder to our understanding of early Christian rhetoric, criticized Wilder's work because 'it significantly fails to relate the developing internal rhetoric of Christianity to the traditions of Judaism of which it is a part'.[4] This criticism introduces crisply the purpose of this second section: to examine the traditions of Judaism in order to relate Kennedy's definition to them. More particularly, *which* traditions of Judaism provide the most significant data for evaluating the veracity of Kennedy's definition of early Christian rhetoric?

A review of early Jewish texts which antedate 135 CE exposes two traditions that provide a backdrop for radical Christian rhetoric and its foundation texts of Mk 13.9-13 and 1 Corinthians 1–2. The first tradition presents the Spirit as the power that overcomes the speaker.

---

by definition. "The poor in spirit will receive the kingdom of heaven" would then be the minor premise.'

1. *New Testament Interpretation*, p. 105.

2. In fact, in conversation Duane Watson pointed out to me that all authoritative judgments, examples, or supernatural occurrences belong to the category of *logos* in classical rhetoric. See his *Invention, Arrangement, and Style: Rhetorical Criticism of Jude and 2 Peter* (SBLDS 104; Atlanta: Scholars Press, 1988), pp. 17, 57-58, 127.

3. C.C. Black's and R. Vinson's articles in this volume on Mk 13 and the Synoptic Gospels, respectively, attest to the rhetorical qualities of Mark's Gospel.

4. *Classical Rhetoric*, p. 128.

It is expressed quintessentially in the writings of Philo Judaeus and Josephus. The second tradition presents the Spirit as the artificer who equips the speaker with wisdom. It is expressed most cogently in Sirach, Wisdom of Solomon, and Susanna. These traditions present two quite divergent views of the means of rhetoric.[1]

1. *The Spirit as Overcomer*

Philo presents Moses and Abraham as prophets. He goes to rather great lengths to explore the nature of their prophetic inspiration.

In *Mos.* 2.188-91 Philo lists three varieties of inspiration which are included in the Scriptures, all of which are related to Moses as prophet (he has already presented Moses as king and high priest). First, some are spoken by God with the prophet as interpreter; these Philo will not discuss because they are too great to be praised by human lips. Second, in some, revelation comes through question and answer; God replies to the prophet's questions. Third, and most important for our purposes, some are spoken by Moses when he is 'possessed by God [ἐπιθειάσαντος] and carried away out of himself'.[2] In this mode of prophecy, God gives foreknowledge to the prophet.

A few sentences later, Philo explains that in this third kind of inspiration 'the speaker appears under that divine possession [ἐνθουσιῶδες ἐμφαίνεται] in virtue of which he is chiefly and in the strict sense considered a prophet'. This mode of inspiration is the quintessential expression of prophecy.

Elsewhere, in *Spec. Leg.* 4.49, Philo clarifies further the nature of this prophetic inspiration by comparing it with false prophecy. He writes:

> For no pronouncement of a prophet is ever his own; he is an interpreter prompted by Another in all his utterances, when knowing not what he does he is filled with inspiration, as the reason withdraws and surrenders the citadel of the soul to a new visitor and tenant, the Divine Spirit which plays upon the

---

1. For general information and bibliography, see J.A. Davis, *Wisdom and Spirit: An Investigation of 1 Corinthians 1.18–3.20 against the Background of Jewish Sapiential Traditions in the Greco-Roman Period* (New York: University Press of America, 1984). He discusses in particular the writings of Philo Judaeus, the Dead Sea Scrolls, and Sirach.

2. Quotations and texts of Philo and Josephus are from the Loeb Classical Library. Translations of all other texts are from the RSV, with the exception of my own translations of Susanna.

vocal organism and dictates words which clearly express its prophetic message.

This passage twice indicates that prophetic speech occurs when the prophet is overcome by the Spirit, that is, when the prophet ceases to be conscious. First, the prophet is unaware of the inspiration that overcomes him or her (ἐνθουσιᾷ γεγονὼς ἐν ἀγνοίᾳ). Second, reason (τοῦ λογισμοῦ) surrenders 'the soul's acropolis' (i.e. the mind), and the Spirit invades and indwells it (ἐπιπεφοιτηκότος δὲ καὶ ἐνῳκηκότος τοῦ θείου πνεύματος). In other words, the Spirit replaces reason as the highest part of the rational soul. Prophetic rhetoric, then, is produced not by reason but by the Spirit through the medium of a prophet who is unaware of this inspiration.

A similar notion of prophetic inspiration appears in the *Antiquitates Judaicae* of Flavius Josephus, in which he retells the episode of Balak's encounter with the prophet Balaam (4.118-19). Following a long quotation of Balaam's blessing (rather than repudiation) of Israel, Josephus summarizes: 'Such was the inspired utterance [ἐπεθείαζεν] of one who was no longer his own master [οὐκ ὢν ἐν ἑαυτῷ] but was overruled [νενικημένος] by the divine spirit to deliver it'.

The nature of being overcome becomes clearer when Balaam defends his oracle to Balak:

> hast thou reflected on the whole matter and thinkest thou that it rests with us at all to be silent or to speak on such themes as these, when we are possessed by the spirit of God? For that spirit gives utterance to such language and words as it will, whereof we are all unconscious.

Josephus has no doubt that true prophecy occurs when the prophet does not employ his or her own rhetorical resources; it occurs instead when the prophets do not know what is being said (οὐδὲν ἡμῶν εἰδότων).

These passages from Philo and Josephus exhibit remarkable agreement on the nature of prophetic rhetoric. First, prophecy occurs when the prophet does *not* know what is taking place; he or she is overcome by the Spirit. Second, the inspiration is described as an aggressive activity of the Spirit, whether by Philo as possessing or invading, or by Josephus as conquering or 'taking us [prophets]'. Inspiration is no mild experience; it is the Spirit's invasion of a prophet, who sacrifices awareness to it, for the sake of communicating its own message through the vehicle of that prophet.

Alongside these texts, which are extremely relevant for evaluating Kennedy's definition of radical Christian rhetoric, another important text is *Virt.* 217, in which Philo describes Abraham's experiences of inspiration (ἐπιθειάζων):

> Thus whenever he was possessed (κατασχεθείη), everything in him changed to something better, eyes, complexion, stature, carriage, movements, voice. For the divine spirit which was breathed upon (καταπνευσθέν) him from on high made its lodging in his soul, and invested his body with singular beauty, his voice with persuasiveness (πειθώ), and his hearers with understanding (τοῖς δ' ἀκούουσι σύνεσιν).

In this text, persuasion is the result of the indwelling of the Spirit rather than rhetorical techniques. In fact, the Spirit not only imbues the speaker with authority but also the audience with comprehension— quite apart from reason!

2. *The Spirit as Artificer*[1]

A second Jewish tradition portrays Spirit-inspired rhetoric in a different way: the Spirit equips the wise person to be intelligent in thought and, consequently, persuasive in speech.

The basis for this viewpoint is the conviction that the Spirit is a Spirit of wisdom and intelligence. In the Wisdom of Solomon, the Spirit is designated a 'Spirit of wisdom' (7.7), while Spirit and wisdom seem to be identified with each other in 9.17: 'Who has learned thy counsel, unless thou hast given wisdom and sent thy Holy Spirit from on high?' Wisdom has 'in her. . . a spirit that is intelligent, holy, unique. . .' (7.22) and is itself a 'breath of power of God' (7.25). So integral is the unity between Spirit and wisdom that, when the author refers to wisdom, the inspiring Spirit is never far from his purview.

The source of rhetoric, then, in the Wisdom of Solomon is identified variously as the Spirit of wisdom, or wisdom which possesses an intelligent Spirit, or the Spirit identified as wisdom. This Spirit as wisdom: (1) gives understanding to the student of rhetoric: 'she understands turns of speech and the solutions of riddles' (8.8); (2) creates prophets (7.27) and gives foreknowledge (8.8); (3) gives to wise people such as Solomon 'understanding, and renown in sharing her words' (8.18);

---

1. For an excellent discussion of the relationship between wisdom and eloquence in early Judaism, see R.A. Horsley, 'Wisdom of Word and Words of Wisdom in Corinth', *CBQ* 39 (1977), pp. 225-29.

and (4) 'opened the mouth of the dumb, and made the tongues of babes speak clearly' during the exodus (10.21).

This wisdom is not something that overcomes the unconscious speaker. Rather, the basic purpose of the Wisdom of Solomon is to encourage Jews to seek the wisdom which is found in the Jewish Scriptures (18.4). Wisdom *is* discoverable and obtainable. It is at once sent from God as a gift (8.21; 9.17) and sought after by wise persons such as Solomon (8.9, 18).

Ben Sira had earlier encapsulated this viewpoint even more succinctly when he wrote:

> If the great Lord is willing, he will be filled with the spirit of understanding;
>> he will pour forth words of wisdom and give thanks to the Lord in prayer (39.6).

Although out of context this passage seems possibly to describe spontaneous, inspired utterance, this is not the case, for the words that precede this description suggest that it portrays rather the scribe who has *learned* wisdom:

> On the other hand he who devotes himself to the study of the law of the Most High
>> will seek out the wisdom of all the ancients, and will be concerned with prophecies;
> he will preserve the discourse of notable men and penetrate the subtleties of parables;
>> he will seek out the hidden meanings of proverbs and be at home with the obscurities of parables (39.1-3).

Wise speech comes from the study of parables, prophecies, and ancient and contemporary discourse. As in the Wisdom of Solomon, God does pour forth wisdom and the Spirit, but it is given in tandem with study and meditation. That is, truly inspired rhetoric belongs not to the spiritually overcome individual but to the diligent scribe. Inspiration and learning are not enemies; they are the closest of associates. The former makes no appearance without the latter.[1]

Alongside the figures of Solomon (Wisdom of Solomon) and the scribe (Ben Sira), wisdom and the Spirit coalesce around the figure of Daniel in early Judaism prior to 100 CE. Josephus associates wisdom and the Spirit when he summarizes the Babylonian king's first words

---

1. On Sirach, see J. Marböck, 'Sir. 38.24–39.11; Der Schriftgelehrte Weise', *La sagesse de l'Ancien Testament* (ed. M. Gilbert; Leuven: Leuven University Press, 1979), pp. 293-316.

to Daniel: 'after telling him that he had learned of him and his wisdom and of the divine spirit that attended him and how he alone was fully able to discover things which were not within the understanding of others. . .' (*Ant.* 10.239).

A yet more impressive presentation of Daniel as a recipient of the 'Spirit of understanding' who speaks persuasively occurs in the deutero-canonical story of Susanna. After Susanna is condemned by the assembly, she prays, and God responds to her cry:

> And behold an angel of the Lord, while she was being led out to be destroyed, the angel gave, as it had been promised, a Spirit of understanding [πνεῦμα συνέσεως] to a younger man by the name of Daniel. When he had split the crowd, he stood in their midst and said. . .[1] (Sus. 44-45, 48).

Only two rhetorical questions and one exhortation of this deliberative speech are recorded. In his plan to expose the false accusers, Daniel's capacity for wisdom is apparent:

> Are you so foolish, children of Israel? Did you not inquire or discover the clear truth when you examined the daughter of Israel? And now, divide these [two men] far from each other so that I may put them on trial! (48b, 51).

Daniel's plan, not just his speech, is persuasive and successful. While he is inspired—for he is by all accounts too young to have such wisdom—his speech constitutes just a portion of the wisdom he possesses. In other words, the speech is a by-product of his intelligence.

In the story of Susanna, Daniel's wisdom allows him to speak persuasively. The story ends with an explicit hope for wisdom and knowledge to characterize all the young people of Israel: 'And let us protect capable young sons. For the young people will be pious, and there will be in them a Spirit of knowledge and of wisdom [πνεῦμα ἐπιστήμης καὶ συνέσεως] for ever' (63).

Here, as in Sirach and the Wisdom of Solomon, the Spirit is characterized predominantly by its association with wisdom. Its primary task is to offer understanding to those who seek it. Within this larger context, the Spirit of Wisdom also inspires people to speak wisely and, concomitantly, persuasively. Whom it chooses to inspire is determined by who seeks wisdom. Solomon, the scribe, and Daniel all receive a

---

1. My translation is based upon the LXX version. The version of Theodotion reads: 'And the Lord heard her voice. And as she was being led out to be destroyed, God raised up the Holy Spirit of a young man by the name of Daniel. And he cried with a great voice. . . And standing in their midst, he said. . .'

Spirit of wisdom as a gracious gift; but they also represent those who seek it diligently (Solomon), who study Torah unceasingly (Ben Sira), and who prepare for it courageously (Daniel). Its presence becomes evident, not in the individual's being overtaken by the Spirit, but in wise sayings of many sorts, some of which instruct and others of which persuade, and all of which catapult the speaker into renown.

This brief foray into early Judaism has no doubt supplied ample evidence for Kennedy's contention that the earliest believers expected God to supply words and to accomplish persuasion. It has also amassed evidence to support an alternative contention: the earliest believers may have expected the Spirit to guide their study and their preparation for speaking. To evaluate which contention is more likely it will be necessary to turn our attention to the NT passages which provide the foundation for Kennedy's definition of early Christian rhetoric.

3. *The Spirit as Overcomer and Radical Christian Rhetoric*
According to Josephus, the Spirit 'gives utterance to such language and words as it will. . .' Philo agrees with Josephus, in his own way, when he presents the Spirit as the invader of the mind which replaces reason and 'dictates words which clearly express its prophetic message'.

It is not difficult to conceive that Jesus' promise in Mark's Gospel took shape in a similar *milieu* to that of the authors of those texts: 'for it is not you who speak, but the Holy Spirit' (13.11). Since the Spirit 'gives utterance' (Josephus) and 'dictates words' (Philo), so it can be counted upon to 'speak' through the earliest Christians (Mark).

Paul's antitheses in 1 Corinthians 1–2 also accord well with this conception of persuasion: 'God's foolishness' vs 'human wisdom' (1.25); 'plausible words of wisdom' vs 'demonstration of the Spirit and of power' (2.4); 'human wisdom' vs 'God's power' (2.5); 'human wisdom' vs 'the Spirit' (2.13). Paul here seems clearly to reject Aristotelian modes of persuasion in favor of relying upon the Spirit to give utterance and even to dictate words that originate in the revelatory Spirit of God.

This inquiry into the plausibility of Kennedy's view of radical Christian rhetoric has provided evidence to corroborate his definition. By exploring the relationship between early Christian rhetoric, as he defines it, and early Jewish rhetoric, we have come upon a context which quite easily could have generated the early Christian conviction that God's Spirit supplies words and accomplishes persuasion.

4. *Unanswered Problems with Kennedy's Definition*

There exist, however, some haunting clues in Mark 13 and 1 Corinthians 1–2 which suggest that this is not the complete story. First, Mk 13.11 occurs in a very specific context:

> . . . for they will deliver you up to councils; and you will be beaten in synagogues; and you will stand before governors and kings for my sake, to bear testimony before them. . . And when they bring you to trial and deliver you up . . . And brother will deliver up brother to death, and the father his child, and children will rise against parents and have them put to death; and you will be hated by all for my name's sake. . . (vv. 9, 11-13).

This description is obviously not a generalized account of early Christianity. It is, first of all, highly eschatological in nature, describing a specific experience prior to 'the end' (13.13). More to the point, it details only one rhetorical situation, and provides the background for only one species of speech, that is, forensic. Jesus in Mark's Gospel provides a promise of the Spirit to those who are on trial and persecuted: God will come to their defense; they need not worry. This limited application within Mk 13.9-13 suggests that Mk 13.11 should not be utilized to characterize radical Christian rhetoric in general, as it does in Kennedy's definition.[1]

A second clue is a disparity between the early Jewish tradition of the Spirit as overcomer and 1 Cor. 2.2. According to the former, persuasion takes place when the Spirit replaces reason or when the speaker becomes unconscious of her or his words. In 1 Cor. 2.2, in contrast, Paul's proclamation is premeditated: 'For I decided to know nothing among you except Jesus Christ and him crucified'. Although Paul did not include words of rhetorical eloquence in his proclamation, he still planned it, not unlike his contemporaries, the rhetors.

Yet another clue is that Paul rejects only certain types of wisdom which he qualifies with genitives (e.g. 'the wisdom of the world', 1.20; 'the wisdom of this age', 2.6) and he rejects this wisdom, not because it is inherently evil, but because of the ill-effects it has brought upon

---

1. The association of wisdom and Spirit is evident, surprisingly, in a Lukan parallel to Mk 13.11. While he retains Mark's reference to the Holy Spirit in Lk. 12.11-12, the closer parallel to Mk 13.11, Lk. 21.14-15, contains a reference, not to the Spirit, but to wisdom: 'Settle it therefore in your minds, not to meditate beforehand how to answer; for I will give you a mouth and wisdom, which none of your adversaries will be able to withstand'. Luke's ability to substitute wisdom for the Holy Spirit is evidence that the two did not exist universally in an antithetical relationship in early Christianity.

the Corinthian church. Specifically, he rejects eloquent wisdom because it provides yet another pretext for boasting among the Corinthians. Twice he cites biblical authority to underscore his aversion to wisdom that causes boasting (1.31; 3.19-21). In contrast, Paul affirms the wisdom to which he himself adheres (2.6-13). It is not, therefore, wisdom in general that Paul rejects, but the sort of eloquent wisdom that the Corinthians have misused.[1]

In summary, Mark 13 fits neatly into the early Jewish tradition of the Spirit as overcomer. Since it cannot be used in a general definition of early Christian rhetoric, however, only 1 Corinthians 1–2 is left on which to base such a definition. Yet Paul's reference to premeditation, alongside his failure to eschew wisdom entirely, is troubling because it implies that the Spirit did *not* overcome him when he preached.

5. *The Spirit as Artificer and Early Christian Rhetoric*

These caveats notwithstanding, Kennedy can refer to Paul's own self-descriptions in 1 Corinthians to support his definition:

> When I came to you. . . I did not come proclaiming to you the testimony of God in lofty words or wisdom. . . and my speech and my message were not in plausible words of wisdom, but in demonstration of the Spirit and of power, that your faith might not rest in human wisdom but in God's power (2.1, 4-5).

Paul's self-evaluation seems indisputably to reject the early Jewish tradition of the Spirit as artificer.

Nevertheless, a disparity exists between *what* Paul says and *how* Paul says it. Although he ostensibly rejects rhetoric, 1 Corinthians 1–2 constitutes a rhetorical tour de force. In other words, although Paul rejects rhetoric, he utilizes rhetoric unreservedly!

These chapters are peppered with figures of thought and speech: antithesis (1.17); anaphora and litotes (1.26); antistrophe (1.26-28); accumulation (2.1-5), etc. In them Paul employs the internal proof of enthymemes (2.10). The bulk of these chapters constitutes an ethical appeal—since Paul's authority is at stake. This wholesale use of

---

1. On Philo's similar bifurcation of σοφός and sophistry, see Horsley, 'Word of Wisdom', pp. 226-27.

rhetoric contrasts sharply with the value Paul seems to place on eloquence in 1 Corinthians 1–2.[1]

Paul relies even more on external logic. His numerous quotations and allusions to biblical texts in these chapters have led H.St.J. Thackeray, W. Wuellner, and others[2] to suggest that Paul has incorporated a midrash into this argument. Although this particular hypothesis is unprovable, it can be said with certainty that Paul's external argumentation reveals a *studied* and prepared display of rhetorical ability.

In light of Paul's ability to navigate successfully the waters of external logic, it is no wonder that H. Conzelmann suggested that Paul had his own wisdom school![3] Like the sage of Sirach 39, Paul knows Torah, quotes from the prophets, and ascertains hidden meanings (1 Cor. 2.7). Like wisdom in the Wisdom of Solomon, he uses terms of speech (cf. Wis. 8.8), and he has studied the prophets whom wisdom created (cf. Wis. 7.28). Like Daniel in the story of Susanna, he courageously overcame physical disability to speak with power.[4]

To return to our problem: a disparity between Paul's explicit rejection of rhetoric and his wholesale use of rhetoric characterizes 1 Corinthians 1–2. Which aspect of this disparity represents Paul's viewpoint? Does he regard the Spirit as overcomer or the Spirit as artificer?

Although Pauline conundrums are never easily unlocked, this one can perhaps be solved by observing Paul's use of irony in 1 Corinthians 1–4. Irony is an intentional clash of meanings between what is said and what is understood. In the *Rhetorica ad Alexandrum*, it is defined as:

> saying something while pretending not to say it, or calling things by the opposite of their real names. . . the following illustrates the device of calling things by the opposite names: 'It appears that whereas these honourable

---

1. There is no need here to recite work which has already been accomplished well by R.A. Humphries in 'Paul's Rhetoric of Argumentation in 1 Corinthians 1–4' (PhD diss., Graduate Theological Union, 1979), pp. 50-104.

2. H.St.J. Thackeray, *The Septuagint and Jewish Worship* (London: Oxford University Press, 1921); N.E. Peterson, '1 Korinther 1.18f. und die Thematik des jüdischen Busstages', *Bib* 32 (1951), pp. 97-103; on these see also Johannes Munck, *Paul and the Salvation of Mankind* (Richmond, VA: John Knox, 1959), pp. 135-36; W. Wuellner, 'Haggadic Homily Genre in 1 Corinthians 1–3', *JBL* 89 (1970), pp. 199-204; see also Robin Scroggs, 'Σοφός and πνευματικός', *NTS* 14 (1967–68), pp. 33-55, esp. pp. 48-50 on Wis. 9.9-18.

3. 'Paulus und die Weisheit', *NTS* 12 (1965–66), pp. 231-44.

4. For Daniel this is youth; for Paul it is unknown (2.1-4).

gentlemen have done our allies a great deal of harm, we base creatures have caused them many benefits'. . . In vituperations also you should employ irony, and ridicule your opponent for the things on which he prides himself.[1]

The most distinctive characteristic of irony is a clash of meaning between what is said and what is meant ('saying something while pretending not to say it').[2] This is precisely what we discover in 1 Corinthians 1–2, where there are two levels to Paul's irony. The first is the explicit level, on which Paul rejects rhetoric and wisdom. Here he concedes that he lacks rhetorical skill. The second level, which clashes with the first, is the deeper level, on which Paul embraces rhetoric and wisdom. Here he writes with reasoned persuasiveness. Rejecting rhetoric while simultaneously demonstrating his rhetorical skill allows Paul to eschew the Corinthians' boastful rhetoric and subtly to show his own rhetorical prowess to those who value rhetorical prowess so highly. A. Lynch, Kennedy's first student of New Testament rhetoric, encapsulated this observation on the penultimate page of his thesis:

> On one level Paul is merely an apologist, explaining away his former ineloquence. On a more literary level, the one most accessible to his sophisticated opponents, he is an orator delivering a rhetorical tour-de-force, blending. . . metaphor[,] enthymeme and antithesis into an artistic whole so impressive as to scatter his critics; turning the tables so that it was not he who was ineloquent, but they who were too immature to grasp true eloquence (3.1-3). . . Throughout his attack on worldly wisdom ... Paul on a higher level is practicing a polished literary rhetoric which serves to refute the claim that he is ineloquent.[3]

Another characteristic of irony is self-depreciation ('we base creatures'). It is apparent in 1 Cor. 4.9-13, in which Paul calls the apostles 'a spectacle', 'fools', 'weak', 'ill-clad', 'the refuse of the world', etc. Although 4.9-13 is an ironic apex, self-depreciation, I suggest, begins

1. As quoted by C. Forbes, 'Comparison, Self-Praise and Irony: Paul's Boasting and Conventions of Hellenistic Rhetoric', *NTS* 32 (1986), p. 10. His references are 1434a and 1441b.23. See also Quint. 9.2.44-46.

2. Secondary sources that refer to primary sources in their helpful explanations of irony include P.D. Duke, *Irony in the Fourth Gospel* (Atlanta: John Knox, 1985), pp. 13-18; K.A. Plank, *Paul and the Irony of Affliction* (SBLSS; Atlanta: Scholars Press, 1987). Plank (p. 35) quotes W.C. Booth: 'regardless of how broadly or narrowly he defines irony. . . every reader learns that some statements cannot be understood without rejecting what they seem to say'.

3. A. Lynch, 'Pauline Rhetoric: 1 Corinthians 1.10–4.21' (MA thesis, University of North Carolina at Chapel Hill, 1981).

already in 2.1-4: although Paul denigrates his eloquence, he does so as the self-depreciating εἴρων.[1] This irony becomes evident in comparison with 1 Thess. 1.5, where eloquence and the Spirit complement each other: 'for our gospel came to you not only in word, but also in power and in the Holy Spirit and full conviction'. In 1 Thessalonians, where Paul can be straightforward and less polemical, his true opinion of his preaching emerges: it is a combination of rhetoric and Spirit. But in 1 Corinthians, where Paul's authority is being challenged forcefully, he plays the role of εἴρων, disarming his opponents by agreeing that he lacks eloquence.

It is irony rather than honesty that gives 1 Corinthians 1-2 its tone. Although what Paul writes is a rejection of rhetoric, how he writes establishes him as a rhetor. Although he concedes that he lacks eloquence, to play the part of εἴρων, in fact he believes that the Spirit does inspire his rhetoric.

What Paul says, then—that he came with power but not eloquence—fits well into the early Jewish tradition of the Spirit as overcomer. *How* he writes—with all the resources of classical rhetoric—indicates that he considers his rhetoric to be a product of the Spirit as artificer. Paul demonstrates the power of the Spirit, not apart from, but by means of his rhetoric. In particular, he demonstrates the power of the Spirit with quotations of, and allusions to, biblical texts which quell Corinthian boastfulness. Paul did come with the power of the Spirit to the Corinthians, but—as much as he plays the εἴρων and depreciates his eloquence—his letter demonstrates that it was an eloquent power of wisdom, one which the Corinthians could not, and still do not, grasp (2.6-13; 3.1-4).[2]

IV

With this observation about Paul's eloquence, our exploration of Kennedy's definition of radical Christian rhetoric is done. We have

1. See Plank, *Affliction*, p. 39; Forbes, 'Comparison', pp. 10-13.
2. The comment by B. Pearson ('Hellenistic-Jewish Wisdom Speculation and Paul', *Aspects of Wisdom in Judaism and Early Christianity* [ed. R.L. Wilken; Notre Dame: University of Notre Dame, 1975], p. 48) is germane because it combines, though without explanation, references to wisdom and irony: 'It is crucial for an understanding of Paul's argument [in 1 Corinthians] to notice his heavy use of irony. It should also be observed, however, that Paul's arguments are themselves based largely on conceptions and traditions at home in the Jewish schools of wisdom. . .'

arrived at a tentative conclusion: Kennedy's definition of radical Christian rhetoric does in fact draw too radical a distinction between the Spirit and rhetoric, between Christian preaching as proclamation and Christian preaching as persuasion.

To be sure, radical Christian rhetoric claimed to be proclamation inspired by the Spirit. In this respect, it fits well into the early Jewish tradition of the Spirit which produces speech by overcoming the speaker. But neither of the two NT passages that Kennedy cites can bear the weight of his definition. Mark 13 deals with a concrete situation of early Christians on trial. 1 Corinthians 1–2, while it appears to support Dr Kennedy's contention that early Christian rhetoric was inspired proclamation rather than reasoned persuasion, actually exhibits considerable irony. Paul appears to disclaim rhetorical eloquence while at the same time writing with considerable rhetorical skill. This communicates that, although he appears to reject rhetoric, he is in fact a masterful proponent of rhetoric. The true rhetoric to which Paul adheres is the studied rhetoric of the sage who pores over ancient wisdom and turns of phrase, and who is renowned for instructive and persuasive speech.

THE TEMPLE CONFLICT SCENE:
A RHETORICAL ANALYSIS OF MATTHEW 21–23

Rollin Grams

'Of the four Gospels, Matthew's makes the widest use of all aspects of rhetoric. He arranges his Gospel into distinct parts which perform specific rhetorical functions. . .'[1] The following study of Matthew's Temple Conflict Scene (chs. 21–23) is inspired by an interest in plumbing the latent possibilities in this comment by Dr Kennedy regarding rhetorical criticism's contribution to studies of thematic units in the Gospels, especially Matthew. I also owe inspiration for this study to a suggestion by Dr Kennedy that this particular section of Matthew would make an interesting study from a rhetorical perspective. I would like not only to elucidate the rhetorical features of Matthew 21–23, but also to demonstrate a more general point: rhetorical criticism is one form of literary criticism which still takes seriously the concern for authorial intention and historical study.[2] This study begins with an overview of Matthew's rhetoric and then offers a rhetorical analysis of Matthew 21–23.[3]

---

1. George Kennedy, *New Testament Interpretation through Rhetorical Criticism* (Chapel Hill, NC: University of North Carolina Press, 1984), p. 101.

2. Literary studies tend to ignore such concerns. See, for example, the recent and helpful study of David R. Bauer, *The Structure of Matthew's Gospel: A Study in Literary Design* (JSNTSup 31; Sheffield: Almond, 1988). Bauer's study would be even more helpful had he taken clues to Matthew's structure and purpose from Matthew's redaction of Mark.

3. Cf. George Kennedy, *New Testament Interpretation*, ch. 1. The rhetorical problems of chs. 21–23 will be considered along with invention and style, since these are integrally related and change from pericope to pericope. See also Duane F. Watson, *Invention, Arrangement, and Style: Rhetorical Criticism of Jude and 2 Peter* (SBLDS 104; Atlanta: Scholars Press, 1988). Note Watson's synopsis of rhetorical criticism, especially for its detailed references to the rhetorical handbooks.

An Overview of Matthew's Rhetoric:
Invention, Arrangement, and Style

The Temple Conflict Scene in Matthew is an example of Matthew's creative rhetoric. A brief (and selective) overview of Matthew's rhetoric will clarify the role that the scene plays in the Gospel as a whole. Since rhetorical criticism's interest in the invention, arrangement, and style of the author is close to redaction-critical concerns, this overview will show how rhetorical criticism may build upon redaction criticism.

Rhetoric, according to Aristotle, is 'the faculty of discovering the possible means of persuasion in reference to any subject whatever'.[1] Rhetorical criticism, then, involves a study of the author's means of persuasion. As Kennedy points out, rhetoric involved five areas of interest in the rhetorical schools:

> *invention*, which deals with the planning of a discourse and the arguments to be used in it; *arrangement*, the composition of the various parts into an effective whole; *style*, which involves both choice of words and the composition of words into sentences, including the use of figures; *memory*, or preparation for delivery; and *delivery*, the rules for control of the voice and the use of gestures.[2]

1. Invention

Assuming Markan priority, Matthew's redactional and rhetorical interests may be described as follows. First, Matthew improves Mark's invention in several ways: by adding proof from the OT, by bringing together the external proof of Jesus' miracles into a unit in chs. 8–9 and increasing the numbers of those involved in the miracles, and by improving Mark's external proof of resurrection witnesses in his Gospel's ending. With respect to internal or artistic proofs, Matthew increases the degree of *pathos* felt toward the Pharisees, increases Jesus' and the disciples' *ethos* by eliminating from Mark's account things which could detract from their character,[3] and expands the

---

1. *Rhet.* 1.2.2.
2. Kennedy, *New Testament Interpretation*, pp. 13-14.
3. Cf. W.C. Allen, *A Critical and Exegetical Commentary on the Gospel According to Matthew* (ICC; 3rd edn; Edinburgh: T. & T. Clark, 1912), pp. 104-105.

argument's *logos* by adding considerably more teaching material of Jesus, particularly parables.[1]

2. *Arrangement*

Matthew's arrangement of the story of Jesus also demonstrates his rhetorical interests.[2] Discussions of Matthew's structure abound, but I shall argue that the Gospel is best understood as a reinforcement of themes found in Mark's loose structure.[3] In fact, Matthew follows Mark's basic outline, but slightly rearranges and greatly expands Mark's outline into a topical arrangement of the story of Jesus. I find the following basic structure in Matthew's Gospel (Part III is more detailed because it needs more proof).

1. Kennedy (*New Testament Interpretation*, pp. 102-104) sees Matthew's concern for 'something close to logical argument' as one of the salient features of this Gospel.

2. Bauer (*Structure*, p. 55) argues from the history of the question of Matthew's structure that any satisfactory explanation of Matthew's structure must concern itself with six matters: '(1) the significance of geographical and chronological references for the structure of Matthew's Gospel; (2) the relationship between narrative and discourse material, including the structural significance of the fivefold formula at 7.28; 11.1; 13.53; 19.1; 26.1; (3) the meaning of the formula repeated at 4.17 and 16.21; and the relationship between this formula and the fivefold formula; (4) the relevance and function of characteristic Matthean literary devices, such as chiasm, *inclusio*, numerical arrangement, for the problem of Matthew's macrostructure; (5) the existence of discrete topical units within the Gospel and, if in fact these units exist, their unity and interrelationships; (6) the implications of Matthew's structure for his theology, especially in terms of Christology and salvation history'. To this I would add (7) that one must attend to the clues to structure and purpose which might be found in Matthew's redaction of Mark. In this paper I address in part all but the first of these matters.

3. For discussions of Matthew's structure, cf. especially Bauer, *Structure*. Another excellent study of suggestions regarding Matthew's structure may be found in Thomas Wolthuis, 'Experiencing the Kingdom: Reading the Gospel of Matthew' (PhD Diss., Duke University, 1987). Also see W.D. Davies and Dale Allison, *The Gospel According to St. Matthew* (ICC; Edinburgh: T. & T. Clark, 1988), I, pp. 58-72. I do not mean to suggest that the discourses may not have unique functions in Matthew (e.g. an ecclesiastical function of the discourses, which build toward the climax of Mt. 28.16-20's affirmation of the Lord's presence with his disciples). This point has also been demonstrated by Bauer (*Structure*, pp. 129-34). Yet the discourses are not structurally separate from Matthew's thematic arrangement (chs. 24–25 being the only exception).

I.   Beginnings (1.1–4.22)
   A.   Infancy Narratives (1.1–2.23)
   B.   John the Baptist Prepares the Way (3.1-17)
   C.   The Beginning of Jesus' Ministry (4.1-22)

II. Jesus' Ministry of Teaching (chs. 5–7) and Miracles (chs. 8–9)
   A.   Ministry Summary (4.23-25)
   B.   Jesus' Ministry of Teaching (5.1–7.29)
   C.   Jesus' Ministry of Miracles (8.1–9.34)
   D.   Ministry Summary (9.35-38)

III. Responses to Jesus' Ministry (10.1–17.27)
   A.   Instruction: Responses to Jesus' Disciples' Ministry (10.1-42)
   B.   Question of John the Baptist and Responses to his and Jesus' Ministries (11.1-30)
   C.   Various Responses to Jesus' Ministry (chs. 12–17)
      1.   The Pharisees' Murderous Response (12.1-14)
      2.   The Crowd's Response and Scripture's Testimony (12.15-21)
      3.   The Pharisees' Blasphemous and Sign-Seeking Response (12.22-45)
      4.   True Response: My mother and my brothers (12.46-50)
      5.   Parables of Response and Judgment (13.1-52)
         a.   Parable: The Response of Soils (13.1-23)
         b.   Parable of Weeds: Delayed Judgment until Fulness of Responses (13.24-43)—Including two other Parables on Slowness of the Time of Fulness (Mustard Seed and Yeast—13.31-33)
         c.   Parables of Treasure and Pearl: Response to Precious Kingdom (13.44-46)
         d.   Parable of the Net: Certainty of Judgment (13.47-52)
      6.   Response of Nazareth (13.53-58)
      7.   Herod's Response to Jesus and John (14.1-12)
      8.   The Crowd's and Disciples' Responses (14.13-36)
      9.   The Pharisees' and Scribes' Response (15.1-20)
      10. A Gentile's Response (15.21-28)
      11. The Crowd's Response (15.29-39)
      12. The Pharisees' and Sadducees' Response (16.1-12)
      13. Peter's Response and Jesus' New Teaching (16.13-28)
      14. God's Response: The Transfiguration (17.1-13)
      15. Response of Faith: Epileptic Boy Healed (17.14-23)
      16. Disciples' Response to Powers of This Age: The Temple Tax (17.24-27)

IV. Greatness and Discipleship—Audience: Disciples (18.1–20.34)

V.   Judicial Conflict at the Temple—Jesus and Jewish Leaders (chs. 21–23)

VI. Jesus' Apocalyptic Teachings to Disciples (chs. 24–25)

VII. Jesus' Passion and Resurrection (chs. 26–28)

In support of this topical structuring of Matthew, note the following:

1. Only once (Jesus' apocalyptic teachings in chs. 24–25) does a discourse function as a theme unto itself. The Sermon on the Mount is clearly part of a larger section introduced by 4.23-25 and concluded by 9.35-38. Chapters 10 and 13 are best taken as expansions of teaching material already in Mark in a larger section dealing with responses to Jesus' ministry.[1] In ch. 18 we again have material from Mark (9.33-37, 42-48) expanded into the theme of Jesus' teaching on greatness in discipleship (chs. 18–20). Chapter 23, which some have taken as part of chs. 24–25 in order to find five discourses in Matthew, is clearly part of the section of Jesus' conflict with Israel's leaders in chs. 21-23.[2] Once again, a Markan suggestion is turned into a discourse by transformation and expansion. Where Mark warned about the scribes and concluded with the widow's gift (which also nicely concludes the scenes at the temple—corresponding to the moneychangers at the beginning of the temple scene) Matthew now has a whole speech of woes against scribes and Pharisees. Thus Matthew's repeated phrase, 'After Jesus finished saying these things', is an obvious conclusion to a section of discourse, but has no significance to the overall structure of the Gospel.[3]

2. Matthew's arrangement is both according to theological topics (e.g. chs. 24–25) and ministerial topics (e.g. 4.23–9.38), and both topics may give shape to a unit. Where miracles appear outside of chs. 8–9 they demonstrate a point other than the fact that Jesus was a miracle-worker, and parables occur in thematic arrange-

---

1. Perhaps this is the most controversial suggestion in my outline. In its defense, I would point out that (1) the stories follow closely Mark's structure and order; (2) the preceding and following thematic units force a definition on the intervening chapters; (3) a loosely defined theme can be seen in these pericopae—responses to Jesus' ministry defined in the previous section (see outline, above).

2. Taking ch. 23 with chs. 24–25, while most frequently associated with B.W. Bacon (*Studies in Matthew* [London: Constable, 1930], and 'The "Five Books" of Matthew against the Jews', *Expositor* 15 [1918], pp. 55-66) is by no means a dated practice, despite the violence it does to the unit formed by chs. 21–23. Cf. e.g. R.H. Gundry, *Matthew: A Commentary on his Literary and Theological Art* (Grand Rapids: Baker, 1982).

3. With Gundry (*Matthew*, pp. 10-11) I would argue that the five formulae which conclude discourses in Matthew have no further function of structuring Matthew as a whole, and the transitional notes at 4.17 and 16.21 mark turning points in Jesus' life, but not in the Gospel's structure.

ments (e.g. ch. 13, responses to kingdom and judgment; chs. 21–22, challenges to leaders' authority; ch. 25, readiness).[1] The topic in chs. 8–9 happens to be that Jesus worked miracles, and that in ch. 13 is, in part, that Jesus taught in parables. Thus Matthew's arrangement includes both narrative topics describing Jesus' ministry and didactic topics covering Jesus' teaching.

3. Matthew follows Mark closely earlier than 14.1, as some scholars assert.[2] From 9.35 Matthew retains Mark's structure. Having removed certain pericopae from Mk 2.23–8.32 to fill in his earlier narrative, Matthew now proceeds with what is left in Mark, expanding Mark at four major points with primarily discourse material: the sending out of the 12 (ch. 10), the teaching of Jesus in parables of the response to his ministry of the kingdom of heaven (ch. 13), Jesus' teaching on the character of a disciple (ch. 18), and the end of Jesus' temple conflict with religious leaders (ch. 23). Each of these is fitted into the Markan narrative, and, by this expansion, the Markan collection of pericopae is given a thematic form. The first two discourses more clearly define Matthew 10–17 as a section of responses to Jesus' teaching; the third more clearly defines Matthew 18–20 as a section of Jesus' teaching on discipleship; the fourth reshapes teaching for disciples in Mark into a discourse spoken as much to scribes and Pharisees as to disciples, thus rounding off a conflict scene at the temple with a pronouncement of judgment. Indeed, the only place where Matthew truly restructures Mark is in chs. 8–9; Matthew primarily attains his thematic structuring of Mark's collection of stories by *adding* material.

---

1. Falling in the *inclusio* of 4.23-25 and 9.35-38 and being a collection of miracles stories, chs. 8–9 surely first and foremost are intended to illustrate Jesus' miracles. That they may have been grouped according to theological themes within this ministerial theme may well also be the case. Cf. Heinz J. Held, 'Matthew as Interpreter of the Miracle Stories', *Tradition and Interpretation in Matthew* (ed. Günther Bornkamm, *et al.*; NTL; Philadelphia: Westminster, 1963), pp. 165-299; Jack D. Kingsbury, 'Observations on the "Miracle Chapters" of Matthew 8–9', *CBQ* 40 (1978), pp. 559-73.

2. E.g. Gundry (*Matthew*, p. 10) believes that Matthew restructured Mark in the first half of his Gospel, but discontinued restructuring in the second half of his Gospel due to editorial fatigue. Cf. Davies and Allison, *Matthew*, I, p. 73, and many others.

3. Style

Redaction criticism can tell us something of Matthew's style. A thorough discussion of Matthew's style may now be found in Davies and Allison.[1] In light of this work, note especially their demonstration of Matthew's preference for threefold examples to illustrate a point.[2] Another stylistic feature of Matthew is interest in shortening the length of Mark's stories and lengthening the overall story of Jesus. Little of Mark is excluded; much is added. Again, the structure of Mark's story is in large part retained, but Matthew imposes a thematic structure upon it.

Rhetorical Analysis of the Temple Conflict Scene (Mt. 21–23)

1. The Rhetorical Unit

The rhetorical unit is established by the place, persons, and topic under consideration. Matthew 20 concludes a section in which Jesus elucidates the characteristics of true discipleship for his disciples. The question about greatness in ch. 18 is still being addressed in 20.20-28, and the pericope about the two blind men receiving their sight (20.29-34) functions as an example of what Jesus has been teaching—discipleship is for the humble and poor. In 21.1ff., Jesus finally comes into Jerusalem, and the story moves from one of teaching the disciples to confrontation with the religious leaders of Judaism. The confrontation may be structured around questions from each side challenging the other's authority, and Jesus' final indictment. The entire section has the character of an ad hoc trial scene in which one is never sure who is on trial and who is prosecuting. In the end (ch. 23) Jesus pronounces God's final verdict of condemnation on the religious leaders of Judaism. With ch. 24 Jesus is again alone with the disciples, teaching on eschatology.

Matthew 21–23 is also defined as a unit christologically, and two *inclusios* demonstrate this. The one who rode into Jerusalem and was rejected (21.1ff.) will not return until Jerusalem says, 'Blessed is the one who comes in the name of the Lord' (23.39). By riding into Jerusalem, Jesus makes royal, messianic claims, and thus the conflicts are also flanked with a story of Jesus seen as Son of David and a ques-

---

1. Davies and Allison, *Matthew*, I, pp. 72-96.
2. Davies and Allison, *Matthew*, I, pp. 58-72.

tioning by Jesus of the adequacy of this title for depicting the Messiah's authority (21.1ff.; 22.41ff.).

2. *The Rhetorical Situation*

The rhetorical situation is established by three pericopae: Jesus' entry into Jerusalem, cleansing of the temple, and cursing of the fig tree. Although the disciples are the only ones present for all three parabolic actions of Jesus (and the Gospel readers as well), the question of the chief priests and elders in 21.23, 'By whose authority are you doing such things?' presupposes all three actions which challenge their authority.

Jesus' triumphal entry into Jerusalem challenges Judaism inasmuch as Jesus unquestionably claims Zech. 9.9 for himself. The crowd recognizes this and appropriately proclaims him to be the Son of David, one sent by God to bring salvation. This is Jesus' most forthright messianic claim in public, and it calls for an explanation.

Since Peter's confession in Caesarea-Philippi, the Gospel's readers have been prepared for this moment, for Jesus has warned his disciples that 'he must go to Jerusalem and suffer many things at the hands of the elders, chief priests and teachers of the law, and that he must be killed and on the third day be raised to life' (16.21). Jesus is well aware that his temple conflict precipitates events leading to this prophecy's fulfillment, as he suggests in 23.37: Jerusalem is the place where the prophets are killed. As Messiah and Servant sent from God (16.16; 12.18; 13.53ff.), Jesus' ultimate fate is confrontation and death at the hands of the sinful people whom he redeems (20.28). Jesus' exigence at this moment is his whole prophetic and messianic ministry: the secrecy as to his identity is now publicly, although parabolically, announced; his proclamation of the kingdom of heaven, entailing the coming of God's righteous judgment, is now in full view as he enters Jerusalem to judge and be judged; his role as Savior is about to be fulfilled as the confrontation leads to his death, which is, ironically, salvific for sinful humanity. The exigence of the leaders of Jerusalem is their inability to ignore Jesus' brave actions and challenges; they must address the situation at the risk of their own leadership positions. Hence they come to him (Jesus never goes to them) and initiate the conflict. But first Jesus performs two more symbolic actions challenging Judaism as a whole.

Jesus' cleansing of the temple involves three challenges. He calls for changes of the worshipers, the worship, and the worship leaders.[1] These three challenges are reflected in the three quotations from Scripture which Jesus gives to defend his action. The first quotation is Isa. 56.7, the context of which speaks of a change of worshipers in God's temple. Jesus actually only quotes, 'My house will be called a house of prayer', but Isaiah goes on to describe how eunuchs and Gentiles will be incorporated into the temple worship.[2] This fits the story of Jesus' cleansing of the temple of money-changers and sales-people in the Gentile court, since immediately after these actions, Jesus heals those unworthy to enter the temple—the blind and the lame—and children in the temple begin shouting, praising Jesus, 'Hosanna to the Son of David'.

The second quotation comes from Jer. 7.11, the context of which elaborates on the false security Israel places in the temple when they in fact practice injustice. The prophet warns all who come through the gates to worship the Lord (7.2) that they will be removed from Israel.

---

1. Cf. E.P. Sanders's discussion of Jewish thoughts on an eschatological new temple in *Jesus and Judaism* (Philadelphia: Fortress, 1985), pp. 77-90. His references are relevant here, although his historical interests and concerns are quite different from those of this study.

2. Mark includes 'for all nations' (11.17). Why should Matthew exclude these words? Matthew's interest in the kingdom for the Gentiles appears at the end of his Gospel (28.18ff.), with proleptic foreshadowings in 8.5-13 and 15.21-28. Perhaps Matthew's omission of these words from Mark and Isaiah is in the interest of greater inclusiveness than the word 'nations' allows: the new worshipers were the unholy generally, not only the Gentiles. Thus Jesus heals the blind and lame, many of whom would not have been permitted into the temple (21.14). Cf. J. Jeremias, *Jerusalem in the Time of Jesus: An Investigation into Economic and Social Conditions during the New Testament Period* (Philadelphia: Fortress, 1969), pp. 117-18. Some see 2 Sam. 5.8 behind this text (e.g. Gundry, *Matthew*, p. 413). But more likely texts such as Mic. 4.6-7, Isa. 35.5-6 and 61.1, which describe the Day of the Lord in terms of restoring the lame and blind, underlie our passage. Also cf. Jn 5 and 9. Subsequently, Jesus says to the chief priests and elders that tax collectors and prostitutes are entering the kingdom of heaven before them (21.31), that the vineyard will be taken from them (now the chief priests and Pharisees, 21.45) and given to a nation producing fruit (21.43, not in Mark), and that the invited guests will be replaced by those off the street (22.9). Earlier Jesus said that some have become eunuchs for the kingdom (19.12), a defect which would have excluded one from temple service (cf. Jeremias, *Jerusalem*, pp. 343-44). Thus I understand Matthew to regard Jesus' coming as significant for the Gentiles' salvation and for Israel's judgment (cf. 23.39). This fact would suggest that he would have understood Jesus' quotation from Isa. 56 in reference to the outcasts, including the Gentiles.

The indictment of Israel which led to the Babylonian captivity is once again applicable in Jesus' day. This second quotation, then, is an indictment of the worship which Israel is offering God. By citing it Jesus announces that both the worship and the worshippers will be changed in God's impending judgment.

Also, as Jesus' third quotation shows, the worship leaders will be exchanged. The chief priests and elders contrast with the children in the pericope, the former passing judgment on Jesus, the latter offering praise. Jesus quotes from Ps. 8.2, which here functions prophetically, saying that the worshipers and worship leaders will be exchanged for children. In Matthew's Gospel the children or little ones are the disciples of the kingdom.[1] Psalm 8 speaks of God's ordaining and accepting humankind's worship of him despite its insignificance in his majestic creation. If worshipers are acceptable only because God has made them so, then worship leaders are acceptable, not because of their status, but because God has ordained the little ones of creation to lead his creation in worship. The disciples, who are given the keys of the kingdom, the power of binding and loosing (Mt. 16.19; 18.18), who have been given clear instruction about greatness and servanthood (chs. 18–20), are now portrayed as the new leaders of Israel through the response of the children in the temple (and this is confirmed in the next pericope).

Jesus' cursing of the fig tree is more than a pericope teaching about faith. The image of bearing fruit is used in various ways in the OT to refer to the life of Israel.[2] The failure of Israel, and of her leaders in particular, has led to this divine curse. In its place are now put the disciples, whose worship will be through faith and prayer, not through works and earthly authority. Thus, like the pericope on the cleansing of the temple, this too involves the idea of a change of worshipers (those who bear fruit), worship (faith and prayer), and worship leaders (the disciples, the little ones, those who can move mountains).

These challenges to the religious authorities cannot go unnoticed, and the situation leads to a series of conflicts between them and Jesus.

---

1. E.g. Mt. 5.1-12; 10.42; 11.25; 18.1-14; 19.13-15; 20.1-16; 21.33-46; 22.1-14; 25.31-46.
2. E.g. Isa. 5.1-7; 11.1; Ezek. 17; Joel 1.7; Mic. 7.1-6.

3. *The Rhetorical Species*

The rhetorical situation as a whole is one of judgment; the species of rhetoric is judicial. The legal issue in this public trial is one called transference, that is, proof and refutation must center around who has the right to proclaim judgment.[1]

At the beginning and ending of the trial, Jesus asks questions which his opponents cannot answer. These two questions form an *inclusio* for the other conflict material, and they serve to demonstrate Jesus' authority from start to finish in the 'trial'. If Jesus is to submit to the role of defendant, he will also be the prosecutor. Indeed, the 'judicial' scene is one in which the roles of prosecutor and defendant shift between Jesus and the leaders, and Jesus wins the trial by virtue of being the final prosecutor, the leaders being unable to reply to his question.

4. *The Rhetorical Arrangement*

The following is an outline of the Temple Conflict Scene.

I. *Narratio*: Three Parabolic Actions: Jesus' Authority (21.1-22)
   A. Triumphal Entry—Jesus as Son of David (21.1-11)
   B. Temple Cleansing—Jesus as Son of David and Judge (21.12-17)
   C. Tree Cursing—Jesus as Judge (21.18-22)

II. First Stage of Proof: Opening Question over Authority (21.22–22.14)
   A. The Chief Priests' and Elders' Question (21.23-27)
   B. Jesus' Three Parabolic Questions Challenging the Leaders' Authority
      (21.28–22.14)
      1. Parable of the Two Sons (21.28-32)
      2. Parable of the Wicked Tenants (21.33-46)
      3. Parable of the Wedding Banquet (22.1-14)

III. Second Stage of Proof: Questions for Entrapment—Tests for Jesus' Authority
      (22.15-40)
   A. Pharisees and Herodians on Taxation (22.15-22)
   B. Sadducees on Resurrection (22.23-33)
   C. Pharisees and Scribes on Greatest Command (22.34-40)

IV. Third Stage of Proof: Closing Question by Jesus on the Authority of the
      Messiah (22.41-46)

V. *Peroratio*: Jesus' Verdict: Epideictic Speech against the Pharisees and Scribes
      (23.1-39)

1. *Her.* 1.11.

A. First Section: Do not do as the scribes and Pharisees (spoken to crowd and disciples) (23.1-12)
1. Reason: scribes and Pharisees sit in Moses' seat (23.2)
2. Conclusion: obey what they say (23.3)
3. Conclusion: do not do as they do (23.3)
4. Reasons:
     a. they do not practice what they preach (23.3)
     b. they burden people down and will not help them (23.4)
     c. they do things for show (23.5)
         (1) Three examples (two parts each)
             (a) Example: they make their phylacteries wide, they make their prayer shawls long (23.5)
             (b) Example: they love the place of honor at banquets, they love the most important seats at synagogue (23.6)
             (c) Example: they love to be greeted in the market-places, they love to be called 'Rabbi' (23.7)
         (2) Three contrasting enthymemes to the last example:
             (a) Do not be called Rabbi (23.8)
             (b) Do not call others 'father' (23.9)
             (c) Do not be called 'teacher' (23.10)
         (3) Conclusion: contrasting maxim (23.11-12)
B. Second Section: Seven Woes (spoken to scribes and Pharisees) (23.13-33)
1. First Woe (23.13-14)
2. Second Woe (23.15)
3. Third Woe (23.16-22)
4. Fourth Woe (23.23-24)
5. Fifth Woe (23.25-26)
6. Sixth Woe (23.27-28)
7. Seventh Woe (23.29-33)
C. Third Section: *Peroratio*—Judgment (spoken to Israel) (23.34-39).
1. Judgment for murdering God's messengers (23.34-36)
2. Delay of Christ's return until they accept God's messenger (23.37-39)

The arrangement of the Temple Conflict Scene is highly rhetorical. Two questions over authority, at the beginning by the chief priests and elders and at the end by Jesus, form an *inclusio* for the whole conflict. The sequence of events fits into groupings of three, a typical feature of Matthew's rhetoric: three action parables, three stages to the conflict scene, three parables, three questions for entrapment, three stages to the speech in ch. 23, three reasons for not following the Pharisees' example, three groupings of six examples of how the Pharisees do things for show, and three concluding enthymemes.

5. *Rhetorical Problems, Invention, and Style*

As noted above, invention has to do with modes of non-artistic (use of witnesses, documents) and artistic (*ethos, pathos, logos*) proof, and the manner of proof (i.e. the *stasis* of the speaker and his/her arguments). Style has to do with the virtues of the speech or narrative (correctness, clarity, ornamentation, propriety), the level of style (plain, middle, grand), and the stylistic features (figures of speech, including tropes, and figures of thought). While one may analyze the invention and style of a passage in great detail, a briefer analysis must suffice here in conjunction with an analysis of the rhetorical problems.

a. *First Stage of the Proof (21.23–22.14).* Several of the leading groups in Judaism (except the Essenes and Zealots) challenge Jesus, whose rhetorical problems may be seen in the difficulty of answering the questions which they pose. Jesus' challenges to the worship, worshipers, and worship leaders of Judaism all constitute a christological challenge: 'Accept that I am the authoritative One about whom Zechariah spoke, worthy to receive praise in the temple, legitimate Judge of Israel's worship'. One claiming such authority must overcome the challenge of Israel's leaders. Thus the *ethos* of the speakers is important, although the means by which it is established is through *logos*, the ability to answer questions rightly. The *stasis* is one of jurisdiction, for Jesus and the leaders reject each other's right to pass judgment.

The first group which challenges Jesus' authority consists of the chief priests, who are first teamed with the scribes against Jesus for his reception of the children's praise (21.15), then with the elders (21.23), and then with the Pharisees (21.45). The chief priests and elders ask, 'By what authority are you doing these things? Who gave you this authority?' How is Jesus to respond? A *stasis* of fact dependent upon Jesus' own testimony ('by God's authority') will carry no weight on a matter where authority is disputed. Previously Jesus had met the Pharisees in debate resting on a *stasis* of quality (what does it mean to pluck grain on the Sabbath?, 12.1-14) and in another debate resting on a *stasis* of fact (does Jesus drive out demons by Satanic power?, 12.22-45). Jesus' coming to Jerusalem moves the *stasis* of his ongoing debate with the Jewish leaders to one of jurisdiction.

Jesus' response is based on a dispute over jurisdiction in three ways. First, in the presence of the crowds, he responds with a question which ultimately undermines the leaders' authority: 'John's baptism, where did it come from? Was it from heaven, or from men?' (21.25) Since the crowds accept that John the Baptist was sent by God, for the leaders to say he was not would destroy their authority over the people, and to say he was would do likewise because they would then be inconsistent, not having previously accepted John's baptism. Second, Jesus' question about John the Baptist is an argument from the *stasis* of authority inasmuch as John testified of Jesus. To accept John was to accept the One about whom he testified. Like the three parables which follow, Jesus requires the chief priests and elders to pass judgment in a situation which has direct consequences for their own credibility as leaders. Third, if answering questions is going to prove one's authority, then Jesus will ask a question which the chief priests and elders cannot answer.

In Jesus' indictment of the chief priests and elders he offers proof by means of fictitious example, that is, through parables (21.28–22.14).[1] These three parables advance the argument that the leaders have no jurisdiction. The first, the parable of the two sons, argues that sinners are entering the kingdom of heaven before the leaders since the latter have not repented and believed the way of righteousness. The second, the parable of the wicked tenants, argues that the leaders will be punished and replaced since they abused their authority. The third, the parable of the wedding banquet, argues that those who have been invited (the leaders are particularly in mind if not exclusively so) will be punished and replaced in the kingdom of heaven by any others since they refused the invitation and abused God's servants who invited them.

These parables could have been formulated as enthymemes: *this* will happen because *that* was done. However, Jesus teaches primarily through the inductive rhetoric of parables, and here we see the effectiveness of this type of teaching. Aristotle saw inductive argument as usually unsuited to judicial speeches when one could speak enthymematically; examples should follow enthymemes and thereby resemble evidence as opposed to induction.[2] However, in Matthew the parables function effectively as interrogation and for self-indictment. The parabolic examples are stated, then the leaders are asked to make a

---

1. Cf. Ar. *Rhet.* 2.20.
2. *Rhet.* 2.20.9.

judgment on the example, but by so doing they indict themselves.[1] Such inductive rhetoric is highly suitable when direct confrontation is either impossible or ineffective. The leaders are on the witness stand, forced to respond to the examples in the parables rather than be called to account for their specific actions. If Jesus had spoken enthymematically, they could have replied, 'No, we are following the way of righteousness, we have not abused our authority, we have accepted the invitation of God'. However, presented through examples, they can only reply that those in the parables have done wrong. The implicit assumption is that those in the parables who have done wrong are to be identified with the leaders. Hence the self-indictment, but only because Jesus makes explicit the connection between the characters in the example and the leaders. Here he introduces enthymemes:

1. 'I tell you the truth, the tax collectors and the prostitutes are preceding you into the Kingdom of God. *For* John came to you. . . and you did not believe him, but the tax collectors and the prostitutes did. And even after you saw this, you did not repent. . .' (21.31-32).

2. After the parable of the wicked tenants, the leaders indict themselves again, and then Jesus quotes Ps. 118.22-23, which is used as a proof that the kingdom will be taken away from them and that they will be 'crushed' (21.42-44). Verse 44 has the character of a maxim: 'The one who falls on this stone will be broken to pieces, but the one on whom it falls will be crushed'.

3. The parable of the wedding banquet does not have a postscript identifying the leaders in it. This would hardly be necessary, since the two previous examples set the pattern. But it does end with a maxim: 'For many are called, but few are chosen' (22.14).[2] The 'for' indicates that the maxim functions as a reason for the judgment rendered in the parable. Jesus' maxims also add to his *ethos*, since they pronounce memorable, eternal truths.[3]

Thus the parables of Jesus function as interrogation and indictment of the leaders. The mode of proof is reason (*logos*), argued through three fictitious examples with enthymemes and maxims. At this point,

---

1. Jesus gives no opportunity for such a response after the final parable, preferring to give the indictment himself.
2. Note the homoeoptoton of this maxim.
3. Ar. *Rhet.* 2.21.16.

the leaders have indicted themselves, and Jesus' authority stands firm. Also at this point, Matthew writes that the Pharisees 'laid plans to trap him in his words' (22.15); they try to put Jesus on public trial (22.15-40).[1]

b. *Second Stage of the Proof (22.15-40)*. The second group which questions Jesus consists of an unlikely mix, the Pharisees and the Herodians. Yet the Pharisees solicit the Herodians' company in order to set a rhetorical trap for Jesus. When the Pharisees approach Jesus they use flattery in an attempt to disarm him so that he will say what he really believes and not be cautious and so avoid their trap (22.16). They ask, 'Is it right to pay taxes to Caesar or not?' An affirmative response would bring Jesus into disfavor with many Jews (and especially the group known as the Zealots); to respond in the negative could have led to Jesus' immediate arrest by the Herodians.

Jesus' response entails an interesting combination of *stases*. He asks them a question of fact, 'Whose portrait is on the denarius?' (the coin used for the tax). Their response, 'Caesar's', shifts the *stasis* of the overall argument to one of definition: 'What does it mean to pay taxes?' Jesus replies, 'Give to Caesar the things that are Caesar's and to God the things that are God's'. His point is that the matter is not one of religious concern; but such a definition would not have been accepted by the crowds if it were not for the undeniable argument of fact: the coin itself testifies to whom it belongs. The potency of Jesus' reply may be better appreciated once one realizes that this very logic operated at the temple: money sacrifices had to be paid in Hebrew or Tyrian currency; Roman currency had to be exchanged. The blasphemous Roman coins (e.g. those which called Tiberius Caesar *divus et pontifex*

---

1. A few additional words might be said about style. The parables themselves can be understood as extended metaphors. As noted, the argument is ornamented with maxims, and there are also examples of homoeoteleuton (21.42), paramoiosis (21.41), vivid description (22.13), and reciprocal change (21.44; cf. *Her.* 4). Jesus' characteristic usage of 'Amen' (21.31) is a feature underscoring his authority. As opposed to elsewhere in the NT where 'Amen' is used in assenting to another's words, in Jesus' words it is used as a solemn formula to strengthen his own words, as in the OT, where the term was used with doxologies, oaths, blessings, curses and execration. So J. Jeremias, *New Testament Theology* (trans. J. Bowden; New York: Charles Scribner's Sons, 1971), p. 35.

maximus) were not fit for Temple worship.[1] Jesus' logic accepts the Jewish distinction of sacred and profane regarding money and temple worship, and also reasons that if money can blaspheme it can also testify. As with his parables and his question about John's authority, Jesus once again makes people respond to a secondary issue or story in a way which they cannot escape and so, by implication, to the real issue.

The third group which questions Jesus is the Sadducees, who try to trap him in the theology of the resurrection. The rhetorical problems Jesus now faces are to answer the Sadducees' *reductio ad absurdum* ('whose wife will the woman who married seven times be in the resurrection?') and to offer some support for the resurrection from that part of the Scripture which the Sadducees accepted, the Torah (22.24). Jesus is able to do both. As to the former theoretical problem, Jesus replies that the resurrection state will be different from life as we know it; we shall be like the angels (cf. Dan. 12.3),[2] and there will be no marriage. As to the latter rhetorical problem, Jesus does not go to Isa. 26.19, Dan. 12.2-3, Ezek. 37.1-14, or Job 19.25-27 to prove the resurrection, since the Sadducees would not accept the authority of these writings. Instead, he quotes from Exod. 3.6. To Moses God identifies himself as the God of the patriarchs, who had died long ago. While this does not prove the resurrection per se it does support the notion that one survives death: God is *still* the God of the patriarchs. The Sadducees denied the resurrection because they denied continued existence after death. In the language of rhetorical analysis, Jesus' first *stasis* is that of fact (accept the Scriptures, not just Torah), his second that of definition (what does Exod. 3.6 mean?).

The fourth and final group which challenges Jesus' authority in the Temple Conflict Scene consists of the Pharisees and the scribes. They pose the third, final, and climactic question of the public trial's second stage (cf. the three action parables of the prologue and Jesus' three parables in the trial's first stage). The climax is also signaled by the Pharisees returning with a scribe, highly trained in Torah, to test him

<hr />

1. Cf. E. Schürer, *The History of the Jewish People in the Age of Jesus Christ (175 BC–AD 135)* (rev. and ed. G. Vermes, *et al.*; 3 vols.; Edinburgh: T. & T. Clark, 1973-87), II, pp. 270-72, 266 n. 32.

2. Cf. 2 Esd. 7.97, 125; *1 Enoch* 104.2; *2 Enoch* 1.5; *2 Bar.* 51.3, 10. The resurrected ones will 'shine'.

with the greatest question of all: 'Teacher, which is the greatest commandment in the Torah?' (22.36).[1]

Jesus' response has merit not only for its appealing content, but also for his use of the Law. Out of the 613 laws of the Torah, by rabbinic reckoning, that to which Jesus points as chief is the one which stands at the conclusion to the Ten Commandments and the beginning of the laws in Deuteronomy. It is the law which follows from the first of the Ten Commandments (Deut. 5.7; 6.4-5) and covers the first four commandments. It is a law which was included in the *Shema* (Deut. 6.4-9; 11.13-21; Num. 15.37-41), was said daily by the Jews in the first century AD, and was part of the synagogue and temple worship: love God with your whole being.

Jesus' response includes a second commandment of similar character: love of one's neighbor as oneself (22.39). While the wording comes from Lev. 19.18, it nevertheless aptly sums up the remaining six commands of the Decalogue as well as the laws of the Levitical holiness code not covered by the command to love God, and it is similar to the primary law. Then Jesus goes one stage further; not only is this the greatest command in Torah, but on it all of Scripture hangs, the Torah *and* the Prophets.

Inquiry into the greatest command is attested in Judaism during this period.[2] Notice, however, that these greatest commandments underlie Jesus' ethic and his criticism of the Pharisees' legal ethic. The greatest commandments are hermeneutical keys for unlocking the whole of the Torah, and, therefore, holiness is no longer a legal exercise, but a matter of the heart. This is the very ground for Jesus' challenge of Israel's worship (using Jer. 7.11 in Mt. 21.13; Hos. 6.6 in Mt. 9.13; 12.7).

c. *Third Stage of the Proof (22.41-46)*. In the third stage of the public trial, the roles are again switched as they were in the first stage. Now the Pharisees are on the defensive. With two questions Jesus concludes the interrogation. In response to the first question, the Pharisees admit that the Messiah is the Son of David, but they cannot respond to the second about why David calls him 'Lord' if he is in fact his son. The rhetorical genius of this move has several dimensions. First, note that

---

1. Mark presents the scribe as an earnest seeker, but Matthew retains the judicial atmosphere and forms the question as the climax of the entrapment questions.
2. Cf. e.g. *b. Shab.* 31a; *b. Makk.* 23b.

Jesus has been asked by the leaders to interpret Scripture and has proven his authority by being able to do so and by being able to answer other questions as well. But Jesus' question for the Pharisees leaves them unable to interpret Scripture. At the trial's beginning, the chief priests and elders *chose not* to answer Jesus' question at the risk of self-incrimination (21.23-27); now the Pharisees simply *cannot* answer Jesus' question. The exchange ends with, 'And no one was able to answer him a word, neither did anyone dare to ask him any more questions from that day' (22.46).

Second, note that the issue is once again authority. The whole confrontation between Jesus and the religious leaders has been over authority, and now Jesus gets to the heart of the matter by inquiring into their understanding of the Messiah's authority. These leaders should understand the Messiah's authority so that, when he comes, they will know how to yield to him. But they are confused on the issue and their confusion explains their attack on Jesus, who has ridden into Jerusalem with messianic claims. If at the beginning of the trial scene Jesus is hailed 'Son of David' by the crowd, now Jesus presses the point to the leaders with the question, 'What do you make of the Messiah's authority?' Indeed, Jesus suggests that 'Son of David' is an inadequate title for the Messiah, since David calls him 'Lord'. How dare these leaders ask the Lord Messiah by what authority he does such things? (21.23). The matter of Jesus' doing all things according to the authorization of God (cf. Jn 5.16-47) does not apply here; Jesus as Messiah stands in his own authority, unwilling to shift the responsibility and, therefore, the authority to God.[1]

At the beginning of the trial, Jesus implies that his authority to do such things rests with the same one by whom John the Baptist did what he did. Now, at the end of the trial, an even stronger claim is being made: the Messiah bears the title 'Lord' and does such things by his own authority. Third, Jesus once again does not simply argue his point; he involves his accusers in their own demise.

In this final exchange, the issue of the trial changes. Having begun on the issue of authority, it now moves to a *stasis* of fact, 'Is Jesus the Messiah?' This of course is the real issue, which was slowly revealed in the trial. The religious leaders have answered the question in the negative, even though they have lost the public trial, whereas the disciples and the crowd are still giving an affirmative answer. Thus Jesus

---

1. Cf. *Her.* 1.25.

turns to the latter as he, having won the trial, proclaims the verdict with an epideictic speech.

4. *The* Peroratio *(Mt. 23.1-39)*

Epideictic speeches are seldom used on their own but are often extensive sections in judicial and deliberative causes.[1] Having silenced his opponents, Jesus concludes the conflict scene with an epideictic speech of blame in the grand style. While the mode of argumentation continues to be *logos*, there is suddenly, though expectedly in epideictic, an increase of *pathos*. Jesus' *ethos* also increases for, having worsted his opponents, he speaks as prophet and Lord, delivering God's judgment on the unfaithful tenants of his vineyard.

The prophetic character of this speech should be given special attention. First, this speech pronounces a series of woes (cf. Amos 5.18; 6.1; Mic. 2.1; Hab. 2.6, 9, 15; Zeph. 3.1; Isa. 5.8, 11, 18, 20-22; Mt. 11.21; Lk. 6.24ff.). Second, Jesus identifies himself with the prophets (23.29-39). Third, prophets often spoke against cities or people in a legal context, since the guilty party had broken God's covenant with them (e.g. Micah 6, where the legal context is explicit). Thus Jesus speaks with all the authority of a prophet speaking with God's authority, and, in light of the preceding pericopae, with the very authority of the Lord Messiah. As prophet and Messiah, Jesus now gives a speech of censure and judgment.

Jesus' cause is 'discreditable'.[2] He turns to the crowds and his disciples, but his audience also includes the scribes and Pharisees and all Israel. With both groups in the audience we may well ask what sort of introduction Jesus should use for his speech—a direct or a subtle introduction?[3] The latter is more suitable for discreditable speeches since the audience must not be alienated. Jesus initially affirms the position of the scribes and Pharisees, even if with a touch of irony. They sit in Moses' seat and should be obeyed (23.2-3). Given the context of this speech, such a subtle introduction comes as a surprise and most assuredly establishes a sense of goodwill for the audience. But Jesus' introduction hardly remains subtle for long: people are to obey but not copy the actions of the scribes and Pharisees, who do not prac-

---

1. Cf. *Her.* 3.15.
2. Cf. *Her.* 1.5.
3. Cf. *Her.* 1.6.

tice what they preach. If any in the audience had misgivings about the honor due these leaders, they are now encouraged in this attitude. If the introduction initially secures the goodwill of all, it quickly becomes clear that Jesus has no interest in securing the goodwill of those who had been his accusers. He had been on trial, and had finally silenced the prosecution. There is little purpose in seeking the goodwill of any in his audience. The preceding trial established his authority, and secured respect from the crowd (21.46; 22.33) and hostility from the Pharisees (*passim*, note particularly 21.46; 22.15). Hence little subtlety is used in the introduction to the speech, even though the cause is discreditable. Yet Jesus does exhibit goodwill as well as good sense and virtue.[1] He opposes the leaders because he is seeking virtue and righteousness, and his earlier arguments have been brilliant (i.e. they have shown good sense).

As to arrangement, the speech has no *exordium*; the previous scene leads up to the speech.[2] Also, as is typical of epideictic speeches, there is no continuous narrative; the facts are introduced throughout the speech.[3] There is no *propositio*, although one knows from the beginning of the speech and the preceding context that this is a conclusion to a trial. Thus the general topic, indictment of the Jewish leaders, has already been proposed. The speech falls into three parts, the last of which may be considered a *peroratio*. The first two sections are part of the proof section of a speech.

In the first section of the speech, Jesus addresses his followers and gives reasons why they should not do as the scribes and Pharisees (23.1-12). The whole section is highly stylized with its antithetic parallelism (23.2-3, 12, 16, 18, 25, 28) and groupings of three (three sections to the speech, in the first section: three examples, three contrasting enthymemes with a maxim which concludes the section).[4] Verse 12 also uses periphrasis or a divine passive (cf. 23.35, 36, 37, 38). Antitheses were said to embellish the style, making the speech impres-

---

1. Cf. Ar. *Rhet.* 2.1.5: these are the three qualities necessary for an orator to produce conviction in his audience.

2. The initial words of the speech do function as an introduction, but there is no proper *exordium*.

3. Cf. Ar. *Rhet.* 3.16.

4. Jeremias (*New Testament Theology*, pp. 14-15) notes that antithetic parallelism occurs over 100 times in Jesus' sayings and is a clear example of the Semitic style of his rhetoric.

sive and distinctive.[1] Jeremias avers, 'Like the Old Testament, the Judaism of Jesus' day used antithetic parallelism predominantly to formulate proverbial wisdom, maxims, legal axioms, truths of life and rules for wise conduct'.[2] Verse 12 could also be considered an instance of reciprocal change.[3]

The second section (23.13-33) addresses the scribes and Pharisees and consists of seven woes, a significant number indicating fullness of judgment (cf. Revelation's 7 seals, 7 bowls, 7 thunders, and 7 trumpets). Six of the seven woes have the same grammatical form (οὐαὶ ὑμῖν, γραμματεῖς καὶ Φαρισαῖοι ὑποκριταί, ὅτι..., 23.13, 15, 23, 25, 27, 29), and in addition to the indictment as ὑποκριταί Jesus also calls them ὁδηγοὶ τυφλοί (23.16), μωροὶ καὶ τυφλοί (23.17), ὄφεις, γεννήματα ἐχιδνῶν (23.33), and, the most repeated epithet τυφλοί (23.16, 17, 19, 26). The repetition of woes and epithets is an instance of epanaphora, and the usage of epithets in place of names is an instance of antonomasia. Both function to censure the scribes and Pharisees all the more.[4] Instances of periphrasis occur again in vv. 21-22, and there is a humorous maxim in v. 24 which shows how ridiculous is the Pharisaic piety.[5] A hyperbolic figure of thought in v. 15 has the same effect. A metaphorical figure of thought adds vividness to the description of the kingdoms of heaven (23.13-14, 'shut', 'enter'). For vividness and censure, Jesus uses a simile of the whitewashed wall to describe the scribes and Pharisees (23.27-28). Jesus, by question and answer, shows the faultiness of their reasoning (23.16-22). He ends this second section with a rhetorical question which could apply to the final woe or to all the woes: 'How will you escape being condemned to hell?' (23.33).

The topics addressed are: entering the kingdom (23.13-15), oaths (23.16-19), offerings (23.23-24), inward and outward cleanliness (23.25-27), and murder of the prophets (23.29-33). With this last topic Jesus argues from the external circumstance of descent that the

1. *Her.* 4.21.
2. Jeremias, *New Testament Theology*, p. 19.
3. *Her.* 4.39.
4. Cf. 'son of hell', v. 15; hypocrites, snakes, brood of vipers, v. 33; blind men and fools, v. 16; blind guides, v. 16.
5. The maxim was probably a pun in Aramaic: 'You strain out a *galma* but swallow a *gamla*'. Cf. M. Black, *An Aramaic Approach to the Gospels and Acts* (3rd edn; Oxford: Oxford University Press, 1967), pp. 175-76.

scribes and Pharisees will treat the prophets as their fathers did.[1] Each of the woes is part of an enthymeme, since reasons are given for them, and the whole section leaves the impression that these leaders are the worst. The awful epithets are fully justified. Their vices are many: they are unjust (23.3-4, 14, 30-31), foolish (23.16-22), proud (23.5ff.), intemperate (23.4, 13), insincere and false (23.23-28).[2]

The third section (23.34-39) concludes the speech and clinches the argument (διὰ τοῦτο, v. 34). It follows from the preceding indictment, but it comes as a surprise that first they will be allowed to do further evil before their judgment. The reference is probably to the Jewish treatment of Christ's disciples. However, from the standpoint of Jesus' speech on this occasion, we hear that these leaders will bring judgment upon themselves once they fill up the measure of their fathers' sins (23.32, 35-36). Here Jesus uses a vivid description of what they will do, and together with an ocular description he charges them for all the sins of their fathers.[3]

In 23.37 Jesus utters a lament which is at once tender, sorrowful, and judgmental.[4] It heightens the legitimacy of judgment, for they have rejected such tenderness. The tenderness is obtained through a simile—'as a hen gathers her chicks under her wings'. Jesus uses a metaphor and ocular demonstration to show future judgment in v. 38: 'Look, your house is left to you desolate'. The meaning of 'house' is uncertain; is it Jerusalem, the temple, or the people? Even the underlying question of Jer. 12.7 and 22.5 leaves some doubt as to the identification of the house.[5] Perhaps the reference is intentionally vague. The meaning (in both Jeremiah and Matthew) is that God will forsake his people and that he will do so by departing from the temple. Thus the desolate house entails the temple and the people, and this prophecy was foreshadowed in Jesus' cleansing of the temple.

---

1. Cf. *Her.* 3.10.
2. Cf. Ar. *Rhet.* 1.9.
3. *Her.* 4.55.68; Quint. 9.2.40-44. Jesus is speaking at the temple, we must remember, and v. 35 is probably an ocular demonstration: 'And so upon you will come all the righteous blood that has been shed on earth from the blood of Abel to the blood of Zechariah son of Berakiah, whom *you* murdered between the *temple* and the *altar*'. The present leaders are said to have committed this crime, and Jesus likely points to the very spot—even though the crime took place hundreds of years earlier.
4. Jesus uses reduplication to enhance a pitiful mood. Cf. *Her.* 4.38.
5. Cf. discussion in Gundry, *Matthew*, p. 473.

At this point in the speech, Jesus' speech is God's speech, prophetic speech. The 'I' of v. 24 sends messengers, and the lament in v. 37 is God's lament over the desolate house, desolate because of God's departure from the temple. But v. 39 again has Jesus as the speaker; while God departs from the temple and people, Jesus will not be seen again until they give the blessing of Ps. 118.26. There is an equating of God and Jesus in this conclusion; the actions of the one are those of the other. Thus in the first verse of ch. 24 Jesus leaves the temple. The judgment has been rendered: Jesus leaves the temple area; symbolically God has forsaken the leaders and Jerusalem. Only Jesus' disciples (that is, the Twelve) figure in the following two chapters.

Stylistically, Jesus' speech may be considered 'grand'. It is forceful, highly ornamented with epithets and metaphors, and uses hyperbole and amplification.[1] Jesus makes use of amplification in various ways. He uses strong words and negative epithets in reference to his opponents, uses comparison (their actions versus righteous actions), and amplifies by offering many reasons and examples. The whole speech thereby builds in intensity and emotion until the final verdict is wholly justified: 'And so upon all of you will come the righteous blood which has been poured out on the earth. . .' (23.35). This judgment follows from the accumulated accusations which precede it, starting with hypocrisy and moving to persecution of the righteous. A final contrast amplifies the justice of this judgment: they have rejected God's merciful and patient appeal, and therefore they receive a second punishment—the departure of the Lord from their midst until they willingly receive him (23.39).

4. *Conclusion*

George A. Kennedy writes,

> For some readers of the Bible rhetorical criticism may have an appeal lacking to other modern critical approaches, in that it comes closer to explaining what they want explained in the text: not its sources, but its power. Rhetoric cannot describe the historical Jesus or identify Matthew or John; they are probably irretrievably lost to scholarship. But it does study a verbal reality, our text of the Bible, rather than the oral sources standing behind that text, the hypothetical stages of its composition, or the impersonal workings of social forces, and at its best it can reveal the power of those texts as unitary messages. The Bible

---

1. For a concise and helpful discussion of these elements of style in relation to the rhetorical handbooks, cf. Watson, *Invention, Arrangement and Style*, pp. 22-28.

speaks through ethos, logos, and pathos, and to understand these is the concern of rhetorical analysis.[1]

Through the preceding rhetorical study which investigated the persuasive art of Matthew's Temple Conflict Scene, something of the unity and power of the section has been discovered which other critical approaches all too often ignore. Also, the place of this section in Matthew's Gospel as a whole has been noted: the Temple Conflict Scene is an assertion of Jesus' authority throughout his public trial and judgment of the Jewish leaders, coming after sections concerned with Jesus' beginnings, ministry, responses to that ministry, and a description of the disciples' leadership; and coming before Jesus' secret arrest, trial, passion, and resurrection. Finally, this study has shown how rhetorical criticism honors Scripture's authority in its concern with the text as it is and in its concern with the author's intentions, while at the same time paying attention to historical-critical insights which contribute to these concerns.

1. Kennedy, *New Testament Interpretation*, pp. 158-59.

AN ORATION AT OLIVET:
SOME RHETORICAL DIMENSIONS OF MARK 13*

C. Clifton Black

Perhaps no section of Mark's Gospel bristles with more problems than the so-called synoptic apocalypse in ch. 13.[1] Beyond the exegetical difficulties posed by specific verses, interpreters have pondered this material's derivation, either from the historical Jesus[2] or from some Jewish or Jewish-Christian *Vorlage*,[3] and the degree, if any, to which this chapter may be properly regarded as 'apocalyptic'. Interestingly, rather less research has been devoted to one of the more obvious features of Mark 13: its character and function as a rhetorical performance.

---

   * My first soundings of the rhetoric of Mk 13 were taken while under the tutelage of this volume's honoree. I am grateful to Professor Kennedy, as well as to those who read various recensions of this paper and offered many helpful observations: Dr Jouette M. Bassler of Southern Methodist University; Dr John R. Levison of North Park College; Ms Vickie E. Pittard, a graduate student in NT at Southern Methodist University; Dr Frank Thielman of Samford University, and Dr Duane F. Watson of Malone College. For the deficiencies that remain, I alone am responsible.
   1. The standard history of modern exegesis, up to 1954, is G.R. Beasley-Murray, *Jesus and the Future: An Examination of the Criticism of the Eschatological Discourse, Mark 13, with Special Reference to the Little Apocalypse Theory* (London: Macmillan, 1954). For research on Mk 13 from 1954 to 1968, see R. Pesch, *Naherwartungen: Tradition und Redaktion in Mk 13* (KBANT; Düsseldorf: Patmos, 1968), pp. 19-47. D. Wenham, 'Recent Study of Mark 13', *TSFBul* 71 (1975), pp. 6-15 (part 1), and 72 (1975), pp. 1-9 (part 2), provides a helpful overview of the most recent, relevant monographs.
   2. Among the most optimistic in tracing the discourse back to the *Sitz im Leben Jesu* is Beasley-Murray, *Jesus and the Future*, pp. 244-50; *idem*, 'The Eschatological Discourse of Jesus', *RevExp* 57 (1960), pp. 153-66.
   3. First proposed by T. Colani, *Jésus Christ et les croyances messianiques de son temps* (2nd edn; Strasbourg: Treuttel & Wurtz, 1864), the theory of a 'little apocalypse' underlying Mk 13 can no longer be regarded, without qualification, as 'a *sententia recepta* of synoptic criticism' (J. Moffatt). Of late the hypothesis has been revived by Pesch, *Naherwartungen*, pp. 207-23.

Precisely at this point the critical approach suggested by George Kennedy[1] may prove helpful. Accordingly, I shall essay here a preliminary assessment of the rhetoric of Mark 13. I begin with certain assumptions: first, in line with what may be reckoned as an emerging scholarly consensus, I regard this chapter to be eschatologically oriented but not an 'apocalypse' as such.[2] Second, the analysis of this material according to the conventions of Greco-Roman rhetoric is appropriate, owing to that discipline's pervasiveness throughout Mediterranean antiquity.[3] Third, the questions attached to the sources and authenticity of the Olivet Discourse, while interesting, are largely immaterial to the question of its rhetorical effectiveness.[4] Therefore, it is with the discourse in its present literary form, as presented by the Markan Jesus, that I shall be concerned.

Toward a Rhetorical Analysis of Mark 13

1. The Rhetorical Unit
For defining the limits of the speech in Mark 13, the signs of *inclusio* are straightforward. At 13.5a a common Markan formula, ὁ δὲ Ἰησοῦς ἤρξατο λέγειν αὐτοῖς,[5] introduces Jesus' discourse, which commences at 13.5b. As the narrator intervenes at 14.1, clearly shifting the time, characters, and circumstances, 13.37 may be regarded as

---

1. *New Testament Interpretation through Rhetorical Criticism* (Chapel Hill, NC: University of North Carolina Press, 1984), pp. 3-38. For a review of the different kinds of 'rhetorical criticism' being practiced by biblical scholars, see C.C. Black, 'Keeping Up with Recent Studies, XVI: Rhetorical Criticism and Biblical Interpretation', *ExpTim* 100 (1989), pp. 252-58.

2. Thus E. Schüssler Fiorenza, 'The Phenomenon of Early Christian Apocalyptic: Some Reflections on Method', *Apocalypticism in the Mediterranean World and the Near East* (ed. D. Hellholm; 2nd edn; Tübingen: Mohr, 1989), pp. 295-316; C. Rowland, *The Open Heaven: A Study of Apocalyptic in Judaism and Early Christianity* (New York: Crossroad, 1982), pp. 9-72, 351-57. For a dissenting view, reasserting the 'apocalypticism' of this passage, see E. Brandenburger, *Markus 13 und die Apokalyptik* (FRLANT 134; Göttingen: Vandenhoeck & Ruprecht, 1984), pp. 21-42.

3. The evidence is conveniently summarized by J.L. Kinneavy, *Greek Rhetorical Origins of Christian Faith: An Inquiry* (Oxford: Oxford University Press, 1987), pp. 56-100.

4. Broadly conceived, the question of sources is not entirely irrelevant: as we shall witness, the *ethos* of Jesus and the employment of septuagintal allusions contribute to the rhetorical power of Mk 13.

5. Cf. Mk 1.45; 4.1; 5.20; 6.2, 34; 8.31; 10.32; 12.1.

the end of the oration. Between these points of opening and closure extends an uninterrupted address of thirty-three verses (vv. 5b-37). Not only is this a unit of considerable magnitude; it is also, indisputably, the longest unbroken speech of Jesus that is presented in the Second Gospel.[1]

2. *The Rhetorical Situation*
According to Lloyd Bitzer, on whose theories Kennedy relies, the rhetorical situation is a

> natural context of persons, events, objects, relations, and an exigence which strongly invites utterance; this invited utterance participates naturally in the situation, is in many instances necessary to the completion of situational activity, and by means of its participation with [the] situation obtains its meaning and its rhetorical character.[2]

Does this state of affairs obtain in Mark 13?

Though its verification depends on closer inspection of the rhetoric of vv. 5b-37, a provisional case can be made for the existence of such a situation. (a) As described by Mark, the audience is appropriate for the somewhat esoteric discourse that will follow. After a period of public instruction within the temple (11.27–12.44), the *dramatis personae* are quickly reduced, first to Jesus and his disciples (13.1-2), then, almost immediately, to Jesus and a quartet from among the Twelve (13.3). Although corresponding with the collocation, evidenced in various rabbinic texts, of 'public retort and private explanation',[3] this movement is characteristic of Mark's narrative: repeatedly therein, a small group of Jesus' intimates are permitted instruction or disclosures that are denied the general populace (cf. Mk 4.10-34; 7.17-23; 9.28; 10.10-12). Indeed, on three occasions besides that recounted in 13.3, Peter, James, and John participate in events closed to others, even to the rest of the Twelve (cf. 5.37; 9.2; 14.33).[4] Therefore, Jesus'

---

1. The only discourses of comparable length are Mk 4.3-32 and 7.6-23, both of which are repeatedly interrupted by the narrator (4.10-11a, 13a, 21a, 24a, 26a, 30a; 7.9a, 14a, 17a, 18a, 20a).

2. L.F. Bitzer, 'The Rhetorical Situation', *PhilR* 1 (1968), pp. 1-14 (quotation, p. 5); cf. Kennedy, *New Testament Interpretation*, pp. 34-35. On the concept of 'exigence', see Bitzer, pp. 6-7.

3. D. Daube, *The New Testament and Rabbinic Judaism* (Salem, NH: Ayer, 1984), pp. 141-50.

4. It may be no coincidence that Simon Peter, Andrew, James, and John are the first disciples called by Jesus (Mk 1.16-20).

oration in 13.5b-37 is privately addressed (cf. v. 3, κατ' ἰδίαν)[1] to a privileged inner circle, three of whom have been informed of their teacher's identity as Messiah (8.29; 9.41) and Son of God (9.7; cf. also 8.31, 38; 9.9, 31; 10.33, 45).

(b) By the beginning of ch. 13, a number of related events are converging in a manner that would render the ensuing speech natural, if not inevitable. In response to a disciple's comment on the seemingly rock-solid stability of the temple (v. 1),[2] Jesus' prophecy of its annihilation (v. 2) overtly proclaims the destruction of Judaism's cultus, which has been foreshadowed in Jesus' prophetic activity (11.12-21) and his subversive teaching within the temple precincts (11.27-44). Jesus' own destruction is also imminent: immediately after the Olivet Discourse, the plot for his arrest and crucifixion is hatched in earnest (14.1-11; cf. 8.31; 9.31; 10.33-34). Moreover, in terms of both narrative and rhetorical logic, this is an appropriate place for Mk 13.5b-37: the sheer length and gravity of this address, laden with images and phraseology that will be echoed in chs. 14–15, comport with the pronounced deceleration of narrative speed and the dark hues of Mark's passion narrative.[3] Occurring on the eve of Jesus' execution, Mk 13.5b-37 appears reminiscent of an *Abschiedsrede*: a 'farewell address of a great man before his death', of which there are numerous examples in Semitic and Greek literature.[4]

1. Interestingly, the audiences for the Olivet Discourse appear to be incrementally enlarged in the Matthean (24.3) and Lukan (21.5-7) renditions.
2. Cf. Jos. *Ant.* 15.11.1.380–7.425; *J.W.* 5.5.1.184–8.247. Although Brandenburger (*Markus 13 und die Apokalyptik*, pp. 91-115) is probably correct that Mk 13.1-2 originated as an independent apophthegm, in their present literary position these verses nevertheless situate the address in vv. 5b-37.
3. On 'The Connexion of Chapter Thirteen with the Passion Narrative', see R.H. Lightfoot, *The Gospel Message of St. Mark* (Oxford: Clarendon, 1950), pp. 48-59. For insight into the 'narrative deceleration' created by Mk 13, I am indebted to W.S. Vorster, 'Literary Reflections on Mark 13.5-37: A Narrated Speech of Jesus', *Neot* 21 (1987), pp. 203-24, esp. p. 212.
4. Cf. Gen. 41.21-49; 48.29–49.33; Deut. 31.1–34.38; Josh. 23.1–24.30; 1 Sam. 12.1-25; 1 Kgs 2.1-9; 1 Chron. 28.1–29.5; Tob. 14.3-11; 1 Macc. 2.49-70; *1 Enoch* 91–105; *Jub.* 23.9-32; the various *T. 12 Patr.*; Xen. *Mem.* 4.7.1-10; Pl. *Ap.*, *Crito*, *Phaedo*; Jn 14.1–17.26; Acts 20.18b-35; 2 Tim. D.E. Aune (*Prophecy in Early Christianity and the Ancient Mediterranean World* [Grand Rapids: Eerdmans, 1983], pp. 186, 399-400 n. 93) notes that the introduction of this discourse reflects a complex entwining of various literary genres: the peripatetic dialogue (13.1-2), the solicitation of an oracular response (13.3-4), and the *Tempeldialog* (13.1-4).

(c) An 'exigence', for Bitzer, refers to an actual or potential imperfection, marked by urgency, which is amenable to positive modification by discourse. Similarly, the exigence that occasions the speech in Mark 13 is indicated by potential imperfection (v. 2: Jesus' prediction of the temple's toppling) and implied urgency (v. 4: the quadrumvirate's inquiry about the accomplishment of these things). Implicit in both of these aspects is an intricate web of rhetorical associations. The prophecy in v. 2 tacitly locates Jesus within a tradition of prophets who announced the temple's desolation.[1] While seemingly detached from the proclamation of a singular catastrophe, the query in v. 4 (πότε ταῦτα ἔσται... ὅταν μέλλῃ ταῦτα συντελεῖσθαι πάντα) echoes the eschatological phraseology of Dan. 12.7 (LXX, συντελεσθήσεται πάντα ταῦτα). By this choice of Danielic expression, Mark seems to suggest that the disciples' reaction to the possibility of the temple's fall was colored by a degree of eschatologically generated excitement.[2] Delivered at a venue with some eschatological associations (cf. Zech. 14.1-5), Jesus' response will attempt in part (in Platonic terms) to bolster the confidence of an audience whose 'soul' is reckoned to be agitated (cf. Pl. *Phdr.* 271a-d; Ar. *Rhet.* 2.5.1382a-83b).

As far as I can determine, rhetorical criticism of Mark 13 cannot resolve the vexed question of whether the tragedy of AD 70 has already occurred. If Mark knew that the temple had already fallen, a *vaticinium ex eventu* to that effect would have amplified the *ethos* of Jesus (a rationale that seems to be at work in Lk. 19.41-44; 21.20-24). On the other hand, a more precise statement of cultic collapse, reflecting the post-70 reality, could have heightened the very eschatological tension that, as we shall see, Mk 13.5b-37 seems designed to relax. On this issue, rhetorical analysis contributes to, but cannot arbitrate, a classic exegetical stalemate.

However, the assessment of this material's rhetorical situation may offer greater help in adjudicating another, no less contentious, scholarly debate. On both stylistic and substantive grounds the very exis-

---

1. Cf. Mic. 3.10-12; Jer. 7.14; 26.6, 18; *1 Enoch* 90.28; Jos. *J.W.* 6.5.3.300-309; Mk 14.58; 15.29; Jn 2.19; Acts 6.13-14; *b. Yom.* 4.1.39b.

2. Jewish reaction to the events of AD 70 was anything but uniform, though the fall of the temple was associated by some with divine judgment (*2 Bar.* 7.1; 80.1-3; *Sib. Or.* 4.115-27) or eschatological hopes for Jerusalem's re-creation (2 Esdr. 11.1–12.3). For further discussion, consult G.W.H. Lampe, 'A.D. 70 in Christian Reflection', *Jesus and the Politics of His Day* (ed. E. Bammel and C.F.D. Moule; Cambridge: Cambridge University Press, 1984), pp. 153-71.

tence of Mark 13, embedded in its present location, has appeared intrusive to some scholars.[1] If the foregoing analysis is accepted, one could conclude that the Olivet Discourse is propitiously, even powerfully, situated, however obtrusive it may seem to certain literary or redaction-critical sensibilities.

3. *The Rhetorical Problem*

Implicated in one's definition of this unit's primary rhetorical problem is a longstanding scholarly puzzlement over the *raison d'être* of Mark 13. How might a rhetorical interpretation clarify the principal issues at stake in this passage?

(a) Presupposing an association of the temple's destruction with the end of all things, the questions of the four disciples in 13.4 invite neither a forensic evaluation of past facts nor a deliberative assessment of actions that might be expedient for their future performance. Essentially, their questions pivot on proper belief (πότε ταῦτα ἔσται) and the evidence that might substantiate that belief (τί τὸ σημεῖον ὅταν μέλλῃ ταῦτα συντελεῖσθαι πάντα). Jesus' address in 13.5b-37 responds to these issues of belief and validation: certain virtues are implicitly or explicitly extolled (wariness, endurance, preparedness, perspicacity), while specific, corresponding vices are censured (cf. Ar. *Rhet.* 1.9.1366a-b; *Her.* 3.6.10-3.8.15; Aug. *De Doctr. Chr.* 4.4.6). Therefore, from among the various species of rhetoric,[2] epideictic, in my judgment, most accurately describes the type of oration in 13.5b-37.

Even if this judgment is accepted, of necessity it requires trimming with some clarifications and provisos. First, by typing the Olivet Discourse as epideictic, I am not suggesting that here Jesus is engaged in oratorical display, calculated chiefly to please his audience (cf. Ar. *Rhet.* 1.3.1358b; Cic. *De Or.* 2.84.340–85.349). By AD 300 Menander Rhetor[3] analyzed and systematized a rhetorical reality that had long existed: the manifold complexity of epideictic as a rhetorical species. Similarly, when viewed in light of Menander's categories, Mk 13.5b-37 begins as a *lalia*, an informal talk (Menander, 2.4). As the speech

1. For example, Pesch, *Naherwartungen*, pp. 48-73; K. Grayston, 'The Study of Mark XIII', *BJRL* 56 (1974), pp. 371-87.
2. Included among the standard classical discussions of this topic are Ar. *Rhet.* 1.3.1358b-1359a; Cic. *Inv.* 1.5.7; *Her.* 1.2.2; Quint. 3.4.1-16; 3.6.80-85.
3. *Menander Rhetor* (ed. with trans. and commentary by D.A. Russell and N.G. Wilson; Oxford: Clarendon, 1981).

progresses, however, it appears to compound the concerns of
paramythetic, or consolation (2.9), with *proemptic*, a speech for one
departing on a journey (2.5). If our prior assessment of this material
is upheld, then the Olivet Discourse would also function, implicitly to
some degree, as *syntactic*, a speech of leave-taking (2.15). I would not
argue that Mk 13.5b-37 fits snugly into any of these oratorical pigeon-
holes of late antiquity, since the speech does not precisely accord with
the topics germane to these types as presented by Menander. My point,
rather, is that the presiding functions of the oration in Mark 13 may
be defensibly described as epideictic, construed broadly yet appropriately with respect to ancient norms. Jesus does not intend to dazzle or
to delight his auditors, but to bolster their confidence and to instruct
them in values that are essential in an eschatological age.

Second, as is frequently the case in epideictic discourse, portions of
Mk 13.5b-37 shade into deliberative rhetoric: at several points, an
undeniable concern for the disciples' behavior in the future is manifested (e.g. vv. 14-16). Both theoretically and practically, this is tol-
erable within epideictic. Classical theorists acknowledge considerable
fluidity among rhetorical species, granting that considerations of past
and future often converge in epideictic (Ar. *Rhet.* 1.3.1358b; cf.
Quint. 3.4.15-16; 3.7.28). Within Mk 13.5b-37 Jesus understandably
responds in terms of circumstances to come, inasmuch as the exigence
triggering the oration is oriented toward the future (vv. 2, 4; cf.
Quint. 3.8.25). Nevertheless, Jesus ultimately denies that the course of
the future, while providentially assured, can be fixed to a timetable
(vv. 32-37); nor, on the basis of expedience or self-interest, can one
prepare beforehand for the upcoming contretemps (v. 11). Indeed, the
thrust of this speech advocates, not activity, but equanimous detach-
ment during a stressful time.[1] Though tinctured with deliberative
elements that carry persuasive force, the center of gravity in this
address thus remains, I believe, epideictic: an attempt by the speaker to
instill into his hearers as well as to enhance among them certain attitudes and feelings in the present regarding things to come, and to
denounce or to extirpate the converse of those values and beliefs.

---

1. So also Grayston ('The Study of Mark XIII', pp. 378-79), who arrives at this
judgment independently of rhetorical premises. Obviously this contravenes the exegesis of W. Marxsen, *Der Evangelist Markus: Studien zur Redaktionsgeschichte des
Evangeliums* (Göttingen: Vandenhoeck & Ruprecht, 1956), pp. 101-40.

(b) Another approach to the question of this unit's overriding rhetorical problem is by means of *stasis* theory: the identification of the point on which the speech pivots and to which the audience's attention is directed (Quint. 3.6.9, 12, 21). Though the discussion of *stasis* in antiquity was exceedingly complex,[1] our present purposes may be adequately served by Cicero's and Quintilian's simpler parsing of alternative rational questions: fact or conjecture (*an sit*, whether a thing is), definition (*quid sit*, what it is), and quality (*quale sit*, of what kind it is).[2]

Evidently, the facts concerning which Jesus prophesies are not, for his audience, at issue. That the temple will totter (and, by extension, that the other calamities foretold by Jesus will come to pass) appears to be intelligible to the disciples; neither do their questions in Mk 13.4 deny the veracity of Jesus' pronouncements. Nor is the quality of these occurrences in dispute: whether or not God is justified in so designing or permitting this eschatological scenario is never broached. The principal question to which Jesus' oration is addressed concerns the proper definition of facts whose reality is, or will be, conceded: when there arise false prophets, wars and rumors of wars, and so forth, how shall they be interpreted? Will they constitute the final consummation, or will they be merely preliminary to it? Jesus argues for the latter construal. After the prophecy in 13.2, the disciples ask for more facts (v. 4). Jesus complies with their request, yet elevates the discussion to a different level: namely, the correct definition or faithful interpretation of those facts (*quid sit*).

4. *Arrangement*

The classical *taxis* or *dispositio* of an epideictic address consists of three major components: the *proemium* (or *exordium*), a narration (*narratio*) of various topics, and the *peroratio* (or *epilogos*). Mk 13.5b-37 appears to exhibit general conformity with, as well as creative adaptation of, this typical *taxis*.

1. Among numerous treatments, see Cic. *Inv.* 1.8-14; 2.4.14-54.177; *De Or.* 2.24.104–26.113; Quint. 3.6.63-82; *Her.* 1.11-16; Hermogenes, 'On Stases: A Translation with an Introduction and Notes', trans. and ed. R. Nadeau, *Speech Monographs* 31 (1964), pp. 361-424.

2. Cic. *De Or.* 2.25.104-109; 2.30.132; Quint. 3.6.66-67, 86. Nevertheless, among classical theorists there is lack of consensus on the exact divisions among *stases* (cf. Ar. *Rhet.* 3.17.1417b; Cic. *Inv.* 1.8.10; *Her.* 1.11.18–15.25; 2.12.17).

(a) The textbook *exordium* prepares the audience by informing it of the object(s) of the discourse and by disposing the listeners to be receptive to what will be said (Ar. *Rhet.* 3.14.1415a; *Her.* 1.4.6-7; Quint. 4.1.1-79). If Mk 13.5b is to be considered the introduction of the Olivet Discourse (as appears to be the case, since the first of the oration's topics is presented in 13.6), then the minimalism and sheer abruptness of βλέπετε μή τις ὑμᾶς πλανήσῃ would seem to flout the criteria for an appropriate *proemium*. Despite its unconventionality, a case can be made for the suitability and effectiveness of this *exordium*. Admittedly, v. 5b does not attempt to ingratiate the speaker to his audience; for this, however, there is no need. Surely this oration is intended to be heard within, not detached from, the context of the Gospel's previous twelve chapters, from which has emerged the commanding yet mysterious authority of Jesus. Nor need the orator at Olivet solicit his listeners' attention: he knows that he has it, as they have already invited his response (vv. 3-4). Indeed, no statement of the objects of the discourse is necessary, since in effect they have already been proposed in the disciples' questions: 'When will these things be?' (a question of time) and 'What will be the sign?' (a question of circumstance). On the other hand, the sudden, authoritative command in v. 5b does satisfy the one, indispensable requirement of a *proemium*: to capture the audience's attention for the ensuing discourse (Quint. 4.1.5). Conjoined with the questions of time and circumstance in v. 4a and 4b, Mk 13.5b economically and effectively accomplishes all that is needful to prepare this audience for this speech.[1]

(b) The bulk of the address, Mk 13.6-36, is the *narratio*, comprising specific topics that appear to have been carefully grouped for their fitness with the *exordium*, their internal coherence, and their maximum amplification. Though none may be completely analyzed here, all of these aspects should at least be observed.

First, there is a chiastic relationship between the implied objects of the *proemium* (the questions in v. 4) and the kinds of topics treated in the *narratio* (vv. 6-36). The disciples' second query, τί τὸ σημεῖον, is addressed by roughly the first three-quarters of the *narratio* (vv. 6-

---

1. Similarly, in the majority of the speeches in Acts, the length of the *exordium* is one sentence or less: 1.16; 2.14b; 3.12; 4.8b; 5.35b; 7.2a; 10.34-35; 13.16b; 15.7a, 13b; 17.22b; 19.35; 22.1; 24.10a; 25.24a; 27.21; 28.17b. Four speeches in Acts contain an extended *proemium* (4.24b-26; 20.18-27; 24.2-4; 26.2-3), and in three there is no *proemium* at all (5.29-32; 11.4-18; 25.14-21).

27); the remainder, vv. 28-36, takes up their first question, πότε ταῦτα ἔσται. Thus the observation of the fifth-century commentator, Victor of Antioch, is not entirely just: 'They asked one question; he answers another'.[1] In fact, they asked two questions; Jesus responds to both, but in a way (disproportionately and in inverse order) that subtly realigns the disciples' assumptions of their force and significance.

Second, the topics in Mk 13.6-36 are formally repetitive but materially progressive. Aside from the pathetical lament and petition in vv. 17-18, Jesus' statements assume one of four basic forms that recur in varying juxtapositions throughout this address:

1. Exhortation, usually to vigilance (vv. 9a, 23a, 28a, 33a, 35a)
2. Prediction of future occurrences (vv. 6, 8a, 9b, 12-13a, 19, 22, 24-27)
3. Commission or prohibition, preceded by a temporal or relative conditional clause (vv. 7a, 11, 14-16, 21, 28b-29)
4. Authoritative pronouncement (vv. 7b, 8b, 10, 13b, 20, 23b, 30-32, 33b-34, 35b-36).

Concentrations of one form or another occur at certain points: thus vv. 24-27 are uninterruptedly predictive: vv. 30-36, nearing the end of the address, are predominantly *Verkündigungen*, peppered with some exhortations. Most striking overall, however, is the high degree of recurrence and entwinement of these forms throughout the speech. In terms of rhetorical effect, their repetition would implicitly afford the listeners some consistent and regular points of orientation in grappling with the equivocal occurrences and uncertain responsibilities associated with the eschatological age.

For all their formal repetitiveness, the topics in Mk 13.6-36 are substantively distinguishable and logically progressive. In response to the question of 'the sign' attending the eschatological consummation (v. 4b), Jesus arranges four topics:

1. General earthly calamities to be experienced by all (vv. 6-8)
2. Particular earthly calamities to be experienced by believers (vv. 9-13)
3. Particular human responses to the calamitous 'Great Tribulation' (vv. 14-23)

---

1. Cited by D.E. Nineham, *The Gospel of St. Mark* (Pelican Gospel Commentaries; Baltimore: Penguin Books, 1963), pp. 343-44.

4. Particular supernatural responses to the 'Great Tribulation' (vv. 24-27).

Then, in response to the question of the time of 'these things' (v. 4a), two topics are considered:

1. Predictable imminence and assurance of the time (vv. 28-31)
2. Unpredictable suddenness and ignorance of the time (vv. 32-36).

In general, therefore, the regularity of these topics' formal expression assists in reassuring those who receive a substantively more complex response than their rather simplistic questions may have envisioned or invited.

A third aspect of this *narratio* warrants mention: its topical arrangement of eschatological circumstances escalates to the climax. 'The troubles' are not randomly enumerated by Jesus; they are amplified, advancing from more familiar, abstract disturbances, which are but the beginning of the world's labor contractions (vv. 6-8), through more intense, personal suffering (vv. 9-13), and ultimately culminating in breathtaking, cosmic turbulence (vv. 24-27). In rhetorical perspective, the technique in use is known as ἀπ' ἀρχῆς ἄχρι τέλους: a progression that moves 'from beginning to end'.[1] With the completion of circumstantial topics, at v. 27, the speech has reached its emotional climax; from here until the end, the address proceeds with somewhat quieter, thoughtful caution. This is more characteristic of Greek than of Roman oratory, which tended to reserve its full passion until the very end.[2] Doubtless this arrangement also reflects one of Mark's theological convictions (the need for Christians' equanimity under eschatological pressure). In any case, the *narratio* of this address arguably exemplifies Quintilian's standards of lucidity, brevity, and plausibility (8.2.1-2), though the latter criterion is better satisfied by the oration's invention and style (to be considered below).

(c) Although a one-sentence *peroratio* would be unusual in classical rhetoric, this seems to be precisely what we find in Mk 13.37.[3] On the

---

1. Hermogenes, *Opera* (ed. H. Rabe; Leipzig: Teubner, 1913), p. 47.
2. As observed by Kennedy, *New Testament Interpretation*, p. 48.
3. An alternative would be to classify 13.32-37 as the *peroratio*. Such an assessment is problematic in that it all but relegates the critical issue of time (cf. v. 4a) to the *epilogos* without the topic's having been previously developed in the *narratio*. Furthermore, vv. 32-37 really do not restate anything that has preceded them other than that which is adequately recapitulated in v. 37 alone: the exhortation to 'watch'.

other hand, by Aristotelian standards (*Rhet.* 3.19.1419b-20b; cf.
Quint. 6.1.1-55), v. 37 (ὃ δὲ ὑμῖν λέγω, πᾶσιν λέγω, γρηγορεῖτε)
does precisely what needs to be done. First, the repetition of λέγω
encourages the audience's favorable estimation of the orator (and, by
implication, its distrust of those who might vitiate his perspective).
Second, the extension of Jesus' address from ὑμῖν to πᾶσιν amplifies
the force of his points, broadening their significance beyond a coterie
of disciples to the larger Markan community. Third, the audience's
emotions are suitably stirred by the final command, γρηγορεῖτε.
Finally, although v. 37 does not summarize the various arguments of
the discourse, it forcefully recapitulates the oration's principal refrain:
'Watch!' (cf. vv. 5, 9, 23, 33, 35). Indeed, one might argue that, at
v. 37, Mark skillfully accomplishes several rhetorical objectives in
one, sharply pointed stroke: (i) He rivets the reader's attention to the
passion narrative, immediately following, which will detail (among
other things) the consequences for disciples who fail 'to watch' (14.32-
42). (ii) The abrupt command on which Jesus' discourse concludes in
13.37 (γρηγορεῖτε) formally and substantively balances the equally
pointed imperative in 13.5b (βλέπετε), which inaugurated the
address. (iii) The form and content of this *peroratio* are
commensurate: the speech ends just as suddenly and without warning
as 'the master of the house' will come (cf. vv. 35-36). Though
violating certain classical sensibilities, this curt *epilogos* arguably
mirrors others: with emphatic concision (βραχυλογία, *Her.* 4.54.68),
Mk 13.37 preserves the 'internal economy' of the address (Quint.
7.10.16-17) and dramatically leaves its audience at the threshold of
decision (Ar. *Rhet.* 3.18.1420b; *Her.* 3.10.18).

To the degree that this analysis is persuasive, how might it contribute to the larger, scholarly conversation, conducted from different
critical premises, about the arrangement of Mk 13.5b-37? In general,
rhetorical criticism may provide some standards, roughly contempo-
raneous with the biblical material, by which competing scholarly
assessments of a passage's literary structure might be adjudicated. I do
not claim that mine is the only possible analysis, based on rhetorical
principles, of the arrangement of Mark 13. I would suggest that such
principles and the sort of interpretive outcome to which they have led
here may be used to corroborate and refine the results that have been
achieved by some other interpreters, primarily on the basis of form

and composition criticism.[1] Moreover, by attempting to construe the Olivet Discourse as a whole, apart from its composite origins, rhetorical analysis may shed some light, in specific cases, on the persuasive function of problematic or seemingly ill-fitted verses.[2]

5. Invention

'Of the. . . tasks of the speaker invention is the most important and the most difficult' (*Her.* 2.1.1 [trans. Caplan]). Commensurately difficult is the analysis of *inventio*, the devising of arguments (or proofs) that lend conviction to a case. The inventional strategies inherent in Mk 13.5b-37 are of sufficient intricacy that only a few of their more conspicuous features may be noted here.

(a) Inartificial proofs (ἄτεχνοι), not created by the orator (laws, contracts, witnesses, oaths, among others), appear to have been characteristic of judicial rhetoric (cf. Ar. *Rhet.* 1.15.1375a); thus their general absence in the Olivet Discourse is understandable. However, if 'law' be broadly defined as any testament, record, or document to which appeal is made for the substantiation or refutation of a claim,[3] then the numerous septuagintal allusions throughout this address would arguably function as inartificial proofs of Jesus' position.[4]

---

1. Cf. the reconstructions by J. Lambrecht, *Die Redaktion der Markus-Apokalypse: Literarische Analyse und Strukturuntersuchung* (AnBib 28; Rome: Pontifical Institute, 1967), pp. 285-97; B.H.M.G.M. Standaert, *L'Évangile selon Marc: Composition et genre littéraire* (Nijmegen: Stichting Studentenpers, 1978), pp. 231-53; Brandenburger, *Markus 13 und die Apokalyptik*, pp. 13-20, 164-65.

2. For instance, if the prediction in v. 6, concerning usurpers of Christ (cf. Mt. 24.5), is to be regarded within the purview of 'general earthly calamities', then it probably does not allude to an intramural, Christian aberration. Further, the putatively intrusive pronouncement regarding universal preaching of the gospel is surely to be coordinated with the particular persecutions that believers will undergo (cf. vv. 9-13). In my judgment, M.D. Hooker ('Trial and Tribulation in Mark XIII', *BJRL* 65 [1982], pp. 78-99, esp. pp. 85-88) has correctly intuited the Evangelist's intentions in both of these cases, for which a rhetorical analysis offers conceptual support.

3. Thus E.P.J. Corbett, *Classical Rhetoric for the Modern Student* (2nd edn; New York: Oxford University Press, 1971), p. 142.

4. The following list is representative, but not exhaustive: v. 7 (δεῖ γενέσθαι), cf. Dan. 2.28-29; v. 8a (ἔθνος ἐπ' ἔθνος), cf. 2 Chron. 15.6; v. 8b (ὠδίνων), cf. Isa. 26.17; 66.8; Jer. 22.23; Hos. 13.13; Mic. 4.9-10); v. 9c, cf. Ps. 118.46; v. 12, cf. Isa. 3.5; 19.2; Ezek. 38.21; Mic. 7.6; v. 14a (τὸ βδέλυγμα τῆς ἐρημώσεως), cf. Dan. 9.27; 11.31; 12.11; 1 Macc. 1.54; 6.7; v. 14c (φευγέτωσαν εἰς τὰ ὄρη), cf. Gen. 14.10; v. 19, cf. Dan. 12.1; v. 22, cf. Deut. 13.1-3; vv. 24-25, cf. Isa. 13.10, 13; 34.4; Ezek. 32.7-8; Joel 2.10, 31; 3.15; Hag. 2.6; v. 26, cf. Dan. 7.13-

Of course, the scriptural echoes that reverberate within Mark 13 have long been recognized by scholars; noteworthy in this regard is Lars Hartman's thesis that the chapter is virtually a midrashic exposition of Daniel.[1] Whatever is to be made of that proposal, one still may ask if sufficient attention has been paid to the rhetorical effect of the biblical appropriation that we encounter in this discourse. Here I would venture two suggestions. First, to hint at such a range of scripture without explicit citation is, in effect, to pay tribute to the 'biblical literacy' of one's audience, if the listeners' recognition of those allusions was presupposed. Second, and more important, by offering scriptural conventionalizations as helps in the interpretation of disruptive and threatening prospects, such tacit ἄτεχνοι could generate no little consolation among anxious auditors.

(b) However such possibilities are evaluated, surely artificial proofs (ἔντεχνοι), those constructed by the rhetor from the circumstances of the case (Ar. *Rhet.* 1.2.1355b-1356a; Quint. 3.8.15), bear the brunt of the persuasive task in Mark 13. As is typical of epideictic, neither inductive nor deductive logic as such looms large in this oration. The various events, recounted by Jesus in the first four topics (vv. 6-8, 9-13, 14-23, 24-27), are roughly analogous to Aristotle's historical arguments by example (παράδειγματα);[2] however, as these are couched as predictions of the future and not yet actual history, the analogy is imprecise. Closer to the Aristotelian model are the examples in the last two topics (vv. 28-31, 32-36): the image of the fig tree (vv. 28-29) is an 'illustrative parallel' (Ar. *Rhet.* 2.20.1393b; = *similitudo*, Quint. 5.10.1);[3] the story of the traveler (vv. 34-36), a 'fable' (Ar. *Rhet.* 2.20.1393b-1394a).[4] Although these παραδείγματα

14; v. 27 (ἀπ' ἄκρου γῆς ἕως ἄκρου οὐρανοῦ), cf. Deut. 13.7; 30.3-4; Zech. 2.6, 10.

1. L. Hartman, *Prophecy Interpreted: The Formation of Some Jewish Apocalyptic Texts and of the Eschatological Discourse Mark 13 Par.* (ConBNT 1; Lund: Gleerup, 1966), esp. pp. 145-77.

2. Ar. *Rhet.* 2.20.1393a; cf. Quint. 5.10.125–11.44; *Her.* 4.3.5; *Rhet. ad Alex.* 7.17.1428a–8.13.1430a.

3. In broader perspective Mk 13.28-29 should be exegetically conjoined with Mk 11.12-21. Cf. W.R. Telford, *The Barren Temple and the Withered Tree* (JSNTSup 1; Sheffield: JSOT Press, 1980), esp. pp. 213-18.

4. Alternatively, the ὡς-clause in 13.34 could be taken as a simile (cf. Quint. 8.3.72-76). On the complex tradition-history of 13.34-36, consult G.R. Beasley-Murray, *A Commentary on Mark Thirteen* (London/New York: Macmillan/St. Martin's, 1957), pp. 114-17.

are intended to carry persuasive value (cf. v. 28a, ἀπὸ δὲ τῆς συκῆς μάθετε τὴν παραβολήν), actually they do not prove anything. And while the speech evinces careful arrangement, as we have seen, it does not proceed in accordance with the dictates of deductive or enthymematic logic.[1] On the other hand, the address is at least partially motivated by a logical fallacy: that of confusing fallible signs (such as persecutions and spurious prophecies) with infallible signs (those that will demonstrably attend the *parousia* of the Son of Man; cf. Ar. *Rhet.* 1.2.1357b). Thus the force of Jesus' argument, while not rigorously logical, is in fact directed toward exposing this logical fallacy.

To this end, it is worth noting that Mk 13.5b-37 employs, in effect if not by design, several of Aristotle's general lines of argument, or κοινοὶ τόποι (Ar. *Rhet.* 2.18.1391b–19.1393a; cf. the discussion of *loci* in Quint. 5.10.20-125). Thus, against various misapprehensions concerning the time and circumstances of the end, Jesus mounts the following kinds of conventional arguments:

1. *The division of genus into species:* Against the possibility of a mistakenly or prematurely realized eschatology, Jesus presents a 'periodization of tribulation'. That is to say, he deflects attention away from 'the end', generically conceived, onto various, complex species of eschatological events (general calamities, believers' trials, the great tribulation, the coming Son of Man).[2]

2. *The relationship of antecedent and consequence:* The species of events into which the eschatological genus is divided occur, not randomly, but in chronological order, with particular consequences following specific antecedents (cf. v. 8c, ἀρχὴ ὠδίνων ταῦτα).

---

1. Mk 13.20b may contain perhaps the only enthymeme in the entire speech. Although it can be syllogistically reconstructed, its major and minor premises would not be considered probable, much less universally true, by those not already disposed to accept the validity of Jesus' definitions:

> Those human beings who will be saved are the elect.
> God shortened the days for the sake of those who will be saved.
> Therefore, God shortened the days for the sake of the elect.

On enthymematic argument, see Ar. *Rhet.* 2.22.1395b–23.1400b; 2.25.1402a; Quint. 5.10.1-6; 5.14.1-35; 8.5.9-11.

2. A similar strategy is adopted by the author of 2 Thess. 2.1-12, a rhetorical analysis of which is offered by G.S. Holland, *The Tradition that You Received from Us: 2 Thessalonians in the Pauline Tradition* (HUT 24; Tübingen: Mohr, 1988). See pp. 134-39 of that monograph for a comparison of 2 Thess. 2.1-12 with Mk 13.

3. *The relationship of contradiction:* Against antagonists who would short-circuit the appointed chronological progression with illegitimate claims that the end is imminent or calculable, Jesus invokes contradictory propositions ('the end is not yet' [v. 7b]; 'you do not know when the time will come' [v. 33; cf. v. 35]).

4. Jesus contends, not that the end is indefinitely delayed (cf. v. 30), but that all of the penultimates of the end must become manifest before the ultimate reclamation of God's elect. This is one form of *the circumstance of future fact*: if the antecedents of something are present, then the natural consequences will occur (cf. Ar. *Rhet.* 2.20.1393a).

In passing, we might ponder a common form of argument that is exploited not once in this discourse: the interrogation of one's opponents. Constructions from silence are always hazardous; still, the accepted use of question and answer in classical rhetoric (cf. Ar. *Rhet.* 3.17.1419a; *Her.* 4.15.22–16.24), as well as the prevalence of this technique by Jesus elsewhere in Mark (some fifty-seven occurrences), would seem to confirm our original assessment of the rhetorical situation of Mark 13: this speech resonates, less as an apologetic rejoinder within a heretically schismatic *Sitz*, more as pedagogical consolation for uneasy Christians.[1]

Either in practice or by assumption, *logos* is but one of the modes of internal persuasion evident in this address. Of greater persuasive power are *pathos*, the emotion stirred among the audience, and *ethos*, the character of the rhetor.[2] Incorporated within Jesus' eschatological scenario are sobering, even fearsome occurrences (wars, persecutions, familial infighting, cosmic ruptures, and so forth), for which an effective counterfoil is the arousal of pity for those especially vulnerable (expectant and nursing mothers [v. 17]; endangered travelers [v. 18];[3] cf. Ar. *Rhet.* 2.8.1385b-86b; Cic. *De Or.* 2.52.211). So vividly rendered are these images that they might be considered examples of ἐνάργεια (Quint. 4.2.63-64; 8.3.61-67; cf. *Her.* 4.55.68-69) or

---

1. Similarly, Grayston, 'The Study of Mark XIII', pp. 375-76; *contra* T.J. Weeden, Sr, *Mark—Traditions in Conflict* (Philadelphia: Fortress, 1971), pp. 52-100.

2. For both Cicero (*De Or.* 2.43.182–46.194) and Quintilian (6.2.7-27), *ethos* and *pathos* can be varying degrees of the same sort of proof.

3. With R. Pesch (*Das Markusevangelium* [HTKNT 2; 2nd edn; 2 vols.; Freiburg: Herder, 1976-80], II, p. 293), I take the reference to χειμῶνος to refer to the season of heavy rains, when passage across the wadis would have been impeded.

visiones (Quint. 6.2.29-36; cf. Long. *Subl.* 15.1-12): exposition that excites the imagination and stirs the emotions. If the exigence and situation of this address have been properly construed, we may wonder what purpose is served by the depiction of such horrifying prospects. Tacitly, the answer seems to lie in the recurrent assurances and exhortations to endurance in vv. 7, 11, 13b, 20, 23, 27, and 30-31: the effective bolstering of confidence presupposes, and to some degree is dependent on, a clear-eyed acknowledgment of fearful potentialities (cf. Ar. *Rhet.* 2.5.1382a-83b). By rhetorically creating in his listeners' minds the experience of terrors to come, Jesus reassures 'the elect' of the ultimate triumph of God's providence and equips them for future trials and tribulations (cf. Ar. *Rhet.* 2.5.1383a).

Implicit throughout this address, indeed throughout the Second Gospel (cf. 1.27-28; 4.41; 9.14-15; 12.32), is an estimation of Jesus 'as [one] possessing genuine wisdom and excellence of character' (Quint. 4.12.1 [trans. Butler]; cf. 1. Pr. 9-12; 1.2.3; 2.15.33; 12.1.1-45). Thus the *ethos* of Jesus lends considerable persuasive weight to various pronouncements in this address (vv. 9 [ἕνεκεν ἐμοῦ], 13a [διὰ τὸ ὄνομά μου], 23b, 26, 31, 37). Even the self-professed qualification of his knowledge (v. 32) redounds to the credit of 'the Son' insofar as it magnifies the surpassing knowledge of God. So rhetorically powerful is the sheer *ethos* of Christ that it can backfire on gullible believers: when suborned by false Christs and false prophets, it can be wielded as an instrument of deceit (vv. 21-22; cf. vv. 5-6), whose potential nefariousness is thwarted only by authoritative forewarnings of the authentic Christ (vv. 5b, 23). On balance, it is probably the case that the *logos* and *pathos* of the Olivet Discourse depend ultimately upon the *ethos* of its orator.[1]

6. *Style*

Kindred to the invention and arrangement of this address is its *elocutio*, 'the fitting of the proper language to the invented matter' (Cic. *Inv.* 1.7.9 [trans. Hubbell]). Our observations on this score may be

---

1. Aristotle (*Rhet.* 1.2.1356a) considered *ethos* to be entirely internal to a speech. However, as Kennedy notes (*New Testament Interpretation*, p. 15), in practice the speaker's authority was often brought to the rhetorical occasion, such that *ethos* in the Bible functions largely as an external means of persuasion.

categorized in accordance with the four virtues of style proposed by Theophrastus: correctness, clarity, ornamentation, and propriety.[1]

(a) For classical theorists, *correctness* (ἑλληνισμός; *purus*) seems to have referred mainly to appropriate grammar (e.g. Cic. *De Or.* 3.40). If 'Atticism' be taken as the touchstone of appropriateness, as was the case in Rome of the mid-first century AD,[2] then Mk 13.5b-37 would probably be regarded as deficient at several points. The Olivet Discourse harbors grammatical constructions that, by classical standards, would be considered inelegant: ὅτι-recitative following λέγειν (vv. 6, 30); the use of εἰς in constructions where ἐν would be favored (vv. 9, 10); the impersonal use of a plural verb, with no subject expressed (vv. 9, 11); the solecistic conjunction of an attributive participle in the masculine case with a neuter noun (v. 14); the use of ἄν, followed by a verb in the indicative mood (v. 20); various Semitisms (redundant pronouns [vv. 11c, 19]; the use of εἰμί followed by a participle [vv. 13a, 25a]; the substitution of an impersonal plural for a passive verb [v. 26]) and probably at least one Latinism (v. 35c). There are also various instances of asyndeta, the absence of connecting particles (vv. 5b-6, 7bc, 8abcd, 23ab, 33a), some of which have been attributed to a putative Aramaic *Vorlage*.[3] That some of these constructions were considered less than felicitous is suggested by their deletion or alteration in the synoptic parallels.[4]

On the other hand, in defense of the overall 'correctness' of Markan style in ch. 13, the following rejoinders could be made. First, with

---

1. Theophrastus' four virtues were to some degree anticipated by Aristotle (*Rhet.* 3.2.1404b-1450b) and later taken up by Cicero (*Or.* 75-121; *De Or.* 3.9.37-39; 3.52.199), Quintilian (1.5.1; 8.1–11.1; cf. 12.10.58), and Hermogenes (*Peri Ideōn*). For further discussion, see G.A. Kennedy, *The Art of Persuasion in Greece* (Princeton: Princeton University Press, 1963), pp. 273-90.

2. Kennedy, *Art of Persuasion*, pp. 330-40.

3. Thus M. Black, *An Aramaic Approach to the Gospels and Acts* (2nd edn; Oxford: Clarendon, 1954), p. 42; cf. pp. 38-43.

4. Cf. Mk 13.6 / Mt. 24.5 = Lk. 21.8 (both delete ὅτι); Mk 13.9 / Mt. 10.17 (ἐν ταῖς συναγωγαῖς), cf. Lk. 21.12; Mk 13.10 / Mt. 24.14 (ἐν ὅλῃ); Mk 13.11c / Mt. 10.19 = Lk. 21.15 (both delete the *casus pendens* followed by τοῦτο); Mk 13.14 / Mt. 24.15 (ἑστός); Mk 13.19 / Mt. 24.21 (deletes τοιαύτη); Mk 13.25a / Mt. 24.29 (πεσοῦνται); Mk 13.35 / Mt. 24.42 = Lk. 12.38, 40 (both delete the allusion to Roman 'watches'). However, Matthew and Luke agree with Mark in preserving some impersonal plurals (Mk 13.9, 11 = Mt. 10.17 = Lk. 21.12; Mk 13.26 = Mt. 24.30 = Lk. 21.27) and the phrase, λέγω ὑμῖν ὅτι (Mk 13.30 = Mt. 24.34 = Lk. 21.32). Note also Matthew's preservation of ἄν plus the indicative (24.22a = Mk 13.20a).

respect to Markan *koine*, an 'ideal' standard of Attic purity is arguably as unrealistic as it is unsuited. Second, the line of demarcation between 'classical' and 'Semitizing' Greek is scarcely hard and fast: thus, for example, the construction of a *casus pendens* with a resumptive pronoun (cf. Mk 13.11c) is not unknown in classical Greek,[1] and (as we shall see shortly) asyndeta need not be automatically identified as 'Semitisms'.[2] Third, assuredly in the case of Mk 13.19 (cf. Dan. 12.1), but possibly elsewhere, the Semitic flavor of this address owes much to Mark's inventional use of the LXX. Fourth, Mk 13.5b-37 is lacking a number of the syntactical excesses often attributed to that Evangelist (such as the heaping of participles, prepositions, and adverbs; excessive use of the historical present and double negatives).[3]

On balance, therefore, the syntax of Mk 13.5b-37 betokens, if not 'classical purity', at least the direct simplicity of *koine* Greek, as appropriated within Hellenistic Judaism. If it does not evince the elegance of the Epistle to the Hebrews, then neither does it manifest the 'barbarism' of Revelation.

(b) For Quintilian (8.2.22), the primary stylistic virtue is *clarity* (*perspicuitas*; τὸ σαφές). In this area, the oration at Olivet merits relatively high marks. In vv. 6-36 most of the referents, if not in every case their precise significations, seem clear enough, and the παραδείγματα in vv. 28, 34-36a are arguably less obscure than the parables in Mk 4.3-32 (cf. Quint. 8.6.52). A glaring exception to this general assessment is presented by v. 14; however, as we shall consider momentarily, its obscurity may be calculated.

(c) It is with respect to *ornamentation* (τὸ μεγαλοπρεπές; *ornatus*) that the style of Mark 13 may hold the greatest surprise. In classical theory, style is divided into two parts: *lexis* (diction), the choice of words for forceful expression, including metaphors and tropes ('turnings', in which one word is substituted for another); and *synthesis*, verbal compositions that manipulate clusters of sounds or words

---

1. Cf. J.H. Moulton, *A Grammar of New Testament Greek*, Vol. I: *Prolegomena* (3rd edn; Edinburgh: T. & T. Clark, 1957), pp. 69-70, and the Attic evidence cited there.

2. On the slippery subject of 'Semitisms', consult the balanced treatment of C.F.D. Moule, *An Idiom Book of New Testament Greek* (2nd edn; Cambridge: Cambridge University Press, 1959), pp. 171-91.

3. V. Taylor, *The Gospel according to St. Mark: The Greek Text with Introduction, Notes, and Indexes* (2nd edn; New York: Macmillan, 1966), pp. 44-66, presents a convenient précis of Markan vocabulary, syntax, and style.

('figures of speech') or ideas ('figures of thought') in striking or unexpected ways.[1] Although it is not exhaustive, the following table offers a conspectus of the diction and composition employed in Mk 13.5b-37.

I. *Tropes*
  A. *Metaphor (translatio)*: the transference of a word applying to one thing to another that is similar (*Her.* 4.34.45).
    ἐκολόβωσεν κύριος τὰς ἡμέρας (v. 20a)
    ἀπὸ δὲ τῆς συκῆς μάθετε τὴν παραβολήν (v. 28a)
    ἐγγύς ἐστιν ἐπὶ θύραις (v. 29)
    οὐκ οἴδατε γὰρ πότε ὁ κύριος τῆς οἰκίας ἔρχεται... (vv. 35b-36)
  B. *Synecdoche (intellectio)*: the suggestion of the whole or genus of something by its part or species (Quint. 8.16.19).
    διὰ τὸ ὄνομά μου (v. 13a)
  C. *Metonymy (denominatio)*: the substitution of some attribute or suggestive word for what is actually meant (*Her.* 4.32.43).
    πᾶσα σάρξ (v. 20a); λόγοι μου (v. 31).

II. *Figures of Speech*
  A. *Parallelism*: the collocation of related words, phrases, or clauses of similar structure.
    καὶ ... δαρήσεσθε καὶ... σταθήσεσθε (v. 9bc)
    ... ἐκολόβωσεν... τὰς ἡμέρας... ἐκολόβωσεν τὰς ἡμέρας (v. 20ad)
    οἱ ἐν τῇ Ἰουδαίᾳ φευγέτωσαν.../ ὁ [δὲ] ἐπὶ τοῦ δώματος μὴ καταβάτω.../ ὁ εἰς τὸν ἀγρὸν μὴ ἐπιστρεψάτω (vv. 14-16)
    ὁ ἥλιος.../ ἡ σελήνη.../ οἱ ἀστέρες.../ αἱ δυνάμεις (vv. 24bc-25ab)
  B. *Homoeoptoton (exornatio)*: the appearance, in the same sentence, of two or more words with like terminations (*Her.* 4.20.28; cf. Quint. 9.3.78).
    ἀποστελεῖ τοὺς ἀγγέλους καὶ ἐπισυνάξει τοὺς ἐκλεκτούς... (v. 27)
  C. *Reduplication (ἀναδίπλωσις)*: immediate repetition of one or more words of identical syntax, for the purpose of amplification (*Her.* 4.28.38; Quint. 9.3.28).
    ὅταν... γινώσκετε ὅτι ἐγγὺς... ἐστίν /...
    ὅταν... γινώσκετε ὅτι ἐγγύς ἐστίν (vv. 28bc, 29bc)

---

1. The standard classical treatments of ornamentation include Ar. *Rhet.* 3.1.1403b–12.1414a; *Rhet. ad Alex.* 22.1434a.35–28.1436a.13; Long. *Subl*; Demetr. *Eloc.*; Cic. *De Or.* 3.37.149–42.168; 3.54.206-208; Quint. 8.6.1-76; 9.1.1-3.102. See also H. Lausberg, *Handbuch der literarischen Rhetorik: Eine Grundlegung der Literaturwissenschaft* (2nd edn; 2 vols.; Munich: Hüber, 1973), I, pp. 248-525.

D. *Transplacement (traductio)*: the reintroduction of a word used in various functions (*Her.* 4.14.20-21; Quint. 9.3.41-42).

γρηγορῇ—γρηγορεῖτε (vv. 34d, 35a)

E. *Polyptoton*: establishing a contrast by variation in a word's declension or inflection (cf. Quint. 9.3.37).

ἀκούσητε πολέμους καὶ ἀκοὰς πολέμων (v. 7a)
κτίσεως ἧς ἔκτισεν (v. 19)
ἐκλεκτοὺς οὓς ἐξελέξατο (v. 20b)

F. *Epanaphora*: repetition of the same word at the beginning of successive clauses (*Her.* 4.13.19).

ἔσονται. . . , ἔσονται. . . (v. 8bc)
Ἴδε. . . , Ἴδε. . . (v. 21bc)

G. *Antistrophe* (ἐπιφορά): repetition of the same word at the end of successive clauses (*Her.* 4.13.19).

. . . παρελεύσονται, . . . παρελεύσονται (v. 31ab)
. . . ὑμῖν λέγω, πᾶσιν λέγω (v. 37ab)

H. *Homoeopropheron*: syllabic correspondence in the beginning of two or more words in close succession (cf. *Her.* 4.12.18).

ψευδόχριστοι καὶ ψευδοπροφῆται (v. 22a)

I. *Homoeoteleuton*: syllabic correspondence in the ending of two or more sentences (Quint. 9.3.77).

βλέπετε ἀγρυπνεῖτε (v. 33a)

J. *Epanalepsis*: repetition of a word at the beginning and end of a clause (Quint. 8.3.51).

ἔθνος ἐπ᾽ ἔθνος καὶ βασιλεία ἐπὶ βασιλείαν (v. 8a)
καὶ παραδώσει ἀδελφὸς ἀδελφόν (v. 12a)

K. *Asyndeton (dissolutio)*: absence of connecting particles (Quint. 9.3.50).

βλέπετε. . . πλανήσῃ—πολλοί. . . (vv. 5b-6)
μὴ θροεῖσθε—δεῖ γενέσθαι (v. 7bc)
ἐγερθήσεται. . . ἔσονται. . . ἔσονται. . . ἀρχή (v. 8abcd)
ὑμεῖς δὲ βλέπετε—προείρηκα ὑμῖν πάντα (v. 23ab)
βλέπετε ἀγρυπνεῖτε (v. 33a)

L. *Polysyndeton*: superfluity of connecting particles (Quint. 9.3.50-52).

καί-parataxis in vv. 9c-13a and 24c-27ab
οὐδεὶς οἶδεν, οὐδὲ. . . οὐδέ. . . (v. 32ab)
πότε. . . ἔρχεται, ἢ. . . ἢ. . . ἢ. . . ἤ. . . (v. 35bc)

M. *Alliteration*: repetition, in adjacent words, of initial or medial consonants (cf. *Her.* 4.12.18).

καὶ δοὺς τοῖς δούλοις (v. 34b)

N. *Assonance*: repetition, in adjacent words, of similar vowel sounds conjoined with different consonants (cf. *Her.* 4.12.18).

μὴ θροεῖσθε—δεῖ γενέσθαι (v. 7bc)
ἐξουσίαν, ἑκάστῳ τὸ ἔργον (v. 34bc)

O. *Hyperbaton:* transposition of word order for emphasis (*Her.* 4.32.44; Quint. 8.6.62-67).

ἀρχὴ ὠδίνων ταῦτα (v. 8d)
ἐγγὺς τὸ θέρος ἐστίν (v. 28c)

P. *Chiasmus* (cf. *commutatio: Her.* 4.28.39): reversal of grammatical structures in adjacent phrases or clauses.

παραδώσουσιν ὑμᾶς εἰς συνέδρια καὶ εἰς συναγωγὰς δαρήσεσθε (v. 9b)
καὶ πατὴρ τέκνον, καὶ . . . τέκνα ἐπὶ γονεῖς (v. 12ab)
καὶ εἰ μὴ ἐκολόβωσεν . . . πᾶσα σάρξ—ἀλλὰ διὰ τοὺς ἐκλεκτοὺς . . . ἐκολόβωσεν (v. 20abcd)

Q. *Antithesis:* juxtaposition of contrary ideas (*Her.* 4.15.21; *Rhet. ad Alex.* 26.1435b.25).

δεῖ γενέσθαι, ἀλλ᾽ οὔπω τὸ τέλος (v. 7cd)
μὴ προμεριμνᾶτε τί λαλήσητε, ἀλλ᾽. . . τοῦτο λαλεῖτε (v. 11bc)
οὐ γάρ ἐστε ὑμεῖς οἱ λαλοῦντες ἀλλὰ τὸ πνεῦμα τὸ ἅγιον (v. 11d)
καὶ ἔσεσθε μισούμενοι. . . ὁ δὲ ὑπομείνας. . . σωθήσεται (v. 13ab)
ὁ οὐρανὸς καὶ ἡ γῆ παρελεύσονται, οἱ δὲ λόγοι μου οὐ μὴ παρελεύσονται (v. 31)
οὐδεὶς οἶδεν, . . . εἰ μὴ ὁ πατήρ (v. 32ac)
γρηγορεῖτε οὖν, οὐκ οἴδατε γάρ (v. 35ab)

R. *Parenthesis (interpositio):* the interruption of the flow of discourse by the insertion of a remark (Quint. 9.3.23).

καὶ εἰς πάντα τὰ ἔθνη πρῶτον δεῖ κηρυχθῆναι τὸ εὐαγγέλιον (v. 10)
ὁ ἀναγινώσκων νοείτω (v. 14b)

S. *Ellipsis:* deliberate omission of a word that is implied by the context (Quint. 9.3.58).

καὶ [sc. ἐγερθήσεται] βασιλεία ἐπὶ βασιλείαν (v. 8a)
καὶ [sc. παραδώσει] πατὴρ τέκνον (v. 12a)

T. *Apposition:* juxtaposition of coordinate elements, the second of which modifies the first.

αἱ δυνάμεις αἱ ἐν τοῖς οὐρανοῖς (v. 25b)
οὐδείς. . . οὐδὲ οἱ ἄγγελοι ἐν οὐρανῷ οὐδὲ ὁ υἱός (v. 32ab)
τοῖς δούλοις. . . τὴν ἐξουσίαν, ἑκάστῳ τὸ ἔργον (v. 34bc)

III. *Figures of Thought*

A. *Aposiopesis:* the incompletion of a thought (*Her.* 4.30.41; 4.54.67; Quint. 9.2.54-57; 9.3.60-61).

ὡς ἄνθρωπος ἀπόδημος. . . ἵνα γρηγορῇ (v. 34)

B. *Controversia*: ambiguous phraseology, designed to excite suspicion or entice discovery (Quint. 9.2.65-95).

ὅταν δὲ ἴδητε τὸ βδέλυγμα τῆς ἐρημώσεως ἐστηκότα ὅπου οὐ δεῖ (v. 14a)

C. *Ecphrasis*: vivid description (cf. *Her.* 4.38.51).

καὶ τότε ὄψονται. . . ἕως ἄκρου οὐρανοῦ (vv. 26-27)
πότε ὁ κύριος. . . ἔρχεται. . . ἢ πρωΐ (v. 35bc)

D. *Arousal* (ἀνάστασις): stirring of emotion (*Her.* 4.43.55-56).

προσεύχεσθε δὲ ἵνα μὴ γένηται χειμῶνος (v. 18)

E. *Pleonasm*: emphatic superfluousness (Quint. 9.3.46-47).

βλέπετε δὲ ὑμεῖς ἑαυτούς (v. 9a)
ὑμεῖς δὲ βλέπετε (v. 23a)

F. *Simile*: comparison of implicitly similar figures (*Her.* 4.49.62).

ὡς ἄνθρωπος ἀπόδημος. . . [sc. ὑμεῖς] (vv. 34-35)

Even on the assumption that the preceding list is incomplete, such a range of ornament in a speech of moderate length is striking. Equally impressive is the skill with which the tropes and figures have been blended into the address: they do not attract to themselves undue attention, and most would probably be missed by those who silently read the speech but did not hear it recited aloud. At the time of the oration's performance, even its auditors probably would not be entirely conscious of this panoply of ornament; at a subconscious level, however, the various techniques would register with persuasive effect (cf. Cic. *De Or.* 3.50.195). Thus the diction and composition of Mark 13 are not merely decorative but functional devices, integral to the purpose of securing an audience's agreement in matters of faith that are beyond deductive, logical proof.[1]

(d) The fourth of Theophrastus' virtues, *propriety* (τὸ πρέπον; *decorum*), refers to the appropriateness of the style to the circumstances of the speech, the *ethos* of the orator, the mood of the audience, and the character of the address. In these respects the Olivet Discourse would probably be judged successful. From among the Ciceronian levels of style,[2] the middle way (*medius et quasi temperatus*: Cic. *Or.* 6.21; *De Or.* 3.45.177) tends to be adopted in Mark 13: befitting a 'cautious' or 'restrained' eschatology, the argument and

---

1. On the interplay of figures and argument, see Quint. 9.1.19, 21; note also the more recent discussion in Ch. Perelman and L. Olbrechts-Tyteca, *The New Rhetoric: A Treatise on Argumentation* (trans. J. Wilkinson and P. Weaver; Notre Dame: University of Notre Dame Press, 1969), pp. 167-79.

2. Cic. *Or.* 5.20–6.21; 21.69–29.101; *De Or.* 3.52.199-200; 3.45.177; cf. also *Her.* 4.8-11; Quint. 12.10.58-72; Aug. *De Doct. Chr.* 4.19.38; 4.24.54–26.56.

diction are neither majestically grandiloquent (cf. Cic. *Or.* 5.20) nor
tepidly plain (cf. Cic. *Or.* 6.20). Although its precise rhythm, based on
metrical quantities in pronunciation, is probably irretrievable,[1] overall
this oration evinces a style that is more 'free-running' than pointedly
'periodic' (cf. Ar. *Rhet.* 3.9.1409ab; Quint. 9.4.19-147). Though this
would be expected in a didactic presentation, a 'running' style seems
especially appropriate for an address that counsels cautious
discernment of a lengthy train of eschatological occurrences: the
longer the phrases and clauses (*commata* and *cola*), such as we find
here, the less hurried and more deliberate the rhetorical effect (cf.
Her. 4.19.26-20.28).[2] The already masterly character of the rhetor
would be enhanced by his command of ornament, whose varying clarity and obscurity are congenial with an eschatological scenario that can
be broadly forecast (cf. Mk 13.23) yet not precisely pinpointed (cf.
13.32).

When compared to studies of its arrangement and 'logical' argument, the style of Mk 13.5b-37 has been relatively neglected in recent
scholarship. Here is another area in which Greco-Roman rhetoric may
throw fresh light on familiar texts: the classical theory and practice of
style afford a useful set of conceptual tools with which to frame some
new inquiries, as well as to reexamine some perennial problems of
interpretation.

A case in point is the notoriously difficult *crux interpretum* at Mk
13.14, τὸ βδέλυγμα τῆς ἐρημώσεως. Beyond the general consensus
on its allusiveness to a similar phrase in Daniel (and 1 Maccabees),
commentators have despaired of precisely identifying to what or to
whom Mark intends this epithet to refer.[3] In all likelihood, rhetorical
criticism will be equally unable to answer the question of reference;
that, however, is neither the sole nor arguably the most productive

1. As Kennedy observes (*New Testament Interpretation*, p. 30), the analysis of
prose rhythms in the NT literature is precluded by the apparent lack of systematic dif-
ferentiation between long and short syllables in the pronunciation of *koine* Greek.
Still, the address at Olivet exhibits some almost poetic features: μὴ θροεῖσθε /δεῖ
γενέσθαι (v. 7ab); καὶ τότε ἀποστελεῖ τοὺς ἀγγέλους/ καὶ ἐπισυνάξει τοὺς
ἐκλεκτούς (v. 27a).

2. In 9.4.83, 91, Quintilian speaks of the different effects created by short and
long syllables, rather than by phrases and clauses of varying lengths. The latter,
however, are implicated in Demetrius' discussion of the degrees of elevated diction
(*Eloc.* 2.36-52).

3. Among others, see Beasley-Murray, *Commentary*, pp. 54-72; Pesch, *Naherwartungen*, pp. 139-44.

question to be raised of this phrase. Within a rhetorical framework, the significance of τὸ βδέλυγμα τῆς ἐρημώσεως resides largely in its provocative mystery and its concomitant resistance to clear interpretation. The technique in question is that of *controversiae*, much admired by clever declaimers in the first century AD,

> whereby we excite some suspicion to indicate that our meaning is other than our words would seem to imply; but our meaning is not in this case contrary to that which we express, as is the case in irony, but rather a hidden meaning which is left to the hearer to discover (Quint. 9.2.65 [trans. Butler]).

That is to say, however unsafe or unseemly it might have been for Mark to speak more plainly at 13.14, for him to have done so would have been assuredly less provocative and pleasurable for his audience. Moreover, this approach may help to explain the presence, in the same verse, of the parenthetical admonition, ὁ ἀναγινώσκων νοείτω. As rhetorically inept as it might first appear, this equally mysterious injunction is probably intended to seize the imaginations of those in Mark's community who are 'overhearing' Jesus' oration, to tease them into an attempted unraveling of the secret of 'the desolating sacrilege *who* stands' (*sic*; cf. Quint. 9.2.78).[1] That the Evangelist's rhetorical strategy at this point was successful is confirmed by the captivated creativity that has been exercised by generations of the Gospel's exegetes.

7. *Evaluation*

Does the Olivet Discourse constitute good rhetoric? As is usually the case in any form of criticism, the answer depends on the relative weighing of varying criteria. The bobtailed *proemium* and *peroratio* of Jesus' address in Mark 13, as well as its grammatical roughness, probably would have jarred most classical rhetoricians. Moreover, those, like Aristotle, who esteemed the persuasive value of closely reasoned proof doubtless would have found this speech disappointing. Judged in strict accordance with such canons as these, Mk 13.5b-37 is a flawed declamation.

On the other hand, this unit is by no means bereft of rhetorical effectiveness and sophistication. It seems appropriate to its situation and exigence: while directly responsive to their queries, the speech encourages its listeners to ponder related questions of a higher order.

---

1. This suggestion was adumbrated by Daube, *Rabbinic Judaism*, p. 426.

It is less concerned with dispensing and verifying abstruse information than with allaying anxiety, bolstering confidence, and instilling vigilance among timorous disciples. To those ends, both the form and substance of the address are tailored: the audience is afforded, not only a proleptic and vicarious experience of the vicissitudes and rescue to come, but also the reassurance and stability implicitly communicated through familiar, rhetorical conventions. Having been immediately established, audience contact is maintained by a chiastic, coherent, and climactic narration. Upon a tacitly logical substructure, a speech of powerful *pathos* and *ethos* has been crafted, whose wide-ranging stylistic devices are not merely decorative but also deftly functional. Characteristic, perhaps, of one disposed to open or equivocal conclusions (cf. 15.39; 16.8), the Evangelist does not say how the original audience reacted to the oration at Olivet. Although Mark is no Cicero, one wonders if, in every respect, Quintilian would have disapproved.

Some Concluding Reflections

En route to my own *epilogos*, I have ventured some judgments on the possible contributions and limitations of a rhetorical analysis, with respect to the broader dimensions of scholarship on Mark 13. Whether such judgments will hold, only time and continued investigation will tell. In any case, the following observations seem to me appropriate points on which to conclude.

Methodologically, much of recent scholarship on the Olivet Discourse has gravitated either to the reconstruction of its tradition-history or to the analysis of its literary composition. Regarding the latter, the usefulness of Greco-Roman rhetorical theory, particularly on the subject of *taxis* or *dispositio* (arrangement), should be evident. For *Traditionsgeschichte*, rhetorical study may seem largely irrelevant; however, throughout most of the history of exegesis, precisely the reverse of this assessment would have been more common! Indeed, it is highly unlikely that the Second Evangelist and his audience would have envisioned, much less intended, that the Olivet Discourse be interpreted by means of discriminating its antecedent tradition(s) from its later redaction(s). Generations of listeners and readers have made intelligible sense of Mark 13 and similar passages by appropriating the material in the rhetorical manner in which it is patently presented. Rhetorical theory provides us with some excellent guidelines from antiquity for understanding and articulating the power of ancient address *qua* address.

On the other hand, the current reclamation of classical rhetoric requires correction by, and coordination with, other appropriate interpretive perspectives. This is necessitated by the complexity of biblical texts, which have been influenced by an array of historical, literary, and religious pressures. Thus, as we have witnessed, rhetorical criticism of Mark 13 entails a candid recognition of the degree to which the Olivet Discourse creatively adapts or even flouts rhetorical norms, owing to its location within a larger narrative and its subjection to not one but several generic constraints.

Finally, if the essence of this essay's argument be accepted, then a reconsideration of Mark's rhetorical versatility may be in order. As was acknowledged earlier, in content and format Mark 13 is like nothing else in that Gospel, which at points actually deprecates the power of verbal persuasion (cf. 4.10-12; 8.14-21).[1] Nevertheless, for whatever historical or theological reasons, in ch. 13 Mark modifies his customary approach and attacks the problem of eschatology with noteworthy directness, depth, and rhetorical sophistication.[2] To that degree, we may wish to qualify Professor Kennedy's otherwise valid assessment[3] that Mark's Gospel tends toward 'radical Christian rhetoric', a form of 'sacred language' that presupposes the believer's immediate and intuitive apprehension of truth, without assistance from the art of persuasion.

---

1. In this connection one might recall Mk 13.11, where the value of practiced rhetorical endeavor seems to be undercut by Jesus' admonition that his disciples not anticipatorily rehearse their apologia but leave all persuasion to the Holy Spirit (cf. Exod. 4.1-17; Num. 22.35; Jer. 1.6-10; contrast Quint. 11.2.1-51). For very different reasons, Plato exhibits a similar paradox: the rhetorician who distrusts rhetoric (*Phaedr.* 257b-58e; 275d-76a).

2. Although modern scholarship has tended to construe 'rhetorical' discrepancies as indicative of Mark's use of composite sources, such inconsistencies may have resulted from the Evangelist's need to provide significant oral and aural clues to the auditors of the Second Gospel. See P.J. Achtemeier, '*Omne verbum sonat*: The New Testament and the Oral Environment of Late Western Antiquity', *JBL* 109 (1990), pp. 3-27, esp. pp. 26-27.

3. *New Testament Interpretation*, pp. 97-113, esp. pp. 104-107.

THE RHETORICAL GENRE OF JESUS' SERMON IN LUKE 12.1–13.9

Wilhelm Wuellner

Introduction

The primary objective of rhetorical criticism for George Kennedy[1] is to understand the effect of the text. The text, whose effect we seek to determine, if not to experience, is a sermon given by Jesus in Lk. 12.1–13.9. The effect of a given text is determined by, among other factors, the text's genre, by which we mean the rhetorical genre and not just its literary genre. The text's effect can also be said to be determined by its intentionality.[2] But how are we to proceed to determine the genre, and with it, the intentionality of Lk. 12.1–13.9?

We could proceed by following the steps outlined by George Kennedy (pp. 33-38), starting with the determination of the rhetorical unit to be analyzed. At once we are confronted by a dual task of seemingly circular analyses: (1) the rhetoric of smaller units, such as this sermon, must be interpreted, according to Kennedy, as part of the overall rhetoric of the larger unit of which it is a part, that is, Luke–Acts; (2) the rhetoric of the larger units—whether that of Luke–Acts, or that of the composite unit that makes up the sermon in 12.1–13.9—has to be seen as built up from an understanding of the rhetoric of the smaller units. Among the smaller units in Luke–Acts are, besides the Prologue(s), the several speeches or sermons of Jesus or other speakers within Luke–Acts, the 'Travel Section' (Lk. 9.51–19.27),[3] etc.; or the smaller units can be seen as the constitutive components that make

---

1. *New Testament Interpretation through Rhetorical Criticism* (Chapel Hill, NC: University of North Carolina Press, 1984), p. 33.

2. See Amos N. Wilder, *The Bible and the Literary Critic* (Minneapolis, MN: Fortress, 1990), pp. 22-25.

3. See e.g. David P. Moessner, *Lord of the Banquet: The Literary and Theological Significance of the Lukan Travel Narrative* (Minneapolis, MN: Fortress, 1989).

up a given sermon. In our case, 'patterns of persuasion' are seen in the combination of chreias with parables, as in 12.13-21,[1] or in such features as 'narratives in speech in narration',[2] as found in 12.42-48.

Whether small or large, whether taken by itself or enclosed within another larger unit, each unit must have a beginning, a middle, and an end.[3] As with narrative, so with argumentation, the rhetorical unit may actually begin 'in the middle of things' (*in medias res*), or even at the end, instead of the beginning; but the unit has to have some identifiable narrative or argumentative beginning.

Each rhetorical unit has its own intentionality, that is, its own rhetorical situation, and, with it a rhetorical genre that is supposedly appropriate to its situation or intentionality. But how do we arrive at the identification of the rhetorical genre of Lk. 12.1–13.9? The rhetorical genre is defined by Burton Mack and Vernon Robbins as the inner logic, or the inner unity and organization, of various forms. We could ask, as Mack and Robbins do,[4] what bearing the discussions of ancient rhetoricians have on our task? Indeed, we do need to be aware of the discussions that have shaped, and continue to shape, our own classifications of *rhetorical* genres, and their numerous subgenres, or species, as distinct from the classification of *literary* genres. However, such classifications, whether those of the ancient or of the modern rhetoricians, have led to a dilemma which is now widely felt and being analyzed. One rhetorician, Thomas Conley, identified the prevailing mood in the genre-debate as 'The Linnean Blues'.[5] How we got to this point in the genre-debate interests me at the moment less than how we get beyond this point. When we return to the discussion of the genre of Jesus' sermon in Lk. 12.1–13.9, we will have to weigh the merits and demerits of the genre-discussions of the classical rhetoricians for our text.

---

1. Burton L. Mack and Vernon K. Robbins, *Patterns of Persuasion in the Gospels* (Literary Facets; Sonoma, CA: Polebridge, 1989), p. 23.

2. See Joseph A. Morris, 'Narrative in Speech in Narration: Analysis of Luke's Rhetorical Strategy in 3 Inaugural Speeches (Luke 4, Acts 2 and 13)' (PhD dissertation, Graduate Theological Union, Berkeley, 1991), and Evelyn Rose Thibeaux, 'The Narrative Rhetoric of Luke 7.35-50: A Study of Context, Text, and Interpretation' (PhD dissertation, Graduate Theological Union, Berkeley, 1990).

3. Kennedy, *New Testament Interpretation*, p. 33.

4. Mack and Robbins, *Patterns of Persuasion*, p. 2.

5. Thomas Conley, 'The Linnean Blues: Thoughts on the Genre Approach', *Form, Genre, and the Study of Political Discourse* (ed. H.W. Simons and A.A. Aghazarian; Columbia, SC: University of South Carolina Press, 1986), pp. 59-78.

No one disputes the familiar critical norm which informs the critic's work with a given text: to ignore the rhetorical genre makes the critic risk clouding rather than clarifying the rhetoric of a text like this sermon we seek to explain.[1] But, as Conley keeps asking, 'does rigorous attention to the generic status of [a text like Lk. 12.1–13.9] becloud, rather than clarify, what goes on in the rhetoric the critic tries to explain or to evaluate?'[2] Conley sees evidence among his peers interpreting rhetoric, as I do among my peers doing biblical exegesis, 'that critical fixation on genre identity may, in fact, obfuscate more than it illuminates'.[3] One can readily agree that all genre classification, whether of rhetorical, literary, or any other genre, is supposed to serve 'clarification mainly by way of simplification. . .' But this otherwise helpful enterprise becomes problematic *only* 'when simplification results in distortion. . .' This led Conley to conclude that 'genre criticism in rhetoric must be seen as an approach that has implications for larger questions of method and what method lets us see. . .'[4]—or prevents us from seeing.

To avoid the danger of distortion in the search for the rhetorical genre of the sermon in Lk. 12.1–13.9, Conley would have us observe the following guidelines. To ensure close attention to this literary sermon, priority should be given to style over all the rest: *topoi*, enthymematic reasoning, motive and intention, and situation. This amounts to 'a truly close reading and analysis of a given rhetorical performance' as we have in Lk. 12.1–13.9. To 'preserve the rhetorical idiom' of the sermon, one could abridge the sermon to its 'arguments' or 'strategies'. For Conley, this has the liability of all 'invention-oriented critical approaches': reducing the critics' efforts to 'motive' and

---

1. See Kathleen Jamieson, 'Generic Constraints and the Rhetorical Situation', *PhilR* 6 (1973); K.K. Campbell and K.H. Jamieson (eds.), *Form and Genre: Shaping Rhetorical Action* (Annandale, VA: Speech Communication Association, 1978); Thomas Conley, 'Ancient Rhetoric and Modern Genre Criticism', *Communication Quarterly* 27 (1979), pp. 47-53; Walter Fischer, 'Genre: Concepts and Applications in Rhetorical Criticism', *Western Journal of Speech Communication* 44 (1980), pp. 288-99.

2. Conley, 'Ancient Rhetoric', pp. 49-50; 'Linnean Blues', p. 71.

3. 'Linnean Blues', p. 71.

4. 'Linnean Blues', pp. 72, 73. In his contribution to the Malherbe Festschrift (see below, p. 99 n. 2), Thomas Olbricht likewise warns us to 'steer clear of esoteric modern rhetorics which obfuscate rather than clarify'. In his contribution to the Hendrikus Boers Festschrift, Steve Kraftchick sounds a similar warning: fixation with rhetorical genres categories has become a new form of methodological captivity.

'message content'. Instead, Conley urges the genre critic 'to cultivate critical sensitivity that is as analogous as it can be to the sort of apprehension audiences do experience. . .'[1] We will be testing this more inductive approach to the identification of the rhetorical genre of the sermon in Lk. 12.1–13.9.

The sort of apprehension with which audiences experience a sermon like Lk. 12.1–13.9 has two distinct aspects to it: (1) *The historical* approach to genre which focuses on the audience in the narrative of which the sermon is a part. This approach also includes the sort of apprehension with which the first readers of Luke's Gospel in the first century were presumed to have experienced sermons as part of such larger rhetorical units as the Gospel of Luke, or the liturgy of the church, as part of which Scripture-sermons, along with other sacred texts, would be experienced. Efforts at defining the rhetorical genre in this historical approach invites, if not demands, comparison with rhetorical genres known and familiar to audiences of the first century. While the sermon audience in the text is presumed to be all Jewish (a non-Jew would not know what to do with the ruling metaphor of the leaven of the Pharisees, with which the sermon opens), the reader of Luke's Gospel need not be Jewish. Yet genre-discussions, whether concerning literary or rhetorical genres, stay almost exclusively with this historical approach, which, to be sure, has its justification, at least up to a point.

But there is another aspect to the sort of apprehension with which audiences experience a sermon like Lk. 12.1–13.9. This is (2) the *rhetorical* approach to genre which focuses on what Kennedy calls the power of the text.[2] If the experience is confined by the historical and cultural constraints of the audience of the early first century, the power of the sermon is experienced differently under the changed constraints at the end of the first century when Luke writes. And even more different the experience of the power of the text will be, if the audience's constraints with which the sermon is apprehended are those of the late twentieth century: whether in the confinements of academic institutions (e.g. classrooms, professional meetings), or in the constraints of a given medium (e.g. Bible study in an adult education pro-

1. 'Linnean Blues', pp. 69, 73. Achtemeier (see p. 115 n. 1) makes a similar case; so does Kraftchick in his essay cited below (see p. 117 n. 5).

2. *New Testament Interpretation*, p. 158: 'rhetorical criticism may have an appeal lacking to other modern critical approaches, in that it comes closer to explaining what [readers] want explained in the text: not its sources, but its power'.

gram of a church or synagogue; prime-time TV religious films shown during holiday seasons; computer-assisted reading).

The historical approach to the rhetorical genre has its justification in the need to recognize the historical constraints with which audiences apprehend a sermon like Lk. 12.1–13.9. The indebtedness of early Jewish and Christian sermons to rhetorical conventions, both Jewish (or Near Eastern) and Hellenistic (Western), continues to lead genre critics to ask related questions of the sermon genre's relation to the diatribe tradition,[1] to the tradition of the protreptic genre,[2] not to speak of other genres known from ancient religious and/or philosophical 'propaganda' and their respective institutional *Sitz im Leben* in temple, school, academy, synagogue, or the like.

What I propose to do in what follows is first, by means of a close reading of the sermon in Lk. 12.1–13.9, to determine, with the tools of rhetorical criticism as outlined by Kennedy and Perelman, its rhetorical genre, that is, the expected audience response in the implied rhetorical situation.

The Sermon in Luke 12.1–13.9

1. *Two Reasons for the Choice of this Text*
One reason for choosing this text is the unfinished business in my essay on 'The Rhetorical Structure of Luke 12 in its Wider Context' written for the annual meeting of the New Testament Society of South Africa in the Spring of 1988.[3] The genre issue was touched upon but not discussed. The other reason is the growing realization that all efforts

---

1. Thomas Schmeller, *Paulus und die 'Diatribe'. Eine vergleichende Stilinterpretation* (NTAbh, ns 19; Münster: Aschendorff, 1987); Stanley Stowers, *The Diatribe and Paul's Letter to the Romans* (SBLDS 57; Chico, CA: Scholars Press, 1981); George L. Kustas, 'Diatribe in Ancient Rhetorical Theory', *Protocol of the 22. Colloquy of the Center for Hermeneutical Studies* (ed. W. Wuellner; Berkeley, CA: Center for Hermeneutical Studies, 1976).

2. Mark D. Jordan, 'Ancient Philosophic Protreptic and the Problem of Persuasive Genres', *Rhetorica* 4 (1986), pp. 309-33; David E. Aune, 'Romans as a LOGOS PROTREPTIKOS in the Context of Ancient Religious and Philosophical Propaganda', *Paulus als Missionar und Theologe und das Antike Judentum* (ed. M. Hengel; Tübingen: Mohr, forthcoming); Abraham J. Malherbe, *Paul and the Thessalonians: The Philosophical Tradition of Pastoral Care* (Philadelphia: Fortress, 1987), pp. 21-28 on 'The Philosophers' Call to Conversion'.

3. 'The Rhetorical Structure of Luke 12 in Its Wider Context', *Neot* 22 (1988), pp. 283-310.

of applying the standards of the rhetorical genres of Hellenistic antiquity to first-century Jewish and Christian texts, as Klaus Berger attempted,[1] have ended in more frustration, dissatisfaction, and obfuscation than in clarification of the task at hand. This is true despite the recognized influence of Hellenistic rhetorical culture on Jewish culture, both in the dispersion and in the homeland; in Galilee as well as in Jerusalem; among the literati as well as the sages, even those associated with Javne and the Mishnaic traditions.[2]

The same principle applies to the study of the rhetorical genre of sermons as was recently noted with respect to the study of the letter genres and sub-genres,[3] namely: the crucial need is the recognition of what White calls 'the types of persuasion [i.e. the *rhetorical* genres] which [are] employed in letter writing',[4] and, as such, serving their epistolary or sermonic *function*. The contributions of Lawrence Wills, refined by Clifton Black,[5] focus on both, the similarities and differences between the three rhetorical genres in Greek speeches and the form of the sermon in early Judaism and Christianity. Besides the recognition of the similarities in the use of various rhetorical conventions (e.g. quasi-logical arguments; varieties of artistic and inartistic 'proofs'; figures and tropes) in Jewish and Christian sermons, Black rightly focuses also on the issue of rhetorical coherence or the unification of different arguments into a sermonic unit. Wills emphasizes the distinctive and innovative nature of the homiletical patterns in Jewish and Christian sermons compared with Hellenistic rhetorical genres. By contrast, Black sees every reason for all kinds of speeches,

---

1. *Exegese des Neuen Testaments* (UTB 658; Heidelberg: Quelle & Meyer, 1977), pp. 128-36; and *Formgeschichte des Neuen Testaments* (Heidelberg: Quelle & Meyer, 1984).

2. Richard E. Cohen, 'The Relationship between Topic, Rhetoric, Logic: Analysis of a Syllogistic Passage in the Yerushalmi', *Judaic and Christian Interpretation of Texts: Contents and Contexts*, vol. II, *New Perspectives on Ancient Judaism* (ed. Jacob Neusner and Ernst S. Frerich; Lanham, MD: University Press of America, 1987), pp. 87-125. Gerald M. Phillips, 'The Practice of Rhetoric at the Talmudic Academies', *Speech Monographs* 26 (1959), pp. 37-46.

3. See e.g. Stanley K. Stowers, *Letter Writing in Greco-Roman Antiquity* (Philadelphia: Westminster, 1986), or John L. White, *Light from Ancient Letters* (FFNT; Philadelphia: Fortress, 1986).

4. White, *Ancient Letters*, p. 202.

5. Lawrence Wills, 'The Form of the Sermon in Hellenistic Judaism and Early Christianity', *HTR* 77 (1984), pp. 277-99, and C. Clifton Black II, 'The Rhetorical Form of the Hellenistic Jewish and Early Christian Sermon: A Response to Lawrence Wills', *HTR* 81 (1988), pp. 1-18.

including Jewish and Christian sermons, necessarily to be 'categorized as either judicial, deliberative, or epideictic'. However, Black is open to 'the possibility that continued research might delineate precise and creative modifications of Greco-Roman oratory by its Hellenistic-Jewish and Christian practitioners'.[1] It is precisely these 'precise and creative modifications' of known genres which interest us in the need for clarification of genre-classifications in the midst of growing obfuscation.

In his 'Aristotelian rhetorical analysis of I Thessalonians', rhetorician Thomas Olbricht asks whether the three rhetorical genres are precisely delineated categories in respect to persuasion strategies of *all* kinds of speech,[2] as Black thinks they are. Olbricht rightly warns that biblical exegetes have applied the traditional genre classifications to biblical texts 'far more perfunctorily than Aristotle contemplated'. The three genres have become freeze frames despite Aristotle's intentions. Olbricht proposes for (Jewish and) Christian literature a fourth genre: synagogue or church rhetoric with its central focus on the reality of God. But Olbricht is forced by the textual data to introduce right away such 'sub-set' categories as 'confrontational' and 'reconfirmational', which remind us of Fisher's motive view of communication. Between the one extreme of simply restoring the classical Aristotelian genre classifications (with or without modifications), and the other extreme of sidestepping the rhetorical genre debate altogether by concentrating exclusively on the literary genre discussion, we hope to find and establish some new middle ground that will help us in resolving the current impasse in our genre debates.

2. *The Rhetorical Situation, or the Intentionality of Luke 12.1–13.9*

a. *Rhetorical Epideixis: Praise/Approval or Reproach/Disapproval.* To inquire into the rhetorical or argumentative situation is to ask what the specific condition or situation there *is* (not *was*, as an historical question) that generates the text as we now have it in Lk. 12.1–13.9. The historical question is as inescapably to be asked of the real author (known as Luke), as it is of the narrative story world created by the author, but the question is also inescapable even for the real reader,

---

1. Black, 'Rhetorical Form', pp. 5-6, 17.
2. Thomas H. Olbricht, 'An Aristotelian Rhetorical Analysis of 1 Thessalonians', *Festschrift Abraham Malherbe* (ed. W. Meeks, D. Balch, and E. Ferguson; Minneapolis: Fortress, 1990), pp. 216-36; see also his earlier unpublished 'Aristotelian Rhetorical Analysis of Galatians'.

past or present. But the historical situation, both inside and outside of the narrative and its sermon, is categorically different from the argumentative situation, the exigency, the 'intentionality',[1] that gives (not 'gave') rise and shape to the text as argument, that is, in its orientation toward convincing/persuading the audience/ reader. Distinct from intentionality, but closely related to it, is the concern for the values contained in, and projected by, the text.[2]

Luke's narrative world identifies the rhetorical situation as conditioned by the scheming of scribes and Pharisees to catch Jesus in saying something wrong or debatable (11.53-54) pursuant to what he had done and said just prior to this. The growing popularity and crowd appeal of Jesus (11.29; 12.1) is perhaps partly motivated by curiosity, if not anxiety, because of the institutional powers in charge of maintaining Israel's cultural identity.

Given Jesus' open shaming or vituperating of the Pharisees and scribes (γραμματεῖς/νομικοί) in the section immediately preceding the sermon, for not *doing* what they 'know', readers may well ask what specific condition, what exigency, is discernible in the sermon? What is the text's intentionality, given its specific 'setting'? Given this specific setting in a manifestly deliberate breach of the halakhic norms the Pharisees sought to uphold for *all* Israel, we might expect, as did the characters in the narrative, that the sermon's rhetorical situation will be forensically apologetic (on his own behalf) or accusatory (against the Pharisees). When Jesus does open his mouth, thereby giving his 'opponents' an opportunity to get himself entangled in arguments, we are confronted with something different, something unexpected: not Halakha, but Aggadah![3]

What we find is not halakhic argumentation, but the 'strong and self-conscious didactic function [of Aggadah, with its] use of every literary and rhetorical technique'. That was the familiar way of Aggadists to deal, often times covertly, with 'the burning issues of the day' which

---

1. Eugene A. Nida, J.P. Louw, A.H. Snyman, and J.v.W. Cronje, *Style and Discourse with Special Reference to the Text of the Greek New Testament* (Cape Town: Bible Society, 1983), p. 46.

2. Mark Ledbetter, *Virtuous Intentions: The Religious Dimension of Narrative* (Academy Series; Atlanta: Scholars, 1989).

3. See Judah Goldin, 'The Freedom and Restraint of Haggadah', *Midrash and Literature* (ed. G.H. Hartman and S. Budick; New Haven: Yale University Press, 1986), pp. 57-76, and Joseph Heinemann, 'The Nature of the Aggadah', *Midrash and Literature*, pp. 41-55.

were frequently synonymous with the aim to 'strengthen faith'.[1] The setting for the speech is not defined or confined by conventions, such as a sabbath homily at home or in one of the synagogue services, where homilies of one or another species (Heinemann's 'folk aggadah' vs 'homiletic or scholarly aggadah') have their *Sitz im Leben*. The setting is outdoors, en route to Jerusalem, and fits Luke's 'literary homily' addressed to the reader.

The rhetorical features emerging from the relationship of the parts to one another, which we find in the sermon's constitutive parts (e.g. its introduction, its several parts, and its parabolic conclusion), can give us some first clues. The findings about these rhetorical features must then be tested against the sermon as a whole (12.1–13.9) as well as the larger argumentative strategy in the narrative unity of Luke's Travel Section and of Luke–Acts as a whole. But unlike those who approach the rhetorical structure of Luke 12 as literary artifact, we approach the text's rhetorical features as a 'system of influence'.[2]

The first clues we have on hand indicate that the exigency which gives rise to the sermon is the adjudication of the praise-worthiness or blame-worthiness of the actions or attitudes of the characters in their interaction with Jesus, and his interaction with them, *in the here and now* of the narrative. The sermon's 'setting' which 'sets the mood' is 11.53-54.[3] The narrator sets the stage by his comment in 12.1 that an unusually large crowd had gathered 'while all this happened' (ἐν οἷς) or gathered because of the scribes and Pharisees being and acting 'terribly resentful' about Jesus and seeking to ambush him by drawing him out with leading questions (11.53-54, and again in 20.20). These questions, however, remain unnarrated, thus creating a certain narrative but creative 'gap'.

Blaming Pharisees for their hypocrisy (12.1), as later in the sermon the multitudes get blamed for their hypocrisy (12.56), the audiences/readers are to be led to approve of the two sides of the same issue: the

---

1. Heinemann, 'Nature of the Aggadah', pp. 47, 49.

2. See Robert C. Tannehill, *The Gospel according to Luke*, vol. I, *The Narrative Unity of Luke–Acts: A Literary Interpretation* (FFNT; Philadelphia: Fortress, 1986), p. 8, and his review of Roland Meynet, *L'Évangile selon saint Luc. Analyse rhétorique* (1988), in *Bib* 70 (1989), pp. 561-64.

3. What Seymour Chatman (*Story and Discourse. Narrative Structure in Fiction and Film* [Ithaca, NY: Cornell University Press, 1978], pp. 138-45) says about 'setting' for narratives, applies also, with modification, to argumentation or didactic discourse.

shamefulness of deplorable attitudes or actions (or lack of action!), and the praiseworthiness of the proper quality of life and leadership, even or particularly in the face of (institutional) adversity. The proverbial saying 'that hypocrisy is the homage that vice pays to virtue' is restated by Perelman 'more precisely' as 'hypocrisy is an homage to a certain value, that which one sacrifices while pretending to follow it, because one refuses to confront it with other values'.[1] On separating fiction and fact about the proverbial hypocrisy of the Pharisees, see Neusner's 'Three Pictures of the Pharisees'.[2] The metaphoric, hence rhetorical, sense of 'the leaven of the Pharisees which is hypocrisy' is quite different from the referential sense of hypocrisy as itemized in Lk. 11.37-52.

In Lk. 12.35-48, for instance, the rhetorical situation is one of being vituperative about this hypocrisy and one of lauding the intended confrontation with other values—those cherished by Jesus and the implied author *in* the narrative, and by the author and reader *out*side the story: the values derived from the unity of intention (or volition) and action.

b. *Composite Audience/Readership, and Perelman's 'Universal Audience'*. The audience for our text is threefold: the very resentful (which is different from 'hostile') scribes and Pharisees, the very eager or apprehensive crowd (as a crowd of many thousands in 12.1; as an unspecified crowd or crowds in 12.13, 54; or as specially introduced reporters of ominous events in Galilee in 13.1), and the narratively unqualified disciples. It is 'his disciples' who get addressed primarily (πρῶτον). The crowd and the disciples are each brought into focus by introducing an individual, either named (Peter among the disciples in 12.41) or unnamed (one of the ὄχλος in 12.13), as well as the multitudes (ὄχλοι in 12.54) and some unnamed reporters (τινες... ἀπαγγέλλοντες in 13.1). Thomas Dochery's study is helpful here in exploring the use of names in narration (= presence of character) as compared with unnamed persons (= 'absent' character);[3] in the latter

---

1. Chaim Perelmann and L. Olbrechts-Tyteca, *The New Rhetoric: A Treatise on Argumentation* (trans. J. Wilkinson and P. Wever; Notre Dame: University of Notre Dame Press, 1969), p. 199.

2. Jacob Neusner, *Formative Judaism: Religious, Historical and Literary Studies.* 5th series: *Revisioning the Written Records of a Nascent Religion* (BJS 91; Chico, CA: Scholars Press, 1985), pp. 51-77.

3. Thomas Dochery, *Reading (Absent) Character. Towards a Theory of Characterization in Fiction* (Oxford: Clarendon, 1983).

case the focus shifts from the individualism of named characters to the collective, communal dimension of the 'absent' character.

Whether we think of the resentful, apprehensive collective of scribes and Pharisees, or the hypocrisy of the collective Pharisees, or think of the collective crowd (and its hypocrisy), the text's intentionality affects the narrative as 'system of influence' for *all* concerned, disciples and non-disciples alike. Better still, as part of Luke–Acts, the sermon is directed not at the characters *in* the narrative, but at the readers, with Theophilus as metonymy in Luke's Prologue. Narration, viewed as argumentation, 'is a function of the audience being addressed'.[1] The text as we have it shows the ways in which it appeals to readers; the rhetorical situation, which gives the text its shape and genre, concerns the choice to be made, and to what ends readers should be directed, and how the readers are expected to feel or act, once narration begins.[2]

The Lukan Prologue states the rhetorical situation for the narrative as a whole: Theophilus, and all other 'real' readers, are to be narratively convinced and persuaded of the certainty about the matters of faith already known (and practiced). Thibeaux's perception of the role of the Prologue introducing the paradigm of Luke–Acts as 'narrative-rhetorical sacred history' offers a completely different interpretation of the rhetorical genre of Luke–Acts from Sterling's perception of Luke–Acts as 'apologetic historiography'.[3]

In reflecting on the relations of Lk. 12.35-48 to the participants in the communication, we encounter other rhetorical features as we pay attention to the typology of audiences in our text. Who are the participants in the communication? They are the real people as characters in Luke's narrative, as we have already outlined. But in addressing or writing for people, every speaker or author constructs or invents his/her audience/readers, just as the speaker/author invents his/her

---

1. Perelman and Olbrechts-Tyteca, *New Rhetoric*, p. 44; see also Walter R. Fisher, *Human Communication as Narration: Toward a Philosophy of Reason, Value, and Action* (Columbia, SC: University of South Carolina Press, 1987).

2. James Phelan, *Reading People, Reading Plots: Character, Progression, and the Interpretation of Narrative* (Chicago: University of Chicago Press, 1989).

3. Thibeaux, 'The Narrative Rhetoric of Luke 7.36-50', ch. 2, 'The Text Genre of Luke–Acts', vs Gregory Sterling, 'Historiography and Self-Definition: Josephus, Luke–Acts, and Apologetic Historiography' (PhD dissertation, Graduate Theological Union, Berkeley, 1989).107

arguments. In either case, the invention or construction 'should be adequate to the occasion'.[1]

But what happens when, as in Luke 12, the speaker addresses 'a composite audience, embracing people differing in character, loyalty, and functions' as the zealous representatives of Jewish culture (Pharisees and 'lawyers'), the partial crowd, and the fearful disciples? Perelman and Olbrechts-Tyteca offer two answers: (1) 'the orator will have to use a multiplicity of arguments'. This is exactly what we find in Luke 12. Also, (2) the orator may 'try to locate [his composite audience] in its social setting'.[2] This is also exactly what we find in Luke 12, for the crowd relates to the cultural leaders, as the disciples relate to Jesus as their teacher, as servants/steward relate to their respective masters in the parables cited by Jesus. The composite audience of this sermon reflects the mood of controversy prevalent since Jesus' opening sermon Lk. 4.16-27 and its enraged (θυμός) reaction. But, if controversy is understood as 'the discussion of conflicting claims in community and their resolution by the discovery of common ends of action',[3] then one can see in Lk. 12.1–13.9 an effort of (re-)discovering, of remembering, or reaffirming the common ends of action.

To get his composite audience convinced and persuaded by what Jesus intends to accomplish with his sermon, the composite audience 'has to be regrouped as a single entity'. It exists as such not as a matter of fact (socially, culturally, economically, etc.), but as 'a universality and unanimity imagined by the speaker'.[4] It is important to note with Perelman and Olbrechts-Tyteca: 'Each individual, each culture, has . . . its own conception of the universal audience'. The study of the variant views of universal audience would yield insight into what people (individually and collectively) 'have regarded as *real, true*, and *objectively valid*'.[5]

1. Perelman and Olbrechts-Tyteca, *New Rhetoric*, pp. 19-23.

2. *New Rhetoric*, pp. 21-22.

3. Thomas M. Conley, 'The Virtues of Controversy: In Memoriam R.P. McKeon', *QJS* 71 (1985), pp. 470-75.

4. Perelman and Olbrechts-Tyteca, *New Rhetoric*, p. 31.

5. *New Rhetoric*, p. 33; see also Golden's essay in '*Practical Reasoning in Human Affairs: Studies in Honor of Chaim Perelman* (ed. J.L. Golden and J.J. Pilotta; Dordrecht: Deidel, 1986).

c. *Typology of Audiences/Readers.* In Lk. 12.35-48, for example, we can discern the ideal reader, the composite audience regrouped as a single entity (Perelman's universal audience) in the following instances:

1. In the arguments presupposing assent by the general reader, such as: (a) sentences with third person singular or plural subjects (impersonal speaker/impersonal audience): the parables: 12.36, 39, 42, 45-46; the macarisms: 12.37a, 38, 43; and the proverbs: 12.47-48; see also 12.2, 15b; (b) sentences with impersonal speaker/'you'—plural addressee: proverb: 12.35, 40; see also 12.3.
2. In arguments expressing a single interlocutor/reader, as in the 'truly I say to you' sayings: 12.37b, 44.
3. In arguments where the speaker argues with himself: in sentences with first singular or plural subject, but no addressee, such as in interior monologue: 12.45a, 12.17-19.

The only seeming exception is the direct question in 12.41, but even here the scope of the question regroups one component (the 'we' of the disciples) of the composite audience as single entity: 'all' or 'everyone'.

We conclude from this typology of audiences in Jesus' argument that the main part of our text is convincing argumentation (12.2-20, 23-27, 51-58). Persuasive argumentation is operative in the opening or closing appeals, such as 12.1b, 21, 22, 28, 31-39, 42-48, 49-50, 59, and the closing appeal in 13.1-9. The opening questions in 12.41-42, as well as the beatitudes in 12.37, 43 can qualify as persuasive argumentation. The two versions of the same paradigm/parable of the employees' varying degrees of readiness or unreadiness for their employer's 'coming' (12.36-39, 42-48) amplify the emotional appeal, as does the parable in 13.6-9 for the preceding argument in 13.1-5. The prevalence of the speaker's appeal to the universal audience shows that throughout the sermon the composite audience is regrouped, reconstituted as a single entity.

3. *Rhetorical Disposition, or Argumentative Sequence, in Luke 12.1–13.9*

The sermon's theme is stated first negatively in the warning about the leaven of the Pharisees, identified as hypocrisy (12.1b). Then it is elaborated positively as known (but anxiety-generating) transformations, first in form of a proverb (12.2), then in two images of contrast (12.3, from dark to light; from inner rooms to housetops). These images apply to what the disciples will be doing, in word or deed—not Jesus. Like Jesus' words and deeds, the believers' private, even secret acts will inevitably become public, and as such relevant socially, politically, and culturally, and hence risky. This is where the soon to be addressed fear and anxiety about loss of life (fear of 'perishing' in 13.1-5) enters the argument of the whole sermon. The pattern of amplification by way of proverbs, parables, and paradigms recurs throughout this sermon. What is said to his disciples is said to all. The warning against the hypocrisy of the Pharisees turns into a warning against hypocrisy in anyone, as the concluding sections of the sermon demonstrate.

A first argumentative sequence (12.4-12) addresses the audience as 'my friends' (φίλοι μου). They are assumed to be in fear for their lives, threatened by 'synagogues and rulers and authorities' (12.11), as Jesus, the speaker, is threatened in the narrative. The rhetorical situation of this argumentation is assurance of the validity of the God-code in all situations, both ordinary and extraordinary. The Jewish culture-specific God-code is implied in the code value of the use of such terms as Pharisees (12.1b), 'reveal' (12.2), and 'proclaim' (12.3), but also in such covert or overt references as in 12.5, 6, 9, 10, 12, and in the enumeration of the three institutions designed to order the public and private lives of all members of the people of God: 'synagogues and rulers and authorities' (12.11). In the concluding argumentative sequence (13.1-5, 6-9) the God-code is reflected in the references to sinners and repentance. Whether threatened by political power (Pilate vs the Galileans in 13.1), or by disastrous 'acts of God' (the collapse of the tower of Siloam in 13.4), the threat of perishing in the last argumentative sequence corresponds to the fear of being cast into hell, the fear of God (12.5) in the opening argument. The argumentative appeal is like that of John the Baptist (3.1-18) and the underlying tradition of both prophets and priests.

The second argumentative sequence (12.13-21) is initiated by an unnamed single interlocutor from the crowd who introduces the topic of attachment to possessions at times of facing property inheritance claims among members of a household. This sequence addresses the improper vs the proper fear of God. The pattern of persuasion is familiar: a chreia (12.13-14—a request answered by a question, as in 12.41-42), followed by its elaboration through an ironic parable

(12.16-20), and a concluding brief appeal (12.21). As here, so in the second to last argumentative sequence (12.49-59) the audience's expectation of the speaker (Jesus, addressed as 'teacher' or 'sage') as a peace-maker (as in 12.13) is reversed: not peace, but fire and division. There may well be intentional irony in the affirmative of 'division' (διαμερισμός) from the one who was expected (in 12.14) to serve as 'arbiter' (μεριστής). As 13.1-5 is followed by a parable (13.6-9), so 12.49-53 is followed by two models: familiar discernment of changes in the weather, the signs of the times (12.54-55), followed by an application (12.56), and the familiar negotiations to make amends to avoid court litigation (12.57-58), with implied God-code and a brief application [12.59]). Also 12.4-12 relates to 13.1-9, with the latter intensifying the former, as 12.13-21 relates to 12.54-59 (both marked as addressed to members of the multitude).

This leaves the argumentative sequence in 12.22-53. All four units that make up this argumentative sequence (12.22-34, 35-40, 41-48, 49-53) address the topic of proper vs improper responses to familiar experiences of someone's 'coming'. The phrase 'for this reason' (v. 22) links the preceding arguments with the statement of the thesis in 12.22-23. Whether as a declared disciple of Jesus, or as a member of the crowd, or perhaps even, or especially, as a member of the religious establishment which is provoked by Jesus' teachings and actions, any anxiety for one's life (ψυχή) is argued in three stages: the first to shame the audience by comparison with the ravens who are cared for by God (12.24, an argument from the lesser to the greater, as in 12.6-7), then by the use of two rhetorical questions in 12.25-26 which evoke a sense of futility in one's anxiety, and finally by comparison with the lilies (12.27-28) which, in growth and glory, outdo the legendary splendor associated with King Solomon.[1] The threefold argumentative sequence climaxes with a shaming or vituperative appeal to the audience as people of little faith (ὀλιγόπιστοι), concluding with the appeal not to be so preoccupied with security for food and drink, and not to live or act like a meteor (μὴ μετεωρίζεσθε). Human beings everywhere (as devotees of *their* gods) act like this, but *your* (emphatic) God is fully cognizant of these needs (12.29-30). Jesus'

---

1. On the function of the argumentative technique which works with 'symbolic relation' as 'bond of participation', see Perelman and Olbrechts-Tyteca, *New Rhetoric*, pp. 331-37.

audience as well as Luke's readers are presumed to know this and to be disposed to act accordingly.

The centrality of the God-code in Jewish culture for the argument continues in the following turn to a more positive appeal (12.30-34): God's βασιλεία, as treasure to be sought, is destined to be given gladly to the timid 'little flock' (12.32). Dissociating true and lasting heavenly treasures, which cannot be disowned, from temporary earthly treasures (12.33) leads to a proverbial conclusion (12.34). This argumentative sequence (12.22-34) is not, as Berger[1] claims, a symbouleutic argumentation, but evokes a sense of reaffirmation (revitalizing one's devotion), or a sense of purification (or transformation of one's devotion).[2] What hypocrisy is for Pharisees and crowds, that is what fear, anxiety,[3] and 'little faith' are for Jesus' disciples, his 'friends'.

The extended sequence of argumentation in Lk. 12.35-48 can certainly be seen as a rhetorical unit all its own, yet it has its argumentative force and function by virtue of its place within the larger rhetorical unit of the sermon as a whole, which, in turn, has its force and function within the larger whole of Luke's 'Travel Section' (9.51–19.27). Arguing for (proper vs improper) readiness for a certain reality, that is, for waiting attentively and appropriately for the beneficent or threatening manifestation of that seemingly absent reality (a familiar and particular example taken from the household or business relationships) is employed as either laudable model to be imitated or as vituperative anti-model to be avoided.[4] What we have in this argumentative sequence are not two different parables but evidence of the model-character of the argument being used to make different applications in the unfolding argumentation.

We linked earlier the second to last argumentative sequence in 12.49-59 with the second argumentation in 12.13-21 which, with irony

---

1. *Formgeschichte des Neuen Testaments*, p. 93.
2. See Walter R. Fisher ('A Motive View of Communication', *QJS* 56 [1970], pp. 131-39) on the four motive views of communication.
3. F.W. Danker (*Jesus and the New Age according to St. Luke* [St. Louis: Clayton, 1974], p. 151) states that 'anxiety is a species of unbelief'.
4. Cf. Perelman and Olbrechts-Tyteca (*New Rhetoric*, pp. 362-68) on 'model and anti-model' designed to incite to an action inspired by it. It is important to remember that the use and function of this technique of argumentation, like the use of any other argumentative technique, is not tied to any one particular social situation or any particular value (e.g. social or economic hierarchies).

in the narration of the parable, forcefully argued for the remodeling of the hypocritical conception of reality shared by the composite audience. The force and function of argumentation by dissociation—dissociating true reality from its appearance—is none other than 'a new structuration of reality'.[1] Hypocrisy is the failure of discernment of the reality in the appearances (12.56); in terms of religion, it is the failure to repent (13.3), or, in the illustration of the parable 13.6-9, it is the failure of tended, even fertilized, fruit trees to bear fruit. Hypocrisy arises when cognition and volition do not correspond and are out of proportion or even incommensurate. Hypocrisy is for relationships (to oneself as much as to others!) what sophistry is for communication (with oneself or with others): the disintegration of the unity of convincing and persuasive argumentation.[2]

4. Stylistic Features: Figures and Tropes in Luke 12.1–13.9

Attention to the employed stylistic devices in a given rhetorical performance involves for Conley[3] a departure from the 'an-aesthetic' concerns operative in most genre criticisms—a departure which could (but need not) 'lead to a virtual repudiation of the form-and-genre approach altogether'. From this cursory exploration of the stylistic features found in the sermon in Lk. 12.1–13.9 we might expect the following: keeping the focus on the textual, that is, linguistic and rhetorical details of this sermon and on the attendant 'pleasures of reading'.[4] In the preceding section, dealing with the disposition or argumentative structure of this particular sermon genre, we became repeatedly aware that 'the main problem with invention-oriented critical approaches [which is to] abridge speeches to their "arguments" or "strategies"'.[5] Attention paid to stylistic devices makes us avoid that lingering 'main problem'.

We noted such stylistic devices as the use of metaphors (e.g. 12.1b leaven; v. 3 speaking in the dark/hearing in the light, or whispering in inner rooms/proclaiming from housetops; v. 32 little flock; etc.) and

---

1. Perelman and Olbrechts-Tyteca, *New Rhetoric*, pp. 411-59; quotation from p. 415.
2. Cf. Perelman and Olbrechts-Tyteca (*New Rhetoric*, pp. 26-31) on 'persuading and convincing', and (pp. 59-62) on 'argumentation and commitment'.
3. 'Linnean Blues', p. 73.
4. See Robert Alter, *The Pleasures of Reading in an Ideological Age* (New York: Simon & Schuster, 1989).
5. 'Linnean Blues', p. 73.

of examples or parables (e.g. 12.16-20, 36-48; 13.6-9). The appeal which the sermon wants to make rests to some degree on these recourses to particular known cases. The argument moves inductively from the particular case to the general application sought in the argument. As an illustration, 12.16-20, though seemingly negative, provides support for the established notion of no need to fear anyone or anything, except 'the One who has authority to cast into hell' (v. 5). Soliloquies, whether as narrative or as argumentation, make generalizations possible (e.g. 12.17-19, 45, maybe also 54-55),[1] like examples.

Another stylistic device, the use of rhetorical questions (e.g. 12.6, 25-26, 42), evokes first an established reality or social value (positive or negative), and then is followed by quasi-logical convincing arguments moving from the lesser to the greater (e.g. 12.6-7, 25-28). The same can be said of the use of proverbial wisdom or maxims (e.g. 12.2, 15, 23, 34, 48b, etc.). Like the illustrations, or parables and metaphors, they evoke agreement with an existing reality or value which then gets argumentatively elaborated in the sermon sections following. The metaphor in 12.1b is elaborated first by the proverb (v. 2) and then by other metaphoric expressions (v. 3) which leads to the introduction of the sermon's main subject (12.4-5): true fear as distinct from false fear or false security (= hypocrisy). This distinction is reached by an important stylistic device: the argumentation by dissociation.[2] This stylistic device is employed also in 12.33 (failing vs unfailing treasures).

The pragmatic aspects of the choice of moods, as well as tense or aspect, has been duly noted in Stanley Porter's reconceptualization of NT Greek grammar.[3] Our text is marked by frequent uses of the interrogative modal (12.6, 14, 17, 20b, 25-26, 41, 42, 51; 13.2, 4), exclamations and vocatives, imperatives and imperatival subjunctives, beatitudes and emphatic statements ('truly I say to you'). From the frequency of the use of imperatives, for instance, one can no more infer that the rhetorical genre at hand *has* to be deliberative, than one

---

1. See Dorrit Cohn's seminal study, *Transparent Minds* (Princeton, NJ: Princeton University Press, 1978); also Perelman and Olbrechts-Tyteca (*New Rhetoric*, pp. 40-45) on 'self-deliberating'.

2. Perelman and Olbrechts-Tyteca, *New Rhetoric*, pp. 411-59.

3. Stanley E. Porter, *Verbal Aspect in the Greek of the New Testament, with Reference to Tense and Mood* (Studies in Biblical Greek 1; New York: Peter Lang, 1989).

can do so on the evidence of the frequent use of examples or models. The latter was done in a recent study of the rhetorical genre of 1 Corinthians.[1] The choice of narrating in detail specific actions or persons—an affective rhetorical figure known as *evidentia*[2]—is made in 12.11, 22, 45, 46-48, 53, 58.

Irony was noted in the chiastic structure of the disposition of the sermon as a whole: the one who refuses to act as arbiter in family matters (12.13-21) turns out to be the great family divider (12.49-59). The fear of perishing at the hands of representatives of the religious establishment (12.4-12) is intensified in the fear of perishing at the hands of God, if hypocrites do not repent, which is to bear fruit born out of readiness for an assured reality which is argumentatively dissociated from given appearances.

Where Fisher sees 'primary motive states', there Lausberg saw *Leitaffekt* as determinative of a given rhetorical genre.[3] For Lausberg such *Leitaffekt* becomes most apparent in the persuasive parts, especially the concluding perorations, such as 12.21, 31-34, 40, 48b, 59; 13.3, 5, and the concluding parable (13.6-9).

5. *The Sermon as Whole: Its Genre and Its Function within Luke's Travel Section*

It was observed at the outset that determination of rhetorical units is circular: (1) the rhetoric of smaller units, such as this sermon, is part of the overall rhetoric of the larger unit of which it is a part, whether the Travel Section or Luke–Acts as a whole; (2) the rhetoric of the larger units is built up from an understanding of the rhetoric of the smaller units and their sequences, as outlined in section 3 above. The very disposition of the arguments, their interaction and their ordered sequence,[4] determines, as it is determined by, the argumentative situation or intentionality faced by the audience/reader. If the choice of

---

1. Margaret Mary Mitchell, *Paul and the Rhetoric of Reconciliation: An Exegetical Investigation of the Language and Composition of 1 Corinthians* (HUT 27; Tübingen: Mohr [Siebeck], 1991).

2. See Heinrich Lausberg, *Handbuch der literarischen Rhetorik* (2nd edn; 2 vols.; München: Hüber, 1973), I, pp. 399-407.

3. Lausberg, *Handbuch der literarischen Rhetorik*, I, pp. 89, 131, 145, 239. A distinct key emotive affect is said to dominate a given rhetorical unity, such as a sermon.

4. See Perelman and Olbrechts-Tyteca (*New Rhetoric*, pp. 460-508) on interaction and order of arguments.

Persuasive Artistry

order and sequence of arguments for the purpose of persuasion is conditioned (among two other factors)[1] by 'the argumentative situation itself', what can be said then of the sermon's genre, or its intended function, in the context of the larger rhetorical unit of which it is a part?

We inferred from the changing rhetorical situations within the sermon (see section 2), from the analyzed sequence and climax of the arguments (see section 3), and from the analysis of select stylistic features (see section 4), that all four of Fisher's 'primary motive states'— affirmation, reaffirmation, purification, subversion—can be seen as operative in this sermon at one point or another. The prevailing dissociative argumentation, however, combined with the reconstituting of the composite audience as a single unity, focuses on the reaffirmation of the reality familiar to the Jewish characters in the sermon, as well as to Christian readers hearing the sermon: the privileges and obligations associated with the flock's claim to the realm of God or the realm of holiness.

The very context for making this reaffirmation is the escalating contest which the Pharisees provoked in Israel by exemplifying their stringent holiness rules in all places of daily living. As a sect they were 'part of the everyday corporate community' that is 'Israel', but, as Neusner points out, their efforts at exemplifying 'their rules in the streets and marketplaces' and at attaining 'influence in the people at large' did not require of this group 'to identify itself as "all Israel"'. The Pharisees were not, nor did they regard themselves as such, 'coexistent with "all Israel"',[2] yet their rules sought to reaffirm the centrality of God's Torah for Israel. The rhetorical genre of Lk. 12.1–13.9 is an integral part of the narrative rhetoric of Luke's Travel Section, and of Luke–Acts as a whole.

6. Difficulties in Applying Hellenistic Rhetorical Genre-Categories to Jewish Contexts

The difficulties in applying Hellenistic rhetorical genre-categories to Jewish contexts seem to be threefold. The first two are related to the

---

1. Perelman and Olbrechts-Tyteca (*New Rhetoric*, p. 491) mention 'the conditioning of the audience' which is 'the changes of attitude brought about by the (sermon)', and 'the reactions occasioned in the [composite] audience by its perception of the order or arrangement adopted in the (sermon)'.

2. Jacob Neusner, *Judaism and Its Social Metaphors: Israel in the History of Jewish Thought* (New York: Cambridge University Press, 1989), p. 244.

cultural differences between Jews and 'Gentiles'. Kennedy raises the issue sharply when he asks: 'How legitimate is it to approach the New Testament [let alone the Old!] in terms of Greek ideas of rhetoric?'[1] It is, indeed, historically justifiable to approach the rhetorical genres of the NT and of contemporary Jewish literature in terms of the rhetorical conventions of late antiquity on the grounds that both Judaism and Christianity—as, later on, Islam, as well as Asian and African cultures through later Christian missions[2]—were profoundly influenced by Greco-Roman rhetoric. But the integrity of each culture asserts itself even with, or because of and in reaction to, the cultural hegemony of Greco-Roman (= Western) culture which exerted itself in numerous ways throughout its empire, and beyond as well.

One of the difficulties pertains to the apparent rhetorical genres in ancient Jewish culture as in other non-Western cultures. To presume that 'the canons and principles of Greek and Latin rhetorical art . . .[were] functional in the ancient Israelite cultures in which the Hebrew Scriptures were produced', is one of two cultural fallacies; the other, according to Rabinowitz, concerns

> the assumptions and beliefs about the nature and powers of words that were handed down and received in ancient Israel, how words were culturally perceived to behave and to act—hence, too, the guiding presumptions of word articulation and text formation—are demonstrably quite different from the beliefs and assumptions about the nature and powers of words held in Graeco-Roman and later Western societies and cultures.[3]

If we add 'and early Christianity' after every reference Rabinowitz makes to ancient Israel, we see its relevance for our study.

In support of Kennedy and others it has to be acknowledged that by NT times the rhetorical theory of the school handbooks had found its application in almost every form of oral and written communication, even in Jerusalem's inner Jewish circles. The culture of biblical Judaism may be said to be different from the culture of post-biblical Juda-

---

1. Kennedy, *New Testament Interpretation*, p. 8.
2. See Vernon J. Jensen, 'Teaching East Asian Rhetoric', *RSQ* 17 (1987), pp. 135-49; Mary M. Garrett, 'The Impact of Western Rhetoric in the East: Three Case Studies. Chinese Responses to the Jesuits' Argumentation during the Late Ming–Early Ch'ing' (Paper presented at the International Society for the History of Rhetoric, Göttingen Meeting, July, 1989).
3. Judah Messer Leon, *The Book of the Honeycomb's Flow. Sêpher Nôpheth Sûphîm* (ed. and trans. Isaac Rabinowitz; Ithaca, NY: Cornell University Press, 1982), p. lxv.

ism under Roman occupation and cultural influence. Rabinowitz's concerns are now being taken up by other scholars working as literary anthropologists.[1] How words were culturally perceived to behave and to act, that is the perception of a culture's guiding presumptions of word articulation and text formation, is an integral part of the beliefs and assumptions about the nature and powers of words operative in each culture.[2] In the contest of Israel's cultural integrity against Hellenistic cultural hegemony, the issue we identified is referred to only obliquely as follows:

> the Greek-speaking Jews of these two centuries [2–1 cent. BC] were able to derive from their extensive exposure to the Greek spirit and Greek culture the impulse to create their *own* cultural achievements in ways that were *originally alien* to them [what Rabinowitz called 'culturally fallacious'] but which they succeeded in assimilating to their *own* faith and philosophy (emphasis mine).[3]

The second reason why Hellenistic rhetorical genres present difficulties in their application to Jewish texts and contexts (perhaps even more so than Christian texts?) is the priority of religious culture in Judaism over all other aspects of culture. The God-code is absolutely essential to the sermon's argumentative and persuasive premises, even, or perhaps especially, when the God-code is *not* explicitly stated (e.g. in the use of the passive voice, 12.7), but remains implicit (Meir Sternberg calls this the ideology of biblical literature).[4]

The third reason why we may run into difficulties is the application of rhetorical genres arising from oral culture to literary documents. Achtemeier singles out only one major issue: the oral performance of

---

1. E.g. Wolfgang Iser, *Prospecting: From Reader Response to Literary Anthropology* (Baltimore: Johns Hopkins University Press, 1989).

2. See Robert T. Oliver, *Culture and Communication: The Problem of Penetrating National and Cultural Boundaries* (American Lecture Series 506; Springfield, IL: Thomas, 1962); H. Samuel Hamod, 'Arab and Moslem Rhetorical Theory and Practice', *Central States Speech Journal* (May 1963), pp. 97-102; Lawrence A. Palinkas, *Rhetoric and Religious Experience: The Discourse of Immigrant Chinese Churches* (Fairfax, VA: George Mason University Press, 1989).

3. Nikolaus Walter, 'Jewish-Greek Literature of the Greek Period', *The Hellenistic Age, Cambridge History of Judaism*, vol. II (ed. W.D. Davies and L. Finkelstein; Cambridge: Cambridge University Press, 1984), pp. 385-408 (quotation from p. 408).

4. Meir Sternberg, *The Poetics of Biblical Narrative. Ideological Literature and the Drama of Reading* (Indiana Literary Biblical Series; Bloomington: Indiana University Press, 1985). For a sophisticated grammarian's view of the pragmatic aspects of the choice of voice, see Stanley Porter, *Verbal Aspect*.

NT literature.[1] The role which literary documents, and even more so, sacred and canonical documents, play in an oral culture (ancient or modern) cannot, however, be *reduced* to the common denominator of orality in cultures. An actual sermon of Jesus (which may or may not be reflected in Lk. 12.1–13.9), like any actual pre-70s synagogue sermon, is one thing; the reconstitution of the oral sermon in a literary work (whether in Luke's Gospel, or in rabbinic homily collections) is quite another thing; and the performative reading of these literary works within religious institutional frameworks (the worshiping community; the religious school house) is yet another distinct matter. Hillis Miller has identified this third aspect as 'the materiality of reading'.[2] We have yet to pay attention to this aspect when devoting ourselves to the task of analyzing and interpreting rhetorical genres.

The Current Discussion about Rhetorical Genres

1. The Problem of Defining the Nature and Purpose of Rhetorical Genres

George Kennedy and others have recalled for us the conventions that determined the definition of the three classical rhetorical genres (forensic, epideictic, and deliberative) in the discussions of ancient rhetoricians, their practices and their theories as laid out in their various handbooks on rhetoric. Genre was, and remains, the name which theorists of rhetoric give to similar responses (by audiences *and* speakers!) to recurrent social or rhetorical situations. For Perelman and Olbrechts-Tyteca, however, the very conventions of 'the division into oratorical genres helped to bring about the later disintegration of rhetoric', because these very conventions were based on 'a false conception of the effects of rhetoric'.[3] These effects have been defined as the 'close connection between argumentative thought and the action it

---

1. Paul J. Achtemeier, '*Omne verbum sonat*: The New Testament and the Oral Environment of Late Western Antiquity', *JBL* 109 (1990), pp. 3-27. Similar concerns were voiced in Lou H. Silberman (ed.), *Orality, Aurality and Biblical Narrative* (*Semeia* 39 [1987]). On 'the breakdown of oral consciousness and its meaning for rhetorical theory and practice', see Robert J. Connors, 'Greek Rhetoric and the Transition from Orality', *PhilR* 19 (1986), pp. 38-65.

2. J. Hillis Miller, 'The Triumph of Theory, the Resistance to Reading, and the Question of the Material Base', *PMLA* 103 (1987), pp. 281-91. This is his Modern Language Association Presidential Address of 1986.

3. Perelman and Olbrechts-Tyteca, *New Rhetoric*, pp. 48-49.

paves the way for or brings about'. It is the connection between argumentation and commitment.[1]

a. *Problem 1*. Rhetorical genres change with historical and cultural context. In any given period of history and in any given culture such similar, if not identical, responses can indeed be taken as 'an objective historical reality'.[2] But even within a given culture (e.g. the Jewish culture at the beginning of the first century vs the end of the century, following Javne), let alone in the move from one culture to another (e.g. from Jesus the Jew to Luke the Hellenist and Christian), there may be significant changes.[3] The three basic kinds of social situation in the Greek city-states (and with it certain social institutions!), which provided the contexts for the three basic kinds of rhetoric, *changed* by the first century in such a way that they no longer dominated public life, or better: they dominated life in *changed* ways.[4]

Related to this change in context is the cultural setting, which is relevant for Lk. 12.1–13.9 as part of the 'Judeo-Christian rhetoric'.[5] Down to the first century, Jewish 'preconceptual' and later literary rhetoric, with its Near Eastern origin[6] and Hellenistic influences, was controlled by its own, distinctly Jewish social environments, whether in exile and dispersion, or in *Eretz Yisrael*. Jesus' sermon is born of just such distinctly Jewish social situation and its associated institutions (mentioned in the sermon are: the συναγωγαί, ἀρχαί, and ἐξουσίαι, 12.11 [see 'Pilate', 13.1]; judge/κριτής, arbiter/μεριστής, constable/

---

1. Perelman and Olbrechts-Tyteca, *New Rhetoric*, pp. 59-62.

2. Conley, 'Linnean Blues', p. 68.

3. See D.A. Russell (*Criticism in Antiquity* [London: Duckworth, 1981], pp. 148-58) on the changes in literary and rhetorical genres in antiquity, and on the 'much more patchy and incomplete' classification of genres in antiquity in contrast to Renaissance genre-theory.

4. Vernon K. Robbins ('Pronouncement Stories from a Rhetorical Perspective', *Forum* 4.2 [1988], pp. 20-25) mentions that only the old social situations which informed the three basic rhetorical genres had *changed* by the time the NT pronouncement stories took shape. Courtroom proceedings, political assemblies, and civil ceremonies were still operative, but now, in Imperial Rome and its various provinces, they dominated life just as much, but in different and changed ways, and that has its effect on the rhetorical genres and the ways they were used and classified.

5. George A. Kennedy, *Classical Rhetoric and Its Christian and Secular Tradition from Ancient to Modern Times* (Chapel Hill, NC: University of North Carolina Press, 1980), pp. 120-25.

6. Ronald C. Katz, *The Structure of Ancient Arguments. Rhetoric and Its Near Eastern Origin* (New York: Shapolsky/Steinmatzky, 1986).

πρακτώρ, and prison, 12.14, 58; wealthy farmers, 12.16; house-holder/οἰκοδεσπότης, 12.36-39; employer/κύριος and employee/ οἰκονόμος [steward] and servants 12.42-48; 13.6-9). The norms set by the social life of a particular culture at a given period in history are so well embedded and reflected in a given speech, like the sermon in Lk. 12.1–13.9, that the study of rhetoric could well serve the goal of social reconstruction as advocated by Burton Mack and Vernon Robbins. Perelman and Olbrechts-Tyteca, too, acknowledge the relation of the study of rhetoric to sociology.[1] Rhetorical criticism can *serve* this goal, but it should not be *reduced* to it; it can be done and has been done, but the heart of rhetoric is then getting lost.

b. *Problem 2*: Rhetorical genres are determined by the social functions exercised by the audience/readers and the assumed or real location of their social and institutional setting.[2] But we have two audiences for the sermon in Lk. 12.1–13.9; one is the composite Galilean audience of the early first century as introduced by the narrator; the other is the real reader of this literary sermon, regardless of the century to which the real reader belongs.

As part of 'the oral environment of late antiquity' it is 'the need of listeners (that is said to determine) what it is the speaker desires to communicate' which, in turn, makes 'some kind of formal pattern necessary for communication'.[3] Those formal patterns are more characteristic of literary genres than of rhetorical genres. What could explain the characteristics of a rhetorical genre (or its species) more adequately is Fisher's 'motive view of communication', which works with a scheme of four primary motive states, that is, four primary rhetorical situations (affirmation, reaffirmation, purification, subversion). These make up the 'motivational genres of discourse'.[4] These genres are seen less as 'the formal categories of ancient classical rhetoric' and more as 'the functionally oriented categories of modern rhetoric'.[5]

---

1. *New Rhetoric*, pp. 20-23.
2. Perelman and Olbrechts-Tyteca, *New Rhetoric*, p. 21.
3. Achtemeier, '*Omne verbum sonat*', p. 19.
4. Cf. Fisher, *Human Communication as Narration*, pp. 131-39; Jackson Harrell and Wil A. Linkugel, 'On Rhetorical Genre: An Organizing Perspective', *PhilR* 11 (1978), pp. 262-81.
5. See Stephen Kraftchick, 'Why do the Rhetoricians Rage?', *Text and Logos. The Humanistic Interpretation of the New Testament* (ed. Theodore Jenning; Homage

2. *The Unfinished Agenda*

We argued at the outset that discussions about literary and rhetorical genres should be kept separate. Thibeaux's study mentioned earlier, as well as Hansen's discussion of Galatians in its epistolary *and* rhetorical contexts,[1] are two recent studies which suggest that we must avoid both extremes: to approach literary and rhetorical genres issues as either-or, or to approach one genre at the expense of the other. What I envision and plead for is an approach which is committed to integrating the two genres (and their respective numerous species and 'mixed genres') in such a way that each is appreciated for its unique contribution; that neither is simply absorbed into, or subsumed under, the other, and that both inform the pleasures, rewards and challenges of reading in its everchanging 'materiality'.

Series; Atlanta: Scholars Press, 1991), pp. 55-79. The motives which generate rhetorical genres are distinct from those described by Michael Steig, 'Motives for Interpretation: Intention, Response and Psychoanalysis in Literary Criticism', *American Critics at Work: Examinations of Contemporary Literary Theories* (ed. Victor A. Kramer; Troy, NY: Whitson, 1984), pp. 251-64.

1. G. Walter Hansen, *Abraham in Galatians: Epistolary and Rhetorical Contexts* (JSNTSup 29; Sheffield: JSOT Press, 1989).

A COMPARATIVE STUDY OF THE USE OF ENTHYMEMES IN THE SYNOPTIC GOSPELS*

Richard B. Vinson

The term enthymeme was used in various ways by ancient rhetoricians: as a term for a disjunctive syllogism (Cic. *Top.* 13.55), as reasoning from any sort of facts that run contrary to the general flow of an argument (*Rhet. ad Alex.* 1430a.23-25), and as a term for a truncated syllogism (Ar. *Rhet.* 1356b). In this paper, the third definition will be employed. An enthymeme is a syllogism with one of the terms suppressed.

This paper will describe the use of the enthymeme by the Synoptic authors, the similarities and differences between them, and some of the ways in which their uses of this particular argumentative form support their various narrative strategies. The examination will focus on enthymemes noted by a causal particle such as ὅτι or γάρ. Greek, of course, has many ways of showing cause, and the lack of a causal conjunction may not mean that an enthymeme was not intended. However, asyndeton is such a major (and we must assume deliberate) part of Markan style that examining possible implied enthymemes would obscure the evidence.

Narrative Enthymemes

1. *Mark*

Mark uses enthymemes 77 times. The instances are almost equally divided between narrative uses (36) and the words of Jesus (35). Mark is infamous for some of his narrative enthymemes which appear to be unnecessary (1.16, 'casting their nets in the sea, for they were

* I wish to express my admiration and appreciation to Dr Kennedy, who is the very essence of the 'gentleman and scholar'. I also wish to thank Averett College for providing a research grant to assist in the preparation of this paper.

fishermen') or non-sequiturs (5.42, 'and immediately the girl rose and walked around, for she was twelve years old'). The narrator infrequently explains Jesus' actions (1.34; 6.34; 11.13) or commands (3.10; 6.31; 9.31; 11.13), preferring to apply this device to the actions of other characters. In fact, of the three enthymemes used to explain Jesus' actions, only 1.34 and 6.34 give reasons for something he did deliberately (11.13 explains why he found no figs on the tree he cursed).

These explanations of the actions of others appear in clusters, holding the narrative together. The healing stories of ch. 5 employ four narrative enthymemes explaining the actions of those healed, and the story of the Baptist's death uses six. In the progression of confrontations between Jesus and his enemies in chs. 11–14, Mark uses the enthymeme to introduce the tag lines showing the development of the plot to put Jesus to death (11.18, 32; 12.12; 14.2). In the pericope of the walking on the water, the narrator uses enthymemes to point out the disciples' difficulty (which forms the exigence for the miracle which follows), their reaction of fear, and finally their complete lack of faith. The empty tomb similarly links the women's puzzlement over what to do about the stone (16.4, assuming Mark means ἦν γὰρ μέγας σφόδρα to explain the rhetorical question in 16.3) with their final reaction of fear and disobedience (16.8).

The narrator uses enthymemes to explain the reactions of characters to Jesus 17 times, and other sorts of actions 13 times. The other sorts of actions include characteristic behavior (1.16, casting nets into the sea; 5.4, the demoniac running around naked; 7.3, Jewish opinions about pots) or reactions to other characters. Thus, while Jesus is the focus of most of the actions or reactions of characters in Mark, sometimes the implied author, through the narrator, allows the reader's focus to drift momentarily before snapping it back to Jesus.

In the early part of the Gospel, the narrator identifies positive reactions to Jesus with enthymemes (1.22; 2.15; 5.28, 42). The only exceptions are the demoniac's fear of Jesus (5.8), which is mitigated by the fact that Jesus is trying to help him, and the neutral statement that Herod had heard of Jesus (6.14). However, beginning with 6.50, which identifies the disciples' fear of Jesus as the reason for their response to him, enthymemes identify only negative reactions to Jesus (6.50, 52; 9.6a, 6b; 10.22; 11.18, 32; 12.12; 14.2, 40, 56). This formal similarity, linking various characters' responses together, lumps the disciples together with the wealthy synagogue ruler, the chief priests, and the lying witnesses at Jesus' trial. Putting the disciples' fear or 'hardness of heart' into an enthymematic form reinforces the negative nature of their reactions, and associates them more strongly with other enemies of Jesus.

Enthymemes also serve the narrator in characterization, by giving motives for actions which also come across to the reader as personality traits. A long and vivid description of psychotic behavior is introduced in 5.4, and in 5.28 (the only soliloquy introduced by an enthymeme in Mark) the faith of the healed woman is described, setting up Jesus' remark in 5.34. Most frequently, Mark assigns fear to characters via the enthymeme (6.20, 50; 9.6; 11.18, 32; 12.12; 14.2; 16.8).

The enthymeme, then, is one of Mark's stock devices for narrative construction and characterization. It is significant that while the narrator uses it widely, he uses it only twice to explain Jesus' own actions. The implied author is not reticent about announcing Jesus' inner feelings as motivations for his behavior (1.41; 2.8; 3.5, etc.), but he does not use the enthymeme in this regard. (In fact, the implied author also never has Jesus give a reason for his actions in enthymematic form. He explains his commands and pronouncements to his followers, but not his actions.) The contrast between the regular use of enthymeme to explain others' actions and the irregular use with respect to Jesus' actions supports the Markan portrait of Jesus as authoritative, yet mysterious and reserved about his purposes. The character of Jesus stands apart from others in the text. The implied author explains why the woman touched Jesus and why the disciples cast their nets, and notes those with enthymemes, but he does not mark out Jesus' motivations that way.

2. *Matthew*

Matthew uses the enthymeme 164 times, only 16 times in narrative, as opposed to 121 times in Jesus' words, 24 times in the words of another character, and three times in the words of a parable character. Only two of the narrative enthymemes are not found in Mark (11.20; 28.2), and in both cases Mark lacks the verse, not just the enthymeme. On the other hand, there are six instances where Mark has a narrative enthymeme and Matthew has a parallel verse without the form, and 14 instances where Mark has a narrative enthymeme but in Matthew it is absent altogether. On any source theory, that evidence would tend to argue that the narrative enthymeme is not a particularly characteristic feature of Matthew.

Nevertheless, it is used. Like Mark, Matthew does not regularly use the enthymeme to explain Jesus' actions or commands. This type appears only twice, once parallel to Mark (Mt. 9.36 = Mk 6.34) and once in a passage Mark does not have (Mt. 11.20). Like Mark, most of Matthew's uses describe reasons for the actions of others. Only six of these examples, however, describe reactions to Jesus, two of which are positive (7.29; 9.21) and four negative (19.22; 21.46; 26.43; 27.18). Only one of the negative reactions involves the disciples (Mark has five examples), which is consistent with Matthew's more generally positive attitude towards that group.

Matthew has one instance of the use of narrative enthymemes to tie a pericope together. The story of the execution of John the Baptist, which Matthew shares with Mark, contains the same string of five enthymemes. Otherwise, the narrative enthymemes appear in isolation from each other.

The narrative enthymeme does not support major themes of Matthew's narrative, as in Mark. It tells us very little about Matthew's narrative strategy.

3. *Luke*

Luke uses enthymemes 165 times. 97 appear in Jesus' words, and 23 in narrative, as compared to 33 in the words of someone other than Jesus, and 14 in the words of characters in parables.

The narrative enthymeme is one of Luke's preferred devices. Even though Luke's numbers are not as great as Mark's (36), Luke's narrator uses the form in 10 places where there are no parallels in Matthew or Mark, and inserts the form into four places where both have parallel material but no enthymeme. It is curious that Luke and Mark do not share more narrative enthymemes (seven). However, Luke shares more with Mark than with Matthew (two).

All but three of Luke's narrative enthymemes explain the actions of a character other than Jesus. Almost all of these actions are really reactions to Jesus, with the exceptions being 2.4, Joseph's reason for going to Bethlehem, and 2.7, Mary's reason for laying Jesus in the manger. This percentage (18/23, 78%) is much higher than Matthew's (6/16, 38%) or Mark's (17/36, 47%). The 18 instances are equally divided between positive and negative reactions to Jesus. The disciples appear only once in this list (9.14), in contrast to Mark, who explains the disciples' actions with enthymemes seven times, five of which are negative reactions to Jesus. Thus, while Luke's narrator tends to reserve the narrative enthymeme for reactions to Jesus, he exempts the disciples from this pattern.

Like the other two Synoptics, Luke does not use the narrative enthymeme to explain Jesus' actions very often. In Matthew's case, where the narrative enthymeme is not a preferred method, this perhaps is not so remarkable; but in the case of Luke and Mark, it shows reserve on the part of the implied author. The narrators of both Gospels give their readers insight into Jesus' motives, but not with this form.

Luke does not utilize the narrative enthymeme string to hold pericopes together as do Mark and Matthew (see the discussion concerning Mark in section 1 above and section 1 below). Luke also does not use the narrative enthymeme to describe characteristic behavior, such as 'casting the nets into the sea, because they were fishermen' (Mk 1.16 = Mt. 4.18).

Luke's narrative enthymemes also do not tie together negative reactions as strongly as Mark's do. Whereas all the narrative enthymemes describing reactions to Jesus from Mk 6.50 on characterize negative reactions, Luke's are more varied. Lk. 4.32 is positive, 4.41 negative, 5.9 positive, the next three negative, the next two positive, etc. Perhaps most importantly, the last four reactions to Jesus described with enthymemes are positive. Mark, using the device to link the disciples to other negative characters, creates a string of negative reactions to Jesus. While this supports his portrait of a more mysterious Jesus, Luke's portrait of a more open, more obviously innocent Jesus is better served by the varied reactions to Jesus.

Jesus' Enthymemes

1. *Mark*

Mark uses enthymemes in Jesus' speech 35 times, and in the words of others seven times. The enthymemes Jesus speaks appear in the following forms: 11 support commands ('Do x, because. . .'), six support prohibitions ('Don't do x, because. . .'), 12 support statements or pronouncements, two support rhetorical questions, six are used to clinch episodes, two are used in narrative extension, and there are two extended blocks that are held together by enthymemes.

When the enthymemes are differentiated by audience, most of them are seen to be used in conversation with disciples. All the commands and prohibitions fall into this category, as well as all but one of the statements. The two rhetorical questions supported by enthymemes are equally divided between friendly and hostile audiences.

Jesus' enthymemes tend to come in clusters: four in the parable collections, five each in the material around the first and second passion predictions, and six in the apocalyptic sermon. In the two passion prediction sections, the multiple enthymemes are the glue binding separate commands and reasons into one unit. Clearly, this is parallel to Mark's narrative use of the enthymeme and indicates an element of Markan style.

Mark's Jesus rarely uses enthymemes to support his commands or teachings to his enemies. Jesus employs only three enthymemes in speech to hostile audiences (7.10; 10.7; 12.25). In the first two, the enthymeme introduces a passage from the OT, and in the last, a commonplace point of doctrine. Jesus also does not often explain his own actions (only 8.2). He does explain his pronouncements and commands to his disciples. Most of these passages come after the Caesarea Philippi pericope (1.38; 4.22, 25; 7.21; 8.2 are the only exceptions), after the focus of the narrative has turned to Jesus' instructions about his impending death to his disciples. In fact, 13 of the 23 enthymemes Jesus utters from 8.33 on deal in one way or another with his death. We see again how the implied author uses this device in support of one of his major themes.

Other enthymemes Jesus speaks identify reasons for commands, and in the process, offer instruction on virtues approved by him. Jesus in 10.14 commends being childlike, in 10.27 having faith in the omnipotence of God, in 12.44 generosity, in 13.11 the courage of martyrs, in 13.22 and 13.35 being alert, and in 14.7 the loving deed of the woman who anointed him. All of these instructions are offered to the disciples just like the instructions on his death. Notice, then, that the author marks the disciples' fear and disobedience and Jesus' instructions on virtues and his death with enthymemes. The enthymematic form contrasts the disciples with Jesus' ideals of discipleship, even as the same form compares the disciples with others opposed to Jesus.

2. *Matthew*
Matthew uses enthymemes in Jesus' speech 121 times. The majority occur in the set speeches: 29 in the Sermon on the Mount, seven in the Sermon on Missions, seven in the Parables Sermon, four in the Church Sermon, 15 in the polemic against the Pharisees, and 18 in the final

speech of chs. 24–25, for a total of 80, two-thirds of the number in Jesus' speech in the entire Gospel.

The forms in the speeches are as follows. Jesus uses enthymemes to support commands 17 times, including four instances in which characters in parables do this. Enthymemes support prohibitions 23 times and support statements or pronouncements 31 times. There are 10 beatitudes supported by enthymemes (nine in the beginning of the Sermon on the Mount, and 13.17) and nine woes (all in ch. 23).

Matthew also uses the enthymemes in patterned ways. Three times the enthymeme is used to tie together speech material within a pericope (5.34-35; 13.16-17; 23.8-10) in the style already seen in Mark. However, rather than linking statements together with 'because', Matthew prefers to use repeating forms, and sometimes the enthymeme is a part of the form; the Beatitudes in ch. 5 and the Woes in ch. 23 are good examples. Episodes are introduced with enthymemes twice, and clinched with enthymemes 10 times. Jesus uses enthymemes as narrative extension four times (7.25; 13.5, 6; 25.3). As in Mark, Jesus rarely uses the enthymeme to explain his own actions; in the speeches, this only happens in 13.13.

Outside the speeches, some of the same forms recur. There are 12 instances of commands supported by enthymemes and 23 instances of statements so supported. Jesus again explains his actions only once (15.32), and explains a parable or a figure of speech three times (11.18; 15.19; 22.14). He uses the form to introduce a parable once, but to clinch an episode 11 times. There is one further beatitude and one enthymeme-supported woe. There are no examples of prohibitions supported by enthymemes outside the speeches, but there are five examples of rhetorical questions supported by enthymemes. Thus there is some difference in the way the argumentation is carried out inside and outside the speeches.

There are also differences if account is taken of Jesus' audience. To non-friendly audiences, Jesus uses enthymemes to answer objections 15 times, to support commands three times, to support rhetorical questions five times, to support statements 15 times, and to clinch episodes six times. To friendly audiences, Jesus uses enthymemes to answer objections once, to support commands nine times (52 times, if we include the speeches), to support statements 15 times (54, including speeches), to clinch episodes five times, but never to support rhetorical questions. Thus the rhetorical question supported by an enthymeme is only used with hostile persons (unlike Mark), and likewise the enthymeme supporting the answer to an objection, with one exception (3.15). Outside the speeches, the statement supported by a reason is used more for hostile persons (unlike Mark). But the clincher is distributed evenly. Matthew, who seems to admire that way of rounding off a pericope, thinks of it as a trope suitable for any audience.

Thus we see some differences in the way that Matthew and Mark use enthymemes in Jesus' speech. Mark uses them almost exclusively for statements, commands, and prohibitions made to the disciples. Matthew reserves most of the commands for the disciples, but uses the other forms in Jesus' speech to his enemies. Jesus, in Matthew, frequently supports his arguments with reasons, relying less on the force of his word alone and more on the support of logic or authority.

Jesus' enthymemes support the themes of Matthew's implied author. About half of them could fall into the general category of discipleship or doing righteousness. Within that number, 18 mention being prepared to die or to suffer for Jesus/the gospel. As one can note from this list, all but one of these enthymemes appear in three large collections. Thus, not only is Matthew's percentage of sayings regarding suffering and death lower than Mark's (18/120, 15%; Mark's ratio is 13/23, 57%), but Matthew has them grouped rather than spread over the narrative.

Matthew's use of Jesus' enthymemes includes other matters. Matthew's Jesus uses enthymemes to support his sayings on practicing righteousness 13 times, on the privileged position of the disciples 10 times, and on the Kingdom of Heaven 14 times. Matthew's Jesus uses the enthymeme as an offensive or defensive weapon against his adversaries 48 times, which Mark's Jesus almost never does. Thus Matthew's implied author chooses to support Jesus' statements on some important topics with enthymemes, which Mark's implied author also does, but Matthew's range is wider and includes hostile persons in the audience.

3. *Luke*
Luke's Jesus speaks in enthymemes 97 times (59% of the total). This percentage is higher than Mark's (35/77, or 45%), but lower than Matthew's (121/164, 74%).

Luke uses enthymemes to support commands 27 times, to support prohibitions nine times, to support statements or pronouncements 47 times, and to support rhetorical questions five times. There are five beatitudes and 12 woes supported by enthymemes. Jesus uses enthymemes to answer objections 11 times, and uses one to clinch an episode 16 times.

The audience for these instances is heavily weighted in favor of characters friendly to Jesus: 25 commands go to friendly audiences, all nine prohibitions, 38 of the statements, three of the rhetorical questions, and 11 of those which clinch an episode. Even the answers to objections have four such responses to friendly audiences (4.43; 8.46; 10.42; 13.33).

These numbers are interesting when compared to the other Synoptic Gospels. All three use the majority of enthymeme-supported commands with friendly audiences (the ratios are: Mk, 11/11; Mt., 26/29; Lk., 25/27). Each Gospel reserves all the prohibitions for friendly persons (the ratios are: Mk, 6/6; Mt., 23/23; Lk., 9/9); one can see that this form is much more characteristic of Matthew. Matthew and Luke allow more of the statements to go to non-friendly audiences (the ratios are: Mk, 1/11; Mt., 15/54; Lk., 9/47). Mark's two enthymeme-supported questions are evenly divided between friendly and unfriendly audiences, as are Luke's examples (3/5 go to friendly persons), but Matthew's five go entirely to hostile persons, making this another distinctive of his style. Matthew and Luke allow Jesus to clinch episodes with both friendly (Mt., 15; Lk., 11) and non-friendly audiences (Mt., 6; Lk., 5), while Mark uses this only for friendly audiences. This is part of a larger pattern: Matthew and Luke both have Jesus speak to persons other than the disciples in enthymemes far more often than Mark. Mark directs only five of Jesus' 35 enthymemes (14%) to persons other than the disciples. Luke's usage reflects a ratio of 37/98 (38%), and Matthew (assuming that the primary hearers in the speeches are the disciples) has a ratio of 43/121 (35%). Matthew and Mark also have blocks of Jesus' sayings held together by enthymemes (Mt., 7; Mk., 2), but Luke has only the famous series common to all three regarding taking up the cross (Mk 8.35-38 = Mt. 16.25-27 = Lk. 9.24-26). As Luke's implied author avoids the narrative enthymeme series, so he avoids using enthymemes to join Jesus' words.

Luke's Jesus explains his actions with enthymemes far more often than Matthew's or Mark's, doing so 11 times (compared with once for Mark and twice for Matthew). In fact, the first two that Jesus uses (4.18, 43) are to tell the crowds something about his purpose. This fits with Luke's characterization of a more open, less mysterious, Jesus.

Luke's Jesus answers objections with enthymemes 11 times and attacks various groups with them eight times; thus his total of 19

offensive or defensive enthymemes is much lower than Matthew's 48.
Mark's Jesus rarely speaks in enthymemes to enemies, preferring not
to argue. Matthew's Jesus uses enthymemes as argumentative weapons,
resting his pronouncements upon various authorities. Luke's Jesus
speaks to plenty of outsiders—37 enthymemes to others than the disciples—but his enthymemes are usually more irenic than those of
Matthew's Jesus. This would support his portrait of Jesus as an obviously innocent person.

Luke's Jesus uses enthymemes to support his theme of rich/poor 20
times. The theme of death/sacrifice is supported by enthymemes six
times, forgiveness of sins four times, and practicing righteousness five
times. Luke's Jesus urges the disciples to prepare for persecution and
supports his statements and commands with enthymemes 12 times. The
rest of the enthymemes in Jesus' speech are spread over a variety of
themes.

Others' Enthymemes

1. Mark

On six occasions, a character other than Jesus uses an enthymeme in
speech. Five of these are in speech addressed to Jesus. The demoniac
(5.9) who explains his name can be considered hostile to Jesus at the
time, as are the Pharisees (12.14) and the Sadducees (12.23). The only
times the disciples explain to Jesus why they have done or said something, they are opposing Jesus' intentions (9.38; 14.5). In the final
instance, a bystander explains to Peter why he thinks Peter is Jesus'
disciple, giving Peter the chance to deny Christ one final time. Thus,
the implied author uses this category of enthymeme carefully. Jesus
used enthymemes in speech far more than any other character in
Mark, but almost exclusively in speech to the disciples. His enthymemes are friendly, explaining his commands and pronouncements.
By contrast, enthymemes of others are unfriendly, including those
spoken by the disciples.

2. Matthew

A character other than Jesus uses an enthymeme 24 times in Matthew.
This is a much higher number than Mark's six, but is about the same
ratio when compared to Jesus' speech (20%). Most of the people who
use the enthymeme are positive characters. An angel uses it six times
(every time an angel speaks, it is an enthymeme), the magi once, the

scribes who answer Herod's question twice, John the Baptist twice, a centurion once, the demoniac's father twice, and Pilate's wife once. The disciples use enthymemes twice, but both times the narrator probably means the reader to consider them contrary to Jesus' point of view. This is certainly true of 26.9, and is probably true of 15.23, where the disciples function to explain some of Jesus' rudeness to the Syro-Phoenician woman. The bystander who confronts Peter in his denial of Christ should probably be considered neutral or hostile (26.73), and the rest are definitely hostile: Satan (4.6), Pharisees (15.2; 22.16), chief priests (21.26), Sadducees (22.28), and the mockers around the cross (27.43).

If we consider the disciples and the bystander as hostile, then nine out of 24 enthymemes fall into this category. The majority, then, are spoken by positive characters. In fact, the first nine enthymemes in Matthew are spoken by someone other than Jesus, including four by an angel. Thus the reliability of that sort of speech pattern is built up by the author before Jesus ever opens his mouth. This is important, because after 4.18, the next 30 enthymemes are spoken by Jesus, without any other person intervening. Mark uses the 'other' enthymemes to isolate and make unique Jesus' speech patterns; Matthew uses them to validate Jesus' speech by comparison with other reliable characters.

The forms of the others' enthymemes are as follows. Enthymemes support commands eight times, prohibitions twice, statements nine times, and questions four times. All the commands and prohibitions go to friendly audiences, just as in the case of Jesus' own words in Matthew. The only 'others' who prohibit things are angels, who quite naturally command persons not to fear. The statements are in a ratio of 5/4, and the questions evenly divided between friendly/unfriendly audiences. The two questions to friendly audiences are nevertheless asked by hostile people (22.28; 26.9), so Matthew's pattern of reserving rhetorical questions as an offensive weapon remains true.

3. Luke

Luke uses the enthymeme in the speech of persons other than Jesus 33 times. To get an impression of how much larger his number is, we may compare the ratios of enthymemes spoken by others to those spoken by Jesus. For Mark, the ratio is 17%, for Matthew 20%, and for Luke 33%. That is, Luke's other category is about a third as large as his Jesus category, Matthew's and Mark's only about a fifth as large.

The forms in this category include three prohibitions, 10 com- mands, 14 statements, and six questions supported by enthymemes. All of these numbers are about what is true for Luke's Jesus, except that the number of questions is disproportionately high. Except for this, most characters in Luke who use enthymemes use them in much the same way as Jesus. All the prohibitions are by angels, telling people not to fear (1.13, 30; 2.10). All but one of the commands (3.8) are spoken to friendly audiences, as are 10 of the statements, and five of the questions. Again, this is comparable with Luke's Jesus.

Luke's others are, like his Jesus, more irenic in their uses of enthy- memes. Matthew's others includes nine instances said by those hostile to Jesus, which is 38% of the total. Luke's list includes seven hostile figures, which is 21% of the total. Luke even includes one instance of a Pharisee using an enthymeme to support a statement friendly to Jesus (13.31). Like Matthew, Luke begins the Gospel with enthymemes by others: six by angels, three by Zechariah, two by Mary, and once each by Elizabeth, Simeon, and John the Baptist. Again, the speech pattern is thus validated by these reliable characters.

Luke's Parable Characters

Luke alone among the Synoptics uses this type of enthymeme to any extent, including 15 enthymemes within the speech of parable charac- ters (Mark never, Matthew 4 times). Seven instances are from negative characters. The enthymemes support six statements, seven commands, and two rhetorical questions. In six cases the enthymeme is used by the character to explain his or her behavior; in one further case, someone else provides the explanation. Three of these cases are soliloquies, in which the character muses about what the next step should be. This sort of enthymeme could have been, instead, a narrative enthymeme used in narrative extension. The fact that Luke's narrator allows the characters to speak for themselves, explaining their own motives, is a mark of Luke's fuller characterization within parables.

Conclusion

The study of a very minor rhetorical device used by the evangelists has shown some interesting stylistic differences. Mark frequently uses narrative enthymemes to tie together negative reactions to Jesus. Mark's Jesus uses enthymemes almost exclusively with friendly audiences to support his commands and pronouncements, but never to explain his actions. Matthew rarely uses narrative enthymemes at all. His Jesus, like Mark's, also supports commands to his disciples with enthymemes, but Matthew's Jesus uses enthymeme-supported pronouncements and rhetorical questions in verbal combat with hostile audiences. Luke uses the narrative enthymeme to note reactions to Jesus, both positive and negative. His Jesus, like Matthew's, uses enthymemes to support conversations with hostile persons. Luke's unique feature is the degree to which characters, including characters in parables, are allowed to use enthymemes in their speech.

No one would suggest that the Gospel writers built their rhetorical or narrative strategies around enthymemes, but the considered ways in which they used them strengthened their presentations. For example, Mark's narrator, who in other ways carefully controls the revelation of the character of Jesus to the reader, also does so by the selective use of enthymemes. Mark's presentations of a more mysterious Jesus and less faithful disciples are also supported by his use of enthymemes. Our understanding of Gospel styles would no doubt be improved further by comparative studies of other seemingly minor tropes.

APPENDIX

Markan Enthymemes: Source Comparison

Mark	Matthew	Luke	Type	Notes
1.16	4.18	abs	N	N = Narrative
1.22	7.29	4.32	N	Enthymemes;
1.34	abs	4.41	N	abs = absent
1.38	abs	4.43	J	J = Jesus'
2.15	abs	abs	N	Enthymemes
3.10	abs	6.19	N	
3.21	abs	abs	N	
3.35	12.50	abs	J	
4.5	13.5	abs	J	
4.6	13.6	8.6	J	
4.22	10.26	8.17	J	
4.25	13.12	8.18	J	
5.4	abs	8.29	N	
5.8	abs	8.29	N	
5.9	abs	8.30	Demoniac	
5.28	9.21	abs	N	

Mark	Matthew	Luke	Type	Notes
5.42	abs	abs	N	
6.14	(14.21)	(9.7)	N	(14.21) = the
6.17a	14.3a	(3.19)	N	verse is present,
6.17c	abs	abs	N	but not the
6.18	14.4	abs	N	enthymeme
6.20	14.5	abs	N	
6.26	14.9	abs	N	
6.31	9.36	abs	N	
6.34	abs	abs	N	
6.48	14.24	abs	N	
6.50	(14.26)	abs	N	
6.52	abs	abs	N	
7.3	abs	abs	N	
7.10	15.4	abs	J	
7.21	15.19	abs	J	
7.27	(15.26)	abs	J	
8.2	15.32	abs	J	
8.33	16.23	abs	J	
8.35	16.25	9.24	J	
8.36	16.26	9.25	J	
8.37	(16.26)	abs	J	
8.38	16.27	9.26	J	
9.6a	abs	(9.33)	N	
9.6b	abs	(9.33)	N	
9.31	(17.22)	(9.24)	N	
9.38	abs	9.49	Disciple	
9.39	abs	abs	J	
9.40	abs	9.50	J	
9.41a	(10.42)	abs	J	
9.41b	(10.42)	abs	J	
9.49	abs	abs	J	
10.7	19.5	abs	J	
10.14	19.14	18.16	J	
10.22	19.22	18.23	N	
10.27	(19.26)	(18.27)	J	
10.45	(20.28)	abs	J	
11.13	abs	abs	N	
11.18	abs	19.48	N	
11.32	21.26	20.6	N	
12.12	21.46	20.19	N	
12.14	22.16	(20.21)	Pharisees	
12.23	22.28	20.33	Sadducees	
12.25	22.30	20.36	J	
12.44	abs	21.4	J	

Mark	Matthew	Luke	Type	Notes
13.8	24.7	(21.10)	J	
13.11	10.20	21.12	J	
13.19	24.21	21.23	J	
13.20	24.22	abs	J	
13.22	24.24	abs	J	
13.35	24.42	12.40	J	
14.2	(26.5)	22.2	N	
14.5	26.9	abs	Some	
14.7	26.11	abs	J	
14.21	(26.24)	22.22	J	
14.27	26.31	abs	J	
14.40	26.43	abs	N	
14.56	(26.60)	abs	N	
14.70	26.73	22.59	Bystander	
15.10	27.18	abs	N	
16.4	abs	abs	N	
16.8	(28.8)	abs	N	

Matthean Enthymemes: Source Comparison

Matthew	Mark	Luke	Type	Notes
1.20	abs	abs	Angel	
1.21	abs	abs	Angel	
2.2	abs	abs	Magi	
2.5	abs	abs	Scribes	
2.6	abs	abs	Magi	
2.13	abs	abs	Angel	
2.20	abs	abs	Angel	
3.2(2)	(1.4)	(3.3)	John the Baptist	
3.9	abs	3.8	John the Baptist	
3.15	abs	abs	J	
4.6	abs	4.10	Satan	
4.10	abs	(4.8)	J	
4.17	(1.15)	abs	J	
4.18	1.16	abs	N	
5.3	abs	6.20	J	
5.4	abs	abs	J	
5.5	abs	abs	J	
5.6	abs	6.21a	J	
5.7	abs	abs	J	
5.8	abs	abs	J	
5.9	abs	abs	J	
5.10	abs	abs	J	

Matthew	Mark	Luke	Type	Notes
5.12	abs	6.23	J	
5.20	abs	abs	J	
5.29	abs	abs	J	
5.30	(9.43)	abs	J	
5.34	abs	abs	J	
5.35(2)	abs	abs	J	
5.36	abs	abs	J	
5.45	abs	abs	J	
5.46	abs	6.32	J	
6.5	abs	abs	J	
6.7	abs	abs	J	
6.14	(11.25)	11.4	J	
6.16	abs	abs	J	
6.21	abs	12.34	J	
6.24	abs	16.13	J	
6.32	abs	12.30	J	
7.2	abs	6.38	J	
7.8	abs	11.10	J	
7.12	abs	abs	J	
7.13	abs	13.24	J	
7.25	abs	6.48	J	
7.29	1.22	4.32	N	
8.9	abs	7.8	Centurion	
9.5	(2.9)	(5.23)	J	
9.13	(2.17)	(5.32)	J	
9.16	(2.21)	(5.36)	J	
9.21	5.28	abs	N	
9.24	(5.39)	8.52	J	
9.36	6.34	abs	N	
10.10	abs	10.7	J	
10.17	(13.9)	(21.12)	J	
10.19	(13.11)	12.12	J	
10.20	13.11	(12.12)	J	
10.23	abs	abs	J	
10.26	4.22	8.17	J	
10.35	abs	12.52	J	
11.13	abs	(16.16)	J	
11.18	abs	7.33	J	
11.20	abs	abs	N	
11.21	abs	10.13	J	
11.23	abs	abs	J	
11.25	abs	10.21a	J	
11.26	abs	10.21b	J	
11.29	abs	abs	J	

Matthew	Mark	Luke	Type	Notes
11.30	abs	abs	J	
12.8	(2.28)	(6.5)	J	
12.33	abs	6.44a	J	
12.34	abs	6.45	J	
12.37	abs	abs	J	
12.40	abs	11.30	J	
12.41	abs	11.32	J	
12.42	abs	11.31	J	
12.50	(3.35)	(8.21)	J	
13.5	4.5	abs	J	
13.6	4.6	8.6	J	
13.12	4.25	8.18	J	
13.13	(4.12)	(8.10)	J	
13.16(2)	abs	(10.23)	J	
13.17	abs	10.24	J	
14.3a	6.17a	(3.19)	N	
14.3b	6.17b	(3.19)	N	
14.4	6.18	abs	N	
14.5	6.20	abs	N	
14.9	6.26	abs	N	
14.24	6.48	abs	N	
15.2	(7.5)	abs	Pharisees	
15.4	7.10	abs	J	
15.19	7.21	abs	J	
15.23	abs	abs	Disciples	
15.32	8.2	abs	J	
16.2	abs	(12.54)	J	
16.3	abs	(12.55)	J	
16.17	abs	abs	J	
16.23	8.33	abs	J	
16.25	8.35	9.24	J	
16.26	8.36	9.25	J	
16.27	8.38	9.26	J	
17.15	(9.17)	9.38	Demoniac's Father	
17.15b	(9.17)	9.39	Demoniac's Father	
17.20(2)	abs	(17.6)	J	
18.7	abs	(17.1)	J	
18.10	abs	abs	J	
[18.11]	abs	19.10	J	
18.20	abs	abs	J	
19.5	10.7	abs	J	
19.12	abs	abs	J	
19.14	10.14	18.16	J	
19.22	10.22	18.23	N	

Matthew	Mark	Luke	Type	Notes
20.1	abs	abs	J	
21.26	11.32	20.6	Chief Priests	
21.46	12.12	20.19	N	
22.14	abs	abs	J	
22.16	12.14	(20.21)	Pharisees/Herodians	
22.28	12.23	20.33	Sadducees	
22.30	12.25	20.36	J	
23.3	abs	abs	J	
23.5	abs	abs	J	
23.8	abs	abs	J	
23.9	abs	abs	J	
23.10	abs	abs	J	
23.13(2)	abs	11.52(1)	J	
23.15	abs	abs	J	
23.17	abs	abs	J	
23.19	abs	abs	J	
23.23	abs	11.42	J	
23.25	abs	(11.39)	J	
23.27	abs	11.44	J	
23.29	abs	11.47	J	
23.39	abs	(13.35)	J	
24.5	(13.6)	21.8	J	
24.6	(13.7)	21.9	J	
24.7	13.8	(21.10)	J	
24.21	13.19	21.23	J	
24.22	13.20	abs	J	
24.24	13.22	abs	J	
24.27	abs	17.24	J	
24.37	abs	(17.26)	J	
24.38	abs	(17.27)	J	
24.42	13.35	abs	J	
24.44	abs	12.40	J	
25.3	abs	abs	J	
25.8	abs	abs	Jp	Jp = Parable
25.13	(13.33)	(21.36)	J	Character
25.14	(13.34)	(19.12)	J	
25.29	abs	(19.26)	J	
25.35	abs	abs	Jp	
25.42	abs	abs	Jp	
26.9	14.5	abs	Disciples	
26.10	(14.6)	abs	J	
26.11	14.7	abs	J	
26.12	(14.8)	abs	J	
26.28	(14.24)	(22.20)	J	

Matthew	Mark	Luke	Type	Notes
26.31	14.27	abs	J	
26.43	14.40	abs	N	
26.52	abs	abs	J	
26.73	14.70	22.59	Bystander	
27.18	15.10	abs	N	
27.19	abs	abs	Pilate's Wife	
27.43	abs	abs	Mockers	
28.2	abs	abs	N	
28.5	(16.6)	(24.5)	Angel	
28.6	(16.6)	(24.5)	Angel	

Lukan Enthymemes: Source Comparison

Luke	Mark	Matthew	Type	Notes
1.13	abs	abs	Angel	
1.15	abs	abs	Angel	
1.18	abs	abs	Zechariah	
1.30	abs	abs	Angel	
1.37	abs	abs	Angel	
1.44	abs	abs	Elizabeth	
1.48(2)	abs	abs	Mary	
1.66	abs	abs	'all'	
1.68	abs	abs	Zechariah	
1.76	abs	abs	Zechariah	
2.4	abs	abs	N	
2.7	abs	abs	N	
2.10	abs	abs	Angel	
2.11	abs	abs	Angel	
2.30	abs	abs	Simeon	
3.8	abs	3.9	John the Baptist	
4.6	abs	(4.9)	Satan	
4.10	abs	4.6	Satan	
4.18	abs	abs	J	
4.32	1.22	7.29	N	
4.36	(1.27)	abs	Crowds	
4.41	1.34	abs	N	
4.43	1.38	abs	J	
5.8	abs	abs	Simon	
5.9	abs	abs	N	
5.39	abs	abs	J	
6.20	abs	5.3	J	
6.21a	abs	5.6	J	
6.21b	abs	abs	J	

Matthew	Mark	Luke	Type	Notes
6.23(2)	abs	5.12	J	
6.24	abs	abs	J	
6.25a	abs	abs	J	
6.25b	abs	abs	J	
6.26	abs	abs	J	
6.32	abs	5.46	J	
6.35	abs	abs	J	
6.38	(4.24)	7.2	J	
6.43	abs	(7.16)	J	
6.44a	abs	12.33	J	
6.44b	abs	(7.16)	J	
6.45	abs	12.34	J	
6.48	abs	7.25	J	
7.5	abs	abs	Crowds	
7.6	abs	(8.8)	Centurion	
7.8	abs	8.9	Centurion	
7.33	abs	11.18	J	
7.39	abs	abs	Pharisee	
7.47	abs	abs	J	
8.6	4.6	13.6	J	
8.17	4.22	10.26	J	
8.18	4.25	13.12	J	
8.29	5.8	abs	N	
8.30	5.9	abs	N	
8.37	(5.17)	(8.34)	N	
8.40	(5.21)	(9.18)	N	
8.42	(5.23)	(9.18)	N	
8.46	(5.32)	abs	J	
8.52	(5.39)	9.24	J	
9.12	(6.35)	(14.15)	Disciples	
9.14	(6.44)	(14.21)	N	
9.24	8.35	16.25	J	
9.25	8.36	16.26	J	
9.26	8.38	16.27	J	
9.38	(9.17)	17.15	Demoniac's Father	
9.44	(9.31)	(17.22)	J	
9.48	abs	abs	J	
9.50	9.40	abs	J	
9.53	abs	abs	N	
10.7	abs	10.10	J	
10.13	abs	11.21	J	
10.21a	abs	11.25	J	
10.21b	abs	11.26	J	
10.24	abs	13.17	J	

Matthew	Mark	Luke	Type	Notes
10.42	abs	abs	J	
11.4	(11.25)	6.14	J	
11.10	abs	7.8	J	
11.18	(3.26)	(12.26)	J	
11.30	abs	12.40	J	
11.31	abs	12.42	J	
11.32	abs	12.41	J	
11.42	abs	23.23	J	
11.43	abs	(23.6-7)	J	
11.44	abs	23.27	J	
11.46	abs	(23.4)	J	
11.47	abs	23.29	J	
11.52	abs	23.13	J	
12.12	(13.11a)	10.19	J	
12.15	abs	abs	J	
12.17	abs	abs	Jp	
12.23	abs	(6.25)	J	
12.30	abs	6.32	J	
12.32	abs	abs	J	
12.34	abs	6.21	J	
12.40	abs	24.44	J	
12.52	abs	10.35	J	
12.58	abs	(5.25)	J	
13.2	abs	abs	J	
13.14	abs	abs	N	
13.24	abs	7.13	J	
13.31	abs	abs	Pharisees	
13.33	abs	abs	J	
14.11	abs	abs	J	
14.14(2)	abs	abs	J	
14.17	abs	abs	Jp	
14.28	abs	abs	J	
15.6	abs	(18.13)	Jp	
15.9	abs	abs	Jp	
15.24	abs	abs	Jp	
15.27	abs	abs	Jp	
15.32	abs	abs	Jp	
16.2	abs	abs	Jp	
16.3	abs	abs	Jp	
16.8	abs	abs	J	
16.13	abs	6.24	J	
16.15	abs	abs	J	
16.24	abs	abs	Jp	
16.28	abs	abs	Jp	

Matthew	Mark	Luke	Type	Notes
17.21	abs	abs	J	
17.24	abs	24.27	J	
18.5	abs	abs	Jp	
18.14	abs	(23.12)	J	
18.16	10.14	19.14	J	
18.23	10.22	19.22	N	
18.25	(10.25)	(19.24)	J	
18.32	(10.34)	(20.19)	J	
19.3	abs	abs	N	
19.5	abs	abs	J	
19.9	abs	abs	J	
19.10	abs	[18.11]	J	
19.11(2)	abs	abs	N	
19.17	abs	(25.21)	Jp	
19.21(2)	abs	(25.24)	Jp	
19.44	abs	abs	J	
19.48	11.18	abs	N	
20.6	11.32	21.26	Chief Priests	
20.19	12.12	21.46	N	
20.33	12.23	22.28	Sadducees	
20.36	12.25	22.30	J	
20.40	abs	abs	N	
20.42	(12.36)	(22.43)	J	
21.4	12.44	abs	J	
21.8	(13.6)	24.5	J	
21.9	(13.7)	24.6	J	
21.15	abs	abs	J	
21.22	abs	abs	J	
21.23	13.19	24.21	J	
21.26	(13.25)	(24.29)	J	
21.35	abs	abs	J	
22.2	14.2	(26.5)	N	
22.16	abs	abs	J	
22.18	abs	abs	J	
22.22	14.21	(26.24)	J	
22.27	abs	abs	J	
22.37	abs	abs	J	
22.59	14.70	26.73	Bystander	
23.8(2)	abs	abs	N	
23.12	abs	abs	N	
23.15	abs	abs	Pilate	
23.29	abs	abs	J	
23.31	abs	abs	J	
23.34	abs	abs	J	

Matthew	Mark	Luke	Type	Notes
23.40	abs	abs	Criminal	
23.41	abs	abs	Criminal	
24.29	abs	abs	Cleopas	
24.39	abs	abs	J	

WRITING AS A RHETORICAL ACT IN PLUTARCH AND THE GOSPELS

Vernon K. Robbins

Introduction

This paper addresses an issue that is pertinent especially for interpretation of literature from antiquity which contains biographical dimensions. The phrase 'biographical dimensions' refers broadly to portrayal of a human being during the span of time from conception to afterlife. Much biblical literature falls within the purview of this discussion, as well as much non-biblical literature. Stories about individuals and sayings attributed to them played an important role in the transmission of culture in antiquity. These stories and sayings have come to us in written form, and here a major challenge arises. How shall we understand the act of writing which produced the story or saying as it comes to us? Or, more importantly, what kinds of acts of writing do we consider possible, and what kind dominates our attention?

From Textual Criticism to Rhetorical Criticism

When interpreters began to develop literary-historical methods of analysis during the 17th, 18th, and 19th centuries, settings in which scribes copied and recopied manuscripts guided this analysis. Scribal copying produced 'errors' and 'corruptions' through accidental omissions or additions, or through intentional revisions to improve the text.[1] The major goal for this analysis was to construct the earliest

---

1. B.M. Metzger, *The Text of the New Testament: Its Transmission, Corruption, and Restoration* (London: Oxford University Press, 1964); J. Finegan, *Encountering New Testament Manuscripts: A Working Introduction to Textual Criticism* (Grand Rapids: Eerdmans/London: SPCK, 1974), pp. 54-177; E.J. Epp and G.D. Fee

version of the text available to us on the basis of extant manuscripts. By the beginning of the 20th century, a significant number of 'critical texts', that is, texts constructed out of critically established early readings, were available to the scholarly community.

Once textual criticism had shown its worth and produced 'better', in the sense of 'earlier' texts, the same literary-historical skills that were attained and refined through textual criticism were applied to reconstructing written sources used by the writers of the earliest texts. This step invited greater creativity than textual criticism, but the literary-historical procedures of textual criticism provided the basic tools for the analysis. Much as textual criticism negotiated different readings in manuscripts to reconstruct the earliest text, so source criticism negotiated different readings to reconstruct written sources used by one or more authors. In other words, the literary-historical skills that had been learned to reconstruct 'early texts' simply were extended to reconstruct 'early sources'.

Analysis especially of stories and sayings in the Gospels invited the extension of the literary-historical skills associated with text and source criticism yet one more step, namely to the reconstruction of 'oral sources'. One might think that biblical scholars used significantly different methods of analysis during the era of form criticism, but perusal of form-critical investigations reveals that no significant break with the literary-historical procedures of text and source criticism occurred. The major shift was to concentrate on the 'life' of individual pericopae. The methods for reconstructing the life-stages of these stories and sayings were the same literary-historical methods used for text and source criticism. In other words, the analytical steps in form criticism proceeded as though oral transmission and variation occurred in a manner analogous to 'scribal' transmission and variation.[1]

Redaction criticism, in contrast to form criticism, has opened the door for interpretive skills significantly different from the literary-historical skills that were formulated to reconstruct written and oral sources of a text on the basis of intertextual similarities and differences. To be sure, most interpreters in Europe stay within the bound-

---

(eds.), *New Testament Textual Criticism: Its Significance for Exegesis* (London: Oxford University Press, 1981).

1. W.H. Kelber, *The Oral and the Written Gospel* (Philadelphia: Fortress, 1983), pp. 1-43.

aries of the literary-historical skills of text, source, and form criticism as they use redaction criticism to envision the theological and historical situation of the Gospels.[1] Yet through the influence of interpreters like Norman Perrin redaction criticism in the United States has from the beginning emphasized the 'whole range of creative activities' in a Gospel.[2] This emphasis has given redaction criticism an open-ended agenda that invites interaction with various kinds of structural, literary, and rhetorical modes of analysis.

One of the renewed interests during the transitional period provided by redaction criticism has been the relation of oral to written speech, and in the midst of the discussion a new problem has arisen. The problem is that a discussion of 'print culture' appropriate for our time has been imposed onto the first centuries of the common era in such a manner that the relation between oral and written culture during early Christian times is badly misconstrued. Werner Kelber's discussion not only typifies the problem but contributes a major voice to the confusion. The confusion arises through a failure to recognize the pervasiveness of rhetorical culture throughout Mediterranean society during the Hellenistic period.[3] Kelber distinguishes between 'oral culture', 'scribal culture', and 'print culture', placing an improper mystique on scribal culture using Elizabeth Eisenstein's statement:

> There is nothing analogous in our experience or in that of any living creature within the Western world at present. The conditions of scribal culture thus have to be artificially reconstructed by recourse to history books and reference guides. Yet for the most part, these works are more likely to conceal than to reveal the object of such a search. Scribal themes are carried forward, post-print trends are traced backward in a manner that makes it difficult to envisage the existence of a distinct literary culture based on hand-copying. There is not even an agreed-upon term in common use which designates the system of written communications that prevailed before print.[4]

---

1. Cf. E.V. McKnight, 'Form and Redaction Criticism', *The New Testament and Its Modern Interpreters* (ed. E.J. Epp and G.W. MacRae; The Bible and Its Modern Interpreters 3; Philadelphia: Fortress/Atlanta: Scholars Press, 1989), pp. 153-60.

2. N. Perrin, *What is Redaction Criticism?* (Philadelphia: Fortress, 1969), p. 66.

3. See M.A. Tolbert, *Sowing the Gospel: Mark's World in Literary-Historical Perspective* (Philadelphia: Fortress, 1989), pp. 44-45 n. 36.

4. E.L. Eisenstein, *The Printing Press as an Agent of Change* (Cambridge: Cambridge University Press, 1979), p. 19; quoted by W.H. Kelber, 'From Aphorism to Sayings Gospel and from Parable to Narrative Gospel', *Foundations & Facets Forum* 1.1 (1985), pp. 26-27.

A major problem with this manner of stating the issue is the lack of reference to rhetorical culture in Mediterranean antiquity. The system of communication that prevailed before print, and during the first phase of print, was called 'rhetoric'. For this reason it would be more helpful for us to distinguish between:

1. oral culture
2. scribal culture
3. rhetorical culture
4. print culture

New Testament documents were produced in a culture characterized by interaction among oral, scribal, and rhetorical environments. The phrase 'oral culture' should be used for those environments where written literature is not in view.[1] The phrase 'rhetorical culture', in contrast, should refer to environments where oral and written speech interact closely with one another.[2] It would be best to limit 'scribal culture' to those environments where a primary goal is to 'copy' either oral statements or written texts. Hand-copying in Mediterranean antiquity produced a distinct literary culture in an advanced rhetorical culture where written and spoken composition were closely related to one another.

If we are to be true to writing activity in antiquity, we must be aware of a spectrum of various kinds of writing.[3] This paper focuses on scribal reproduction and progymnastic composition. 'Scribal reproduction' consisted of making copies of extant texts, transcribing messages and letters from dictation, and reproducing stock documents like receipts. A person received training in these skills during the elementary and grammatical phases of education.[4] 'Progymnastic composition', in contrast to scribal reproduction, consisted of writing traditional materials clearly and persuasively rather than in the oral or

---

1. A.B. Lord, *The Singer of Tales* (Harvard Studies in Comparative Literature 24; Cambridge, MA: Harvard University Press, 1960); W.J. Ong, *Orality and Literacy* (New York: Methuen, 1982).

2. T.M. Lentz, *Orality and Literacy in Hellenic Culture* (Carbondale, IL: Southern Illinois University Press, 1989).

3. The primary spectrum of writing in Mediterranean antiquity, in our view, consists of five kinds of writing: (1) scribal reproduction; (2) progymnastic composition; (3) narrative composition; (4) discursive composition; (5) poetic composition.

4. S.F. Bonner, *Education in Ancient Rome: From the Elder Cato to the Younger Pliny* (Berkeley: University of California Press, 1977), pp. 165-211.

written form it came to the writer. The full spectrum of progymnastic composition is outlined and discussed in documents entitled *Progymnasmata* (Elementary Exercises),[1] and we recommend the phrase 'progymnastic rhetoric' to refer to the phenomenon and the phrase 'progymnastic composition' to refer to the writing activities associated with it. Progymnastic composition was intended for the end of grammatical training in preparation for rhetorical training, but there were disagreements during the early centuries of the common era concerning how much grammatical training a student needed to complete before beginning to compose at the progymnastic level.[2] A major thesis of this paper is that progymnastic composition is the activity that bridges the gap between the kind of rhetorical analysis performed by people like George A. Kennedy, in whose honor this volume of studies is offered, and text, source, form, and redaction analysis.

In order to display the nature of progymnastic composition and to distinguish it from scribal reproduction, this paper exhibits multiple versions of Lysander's use of his sword to discuss territorial boundaries, Jesus' healing of Peter's mother-in-law, Jesus' calling of two sets of brothers, Alexander's refusal to run in the Olympic footrace, and the woman who touched Jesus' garment. The documents entitled *Progymnasmata* which were written by Aelius Theon of Alexandria (c. 50–100 AD) and Hermogenes (2nd cent. AD) will serve as guides for analysis of these short units in Plutarch and the Synoptic Gospels.[3]

Recitation Composition in Traditional Rhetorical Culture

In traditional rhetorical culture, repetition of words and phrases in a written document regularly is the result of 'recitation composition' rather than 'copying'. Aelius Theon explains recitation composition in the following manner:

---

1. See R.F. Hock and E.N. O'Neil, *The Chreia in Ancient Rhetoric*, vol. I, *The Progymnasmata* (Atlanta: Scholars Press, 1986), pp. 9-22; B.L. Mack and V.K. Robbins, *Patterns of Persuasion in the Gospels* (Sonoma, CA: Polebridge, 1989), pp. 33-35; J.R. Butts, 'The "Progymnasmata" of Theon: A New Text with Translation and Commentary' (PhD dissertation; Ann Arbor: University Microfilms International, 1987); Bonner, *Education in Ancient Rome*, pp. 250-76.

2. Quintilian, in *Institutio Oratoria*, especially book 1, refers to some of these discussions and clarifies his position in the midst of them.

3. See Butts, 'The "Progymnasmata" of Theon'; Hock and O'Neil, *The Chreia in Ancient Rhetoric*.

and so 1) 'Recitation' (ἀπαγγελία) is obvious. For we try to the best of our ability to report (ἑρμηνεῦσαι) the assigned chreia very clearly in the same words or in others as well.[1]

When Theon refers to 'reporting' a chreia (a statement or action attributed to a specific person), he is talking about writing it. A traditional rhetorical culture is based on stories and sayings that people use in different ways for different purposes. Recitation composition in Hellenistic education built on this insight and, as a result, marked the transition from scribal copying to rhetorical writing. The dynamics and presuppositions surrounding recitation composition emerged as a teacher recited a traditional fable, anecdote, event, or saying in his own words to one or more students and the students wrote the brief unit in their own words, using as much or as little of the teacher's wording as worked well for them. It is not accidental that the recitation exercise marked the transition from scribal copying to rhetorical writing, since once a student moves away from verbatim reproduction of an oral or written text, the dynamics of rhetorical culture invade the act of writing itself. John Dominic Crossan has seen the variations that result from recitation composition in his study of early Christian aphorisms, and he refers to them as 'performancial variations'.[2] Unfortunately, as an heir of literary-historical criticism, he does not use insights from rhetorical criticism or information about different kinds of writing during the Hellenistic period to inform the analysis.

Since recitation composition stands at the entrance to rhetorical culture as it functioned in Mediterranean society, writing and speaking are closely intertwined in much Mediterranean literature. The customary introductory phrase 'it is said' (λέγεται), 'they say' or 'they were saying' (λέγουσιν or ἔλεγον), or some such variation, exhibits the pervasive nature of recitation in the culture. When people transferred material from one written document to another, they regularly performed the material anew. The new performance contained as much or as little verbatim reproduction as was congenial to the writer. An author attributed specific words to specific past authors, and this act produced arguments from ancient authorities or witnesses. The result appears in references to specific people like Xenophon, Homer, Isaiah, or David; and authors regularly refer to these citations through

---

1. Hock and O'Neil, *The Chreia in Ancient Rhetoric*, p. 95.
2. J.D. Crossan, *In Fragments: The Aphorisms of Jesus* (San Francisco: Harper & Row, 1983), pp. 37-66.

'according to' (κατά with accusative) or some form of reference to something 'written' (γέγραπται, ἐστίν γεγραμμένον, etc.). As a result of recitation composition, even specific citations often exhibit variation rather than verbatim transmission.

The dynamic relation between oral speech and written literature is evident from the opening discussion in the *Progymnasmata* of the first-century rhetorician and sophist Aelius Theon. Theon tells his reader that the only way to become a skillful orator is to 'write every day':

> For those who are going to be orators, not the words of the older writers, not their wealth of thoughts, not the purity of their style, not their well-proportioned arrangement, not their elegant oral presentation, in a word, not any of the good elements in rhetoric, are at all useful unless each one practices writing every day for himself.[1]

For Theon, a primary dimension in practicing writing every day is learning to present something well in varying ways. As Theon says:

> For thinking is stirred by one subject in not just one way (so that the sense impression falling upon it is conveyed the same way), but rather in several ways. And since we sometimes make statements, sometimes ask questions, sometimes make inquiry, sometimes express a wish, and sometimes express our thought in some other way, nothing prevents our expressing the same impression equally well in all these ways.[2]

Writing in a rhetorical culture builds on speaking and writing from the past, and the goal is to learn to present the thoughts and actions of the past equally well in varying ways.

The issue is, then, where is the line to be drawn between scribal reproduction, which includes 'corrections and improvements', and recitation composition? Many Gospel units that have been discussed from the perspective of scribal revision are more appropriately described as different recitation performances. Since the person thinks the sounds, and perhaps says them during the writing, written speech remains closely related to oral speech. The person hears the words, and the sounds influence the written form. If we wonder why the Synoptic Gospels contain so much variation in settings of so much verbatim agreement, the answer surely lies here. These authors are working in close relation to one another or to common sources, yet they continually recast the material by adding to it, subtracting from it, rear-

---

1. Theon I, 88-92 (Butts).
2. Theon I, 96-102 (Butts).

ranging it, and rewording it. To posit an 'oral source' for these variations is wrong, because it merges the literary-historical approach
associated with text and source criticism directly with oral transmission without bringing into view the kind of culture in which oral and
written speech interact closely with one another. In other words, those
who posit oral sources for the variation are presupposing a 'copying
culture' linked directly to an 'oral culture'. The evidence we have in
the *Progymnasmata* and other documents suggests that this approach
bypasses a pervasive culture in Mediterranean society in which oral
and written speech interacted closely with one another.[1]

A reader of texts from antiquity can see the kind of variation that
results from recitation composition in Plutarch's three versions of
Lysander's use of his sword in a discussion of territorial boundaries.[2]
The texts are as follows:

Plutarch, *Lysander* 22.1	Plutarch, *Moralia* 190E	Plutarch, *Moralia* 229C
Ἀργείοις μὲν γὰρ ἀμφιλογουμένοις	Πρὸς δὲ Ἀργείους	Πρὸς Ἀργείους δὲ
	δικαιότερα τῶν Λακεδαιμονίων λέγειν	
περὶ γῆς ὅρων καὶ	περὶ τῆς ἀμφισβητουμένης χώρας	περὶ γῆς ὅρων ἀμφισβητοῦντας
δικαιότερα τῶν Λακεδαιμονίων οἰομένοις λέγειν	δοκοῦντας,	πρὸς Λακεδαιμονίους καὶ δικαιότερα λέγειν αὐτῶν φάσκοντας,
δείξας τὴν μάχαιραν, 'ὁ ταύτης', ἔφη, 'κρατῶν βέλτιστα περὶ γῆς ὅρων διαλέγεται'.	σπασάμενος τὴν μάχαιραν, 'ὁ ταύτης', ἔφη, 'κρατῶν βέλτιστα περὶ γῆς ὅρων διαλέγεται'.	σπασάμενος τὴν μάχαιραν, 'ὁ ταύτης', ἔφη, 'κρατῶν βέλτιστα περὶ γῆς ὅρων διαλέγεται'.
For instance, when the Argives were arguing	To the Argives when they seemed to state a better case	To the Argives

---

1. Mack and Robbins, *Patterns of Persuasion in the Gospels*.
2. More versions of this story are displayed in V.K. Robbins, *Ancient Quotes and Anecdotes: From Crib to Crypt* (FFNT; Sonoma, CA: Polebridge, 1989), pp. 23-24.

about boundaries of land,	than the Spartans about the disputed territory,	who were disputing with the Spartans about boundaries
and thought they stated a better case than the Spartans,		and said they stated a better case than them,
he pointed to his sword, and said, 'He who is master of this discourses best about boundaries of land'.	he drew his sword, and said, 'He who is master of this discourses best about boundaries of land'.	he drew his sword and said, 'He who is master of this discourses best about boundaries of land'.

The variations among these three accounts look very much like variations among Synoptic Gospel versions. All three versions share verbatim reference to the Spartans' stating (λέγειν) of a better case (δικαιότερα) concerning (περί) the boundaries, reference to the sword (τὴν μάχαιραν), and reference to the saying, 'He who is master of this discourses best about boundaries of land'. In the midst of this verbatim reproduction, however, significant variation exists. The second and third accounts have 'to the Argives' (with variation in the placement of δέ), and agree on 'drawing' rather than 'pointing to' the sword, the first and second have 'a better case than the Spartans' (but in inverted order in the clause), and the first and third have 'about boundaries of land'. Beyond these agreements, each account contains slightly variant wording.

These phenomena display well the results of recitation composition. It is obvious from the verbatim reproduction that one or more of the accounts functioned as a reference text when one of the other accounts was written. Yet the variation among the accounts indicates that there was no concern to copy another text word for word. If the guiding principle had been to copy another text verbatim, the variations among the accounts would have taken the form of different separations of words that create different punctuations of the text, minor variations in spelling and/or wording that correct or improve the text, or absence or presence of clauses through omission, attempts at restoration, and/or conflations of corrected texts.[1] Instead, the three versions of the Lysander account contain multiple variations of wording and rearrangements of phrases prior to the saying. Only the reference to the

---

1. For an excellent example, see the analysis of Jn 1.1-18 in Finegan, *Encountering New Testament Manuscripts*, pp. 111-77.

sword and the saying which follows it stand in verbatim agreement in the three accounts, and this is one kind of verbatim overlap that is natural, though not mandatory, in an environment of recitation composition. Here, then, the interpreter sees a good example of the kind of verbatim repetition that may exist in the midst of significant variation in a text produced within the guidelines of recitation composition. There has been no attempt to copy an entire text verbatim, nor has there been complete modification of everything in another text. Rather, the performance of the traditional story combines significant variation with significant verbatim overlap.

There is dispute among interpreters whether the materials in one or both of the accounts in the *Moralia* were notes Plutarch made and subsequently used when he wrote his *Lysander*, or the materials were excerpted from the *Lysander* by himself or some other person for the two accounts in the *Moralia*.[1] Thus, similar disputes exist in scholarship about the source relationships of the accounts in Plutarch and the Synoptic Gospels. The important thing is for us to see that the same kind of recitation reproduction and variation among multiple accounts exists among documents attributed to Plutarch as among the Gospels. This phenomenon displays, in our opinion, the widespread activity of recitation composition of stories and sayings attributed to specific persons in Mediterranean literature during the early centuries of the common era.

A generally analogous relation of texts exists among the three versions of Jesus' healing of Peter's mother-in-law in the Synoptic Gospels. The texts are as follows:

Mt. 8.14-15	Mk 1.29-31	Lk. 4.38-39
Καὶ	Καὶ εὐθὺς	Ἀναστὰς δὲ
	ἐκ τῆς συναγωγῆς	ἀπὸ τῆς συναγωγῆς
ἐλθὼν ὁ Ἰησοῦς,	ἐξελθόντες ἦλθον	εἰσῆλθεν
εἰς τὴν οἰκίαν	εἰς τὴν οἰκίαν Σίμωνος	εἰς τὴν οἰκίαν Σίμωνος.
Πέτρου	καὶ Ἀνδρέου μετὰ	
	Ἰακώβου καὶ	
	Ἰωάννου.	
εἶδεν		
τὴν πενθερὰν αὐτοῦ	ἡ δὲ πενθερὰ Σίμωνος	πενθερὰ δὲ τοῦ Σίμωνος
βεβλημένην καὶ	κατέκειτο	ἦν συνεχομένη

---

1. F.C. Babbitt, *Plutarch's Moralia* (Cambridge, MA: Harvard University Press/ London: Heinemann, 1968), III, pp. 3-7.

πυρέσσουσαν·	πυρέσσουσα,	πυρετῷ μεγάλῳ,
	καὶ εὐθὺς λέγουσιν	καὶ ἠρώτησαν αὐτὸν
	αὐτῷ περὶ αὐτῆς.	περὶ αὐτῆς.
καὶ	καὶ προσελθὼν	καὶ ἐπιστὰς ἐπάνω
		αὐτῆς
	ἤγειρεν αὐτὴν	
		ἐπετίμησεν τῷ πυρετῷ,
ἥψατο τῆς χειρὸς	κρατήσας τῆς χειρός·	
αὐτῆς		
καὶ ἀφῆκεν αὐτὴν	καὶ ἀφῆκεν αὐτὴν	καὶ ἀφῆκεν αὐτήν·
ὁ πυρετός·	ὁ πυρετός,	
		παραχρῆμα δὲ
καὶ ἠγέρθη,		ἀναστᾶσα
καὶ διηκόνει αὐτῷ.	καὶ διηκόνει αὐτοῖς	διηκόνει αὐτοῖς.

And	And immediately he left the synagogue and entered the house of Simon and Andrew, with James and John.	And he arose from the synagogue and entered the house of Simon.
when Jesus entered the house of Peter		
he saw		
his mother-in-law lying	Now the mother-in-law of Simon lay	Now Simon's mother-in-law was '
sick with a fever;	sick with a fever and immediately they told him of her.	ill with a high fever, and they besought him for her.
and	And he came	And he stood over
he touched her hand	and took her by the hand and lifted her up,	her
		and rebuked the fever,
and the fever left her, and she rose	and the fever left her;	and it left her; and immediately she got up
and she served him.	and she served them.	and served them.

Among these three versions the dynamics of recitation composition are fully evident. All three versions share verbatim reference to going 'into the house' of Simon, to the 'mother-in-law', to the fever 'leaving her', and to her 'serving'. Some agreements, however, exist only among two versions. The second and third accounts have Jesus come from 'the synagogue', use the name 'Simon' rather than 'Peter', have the disciples tell or ask Jesus 'about her', and have the mother-in-law serve 'them' rather than 'him'. The first and second accounts agree in wording as they refer to being 'sick with a fever', to touching or grasping 'the hand' of the woman, and to 'the fever' leaving her. In the midst of this kind of agreement, each account varies slightly from the other in wording and arrangement of phrases.

Whether Matthew and/or Luke used Mark as a source or Mark used Matthew and/or Luke is less significant than the fact that whoever used whom as a source has exercised freedom in varying the wording. In other words, each writer has proceeded according to the guidelines of recitation composition rather than copying.

Once we become aware of the phenomena common to recitation composition in texts in Hellenistic culture, we may acquire new eyes for understanding Synoptic texts that we usually perceive to stand in a relation of 'scribal revision'. The Matthean and Markan versions of the calling of two sets of brothers present a good example of the kind of variation that usually would be considered to be the product of scribal revision, because of the nature and extent of the verbatim agreement. The texts look as follows:

Mt. 4.18-22	Mk 1.16-20
περιπατῶν δὲ	καὶ παράγων
παρὰ τὴν θάλασσαν τῆς	παρὰ τὴν θάλασσαν τῆς
Γαλιλαίας εἶδεν δύο ἀδελφούς,	Γαλιλαίας εἶδεν
Σίμωνα	Σίμωνα
τὸν λεγόμενον Πέτρον	
καὶ Ἀνδρέαν τὸν ἀδελφὸν αὐτοῦ,	καὶ Ἀνδρέαν τὸν ἀδελφὸν Σίμωνος
βάλλοντας ἀμφίβληστρον	ἀμφιβάλλοντας
εἰς τὴν θάλασσαν· ἦσαν γὰρ	ἐν τῇ θαλάσσῃ· ἦσαν γὰρ ἁλεεῖς.
ἁλεεῖς.	
Καὶ λέγει αὐτοῖς·	Καὶ εἶπεν αὐτοῖς ὁ Ἰησοῦς·
δεῦτε ὀπίσω μου, καὶ ποιήσω	δεῦτε ὀπίσω μου, καὶ ποιήσω
ὑμᾶς	ὑμᾶς
	γενέσθαι
ἁλεεῖς ἀνθρώπων.	ἁλεεῖς ἀνθρώπων.
οἱ δὲ εὐθέως ἀφέντες τὰ δίκτυα	Καὶ εὐθὺς ἀφέντες τὰ δίκτυα
ἠκολούθησαν αὐτῷ.	ἠκολούθησαν αὐτῷ.
Καὶ προβὰς ἐκεῖθεν	Καὶ προβὰς ὀλίγον
εἶδεν	εἶδεν
ἄλλους δύο ἀδελφούς,	
Ἰάκωβον τὸν τοῦ Ζεβεδαίου καὶ	Ἰάκωβον τὸν τοῦ Ζεβεδαίου καὶ
Ἰωάννην τὸν ἀδελφὸν αὐτοῦ,	Ἰωάννην τὸν ἀδελφὸν αὐτοῦ,
	καὶ αὐτοὺς
ἐν τῷ πλοίῳ	ἐν τῷ πλοίῳ
μετὰ Ζεβεδαίου τοῦ πατρὸς αὐτῶν	
καταρτίζοντας τὰ δίκτυα αὐτῶν·	καταρτίζοντας τὰ δίκτυα,

καὶ ἐκάλεσεν αὐτούς·
οἱ δὲ εὐθέως ἀφέντες

τὸ πλοῖον
καὶ τὸν πατέρα αὐτῶν

ἠκολούθησαν αὐτῷ.

As he walked
by the Sea of Galilee, he saw
two brothers,
Simon
who is called Peter
and Andrew his brother,
casting a net into the sea; for they were

fishermen.
And he says to them,
'Follow me, and I will make you
fishers of men'.
Immediately they left their
nets and followed him.
And going on from there
he saw
two other brothers,
James the son of Zebedee and
John his brother,
in the boat
with Zebedee their father,
mending their nets,
and he called them.
Immediately they left

the boat
and their father,

and followed him.

καὶ εὐθὺς ἐκάλεσεν αὐτούς.
καὶ ἀφέντες
τὸν πατέρα αὐτῶν Ζεβεδαῖον
ἐν τῷ πλοίῳ

μετὰ τῶν μισθωτῶν
ἀπῆλθον ὀπίσω αὐτῷ.

And passing along
by the Sea of Galilee, he saw

Simon

and Andrew the brother of Simon
casting in the sea; for
they were
fishermen.
And Jesus said to them,
'Follow me and I will make you
become fishers of men'.
And immediately they left their nets and
followed him.
And going a little farther,
he saw

James the son of Zebedee and
John his brother,
who were in their boat

mending the nets.
And immediately he called them;
and they left
their father Zebedee
in the boat

with the hired servants,
and went away behind him.

The verbatim overlap in these two accounts is extensive, and most of the variations have the nature of addition or omission from the other account. Thus, the phrases 'two brothers', 'who is called Peter', 'become', 'two other brothers', 'with Zebedee their father', and 'with the hired servants' have been added or subtracted by one of the writers. Yet there also is variation in wording, and this rewording combines with rearrangement of the order of phrases near the end of the account. Thus, Matthew has 'as he walked' for Mark's 'and passing along', Matthew has 'casting a net' for Mark's 'casting', Matthew has 'says' for Mark's 'Jesus said', and Matthew has 'they followed him' for Mark's 'they went away behind him'. The overall impression is that each composition contains more and more freedom from the wording of the other as the unit progresses, for the end of the accounts have the most variation in wording and arrangement of phrases. When all is said and done in the investigation of these accounts, what we must consider most remarkable in the setting of this much overlap are the variations. There is no embarrassment with extensive verbatim reproduction, yet there is no commitment to verbatim copying. This, I submit, reveals the presence of 'recitation composition' as a guiding principle.

Argumentation in Progymnastic Composition

A major reason for insisting that variations among Gospel texts are the result of 'recitation composition' is the range of progymnastic composition throughout the Gospels. The nature of the relationship of texts when there is a greater degree of variation than we have analyzed in the preceding section is explained well in the *Progymnasmata* of Aelius Theon, and initial interpretations have been offered in *Patterns of Persuasion in the Gospels*.[1] In Hellenistic education, after the student became proficient in recitation composition, the teacher continued with exercises in inflexion, positive comment, negative comment, expansion, abbreviation, refutation, and confirmation.[2] More often than we might suppose, these variations create different kinds of argumentation, something of great importance in a rhetorical culture. In order to see how variations in rhetorical argument accompany small variations in wording, we will examine multiple accounts in Plutarch of Alexander's refusal to compete in the footrace at Olympia and multiple accounts in the Synoptic Gospels of the woman who touched Jesus' garment.

In three extant accounts of the young Alexander's refusal to run in the footrace at Olympia he responds that he would compete if he had kings as competitors. The agreement and variation look as follows:

1. Mack and Robbins, *Patterns of Persuasion in the Gospels*.
2. Hock and O'Neil, *The Chreia in Ancient Rhetoric*, pp. 95-106; Mack and Robbins, *Patterns of Persuasion in the Gospels*, pp. 35-41; Bonner, *Education in Ancient Rome*, pp. 25-76.

Moralia 179D	*Alexander* 4.10	*Moralia* 331B
Ἐλαφρὸς δὲ ὢν καὶ ποδώκης	ἀλλὰ καὶ	ποδωκέστατος γὰρ τῶν ἐφ᾽ ἡλικίας νέων γενόμενος
καὶ παρακαλούμενος ὑπὸ τοῦ πατρὸς	τῶν περὶ αὐτὸν ἀποπειρωμένων εἰ βούλοιτ᾽ ἂν	καὶ τῶν ἑταίρων αὐτὸν
Ὀλύμπια δραμεῖν	Ὀλυμπίασιν ἀγωνίσασθαι	ἐπ᾽ Ὀλύμπια παρορμώντων,
στάδιον,	στάδιον, ἦν γὰρ ποδώκης,	
		ἠρώτησεν,
'εἴγε', ἔφη,	'εἴγε', ἔφη,	εἰ
'βασιλεῖς ἕξειν ἔμελλον ἀνταγωνιστάς'.	'βασιλεῖς ἔμελλον ἕξειν ἀνταγωνιστάς'.	βασιλεῖς
		ἀγωνίζονται· τῶν δ᾽ οὐ φαμένων, ἄδικον εἶναι τὴν ἅμιλλαν, ἐν ᾗ νικήσει μὲν ἰδιώτας, νικηθήσεται δὲ βασιλεύς.
Being nimble and swiftfooted,	In contrast,	Since he was the swiftest of foot of the young men of his age,
when he was appealed to	when those around him inquired whether he would be willing	and his comrades urged him to enter
by his father to run at the Olympic footrace,	to compete in the Olympic footrace, for he was swift-footed,	at Olympia,
he said: 'Indeed, if I were to have kings as competitors'.	he said: 'Indeed, if I were to have kings as competitors'.	he asked if kings were competing. And when they replied in the negative, he said that the contest was unfair in which a victory would be over commoners, but a defeat would be the defeat of a king.

In the version in the first column, Alexander's father is the person who raises the issue with Alexander, and Alexander responds with a conditional affirmative, namely, only on the condition that his competitors be kings. This story stands in a collection of apophthegms of kings and commanders, and it is preceded by this story:

> While Alexander was still a boy and Philip was winning many successes, he was not glad, but said to his playmates, 'My father will leave nothing for me to do'. 'But', said the boys, 'he is acquiring all this for you'. 'But what good is it', said Alexander, 'if I possess much and accomplish nothing?' (*Moralia* 179D)

In this context it appears to be important that Alexander's father Philip is the one who appeals to Alexander to compete. The effect of Alexander's response is to suggest that he will not be distracted by activities that are less prestigious than the exploits of his father. The unstated premises with the conclusion, therefore, appear to be something like this:

Major premise	Alexander will do nothing less prestigious than his father Philip.
Minor premise	Philip wins many successes competing with kings.
Conclusion	Alexander will compete at the Olympic footrace only if kings are his competitors.

The presence of Alexander's playmates in the preceding story may play a role, since they imply that they would simply enjoy the successes their fathers won. Alexander, in contrast to his playmates, displays the true spirit of the son of Philip by remaining unhappy until he competes with kings themselves—which, of course includes his father. Thus, another implication may be that Alexander would run at Olympia if his own father were willing to run against him.

The version in *Alexander* 4.10 shares nine Greek words in common with *Moralia* 179D: ποδώκης (swiftfooted); Ὀλύμπια... στάδιον (Olympic footrace); 'εἴγε', ἔφη, 'βασιλεῖς ἔμελλον ἕξειν ἀνταγωνιστάς' ('Indeed', he said, 'if I were to have kings as competitors'). The saying of Alexander contains exactly the same words, but the order of ἔμελλον and ἕξειν is reversed in the two versions. Despite the verbatim agreement, those around Alexander, rather than his father, ask if he will compete. The issue in this instance appears to be whether Alexander will seize the opportunity to display his swiftness of foot. In its narrative context, the story is an illustration that it was neither every kind of fame nor fame from every source that he [Alexander] courted, as Philip did, who plumed himself like a sophist on the power of his oratory, and took care to have the victories of his chariots at Olympia engraved upon his coins (*Alexander* 4.9).

In this instance, therefore, the story does not concern competition with Philip's successes but self-restraint and maturity of purpose greater than Philip, who seeks and flaunts his successes. The change of interlocutors from Philip himself to Alexander's playmates appears to contribute to the broader goal. Instead of responding sharply to his father, Alexander responds to the inquiry of his playmates with restraint and maturity by showing an unwillingness to flaunt his swiftness before his peers. He will use his skills only for his major task at hand—competition with kings. Thus, the premises and conclusion of this version appear to be something like this:

Major premise	Alexander possessed self-restraint and maturity of purpose in contrast to his father who sought and displayed every kind of fame.
Minor premise	If Alexander ran in the Olympic footrace without the most rigorous competition, he simply would be seeking and displaying childhood fame, since he was swiftfooted.
Conclusion	Alexander will compete at the Olympic footrace only if kings are his competitors.

This version of the story evokes a fully epideictic situation as it praises Alexander at Philip's expense. Through the technique of comparison (σύγκρισις), Alexander emerges as a personage of restraint and maturity of purpose while Philip lives on as a personage who sought prizes and flaunted them when he attained them.

Why would a transmitter of this story feel free to substitute Alexander's playmates for his father Philip as the one who asks if he will compete in the Olympic footrace? The answer lies in the dynamics of recitation in rhetorical culture. A person feels free to vary the story to bring clarity and persuasiveness to the argument at hand. One may be concerned to establish if the first version of the story is earlier, later, or more authentic than the other, or if it was composed by someone other than Plutarch. But these concerns, which focus on 'copying' and 'sources', may have no certain answer, while an interpreter may uncover and explore the different strategies of argumentation in the two versions with considerable precision.

A third version in *Moralia* 331B also features Alexander in conversation with his playmates. In this instance, the performance expands the dialogue by having Alexander respond with a question that seeks information before he gives his final response. The result is a dialogue that creates an occasion for Alexander to explain why he would not compete unless kings were his competitors. The reasoning appeals to that which is just and unjust:

Major premise	The principle of justice requires that people of equal status compete with one another.
Minor premise	If Alexander competes in the Olympic footrace, his defeat would be the defeat of a king but his victory would be over commoners.
Conclusion	Alexander will not compete in the footrace at Olympia.

There are two dynamics within this reasoning that make the account especially interesting. First, Alexander's statement implies that he himself is a king. Neither of the other versions takes this step: the only assertion was that Alexander would not compete unless kings were his competitors (or at least were among his competitors). Second, while the saying of Alexander articulates a principle of justice as the reason for the refusal to run, the overall saying intermingles a dynamic of honor with a concern about justice. If a king defeats commoners, the primary issue would appear to be justice; but if commoners defeat a king, the primary issue would appear to be the king's honor. So here the reasoning becomes subtle and witty. Once Alexander calls himself a king, he need not compete with commoners. Since he is a king's son but not yet actually a king, however, one might think he would display his royal abilities like he does in other boyhood stories.[1] According to the narrator, this should have been no problem for Alexander, since he was the 'swiftest' of the young men of his age (an assertion only this version makes). But the issue appears to concern the ambiguous nature of athletic victories. As the narrator says:

> Alexander appears to have been averse to the whole race of athletes; at any rate, though he instituted very many contests, not only for tragic poets and players on the flute and players on the lyre, but also for rhapsodists, as well as for hunting of every sort and for fighting with staves, he took no interest in offering prizes either for boxing or for the pancratium (*Alexander* 4.11).

---

1. Cf. Plutarch, *Alexander* 5-7.

Kings, then, cannot display their true character competing at Olympia; those abilities must emerge in the unexpected situations that confront a person who pursues 'a king's business'.

But there appears to be yet one more attribute of character to be valued in a king when this attribute intermingles with a sense of justice, namely cleverness (μῆτις)—the wit and candor that give a person the ability to handle difficult situations skillfully, quickly, and definitively.[1] To the extent that the story seriously raises the issue of 'fairness' among different ranks of people, it contributes well to Plutarch's presentation of Alexander as 'a philosopher in his purpose not to win for himself luxury and extravagant living, but to win for all people concord and peace and community of interests' (*Moralia* 330E). Alexander's suggestion that commoners might defeat a king, however, reveals a moment of candor about himself as well as an ability to get out of a potentially embarrassing situation with skill. In each version, then, the act of composition has produced a significantly different rhetorical argument. It is not necessary to posit the existence of an oral source for each new form of the story. Rather, the dynamics of progymnastic composition have created an environment for writing as a rhetorical act.

A similar relation exists among the Synoptic versions of the woman who touched Jesus' garment:

Mt. 9.20-22	Mk 5.24b-34	Lk. 8.43-48
Καὶ ἰδοὺ γυνὴ αἱμορροοῦσα δώδεκα ἔτη	Καὶ γυνὴ οὖσα ἐν ῥύσει αἵματος δώδεκα ἔτη,	Καὶ γυνὴ οὖσα ἐν ῥύσει αἵματος ἀπὸ ἐτῶν δώδεκα,
	καὶ πολλὰ παθοῦσα ὑπὸ πολλῶν ἰατρῶν καὶ	ἥτις οὐκ ἴσχυσεν ἀπ' οὐδενὸς θεραπευθῆναι,
	δαπανήσασα τὰ παρ' ἐαυτῆς πάντα, καὶ μηδὲν ὠφεληθεῖσα ἀλλὰ μᾶλλον εἰς τὸ χεῖρον ἐλθοῦσα, ἀκούσασα τὰ περὶ τοῦ Ἰησοῦ,	
προσελθοῦσα	ἐλθοῦσα ἐν τῷ ὄχλῳ	προσελθοῦσα

---

1. M. Detienne and J.-P. Vernant, *Cunning Intelligence in Greek Culture and Society* (Atlantic Highlands, NJ: Humanities Press, 1978).

ὄπισθεν	ὄπισθεν	ὄπισθεν
ἥψατο τοῦ κρασπέδου	ἥψατο	ἥψατο τοῦ κρασπέδου
τοῦ ἱματίου αὐτοῦ·	τοῦ ἱματίου αὐτοῦ·	τοῦ ἱματίου αὐτοῦ,
ἔλεγεν γὰρ ἐν ἑαυτῇ ἐὰν	ἔλεγεν γὰρ ὅτι ἐὰν	
μόνον ἅψωμαι τοῦ	ἅψωμαι κἂν τῶν	
ἱματίου	ἱματίων	
αὐτοῦ, σωθήσομαι.	αὐτοῦ, σωθήσομαι. καὶ	καὶ παραχρῆμα
	εὐθὺς ἐξηράνθη ἡ πηγὴ	ἔστη ἡ ῥύσις
	τοῦ αἵματος αὐτῆς,	τοῦ αἵματος αὐτῆς.
	καὶ ἔγνω τῷ σώματι ὅτι	καὶ εἶπεν ὁ Ἰησοῦς,
	ἴαται ἀπὸ τῆς μάστιγος.	Τίς ὁ ἁψάμενός μου;
	καὶ εὐθὺς ὁ Ἰησοῦς	ἀρνουμένων δὲ
	ἐπιγνοὺς ἐν ἑαυτῷ τὴν	πάντων
	ἐξ αὐτοῦ δύναμιν	εἶπεν ὁ Πέτρος,
	ἐξελθοῦσαν,	Ἐπιστάτα, οἱ ὄχλοι
	ἐπιστραφεὶς ἐν τῷ ὄχλῳ	συνέχουσίν σε καὶ
	ἔλεγεν·	ἀποθλίβουσιν.
ὁ δὲ Ἰησοῦς στραφεὶς	τίς μου ἥψατο τῶν	ὁ δὲ Ἰησοῦς εἶπεν,
	ἱματίων;	Ἥψατό μού τις, ἐγὼ
		γὰρ ἔγνων δύναμιν
	καὶ ἔλεγον αὐτῷ οἱ	ἐξεληλυθυῖαν ἀπ᾽
	μαθηταὶ αὐτοῦ· βλέπεις	ἐμοῦ.
	τὸν ὄχλον	
	συνθλίβοντά σε, καὶ	
	λέγεις· τίς μου ἥψατο;	
καὶ ἰδὼν αὐτὴν	καὶ περιεβλέπετο ἰδεῖν	ἰδοῦσα δὲ ἡ γυνὴ
		ὅτι οὐκ
	τὴν τοῦτο ποιήσασαν.	ἔλαθεν τρέμουσα
	ἡ δὲ γυνὴ φοβηθεῖσα	ἦλθεν
	καὶ τρέμουσα,	καὶ προσπεσοῦσα
		αὐτῷ δι᾽
	εἰδυῖα ὃ	ἣν αἰτίαν ἥψατο
		αὐτοῦ
	γέγονεν αὐτῇ, ἦλθεν καὶ	ἀπήγγειλεν ἐνώπιον
	προσέπεσεν αὐτῷ καὶ	παντὸς τοῦ λαοῦ καὶ
		ὡς
	εἶπεν αὐτῷ πᾶσαν τὴν	ἰάθη παραχρῆμα.
	ἀλήθειαν.	
εἶπεν· θάρσει,	ὁ δὲ εἶπεν αὐτῇ	ὁ δὲ εἶπεν αὐτῇ,
θύγατερ·	θυγάτηρ,	θυγάτηρ,
ἡ πίστις σου σέσωκέν	ἡ πίστις σου σέσωκέν	ἡ πίστις σου σέσωκέν
σε.	σε·	σε·
καὶ ἐσώθη ἡ γυνὴ	ὕπαγε εἰς εἰρήνην, καὶ	πορεύου εἰς εἰρήνην.
	ἴσθι ὑγιὴς	
ἀπὸ τῆς ὥρας ἐκείνης.	ἀπὸ τῆς μάστιγός σου.	

And behold, a woman who had suffered from a hemorrhage for twelve years	And there was a woman who had had a flow of blood for twelve years, and who had suffered much under many physicians, and had spent all that she had, and was no better but rather grew worse. She had heard the reports about Jesus,	And a woman who had a flow of blood for twelve years and could not be healed by any one,
came up behind him and touched the fringe of his garment; for she said to herself, 'If I only touch his garment, I shall be made well'.	and came up behind him in the crowd and touched his garment. For she said, 'If I touch even his garments I shall be made well'. And immediately the hemorrhage ceased; and she felt in her body that she was healed of her disease. And Jesus, perceiving in himself that power had gone forth from him, immediately	came up behind him, and touched the fringe of his garment; and immediately her flow of blood ceased. And Jesus said, 'Who was it that touched me?' When all denied it, Peter said, 'Master, the multitudes surround you and press upon you!'
Jesus turned	turned about in the crowd, and said, 'Who touched my garments?' And his disciples said to him, 'You see the crowd pressing around you, and yet you say, "Who touched me?"' And he looked around to	But Jesus said, 'Someone touched me; for I perceive that power has gone forth from me'.
and seeing her	see who had done it. But the woman, knowing what had been done to her, came in fear and trembling and fell down before him,	And when the woman saw that she was not hidden, she came trembling and falling down before him

	and told him the whole truth.	declared in the presence of all the people why she had touched him, and how she had been immediately healed.
he said, 'Take heart, daughter, your faith has made you well'.	And he said to her, 'Daughter, your faith has made you well;	And he said to her, 'Daughter, your faith has made you well;
And instantly the woman was made well.	go in peace and be healed of your disease'.	go in peace'.

As with the two accounts in Plutarch, there is enough verbatim language to suggest some kind of dependence among the three versions. Yet the final form of each account is the result of a compositional act that produces a significantly different version. This kind of relationship should, in our view, be seen as the result of composition at the level of progymnastic rhetoric.

The Matthean version of the woman who touched Jesus' garment (9.20-22) contains abbreviated narrative,[1] a saying by the woman, and a saying by Jesus. This story, like the first two versions of the account of Alexander's refusal to compete in the Olympic footrace, contains only one exchange of conversation among the featured characters. In this instance, however, the display of the logic behind the woman's act creates a setting in which Jesus' speech turns the woman's logic into an actualized syllogism containing a dimension the woman did not articulate and the auditor probably would not supply. In other words, the woman's statement evokes the following conditional syllogism:

Unstated premise	Touching any part of Jesus can make a person well.
Conditional premise	If I touch only his garment,
Conditional conclusion	I will be made well.

---

1. Hock and O'Neil, *The Chreia in Ancient Rhetoric*, p. 101; V.K. Robbins, 'Pronouncement Stories and Jesus' Blessing of the Children: A Rhetorical Approach', *Semeia* 29 (1983), p. 49; *idem*, 'The Chreia', *Greco-Roman Literature and the New Testament* (ed. D.E. Aune; Atlanta: Scholars Press, 1988), p. 17; *idem*, 'Pronouncement Stories from a Rhetorical Perspective', *Foundations & Facets Forum* 4.2 (1988), p. 10; Mack and Robbins, *Patterns of Persuasion in the Gospels*, pp. 17-18.

When Jesus says, 'Your faith has made you well', he has introduced a premise that changes the initial premise of the woman's conditional logic, and therefore changes the syllogism. The resultant syllogism is:

Major premise	An act of faith can make a person well.
Minor premise	The woman's act of touching was an act of faith.
Conclusion	Therefore, the woman was made well.[1]

The logic has moved the term 'Jesus' out of the unstated premise and introduced a general principle that could be made concrete in various ways. The faith simply could be confidence that healing would occur, or it could be confidence that Jesus or God could make it happen. The logical progression has transformed the initial premise, and therefore the entire logic, into a multi-valent form of reasoning which perpetuates Jewish heritage, attributes distinctive power and understanding to Jesus, and engages cultural beliefs in Asklepios' ability to heal.[2] The special dynamic of the story, however, is that Jesus' interpretation of the woman's logic enacts the healing. With this version, then, appropriate logic and healing occur simultaneously.

Mk 5.25-34 presents the story in the mode of an expanded chreia.[3] The writer presents extended narration, verbal exchange between Jesus and his disciples, and a saying of Jesus that not only announces that the woman's faith has made her well but gives a blessing of peace and health at the end. First, this version narrates the plight, actions, and inner thoughts of the woman, and the inner thoughts present the same logic of the woman that is in the Matthean version (vv. 25-28). Then, inner perception of healing by the woman occurs simultaneously with inner perception by Jesus that power has gone forth from him (v. 30b). Next, Jesus' speech in the form of a question calls forth a response from his disciples. This response repeats Jesus' question in a manner that intensifies emotions between Jesus and his disciples as Jesus looks around to see who touched him (v. 32). This sequence is

1. V.K. Robbins, 'The Woman who Touched Jesus' Garment: Socio-Rhetorical Analysis of the Synoptic Accounts', *NTS* 33 (1987), p. 507.
2. G. Theissen, *The Miracle Stories of the Early Christian Tradition* (Edinburgh: T. & T. Clark, 1983), pp. 130-33.
3. Hock and O'Neil, *The Chreia in Ancient Rhetoric*, pp. 100-103; Robbins, 'Pronouncement Stories and Jesus' Blessing of the Children', p. 50; *idem*, 'The Chreia', p. 18; *idem*, 'Pronouncement Stories from a Rhetorical Perspective', pp. 15-16; *idem*, 'The Woman who Touched Jesus' Garment', p. 508; Mack and Robbins, *Patterns of Persuasion in the Gospels*, pp. 17-18.

based on Jesus' statement of a conclusion that is based on an unstated major premise and a narrated minor premise:

Major premise	Touching causes healing power to go forth from Jesus.
Minor premise	Jesus felt power go forth from him.
Conclusion	Someone touched Jesus.

While the major premise that touching causes healing power to go forth from Jesus lies implicitly in the Matthean version, that version of the story does not develop either the minor premise or the conclusion that is present in the Markan version. In the next step in the Markan version, Jesus' search for the person produces emotions in the woman which cause her to come forth and tell him the whole truth (v. 33). At the end of the story, Jesus responds to the woman's truth-telling with an interpretation of her act as faith and with a double blessing to 'go in peace'; and 'be healthy'. Since the healing already occurred earlier in the story, Jesus' saying does not enact the healing, as it does in Matthew, but registers approval of the woman's act. Jesus' saying in the Markan version, therefore, functions as the positive comment (ἐπιφώνειν) that students were taught to add to a brief unit as they were learning the techniques of progymnastic composition.[1]

Thus, the Markan version contains interaction between the main character and his associates as well as between the main character and his primary counter character. Also, it presents argumentative logic about healing power flowing from Jesus' body that the Matthean version does not explore. This way of writing the episode enriches the display of *ethos* and broadens and intensifies the range of emotions (*pathos*). The longer version of Jesus' saying that contains a double blessing of peace and health also is part of this way of writing the episode. The act of writing this story using the technique of amplification, one of the approaches in progymnastic composition, then, changes the function of the saying and introduces a range of rhetorical features not in the Matthean version. Whether Matthew abbreviated Mark's version or Mark expanded Matthew's version can remain a matter for debate, but the rhetorical differences between the two accounts are amazingly clear and should not be missed in interpretation of either story.

The Lukan version (8.43-48) is different yet from the other two versions, featuring no speech by the woman but attributing speech to

---

1. Hock and O'Neil, *The Chreia in Ancient Rhetoric*, pp. 69-70, 98-101.

Peter (v. 45) and containing more speech by Jesus than the other two versions (v. 46). The opening part simply presents the woman touching the fringe of Jesus' garment and being healed (vv. 43-44). Then, in the next two verses (vv. 45-46) Jesus explicitly articulates the syllogism that lies partly in narrative comment and partly in Jesus' speech in Mark:

Major premise	Touching causes healing power to go forth from Jesus.
Minor premise	Jesus felt power go forth from him.
Conclusion	Someone touched Jesus.

After this, the woman not only reveals to everyone the inner logic present in Matthew and Mark about touching and being healed, but she also tells them how she touched Jesus and immediately was healed. When Jesus responds in the final part of the story, then, he is not responding simply to the woman's act, but responding to her public announcement of the logic and success of her act. Since the woman's statement makes Jesus the object of praise in this public setting, Jesus' final saying now guards against offensive self-praise by calling attention to the woman's faith rather than the power that went forth from him. Thus it functions like Epameinondas' saying when he told the men of Thebes:

But it is *your doing*, men of Thebes; with *your help alone* I overthrew the Spartan empire in a day (Plutarch, *Moralia* 542C).[1]

In essence, Jesus is telling the woman;

But it is *your doing*, daughter; with *your faith alone* the power in me caused your flow of blood to cease.

In this instance, then, the saying of Jesus deflects praise the woman has bestowed dramatically upon him in a public setting where he has just insisted that he felt power go forth from him. If he accepts her praise without demurral, he emerges as a person who loves to flaunt his powers and make women recount them in public. His quick response, giving the woman the credit rather than taking the credit himself, escapes this danger and establishes his status as the gracious patron of a needy client.[2]

---

1. Robbins, 'The Woman who Touched Jesus' Garment', p. 513.
2. J.H. Elliott, 'Patronage and Clientism in Early Christian Society: A Short Reading Guide', *Foundations and Facets Forum* 3.4 (1987), pp. 39-48.

In all of the instances cited from Plutarch and the Synoptic Gospels, then, different argumentation accompanies internal variations in the stories. The variations are part of writing in a rhetorical culture. While recitation composition begins the process, techniques like abbreviation, expansion, and commentary create different kinds of argumentation using the same story. These kinds of variations, which are typical in the Synoptic Gospels, exhibit composition as influenced by rhetorical culture rather than scribal culture focused on copying previous documents.

Conclusion

In previous research, verbal similarities among written versions of stories and sayings regularly have been discussed in terms of 'dependence' on written or oral sources. This terminology emerges from a presupposition that written performance of the material was guided by copying an oral or written antecedent. This language and this perception impose goals and procedures on the writers which are inaccurate, since, even if the writer recently had heard or was looking at a version of the story, the version existed in the eye, ear, and mind of the writer as a 'recitation' that should be performed anew rather than a verbal text that should be copied verbatim. Within a rhetorical culture, then, similarity in wording exhibits 'recitation composition'. A writer in rhetorical culture perceives an antecedent oral or written version of a story or saying as a performance, and a new performance can perpetuate as much or as little verbatim wording as is congenial to the writer. The similarities and variations in wording in both Plutarch and the NT Synoptic writers should make it obvious to us that the guiding principle behind their transmission of stories and sayings is recitation composition.

In this paper we have tried to introduce some markers for identifying progymnastic composition. Also, we have explored some argumentative features that accompany variations among versions of stories produced by progymnastic composition. In addition, we have proposed that recitation composition—writing that presupposes that sources and new compositions are performances in particular contexts—marks the boundary between scribal reproduction and progymnastic composition. We have not explored the boundaries between progymnastic composition and other kinds of writing, because this is a topic too large for this paper. As implied earlier in this paper, the documents entitled *Progymnasmata* in antiquity show the outer parameters. The book *Patterns of Persuasion in the Gospels* displays a broader range of progymnastic composition in the Synoptic Gospels than has been displayed here, and it explores more complex rhetorical strategies. A discussion of the ways in which composition in Plutarch's writings goes beyond the progymnastic level of composition in the Synoptic Gospels also must await another context. It has seemed fitting, however, to discuss the place where progymnastic composition begins, since the art of rhetorical interpretation itself is in a new stage of beginnings. With the help of such people as George A. Kennedy, interpreters are challenging the view that writers come into view in biblical texts as copiers of oral and written sources. In fact, most of the writers who produced biblical texts probably were trying to persuade readers to think, feel, and act in particular ways for particular reasons. From our perspective, this means that their placing of writing instrument upon writing material was a rhetorical act.[1]

1. I am grateful to David B. Gower and Mark Ledbetter for their insightful responses to earlier versions of this paper.

THE STYLE OF THE FOURTH GOSPEL AND ANCIENT
LITERARY CRITICAL CONCEPTS OF RELIGIOUS DISCOURSE

Frank Thielman

One of the most puzzling of the Fourth Gospel's many puzzles is its peculiar style. From the standpoint of grammar a number of mysteries emerge. Why, for example, does the author use ἵνα instead of ὅτι in 9.22, instead of ὅτε in 16.2, and instead of an infinitive in 8.56 and 16.7?[1] Why does he use common subordinating conjunctions like μέν, δέ, and γάρ less than the Synoptic Gospels, and connect his sentences, when he does connect them, with καί alone?[2] Why the redundant use of pronouns,[3] the ubiquitous presence of the emphatic personal pronoun,[4] and the variation in words or phrases for the same concept within the space of a few verses?[5]

On the level of the Gospel's narrative structure the list of puzzles is even more extensive and has evoked more frequent comment. Three features of the narrative are especially enigmatic. First, the evangelist makes the most of ambiguity. For example, he frequently makes a statement and then clarifies or refines it. The best known instance of this comes in chs. 3 and 4 where he says first that Jesus entered Judea,

---

1. See also 1.8; 1.22; 6.50; and 9.3.
2. See, for example, 1.24-25. For a comparison of John's use of μέν, δέ, and γάρ with the Synoptic use of these conjunctions see C.F. Burney, *The Aramaic Origin of the Fourth Gospel* (Oxford: Clarendon, 1922), pp. 68-69.
3. The relative in 1.12; 3.32; the demonstrative in 1.33; 4.25; 5.11; 7.18, 45; 10.1; and the third person personal pronoun in 18.11.
4. In all three persons. See, for example, the use of ἐγώ in 18.19, 35, 37, and 19.6; of ὑμεῖς in 14.19, and of αὐτοί in 17.19.
5. See, for example, the three different ways of expressing the phrase 'which when translated says' in 1.38, 41, 42; the different words for 'evil' in 3.19, 20; the variation between καιρός, ὥρα, and χρόνος in 7.6, 30, 33; the two different words for 'rejoice' in 8.56; and the well-known variation between ἀγαπάω and φιλέω in 21.15-19. In addition to these examples, see those provided by E.D. Freed, 'Variations in the Language and Thought of John', *ZNW* 55 (1964), pp. 170-71.

remained there with his disciples, 'and baptized' (3.22; cf. 3.26; 4.1), but later modifies this information by saying, 'Jesus himself did not baptize, but his disciples' (4.2).[1] Something similar occurs twice in ch. 7: Jesus tells his brothers that he is not going to the feast because his time has not yet come (7.8), but then goes to the feast after his brothers had already left (7.10). Similarly, Jesus modifies his statement that Moses gave circumcision to the Jews to mean not that Moses alone gave it, but 'the fathers' (7.22).

Some ideas, moreover, are allowed to stand without clarification as simply ambiguous.[2] Does Jesus execute judgment (cf. 3.17-21, 12.46-48, and 8.50 with 5.22-30, 8.12-20, 8.26, and 12.47)? Does he bear witness to himself (cf. 5.31 with 8.14)? Has the hour come (4.21, 23; 5.25)? John may intend the reader to realize that the answers to these questions are in some senses yes and in others no, but he does not explain the ambiguity explicitly in those terms.

Second, the discourse in the Gospel frequently, although certainly not always, takes place on two levels. People come to Jesus with 'earthly' concerns, but Jesus answers them in 'spiritual' terms. Jesus' conversation with Nicodemus in ch. 3 is perhaps the best illustration of this feature of the Gospel's style. Nicodemus comes to Jesus with the practical concern of wanting to know who Jesus is in light of the signs which he has performed. Jesus does not answer this concern directly but instead uses the ambiguous word ἄνωθεν to describe how one can enter the kingdom of God. Likewise in ch. 4 it is not immediately clear why Jesus responds to the official's request with the statement, 'If you do not see signs and wonders you will not believe' (4.48). The text does not tell us that the official had said or done anything which indicated his unwillingness to believe without seeing a sign. Much the same happens in Jesus' answer to the report of Andrew and Philip that some Greeks wanted to see him (12.20-26), and in his response to Judas' question concerning Jesus' appearance to the disciples but not to the world (14.22-24).

Finally, it has long been recognized that John's narrative contains several abrupt breaks in chronological sequence. The most famous of these are located in 5.47–6.1 and 14.31–15.1. Throughout ch. 5 Jesus is engaged in a heated discourse with the Jews in Jerusalem, but ch. 6

---

1. Translations of all Greek texts are mine unless otherwise indicated in the notes.

2. Freed, 'Variations', pp. 177-92. See also H.M. Teeple, *The Literary Origin of the Gospel of John* (Evanston: Religion and Ethics Institute, 1974), pp. 1-7.

opens with the statement that 'after these things' Jesus crossed the Sea of Galilee. A similar problem appears in 14.31, where the present text creates the strange picture of Jesus asking his disciples to get up and leave in the middle of a discourse that goes on for two more chapters.

There has been no shortage of attempts to account for both the grammatical and the compositional peculiarities of John's style. Compositional peculiarities have frequently been viewed as evidence of clumsy editing or dislocation of the text through some accident.[1] Grammatical problems, on the other hand, have sometimes been explained as evidence of Aramaic influence or, alternately, of John's humble origins as a writer and speaker of simple, Hellenistic Greek.[2]

---

1. On the location of ch. 6 and the problem presented by 14.31 see, among others, Rudolf Bultmann, *The Gospel of John: A Commentary* (trans. G.R. Beasley-Murray; Philadelphia: Westminster, 1971), pp. 209, 631 n. 5; James Moffatt, *The New Testament: A New Translation* (New York: Harper, 1935), p. 159; Barnabas Lindars, *The Gospel of John* (NCB; Grand Rapids: Eerdmans, 1972), pp. 234, 486. Even minute irregularities appear to some scholars to be evidence that the evangelist composed his Gospel in part from various sources at his disposal. Rudolf Bultmann is the Gospel's most famous source critic, although his efforts have not been well received. See D. Moody Smith, *Johannine Christianity: Essays on Its Setting, Sources, and Theology* (Columbia: University of South Carolina Press, 1984), p. 53.

2. A vigorous debate raged during the first half of this century over which of these two possibilities was correct. According to Burney (*Aramaic Origin*, p. 2) students of the Fourth Gospel had raised the possibility of an Aramaic original as early as the seventeenth century. The possibility was not argued in earnest in modern times, however, until the appearance of C.J. Ball's short study, 'Had the Fourth Gospel an Aramaic Archetype?' *ExpTim* 21 (1909), pp. 91-93, Burney's comprehensive monograph, and C.C. Torrey's lengthy article, 'The Aramaic Origin of the Gospel of John', *HTR* 16 (1923), pp. 305-44. The claim that John wrote in the simple Greek of the common person had already been opposed to the argument for Semitic (if not specifically Aramaic) influence by Adolf Deissmann, *Light from the Ancient East* (trans. Lionel R.M. Strachan; 4th edn; London: Hodder & Stoughton, 1927; 1st German edn, 1908), pp. 131-45. Devastating arguments specifically against the claims of Burney and Torrey came from, among others, O.T. Allis ('The Alleged Aramaic Origin of the Fourth Gospel', *Princeton Theological Review* 26 [1928], pp. 531-72) and E.C. Colwell (*The Greek of the Fourth Gospel: A Study of Its Aramaisms in the Light of Hellenistic Greek* [Chicago: University of Chicago Press, 1931]). Colwell concluded (p. 130) that the Gospel's Greek is what we should expect of an author, writing in Greek, who was familiar with the Synoptic Gospels and possibly the LXX. This conclusion seems to have carried the day. See, for example, the comments of C.K. Barrett, *The Gospel according to St. John* (2nd edn; Philadelphia: Westminster, 1978), p. 11; *The Gospel of John and Judaism* (trans. D. Moody Smith; Philadelphia: Fortress, 1975), pp. 23, 31; Rudolf Schnackenburg,

There are indications within the Gospel itself, however, that John's peculiar grammar and his unusual compositional style are related, for in at least one important respect they complement each other. Redundancy is a feature of John's style both at the grammatical and the compositional level. Not only does the evangelist unnecessarily repeat demonstrative and personal pronouns,[1] but he frequently repeats the important words and actions of the leading characters in his narrative. In 1.30 he repeats the words which John the Baptist originally spoke in 1.15; in 4.39 he repeats the Samaritan woman's words from 4.29; in 8.52 the Jews repeat Jesus' words from 8.51; Jesus repeats his own words from 13.16 in 15.20; the story of the blind man in ch. 9 is recalled in 10.21 and 11.37; and a reminder of the raising of Lazarus in ch. 11 appears three times in ch. 12.[2] The ponderous nature of the Greek grammar, attributed by C.F. Burney and his allies to Aramaic influence and by Adolf Deissmann and E.C. Colwell to the unsophisticated nature of John's Greek, therefore, seems instead to be a calculated feature of the book as a whole.

Can a single hypothesis about the nature of the Gospel account both for the Gospel's compositional shape and the unusual nature of its grammar?[3] The answer to this question may lie buried in the works of several ancient literary critics who possessed distinct ideas about the kind of writing appropriate to religious themes.[4]

The Gospel according to St. John (trans. Kevin Smith *et al.*; 3 vols.; New York: Herder & Herder, 1968-83), I, pp. 111-14.

1. See p. 169 nn. 3 and 4.

2. See 12.1-2, 9-10, 17. Other examples of this phenomenon appear in 4.46, 54; 18.9, 14; 19.39; 21.20.

3. Bultmann has already asked this question and answered it affirmatively, for he regarded the Semitic cast of certain parts of the Gospel's grammar as a clue, along with narrative peculiarities, to the presence of the evangelist's sources. See, for example, *John*, p. 122 n. 2, and the comments of Smith, *Johannine Christianity*, pp. 41-42.

4. That I am able to speak intelligibly of such matters at all is due in large measure to the pedagogical skill and immense learning of Professor Kennedy. Those of us who studied with him will not forget the inspiration of his warmth, humor, and intellectual rigor.

The Relationship between Theological Content and Literary Style in Antiquity

Three stylistic characteristics are often connected with religious themes in literary critical treatises from the first century BC to the second century AD: sublimity (*hypsos*), obscurity (*asapheia*), and solemnity (*semnotēs*). These concepts cannot be neatly separated from one another in the sources, but we shall view them separately here in order to observe their distinctives.

1. *Sublimity*

Two ancient literary scholars, Philo and 'Longinus', connect the stylistic quality of lofty or sublime expression with religious themes.[1] Philo uses the term *hypsēgoria* for this quality whereas 'Longinus' uses *hypsos*; but the two terms, at least for these authors, mean much the same thing. In *Det.* 79 Philo uses the term *hypsēgoria* to show the necessity of combining eloquent speech with lofty thoughts. The wise person who cannot communicate wisdom, he says, will be ineffective (43-44). 'Longinus', approaching the subject from a different angle, says that 'it is impossible that those whose thoughts and habits all their lives long are petty and servile should flash out anything wonderful, worthy of immortal life' (9.3).[2] Philo hopes that the wise person will use lofty expression while 'Longinus' hopes that the person aspiring to lofty expression will be wise; but in both authors great thoughts and lofty expression go hand in hand.[3]

Similarly, in *Quis Her.* 4 Philo explains why Moses was 'a man of slight voice and slow of speech from the time when God first began to converse with him' (Exod. 4.10).[4] The reason, he says, is that the natural organs of his speech were hindered in proportion to the lofty expression (*hypsēgoria*) of the thoughts within his mind. At issue here

---

1. Aristophanes' *The Frogs* is the earliest extant source which uses the term *hypsos* in a literary connection. The play makes Aeschylus say that 'greatness' (*megalos*) of thought requires lofty expression (1057-1060). Here, however, the concept is not tied to religious themes as it is in Philo, and later in 'Longinus'.

2. Translations of 'Longinus' come from *'Longinus', On the Sublime* (trans. W. Hamilton Fyfe; LCL; Cambridge, MA: Harvard University Press, 1932).

3. See also D.A. Russell, *Longinus, On the Sublime* (Oxford: Clarendon, 1964), pp. xl-xli, and T. Mommsen, *The History of Rome* (trans. W.P. Dickson; New York: Scribners, 1899), II, pp. 182, 251.

4. Translations of Philo are from *Philo* (trans. F.H. Colson and G.H. Whitaker; LCL; 10 vols.; Cambridge, MA: Harvard University Press, 1929-53).

is not the *presence* of the lofty verbal expression of ideas (as in *Det.* 79), but the *lack* of lofty verbal expression as a direct consequence of the loftiness of one's mental discourse.

Admittedly, the connection between Philo's concept of *hypsēgoria* and 'Longinus'' ideas on *hypsos* in this passage is less than direct. Three similarities, however, are clear. First, for 'Longinus', as for Philo, sublimity is viewed as a point of contact with the eternal and the divine. Just as the *hypsēgoria* of the Philonic Moses derived from his discourse with God, so *hypsos* in 'Longinus' connects humankind with eternity and allows it to 'rise near to the mighty mind of God' (36.1). Thus, 'Longinus' admonishes Terentianus that 'it is not right to display an unseemly triviality before an audience of all the ages' (πρὸς τὸν αἰῶνα, 4.7) and claims that the sublime is what gave to the greatest historians and poets 'immortal fame' (τὸν αἰῶνα, 1.3).[1]

Second, just as in Philo, so in 'Longinus', inspiration gives the student the ability to achieve sublimity of expression. Inspiration, it is true, comes through 'imitation' of the great poets (13.2), but 'imitation' is not conceived of here as the rote exercise of copying. Rather it is an infusion of the 'genius of those old writers' into the souls of 'their admirers' in a way comparable to the inspiration of the Pythian priestess by 'the divine power' (13.2).[2]

Finally, just as Philo views Moses as dumbfounded by the sublimity of eternal thoughts, so 'Longinus' does not understand *hypsos* as impeccable diction or clear expression, but as 'that which contains much food for reflection' (7.3).[3] It can, therefore, be expressed in silence (9.2) and is most often found among those whose style is not pure according to the common canons of grammar and rhetoric (33.2). It may, in fact, be incomprehensible to those of the author's own time:

> But if a man shrinks at the very thought of saying anything that exceeds the comprehension of his own time, then must all the conceptions of that man's nature be like some blind, half formed embryo, all too abortive for the life of posthumous fame (14.2).

1. C.P. Segal, '*Hypsos* and the Problem of Cultural Decline in the *De Sublimitate*', *Harvard Studies in Classical Philology* 64 (1959), p. 124; G.K. Kustas, *Studies in Byzantine Rhetoric* (Analekta Vlatadon 17; Thessaloniki: Patriarchal Institute for Patristic Studies, 1973), p. 73.

2. Segal, '*Hypsos*', pp. 126-27.

3. Quint. 8.3.83-86 uses the Greek term *emphasis* and *Her.* 4.53.67 uses the Latin word *significatio* to describe this quality.

Once again, loftiness of expression is connected with obscurity of expression, and the whole concept appears in the context of discussions about God and the eternal.[1]

2. *Obscurity*

It thus becomes crucial to discuss the second characteristic of religious style according to the literary critical texts of antiquity: 'obscurity' (*asapheia, obscuritas*). Obscurity was viewed in two ways by literary theorists from Aristotle to Hermogenes.[2] On one hand, it was regarded as a stylistic fault, as in Aristotle's *Rhet.* 3.3.3 where Aristotle criticizes those who attempt to dress prose as if it were poetry and thus produce tiresome redundancies because 'they create by their idle chatter... obscurity'.[3] Alternatively, it was considered useful for three purposes. First, it allowed one to avoid the pitfall of being so 'clear' as to be unadorned. Although Aristotle does not use the word *asapheia* in a positive way of style, he does say that 'it is necessary to make speech exotic (*xenen*); for people marvel at what is remote, and the marvellous is pleasant' (*Rhet.* 3.2.2-3). Much later the second-century rhetor Hermogenes, although still uneasy about using the word *asapheia* positively, says that *asapheia* is not on its own a vice of speech because it shares certain properties with 'emphasis' and other figures which are used to moderate clarity with 'a certain grandeur and dignity' (240.24–241.9).[4]

Second, it was useful for a variety of purposes in declamation. In judicial settings it could be used to confuse the judge when the evidence did not favor the speaker[5] or to ready the judge for receiving

---

1. Kustas, *Studies*, pp. 72-75, and Segal, '*Hypsos*', *passim*.

2. See the useful comments of Kustas, *Studies*, pp. 63-100.

3. See Kustas, *Studies*, pp. 64-67.

4. References to Hermogenes are to page and line numbers in Hugo Rabe, ed. *Hermogenis: Opera* (Rhetores Graeci VI; Stuttgart: Teubner, 1969). I am indebted to Kustas, *Studies*, p. 82, for bringing this passage to my attention.

5. Kustas (*Studies*, p. 78 n. 2) mentions in this regard an anonymous work, 'the Seguerianus', which advises the aspiring rhetor, 'you will also produce obscurity (*asapheian*) if you dissolve the proper sequence of events into an illogical narrative, pass over some things and put others out of order. One who desires to deceive the judge by means of obscurity (*anakolouthia*) will do these things in this way' (my translation). See also the comment of Philodemus, to which Kustas (*Studies*, p. 66 n. 1) refers, that 'some obscurity is purposeful and some is not. Purposeful obscurity occurs when one knows nothing or has nothing to say and hides this through obscurity in order that he might seem to write or say something useful' (my translation).

instruction,[1] and in declamation in general it proved useful for creating the 'figure' of 'emphasis'.[2] Third, and most important for our purposes, it provided an appropriate means of expressing religious themes. It was already used to this end in Greek society by the oracle at Delphi whose obscure utterances could be understood in a number of ways.[3] Much later, Diogenes Laertius speaks of the notoriety which Heraclitus' treatise *Concerning Nature* had achieved because of its obscurity. The work was so difficult, says Diogenes, that the king of Persia asked Heraclitus to come to his palace and explain it (4.13-14), and the poet Scythinus composed a jingle in its 'honor':

> Do not be in too great a hurry to get to the end of Heraclitus the Ephesian's book: the path is hard to travel. Gloom is there and darkness devoid of light. But if an initiate be your guide, the path shines brighter than the sunlight (9.16).[4]

The last sentence is reminiscent of another statement of Diogenes' description which specifically connects the obscurity of the book with religious concerns:

> This book he deposited in the temple of Artemis and, according to some, he deliberately made it the more obscure (*asaphesteron*) in order that none but adepts should approach it, and lest familiarity should breed contempt (9.6).[5]

Demetrius' treatise *On Style* also mentions the appropriateness of obscurity to religious themes. In a discussion of *allegoria* he uses the mysteries as an example:

> The Mysteries are revealed in an allegorical form in order to inspire such shuddering and awe as are associated with darkness and night. Allegory also is not unlike darkness and night (2.101).[6]

---

1. See Quint. 4.3.41-42, and Kustas, *Studies*, p. 78.

2. *Her.* 4.53.67.

3. M. Fuhrmann, 'Das Problem der Dunkelheit in der rhetorischen und literaraesthetischen Theorie der Antike', *Immanente Aesthetik Kolloquium Köln, 1964*, II, *Poetik und Hermeneutik* (ed. W. Iser; Munich: W. Fink, 1966), pp. 51-54.

4. Translations of Diogenes Laertius are from his *Lives of Eminent Philosophers* (trans. R.D. Hicks; LCL; Cambridge, MA: Harvard University Press, 1959).

5. Kustas (*Studies*, p. 81) brought this passage to my attention. Diogenes, who wrote in the latter half of the third century AD, based his work on earlier sources and thus is helpful for understanding literary concerns around the time that John's Gospel was composed.

6. See also Kustas, *Studies*, p. 69. Translations of Demetrius come from *Demetrius, On Style* (trans. W. Hamilton Fyfe and W. Rhys Roberts; LCL; Cambridge, MA: Harvard University Press, 1932).

Thus the stylistic device of 'obscurity' was not only an appropriate means of elevating style in order to keep it from becoming too commonplace, or of emphasizing a point in judicial declamations, but of leading the adept from the earthly to the spiritual and of preserving the mysterious nature of the religious.

3. *Solemnity*

Solemnity (*semnotēs*) begins to receive considerable attention in the second century AD, and like sublimity and obscurity is said to be particularly suited for religious themes. Like sublimity, moreover, solemnity could be achieved by means of obscurity. Hermogenes' treatise *On Types* discusses solemnity as the first part of a larger treatment of the way in which one can achieve 'grandeur' (*megethos*) or 'dignity' (*onkos*). The discussion of 'grandeur' follows directly upon a discussion of clarity and serves as a corrective to those who have allowed their lucid expressions to lapse into the commonplace (241). Thus, although Hermogenes does not use the word 'obscure' to describe solemnity, the two concepts are related in his thinking. In fact, at the end of his discussion of clarity, and apparently by way of transition to the subject of solemnity, Hermogenes explicitly says that 'obscurity is not in itself a defect of speech' (οὐ γὰρ ἥ γε ἁπλῶς ἀσάφεια κακία ἂν εἴη λόγου, 240.25).

Solemnity, says Hermogenes, is appropriate to the treatment of four kinds of 'thoughts' (ἔννοιαι). It should accompany, first, general statements 'about the gods as gods' (such as God's impassivity and goodness as described by Plato, 242.21–243.16); second, statements about 'truly divine matters' (such as the functions of nature, 243.22–245.3); third, 'matters which are by nature divine, but are seen for the most part in human life' (the immortality of the soul, righteousness, and prudence, for example, 245.3–246.1); and finally, matters which 'concern humanity alone, but which are great and glorious' (such as notable battles, 246.1-9). All except the last of these are clearly religious in character.

An understanding of the type of style that was appropriate to religious writing, therefore, was articulated by grammarians and rhetorical theorists for a hundred years on either side of the composition of the Fourth Gospel. The connection of sublimity, obscurity, and solemnity with religious writing is explicit in the sources of Diogenes, as well as in Philo, Demetrius, and Hermogenes. Although it is less explicit in 'Longinus', it comes to the surface in his concern for inspiration and eternity.

The Fourth Gospel and Ancient Concepts of Religious Style

If we compare the language and organization of the Fourth Gospel with the ancient stylistic philosophy outlined above, several parallels emerge which are pertinent to the discussion of the Gospel's unusual style. If the stumbling of Moses' speech can be attributed to the *hypsēgoria* of his thoughts in Philo, and if in 'Longinus' one of the characteristics of sublime writing is its use of asyndeton (19),[1] then the Gospel's halting, at times epigrammatic, quality should probably not be ascribed to an Aramaic background. It is instead 'intentional, to recount the sacred events in a grave and simple manner, and to present the discourses of Jesus in the solemn style of revelation'.[2]

This tends to confirm the findings of A.-J. Festugière. He compared the style of John's Gospel with that of Xenophon, Luke, *Corpus Hermeticum IV*, Mark, and a non-literary epistle, and he found that John's use of asyndeton did not derive from 'méconnaissance des lois élémentaries de la prose antique',[3] but that his was a literary use of this figure, comparable to that in Aristophanes and *Corpus Hermeticum IV*.[4]

Furthermore, the concepts of emphasis and obscurity already addressed by Philo and 'Longinus' with respect to elevated spiritual discourse, mentioned in the sources of Diogenes Laertius, and related specifically to religious literature by Demetrius and Hermogenes, go a long way toward explaining other stylistic puzzles of the Gospel. The quality of 'emphasis' which 'Longinus' extols as a characteristic of sublimity (7.3), and Hermogenes describes as an aid to the desirable kind of obscurity (240.25) appears in John's prologue, which becomes comprehensible only after reading the entire Gospel.[5] It is likewise present in the frequently obscure two levels of discourse which begin to become clear only after information from the rest of the Gospel has

---

1. Polysyndeton, says Longinus, deadens sublimity (21.2).
2. Schnackenburg, *John*, I, p. 110.
3. *Observations stylistiques sur l'Evangile de S. Jean* (Paris: Editions Klincksieck, 1974), p. 34).
4. Festugière, *Observations*, pp. 35-39.
5. George A. Kennedy, *New Testament Interpretation through Rhetorical Criticism* (Chapel Hill, NC: University of North Carolina Press, 1984), p. 120.

been digested. And finally, it appears in the frequent use of double meanings[1] which give the reader pause and serve to 'emphasize' the point at hand (*Her.* 4.53.67).

The variety of ways in which John refers to the names of his chief characters, his variation of OT quotations formulas, and his seemingly contradictory statements[2] might also be the result of an intentional attempt to give emphasis and obscurity to his style. John's variations in language are illumined both by 'Longinus'' praise of Demosthenes for the 'reckless audacity of his inversions' (23.4) and by his advice to use grammatical variation as an aid to obtaining sublimity (23.1). Likewise, the evangelist's apparent contradictions in thought—although they go beyond what Quintilian, the *Rhetorica ad Herennium*, and even 'Longinus' would consider proper—can be explained in terms of the Alexandrine doctrine[3] that apparent contradiction and obscurity lead the reader to pursue a meaning higher than mere words can convey. The large number of variations and the seemingly contradictory statements in John, therefore, shroud the document with a mystery which was entirely appropriate to religious writing in the ancient world.

The Gospel's celebrated symbolism, by its obscurity, also contributes to its mysterious aura. C.H. Dodd points out that whereas in the Synoptic Gospels Jesus teaches chiefly through parables, in the Fourth Gospel he does so principally through symbols and allegory.[4] Thus the allegory of the good shepherd (ch. 10) does not contain one point, like most of Jesus' Synoptic parables; but symbol and reality inter-penetrate in such a way that numerous qualities of the good shepherd are derived from the comparison: he is the guardian of the flock, door of the sheep pen, and the one who calls his sheep by name. A similar quality can be seen in the allegory of the vine (ch. 15)[5] and in the symbols of water (ch. 4) and bread (ch. 6). J. Sugitt contends, moreover, that Torah is also vested with symbolic value in the Gospel. It is particularly interesting, says Sugitt, that although the equation 'Jesus equals the Torah' is never stated in so many words, the Jewish

---

1. See, for example, ἄνωθεν for 'anew' and 'again', 3.7; πνεῦμα for 'spirit' and 'wind', 3.8; and ὑψόω for 'exalt' and 'crucify', 3.14.
2. See Freed, 'Variations', pp. 167-97.
3. See Philo, *Det.* 81.
4. *The Interpretation of the Fourth Gospel* (Cambridge: Cambridge University Press, 1953), p. 134.
5. Dodd, *Interpretation*, pp. 135-36.

reader of the Gospel could not help but realize that Jesus has been systematically presented in John as a replacement for the Torah. John seeks 'to assist his reader to understand the meaning of the Old Testament, and he does this not by spelling out the exact meaning of the Old Testament texts but by supplying hints and allusions to awaken and enlarge the imagination. . .'[1] A better example of what it means to give the reader 'more food for thought than the mere words themselves suggest' (Long. *Subl.* 7.7) could hardly be found.

Finally, is it not possible to regard the abrupt transitions which we encounter at such places as 5.47–6.1 and 14.31–15.1 as a purposeful attempt at obscurity? There was certainly precedent for such a procedure, as Dionysius of Halicarnassus demonstrates in his criticisms of Thucydides.[2] Dionysius is not only unhappy with Thucydides' obscure language, but with the arrangement of his work as well. In ch. 9 of *On Thucydides* he complains that unlike other historians, Thucydides did not arrange his history according to place or simple chronology, but by 'summers and winters'. In doing so, says Dionysius, he did not give greater clarity to his history, but 'greater obscurity' (here, *dysparakolouthētotera*).[3] Dionysius' illustration of this obscurity is revealing:

> Thus in the third book. . . he begins his account of the Mitylenean episode, but before completing this he turns to the Lacedaemonians; and he does not even round these off before describing the siege of Plataea.[4]

Furthermore, Dionysius hints that Thucydides composed his history obscurely on purpose, so that it would not be understood by the common person, but by 'those who have passed through the standard courses to the study of rhetoric and philosophy' (50).[5]

A similar obscurity of arrangement, but in a purely religious context, is found in Philo and Clement of Alexandria. In his massive commentary on Genesis, Philo reveals no principles of organization, for he is addressing himself to the initiate and does not desire to make

---

1. 'John XVII.17: HO LOGOS HO SOS ALĒTHEIA ESTIN', *JTS* 35 (1984), p. 114.

2. Cf. Kustas, *Studies*, pp. 66-68.

3. This was a technical term in Greek for the stylistic quality of obscurity. See Quint. 4.1.40.

4. Translations of Dionysius come from *Dionysius of Halicarnassus: The Critical Essays in Two Volumes* (trans. Stephen Usher; LCL; Cambridge, MA: Harvard University Press, 1974).

5. I am again indebted to Kustas's study for bringing Dionysius' critique of Thucydides to my attention. See his helpful comments in *Studies*, pp. 66-67.

himself clear to the masses.[1] The same idea is at work in Clement's *Stromata*, which is constructed in its patch-work manner specifically to keep out those who are not 'gnostics' (6.1).

It is true that the structure of John's Gospel parallels none of these examples exactly. The similarity is sufficiently close, however, to suggest that the evangelist may have obscured the organizational pattern of his Gospel by design—to keep out those whose eyes were blind and whose hearts hard (12.40).[2]

This contention is further supported by the remarkable similarity between Hermogenes' treatment of solemnity (*semnotēs*), and certain aspects of John's style. Hermogenes divides his essay on solemnity into two parts. In the first, as we saw above, he discusses the thoughts (ἔννοιαι) appropriate to solemn discourse. In the second he treats the three means (μέθοδοι) by which solemnity can be obtained.

Of the four types of solemn thoughts treated in the first section, only two are strictly relevant to the Gospel of John: thoughts about 'God as God', and thoughts about 'truly divine matters'. In discussing the first of these Hermogenes says that statements about divinities which make them appear human do not possess solemnity. The writer produces solemn statements about the gods when he describes qualities which only gods possess. Hermogenes illustrates what he means with three general statements drawn from Plato's *Timaeus*:

> [God] was good, and for one who is good no envy springs up concerning anything. . . For God desired that all things be good and nothing bad, according to his power. . . For God took everything which was visible, not when it was still, but when it was moving in an erroneous and disorderly fashion. . . (243.6-11).

When he treats the subject of 'divine matters' Hermogenes says explicitly what these illustrations have demonstrated—that universality is the key to solemn expression:

---

1. Helmut Koester, *History, Culture, and Religion of the Hellenistic Age*, vol. I, *Introduction to the New Testament* (Philadelphia: Fortress, 1982), pp. 277-78.

2. This explanation seems at least as plausible as theories of physical damage to the text or clumsy redaction and is consistent with the findings of Wayne Meeks's now widely accepted argument that John is a 'book for insiders' in 'The Man from Heaven in Johannine Sectarianism', *JBL* 91 (1972), pp. 44-52. Smith (*Johannine Christianity*, p. 3), summing up his own conclusions as well as those of several scholars' comments that '. . . on any reading of the Gospel and Epistles there appears. . . a sense of exclusiveness, a sharp delineation of the community from the world'.

> To put it simply, whatever is said in a universal and general way possesses some measure of solemnity of thought, and especially if one continues to do these things throughout [the discourse] (245.15-18).

These ideas, in their emphasis upon universality, describe the character of many of the statements about Jesus and God in the Fourth Gospel. Consider, for example, these two descriptions:

> Everything was made through him and without him not one thing was made (1.3).
> God is spirit and those who worship him must worship him in spirit and truth (4.23).

In the second part of his section on solemnity Hermogenes speaks of the methods by which solemnity is obtained. There are three, and the Gospel uses each of them. First, the orator must speak exactly and directly, without hesitation (cf. John's use of parataxis and asyndeton). Second, he should make use of allegory (cf. Jn 4; 6; 10; 15). Third, and most important, he should

> hint at something that would be a solemn thought, as is done in initiation ceremonies in mystery religions. . . . If it seems that we ourselves know something that we cannot reveal clearly, we thereby create a certain amount of Grandeur and Solemnity as far as the thought is concerned. . . (246.23–247.3).[1]

In this last statement we can detect the same concept which appears in Philo's contention that Moses was struck dumb by the elevation of his thoughts, 'Longinus'' idea that sublime writing should mean more than what it says on a surface reading, and John's use of symbolism, ambiguity, and two-level discourse.

Conclusion

If the above proposal is correct, then the unusual features of John's grammar and narrative are intentional. They are due, not to the accidental rearrangement of codex leaves, to the inelegant handling of sources or to a translator who knew Aramaic better than Greek. Rather they are a product of the evangelist's desire to write in a way appropriate to the mysterious and profound nature of his subject. Following certain canons of ancient religious literary style, he has

---

1. Here I have used the translation of Cecil W. Wooten, *Hermogenes' On Types of Style* (Chapel Hill: University of North Carolina Press, 1987), p. 21.

attempted to produce a narrative which would mean more than was immediately apparent in the words themselves and would therefore lead the reader to appreciate the higher wisdom of the Gospel's teaching. Perhaps Clement of Alexandria, himself a master of obscurity, was not so wide of the mark when he offered the following explanation of the Gospel's origin:

> John, last of all, aware that the outward facts were revealed by the gospels, was encouraged by his pupils and divinely inspired by the Spirit to fashion a spiritual gospel.[1]

---

1. Euseb. *Hist. Eccl.* 6.14.

PAUL'S SPEECH TO THE EPHESIAN ELDERS (ACTS 20.17-38): EPIDEICTIC RHETORIC OF FAREWELL*

Duane F. Watson

The speeches in Acts have received much attention in the scholarship of this century. Many have yielded to rhetorical analysis in recent years,[1] but the unique speech of Paul to the Ephesian elders has not. Part 1 of this essay summarizes the main issues involved in interpreting the speech, and Part 2 presents a detailed rhetorical analysis of the speech which addresses these and other issues. The analysis is informed by Greco-Roman rhetorical handbooks[2] and is conducted according to the methodology proposed by Dr Kennedy in his work, *New Testament Interpretation through Rhetorical Criticism*.[3]

The Speech in Critical Study

Whereas speeches prior to Acts 20 are deliberative and addressed to potential converts, and those following Acts 20 are forensic speeches of defense against charges, this speech is the only one that Paul delivers to Christians. It marks the conclusion of Paul's missionary enterprises in the East and is addressed to the elders of the city of his most extensive work.

---

    * This essay is written in honor of Dr Kennedy, from whom I learned the art of rhetorical criticism, and for whom I have the deepest respect.

    1. E.g. Jerome Neyrey, 'The Forensic Defense Speech and Paul's Trial Speeches in Acts 22–26: Form and Function', *Luke–Acts: New Perspectives from the Society of Biblical Literature Seminar* (ed. Charles H. Talbert; New York: Crossroads, 1984), pp. 210-24.

    2. These handbooks are given in the list of abbreviations introducing this volume.

    3. (Chapel Hill, NC: University of North Carolina Press, 1984). Kennedy provides a brief analysis of this speech on pp. 132-33.

Regarding literary genre, the speech is usually identified as a farewell address.[1] Several topics of the farewell address are found here: the testator assembles the elders of the community, his sons, and/or family (v. 17); rehearses his irreproachable conduct, protests his innocence, and calls others to imitate his life (vv. 18-27, 33-35); announces his impending death (vv. 22-25, 29, 38); appeals to the community tradition and explains the reward and punishment meted out for obedience or disobedience to it (v. 32); transmits the tradition to his descendants or disciples (v. 28); gives moral exhortation (vv. 28, 35); warns of persecution and false teachers to come after his death (vv. 29-30); and closes with prayers and tears (v. 37).[2]

Unlike the identification of genre, no consensus exists about the origin of the speech.[3] Often the same data are used to support a variety

---

1. Johannes Munck, 'Discours d'adieu dans le Nouveau Testament et dans la littérature biblique', *Aux Sources de la tradition chrétienne. Mélanges offerts à M. Maurice Goguel à l'occasion de son soixante-dixième anniversaire* (ed. Oscar Cullmann and Philippe Menoud; Bibliothèque Théologique; Neuchâtel: Delachaux & Niestlé, 1950), pp. 155-70; Hans-Joachim Michel, *Die Abschiedsrede des Paulus an die Kirche Apg 20,17-38: Motivgeschichte und theologische Bedeutung* (SANT 35; Munich: Kösel, 1973). William S. Kurz ('Luke 22.14-38 and Greco-Roman and Biblical Farewell Addresses', *JBL* 104 [1985], pp. 251-68) and Jerome Neyrey (*The Passion According to Luke* [Theological Inquiries; New York: Paulist, 1985], pp. 43-48) compare Acts 20.17-38 with the farewell address of Jesus in Lk. 22.14-38. Cf. J.W. Bowker ('Speeches in Acts: A Study in Proem and Yelammedenu Form', *NTS* 14 [1967], pp. 96-111) who argues that the form of the Acts speeches may be explained as the modification of the Jewish proem homily of the synagogue.

2. There is some debate about identifying the genre of the speech as a farewell address. Farewell addresses are usually given by someone on the verge of death, and this is not the case here. Chr. Burchard, 'Paulus in der Apostelgeschichte', *TLZ* 100 (1975), p. 889; Jan Lambrecht, 'Paul's Farewell-Address at Miletus (Acts 20,17-38)', *Les Actes des Apôtres: Traditions, rédaction, théologie* (ed. J. Kremer; BETL 48; Gembloux: Leuven University Press, 1979), pp. 332-33.

However, as Paul is portrayed he may not know exactly what the afflictions and imprisonment awaiting him will entail, but he does know that he will never see the Ephesians again (vv. 25, 38). Cf. Evald Lövestam, 'Paul's Address at Miletus', *ST* 41 (1987), pp. 2-3.

3. The question of the historicity of the setting of the speech is also raised. The waiting at Miletus while the Ephesian elders traveled 50 kilometers does not seem congruous with Paul's expressed haste (Acts 20.16). W. Grundmann ('Paulus in Ephesus', *Helikon* 4 [1964], pp. 71-78), Charles K. Barrett ('Paul's Address to the Ephesian Elders', *God's Christ and His People. Studies in Honour of Nils Alstrup Dahl* [ed. Jacob Jervell and Wayne A. Meeks; Oslo, Bergen, Tromsö: Universitetsforlaget, 1977], pp. 108-109) and Gerd Lüdemann (*Early Christianity According to the Traditions in Acts* [trans. John Bowden; Philadelphia: Fortress, 1989], pp. 229-

of positions depending upon an author's presuppositions. On one hand, F.F. Bruce writes, 'Almost certainly Luke heard it [the speech] himself. . . , and may even have taken shorthand notes'.[1] Since the speech is in a 'we' section (20.5–21.18), it is also argued that Luke was an eyewitness, and the many expressions paralleled in the Pauline epistles are viewed as the natural result of authentic reminiscence of Paul's own speech.[2] On the other hand, Hans Conzelmann states, 'He [Luke] has composed the details as well as the speech itself'.[3] This more

30) suggest that the setting in Miletus is authentic, but calling for the Ephesian elders is not.

   1. *The Acts of the Apostles* (Grand Rapids: Eerdmans, 1951), p. 377 (hereafter *Acts*). Cf. his *The Speeches in the Acts* (London: Tyndale, 1942), pp. 8, 26-27 (hereafter *Speeches*); 'The Speeches in Acts—Thirty Years After', *Reconciliation and Hope: New Testament Essays in Atonement and Eschatology, Presented to L.L. Morris on his 60th Birthday* (ed. Robert Banks; Grand Rapids: Eerdmans, 1974), pp. 55-58; *The Book of the Acts* (rev. edn; NICNT; Grand Rapids: Eerdmans, 1988), p. 388. See also Percy Gardner, 'The Speeches of St. Paul in Acts', *Cambridge Biblical Essays* (ed. H.B. Swete; Cambridge: Macmillan, 1909), p. 403; Colin J. Hemer, 'The Speeches of Acts. I. The Ephesian Elders at Miletus', *TynBul* 40 (1989), pp. 77-85. I. Howard Marshall (*The Acts of the Apostles* [TNTC 5; Leicester: InterVarsity/ Grand Rapids: Eerdmans, 1980], pp. 329-30) and David John Williams (*Acts* [GNC; New York: Harper & Row, 1985], p. 347) both posit a considerable role for Luke as author. Henry Cadbury (*The Making of Luke–Acts* [London: SPCK, 1958], pp. 189-90) posits Luke's extensive editing of an oral or written source. Kennedy (*New Testament Interpretation*, pp. 114-15, 133) says that Luke either was an eyewitness or used an eyewitness account.
   2. Hemer, 'Speeches', pp. 77, 79, 81, 85; Colin Hemer, *The Book of Acts in the Setting of Hellenistic History* (ed. Conrad H. Gempf; WUNT 49; Tübingen: Mohr, 1989), pp. 418-27; Kennedy, *New Testament Interpretation*, p. 133. For lists and discussions of these parallels, see Henry Cadbury, 'The Speeches in Acts', *The Beginnings of Christianity* (ed. F.J. Foakes Jackson and Kirsopp Lake; 5 vols.; London: Macmillan, 1920–33; repr. Grand Rapids: Baker, 1979), V, pp. 412-13; Bruce, *Acts*, pp. 377-83; Lambrecht, 'Farewell-Address', pp. 319-28; Barrett, 'Ephesian Elders', pp. 109-16; Hemer, 'Speeches', pp. 82-85.
   3. Hans Conzelmann, *Acts of the Apostles* (trans. James Limburg *et al.*; ed. Eldon Jay Epp; Hermeneia; Philadelphia: Fortress, 1987), p. 173. Cf. Ernst Haenchen, *The Acts of the Apostles* (ET from KEKS 14th edn, 1965; Oxford: Basil Blackwell, 1971), p. 590; Martin Dibelius, 'The Speeches in Acts and Ancient Historiography', *Studies in the Acts of the Apostles* (trans. Mary Ling and Paul Schubert; ed. Heinrich Greeven; New York: Charles Scribner's Sons, 1956), pp. 138-45, 157-58, 164, 182; J. Dupont, *Le Discours de Milet* (LD 32; Paris: Les Éditions du Cerf, 1961), pp. 26-30; Eduard Schweizer, 'Concerning the Speeches in Acts', *Studies in Luke–Acts* (ed. Leander E. Keck and J. Louis Martyn; Philadelphia: Fortress, 1980), pp. 208-16 = *ThZ* 13 (1957), pp. 1-11; John T. Townsend, 'The Speeches in Acts', *ATR* 42 (1960), pp. 153, 159; Cadbury, 'Speeches', pp. 402-403, 405, 421;

closely reflects the position of the majority of scholars writing on this issue. Pauline parallels are explained as Luke's attempt to give his composition a Pauline ethos. It is pointed out that the speeches of Acts are similar enough in structure and content, and share enough Lukan features to posit Lukan authorship for all of them.[1] Also, the strong similarities with Jesus' farewell address in Luke 22 make the Lukan authorship of this farewell address very probable.[2]

Also debated is the probability of Luke's use of oral and/or written tradition in the composition of the speech. Luke has been said to use: (1) abstracts of sources traceable to Paul's actual address;[3] (2) 1 Thessalonians as a model;[4] (3) Paul's letters, especially 1 Thessalonians and perhaps Ephesians;[5] (4) biographical traditions about Paul or Pauline legend;[6] (5) a written source, part placed here and part in 22.1-21;[7] (6) a local cult history tied to the church at Ephesus which took the shape of a farewell address of Paul;[8] and (7) the shepherd motif of Ezekiel 33–34 (vv. 28-35).[9]

The structure of the speech has evaded scholarly consensus as well.[10] C.K. Barrett writes, 'It is formless and repetitious, and does little

---

Max Wilcox, 'A Foreword to the Study of the Speeches in Acts', *Christianity, Judaism and Other Greco-Roman Cults: Studies for Morton Smith at Sixty* (ed. Jacob Neusner; SJLA 12; Leiden: Brill, 1975), I, pp. 206-25.

1. Schweizer, 'Speeches', p. 214.

2. Lambrecht, 'Farewell-Address', p. 326; Gerhard A. Krodel, *Acts* (Augsburg Commentary; Minneapolis: Augsburg, 1986), p. 382; Neyrey, *Luke*, pp. 43-48. Not all farewell addresses are fictitious. The genre of the speech cannot determine the historical question, for genuine farewell addresses have the same form as fictitious ones (Munck, 'Discours d'adieu', p. 163; Barrett, 'Ephesian Elders', p. 109; Lövestam, 'Paul's Address', p. 3; Hemer, 'Speeches', p. 79).

3. Hemer, *Acts*, pp. 418-27.

4. S. Schulze, 'Die Unterlagen für die Abschiedsrede zu Milet in Apostelgesch 20,18-38', *TSK* 73 (1900), pp. 119-25.

5. Lars Aejmelaeus, *Die Rezeption der Paulusbriefe in der Miletrede (Apg 20.18-35)* (Suomalaisen Tiedeakatemian Toimituksia; Annales Academiae Scientiarum Fennicae B/232; Helsinki: Suomalainen Tiedeakatemia, 1987).

6. Barrett, 'Ephesian Elders', p. 110; Lambrecht, 'Farewell-Address', pp. 322-23.

7. Thomas Budesheim, 'Paul's *Abschiedsrede* in the Acts of the Apostles', *HTR* 69 (1976), pp. 9-30, esp. 9-10, 29-30.

8. Lewis Donelson, 'Cult Histories and the Sources of Acts', *Bib* 68 (1987), pp. 1-21, esp. 11-12.

9. Lövestam, 'Paul's Address', pp. 1-10.

10. For a review of proposed structures, see Dupont, *Discours*, pp. 21-26; Lambrecht, 'Farewell-Address', pp. 314-18; cf. Haenchen, *Acts*, pp. 595-96.

credit whether to Paul or to Luke as a composer of an original and effective farewell address'.[1] Among other things it has been structured according to formal elements, content, and/or time perspective, the main purpose being defined accordingly. Structuring by content, Martin Dibelius finds four paragraphs which each end with reference to Paul's example, the purpose being to uphold Paul as exemplar.[2] Cheryl Exum and Charles Talbert find an elaborate chiasm with the main point being v. 25, the pivot point of the chiasm: 'You will see my face no more'.[3] H.-J. Michel finds a fourfold parallelism between 20.18-24 and 20.28-35, with vv. 25-27 being the main point.[4] Jan Lambrecht gives two divisions with chiasms composed of three smaller units within each, the purpose being exhortation rather than apology.[5] E. Lövestam argues that the order of the presentation in the speech can be explained by Paul's use of Ezekiel 33–34.[6]

The purpose of this speech is also a source of contention. It is sometimes seen as an authentic speech of Paul in which he calls and commissions the elders to missionary service modeled on his own life.[7] Seen as a construct by Luke, purposes of exemplification and apologetic are offered. Luke may be upholding Paul as an example of the Christian leader for second generation Christian leaders in Pauline churches.[8] Luke may be admonishing the then current leadership to help the poor, possibly because leaders took their right to wages too seriously (cf. Lk. 10.7), or Luke presents an apology to counter anti-Pauline accusations in his own era, accusations that Paul was a money-grubber.[9]

---

1. Barrett, 'Ephesian Elders', pp. 110. For similar sentiments, see Gardner, 'Speeches', p. 403; Dibelius, *Speeches*, p. 157; Haenchen, *Acts*, pp. 595-96.

2. Dibelius, *Speeches*, p. 157 (adopted by Conzelmann, *Acts*, p. 173).

3. Cheryl Exum and Charles Talbert, 'The Structure of Paul's Speech to the Ephesian Elders (Acts 20,18-35)', *CBQ* 29 (1967), pp. 233-36.

4. Michel, *Abschiedsrede*, p. 27.

5. Lambrecht, 'Farewell-Address', p. 318.

6. Lövestam, 'Paul's Address', pp. 1-10.

7. Bruce, *Speeches*, pp. 26-27; 'Is the Paul of Acts the Real Paul?', *BJRL* 58 (1976), p. 304; Williams, *Acts*, p. 347.

8. Haenchen, *Acts*, pp. 596-97; Barrett, 'Ephesian Elders', p. 108; Krodel, *Acts*, p. 381; Budesheim, 'Paul's *Abschiedsrede*', pp. 22-23. Cf. 1 Cor. 4.16; 11.1; Gal. 4.12. Lövestam ('Paul's Address', p. 2) denies that Paul is held up as a model for missionary work.

9. Lambrecht, 'Farewell-Address', pp. 321, 335-36; Barrett, 'Ephesian Elders', pp. 116, 118; Lüdemann, *Traditions*, pp. 227-28.

Luke, through Paul, may be warning the whole church against heresy as it first appeared in Gnosticism.[1] He combats Gnosticism by dissociating Paul from the image of a Gnostic hero. He emphasizes that Paul preached the same gospel as the apostles, and preached the entire gospel to the entire congregation—not a special knowledge to an elite few.[2] By portraying Paul as investing the Ephesian elders with authority and the whole counsel of God, Luke insures that false teachers of his day cannot claim secret Pauline teaching unknown to those in apostolic succession. There is a continuity of faith from Paul to his successors who possess the deposit of faith.[3]

When these questions are viewed rhetorically, it is generally agreed that Luke has followed the Greco-Roman conventions handed down from Herodotus and Thucydides for the composition of speeches in historical works.[4] As expected, the speech suits the context of his narrative (whether fictional or historical) and the person involved, and makes explicit the meaning of the events narrated.[5] However, unlike the typical historiographical speech, the speeches of Acts are essential parts of the story, not just amplification of the meaning and power

---

1. Dibelius, 'Speeches', p. 157; Haenchen, *Acts*, pp. 596-97.

2. Haenchen, *Acts*, pp. 591, 596; Conzelmann, *Acts*, p. 173; Barrett, 'Ephesian Elders', p. 111; Lüdemann, *Traditions*, p. 227. Cf. Lambrecht, 'Farewell-Address', p. 323.

3. Günter Klein, *Die zwölf Apostel: Ursprung und Gehalt einer Idee* (FRLANT 59; Göttingen: Vandenhoeck & Ruprecht, 1961), pp. 178-84; Heinz Schürmann, 'Das Testament des Paulus für die Kirche, Apg 20,18-35', *Traditiongeschichtliche Untersuchungen zu den synoptischen Evangelien* (KBANT; Düsseldorf: Patmos, 1968), pp. 310-40; Otto Knoch, *Die 'Testamente' des Petrus und Paulus: Die Sicherung der apostolischen Überlieferung in der spätneutestamentlichen Zeit* (SBS 62; Stuttgart: KBW, 1973), pp. 32-43; Michel, *Abschiedsrede*, p. 97.

4. For important discussions, see Dibelius, 'Speeches', esp. pp. 138-45, 155-58; Henry J. Cadbury, *The Making of Luke-Acts* (London: SPCK, 1958), pp. 184-93; Cadbury *et al.*, 'The Greek and Jewish Traditions of Writing History', *The Beginnings of Christianity*, II, pp. 7-29; Donelson, 'Cult Histories', esp. pp. 11-16; Wilcox, 'Forward to the Study of the Speeches in Acts', I, pp. 206-25. See also Kenneth S. Sacks, 'Rhetorical Approaches to Greek History Writing in the Hellenistic Period', *SBL 1984 Seminar Papers* (ed. Kent Richards; Chico: Scholars Press, 1984), pp. 123-33. For a critical appraisal of this position, see Hemer, *Acts*, pp. 415-27.

5. Theodore C. Burgess, *Epideictic Literature* (Studies in Classical Philosophy 3; Chicago: University of Chicago Press, 1902; repr. New York: Garland, 1987), pp. 202, 208-209; Dibelius, 'Speeches', pp. 138-45; Cadbury, 'Speeches', pp. 402-406; Cadbury, *Making of Luke–Acts*, pp. 184-90; Sacks, 'Greek History Writing', pp. 123-33; Kennedy, *New Testament Interpretation*, pp. 114-16.

behind the event.[1] Thus the speeches must be interpreted in light of their function in the entire work, not solely in their immediate narrative contexts.[2]

Dibelius argued that Paul is concluding his missionary work in the East and Luke provides Paul with 'an encomium of the kind that biographies are wont to give to their heroes'.[3] I believe Dibelius was correct. Paul is portrayed as giving his own encomium to the Ephesian elders using a farewell address.[4]

An objection needs to be addressed at this point. Dibelius has been criticized because the vast majority of encomiums in historiography and elsewhere are in the third person.[5] In fact Dibelius supported this assertion with only one reference—Lucian, *De peregrini morte* 32—where Peregrinus speaks on his deathbed of his life, about the dangers he has undergone.[6] However, other examples of first person encomiums can be found.[7] More importantly, a recognized rhetorical device explains the first-person stance, *prosopopoeia*, a technique used in historiography in which an historical character is made to speak in the first person with delineation of his or her character and deeds being central.[8]

Of the three species of rhetoric (judicial, deliberative, epideictic), this speech is to be classified as epideictic.[9] Speeches within historical works generally were epideictic,[10] and one type of epideictic speech

---

1. Paul Schubert, 'The Final Cycle of Speeches in the Book of Acts', *JBL* 87 (1968), p. 16.
2. Dibelius, 'Speeches', p. 145.
3. Dibelius, 'Speeches', p. 155.
4. Burgess (*Epideictic*, pp. 113-26) describes the encomium.
5. Hemer, 'Speeches', pp. 78-79.
6. Dibelius, 'Speeches', p. 155 n. 42.
7. Burgess, *Epideictic*, pp. 207-208.
8. Quint. 3.8.49-54; G.A. Kennedy, *The Art of Rhetoric in the Roman World: 300 BC–AD 300* (Princeton: Princeton University Press, 1972), p. 412; Kennedy, *New Testament Interpretation*, pp. 114-15, cf. pp. 23, 37-38.
9. For full discussions of epideictic, see Ar. *Rhet.* 1.9; *Rhet. ad Alex.* 3, 35; Cic. *De Or.* 2.11.45-46; 2.84-85; *Part. Or.* 4.12; 21-23; *Her.* 3.6-8; Quint. 3.7; *Menander Rhetor* (ed. D.A. Russell and N.G. Wilson; Oxford: Clarendon, 1981); Heinrich Lausberg, *Handbuch der literarischen Rhetorik: Eine Grundlegung der Literaturwissenschaft* (2nd edn; 2 vols.; Munich: Hüber, 1973), I, pp. 129-38, §239-54; J. Martin, *Antike Rhetorik: Technik und Methode* (Handbuch der Altertumswissenschaft 2.3; Munich: Beck, 1974), pp. 177-210; Burgess, *Epideictic*; Kennedy, *The Art of Rhetoric*, pp. 21-23.
10. Burgess, *Epideictic*, pp. 195-214.

was the farewell speech (*syntaktikos logos*).[1] Epideictic rhetoric and such rhetoric in speeches in historiography is not primarily apologetic. In epideictic, debate on uncertain things would not be expected,[2] and true encomium is unapologetic.[3] The speech would be expected to uphold Paul as a model or example of Christian leadership, not to provide an apology for Paul. We must concede that all three species of rhetoric rely upon one another,[4] and that Luke had the option of weaving deliberative or judicial rhetoric into an epideictic encomium. As T.C. Burgess notes,

> the speeches found in the works of Greek historians naturally deal with a great variety of themes. They grow from the situation arising in the narrative and throw light upon this situation, or argue some question connected with the state or the individuals involved.[5]

However, the piece overall would remain epideictic. The difficulty of distinguishing apologetic and exemplification must be conceded, but so must the primary purpose of exemplification over apologetic.[6]

A Rhetorical Analysis

Rhetorical analysis of the speech will be conducted primarily according to the methodology proposed by Dr Kennedy.[7] I hope to demonstrate that the speech is carefully crafted and structured according to the Greco-Roman conventions of epideictic rhetoric. My thesis is that careful composition indicates that Luke did not merely summarize, but, as an historian with rhetorical training, is chiefly responsible for

---

1. *Menander Rhetor* 2.15 (although the *topoi* he discusses are not found in this speech); Burgess, *Epideictic*, p. 112; Kennedy, *New Testament Interpretation*, pp. 76-77, 132-33. Kennedy (p. 76) identifies this speech as a *syntaktikos logos*.

2. Cic. *Part. Or.* 21.71.

3. Burgess, *Epideictic*, p. 118. Quint. 3.7.4-6 allows for some apology in encomium.

4. *Rhet. ad Alex.* 5.1427b.31; Quint. 3.4.16; cf. *Her.* 3.8.15; Quint. 3.4.11.

5. Burgess, *Epideictic*, pp. 208-209, cf. 202; Kennedy, *New Testament Interpretation*, p. 117.

6. Many concede the dual purpose of apologetic and exemplification in the speech: Haenchen, *Acts*, pp. 596-97; Bruce, 'Speeches', p. 27; Lambrecht, 'Farewell-Address', p. 318.

7. *New Testament Interpretation*, pp. 33-38. All quotations of the Bible and the Greco-Roman handbooks are from the RSV and the LCL respectively.

the content of the speech.[1] Luke provides a fitting encomium to Paul as he ends his missionary journeys in the East, an encomium within a farewell address using the rhetorical technique of *prosopopoeia*.

1. *The Rhetorical Unit*
The Ephesian elders' speech in Acts 20.18b-35 is a complete rhetorical unit found in the larger context of 20.17-38. It is preceded by an historical preface (20.17-18a) and followed by a narrative summary of the audience reaction and subsequent events (20.36-38).

2. *The Species of Rhetoric and the* Stasis
The species of rhetoric has already been identified as epideictic.[2] Epideictic rhetoric as classically conceived concerns itself mainly with praise and blame,[3] and its end is the honorable or the dishonorable with the intent of increasing or decreasing assent to some value.[4] The main subject is praise and exemplification of Paul the man and missionary for his honorable mission and its execution.

The characteristic time reference for epideictic is present,[5] but the past is often recalled and the future anticipated.[6] Being a farewell address and incorporated within an historical work, this speech is dominated by the recall of the past actions of the main character, Paul. As a farewell address, the future is anticipated for both Paul (vv. 22-24) and his audience (vv. 28-30). However, the present is created in the speech as Paul actively delivers his final farewell.

There is a hint of judicial or forensic rhetoric as well, the rhetoric of accusation and defense.[7] All three species of rhetoric relied upon each other, with one dominating the work.[8] The speech in historio-

---

1. For similar argumentation on all the speeches of Acts, see C.F. Evans, ' "Speeches" in Acts', *Mélanges Bibliques en hommage au R.P. Béda Rigaux* (Gembloux: Duculot, 1970), p. 296.
2. Cf. Bruce (*Speeches*, pp. 5, 26-27) who classifies the speech as 'hortatory'.
3. Ar. *Rhet.* 1.3.1358b.3; Cic. *Inv.* 1.5.7; 2.4.12; *Part. Or.* 21.70; *Her.* 1.2.2; Quint. 3.4.6-9, 12-14; cf. *Rhet. ad Alex.* 3.1425b.35; Cic. *Inv.* 2.59.177; *De Or.* 1.31.141.
4. Ar. *Rhet.* 1.3.1358b.5; *Rhet. ad Alex.* 3.1425b.36-39; Cic. *Inv.* 2.4.12; 2.51.155-56; *Top.* 24.91; *Her.* 3.6.10; cf. Quint. 3.4.16.
5. Ar. *Rhet.* 1.3.1358b.4; cf. Cic. *Part. Or.* 3.10; 20.69.
6. Ar. *Rhet.* 1.3.1358b.4; Quint. 3.4.7; cf. Cic. *Part. Or.* 21.71.
7. For full discussion, see Lausberg, *Handbuch*, I, pp. 86-123, §140-223; Martin, *Rhetorik*, pp. 15-166; Kennedy, *The Art of Rhetoric*, pp. 7-18.
8. *Rhet. ad Alex.* 5.1427b.31ff.; Quint. 3.4.16; cf. *Her.* 3.8.15; Quint. 3.4.11.

graphy 'often sums up a situation, or it presents the arguments on both sides of a question. . .',[1] particularly questions connected with the individuals involved.[2] It 'must arise from the narrative and deal with some question of abiding interest'.[3] Following the conventions of Greco-Roman historiography, Luke needed to make the speech suitable to Paul and his audience. Paul may be portrayed as addressing charges in the speech because they were known to have concerned the Ephesian church, or were merely stock charges commonly brought against Paul in Paul's and/or Luke's own day.

In any case, Paul does seem to be refuting two charges: (1) he failed to declare everything that was profitable to his audience (vv. 20-21, 26-27; cf. v. 31), and (2) he took financial advantage of his converts (vv. 33-35). However, as demonstrated below, these bold declarations of innocence are *topoi* of encomium and farewell addresses, and each needs to be assessed individually whether or not it possesses apologetic intent.

The *stasis* is the basic question at issue in a speech.[4] Of the three basis *stases* (fact, definition, and quality), the one of quality usually characterizes epideictic, for epideictic is concerned with the nature of a thing.[5] Here the nature of Paul and his conduct is being praised. If there is a forensic undercurrent, those portions of the speech are based on the *stasis* of fact. In this *stasis*, the question is whether something was ever done, or was done by the person accused.[6] Paul would be flatly denying the charges that he shrunk from declaring the full gospel (vv. 20, 26-27; cf. 31), and that he took advantage of the generosity of others (v. 33).

3. *Invention, Arrangement, and Style*

The following is a detailed consideration of Luke's use of invention, arrangement, and style in composing the speech. Special attention will

---

1. Burgess, *Epideictic*, p. 202.
2. Burgess, *Epideictic*, pp. 208-209.
3. Burgess, *Epideictic*, p. 202.
4. For full discussion of *stasis*, see Quint. 3.6.63-82; Lausberg, *Handbuch*, I, pp. 64-85, §79-138; Martin, *Rhetorik*, pp. 28-52; Hermogenes, 'Hermogenes' *On Stases*: A Translation with an Introduction and Notes', trans. and ed. Ray Nadeau, *Speech Monographs* 31 (1964), pp. 361-424.
5. Quint. 3.7.28; 7.4.1-3.
6. Cic. *Inv.* 1.8.11; Quint. 3.6.83. For full discussion, see Cic. *Inv.* 2.4.14–16.5; *De Or.* 2.25.105; *Part. Or.* 10.34–11.40; *Top.* 23.87; *Her.* 1.11.18; 2.2.3–8.12; Quint. 7.2; cf. Cic. *De Or.* 2.30.132.

be given to the rhetorical role of standard features of the farewell address and speeches in historiography.

a. *The Historical Preface (vv. 17-18a)*. The speech is preceded by an historical preface which sets the speech within Luke's account of Paul's mission: 'And from Miletus he [Paul] sent to Ephesus and called to him the elders of the church. And when they came to him, he said to them. . .'

b. *The* Exordium *(vv. 18b-24)*. The *exordium* of the speech proper is composed of vv. 18b-24.[1] The *exordium* is the beginning element of a rhetorical piece which has the three purposes or aims of eliciting the audience's attention, receptivity, and goodwill so that it will give the speech a hearing.[2] The *exordium* is divided into two parts: a review of Paul's previous hardships and achievements (vv. 18b-21), and a preview of the same fare in his future (vv. 22-24). The shift between the two parts of the *exordium* is marked by the formula 'and now behold' (καὶ νῦν ἰδού) in v. 22.[3]

The rhetorical handbooks recommend several techniques for obtaining the audience's attention.[4] One is to show that the matter at hand is agreeable to both the rhetor and the audience. Paul's reliance upon the audience's knowledge of his conduct among them (vv. 18-21) is premised upon his assumption that the Ephesian elders agree with him that his conduct among them was exemplary.

1. I disagree with Kennedy (*New Testament Interpretation*, p. 133) that the *exordium* extends through v. 27. There is a decided break at v. 25 (καὶ νῦν ἰδού) and vv. 25ff. is better thought of as the *probatio* for reasons to be given below.

2. Ar. *Rhet.* 3.14.1415a.7; *Rhet. ad Alex.* 29.1436a.33ff.; Cic. *Inv.* 1.15.20; *Or.* 14.122; *Part. Or.* 8.28; *Top.* 26.97; *Her.* 1.3.4; 1.4.6; Quint. 4.1.5, 37, 41, 50-51; cf. Cic. *De Or.* 1.31.143; 2.19.80; *Or.* 15.50; Quint. 4.1.61-62; 4.2.24; 10.1.48. For discussions of the *exordium* of epideictic, see Ar. *Rhet.* 3.14.1414b.1–1415a.4; *Rhet. ad Alex.* 35; *Her.* 3.6.11-12. For detailed discussions of the *exordium* in general, see Ar. *Rhet.* 3.14-15; *Rhet. ad Alex.* 29; Cic. *Inv.* 1.15-18; *De Or.* 2.77.315-80.325; *Part. Or.* 8.28-30; *Her.* 1.3.4-7.11; Quint. 4.1; Lausberg, *Handbuch*, I, pp. 150-63, §263-88; Martin, *Rhetorik*, pp. 60-75.

3. I disagree with Conzelmann (*Acts*, p. 173) who argues that καὶ νῦν ἰδού in vv. 22, 25 and καὶ τὰ νῦν in v. 32 do not mark major sections of the speech.

4. For these techniques, see Ar. *Rhet.* 3.14.1415a.7–1415b.7; *Rhet. ad Alex.* 29.1436b.5-15; Cic. *Inv.* 1.16.23; *Part. Or.* 8.29-30; *Her.* 1.4.7; Quint. 4.1.33-34; 10.1.48.

Another technique for obtaining audience attention is to clarify that the speech pertains to the welfare of all the audience and to the worship of the gods (or God). Paul accomplishes this in his review with reference to his dedicated service to the Ephesian church (vv. 18-21), especially that what he declared to them was 'profitable' (v. 20) and pertained to the 'repentance to God and of faith in our Lord Jesus Christ' (v. 21).[1] Paul's preview also employs this technique, noting that his ministry is directed by the Holy Spirit (vv. 22-23), and his desire 'to testify to the gospel of the grace of God' without regard for his physical life (v. 24).

Audience receptivity was assumed to follow naturally from obtaining audience attention,[2] and no specific techniques are offered in the handbooks for garnering receptivity. Audience goodwill can be derived from either the facts of the case or persons involved in it. Here the emphasis is solely upon gaining goodwill from the person of Paul. This is expected given the nature of the speech as an epideictic encomium within a farewell address. In fact, the *exordium* of epideictic is usually drawn from the person discussed or from the audience.[3]

The primary function of the *exordium* is to establish the *ethos* of Paul.[4] *Ethos* is moral character and conduct, the course of life.[5] It 'is related to men's nature and character, their habits and all the intercourse of life. . .'[6] *Ethos* is an artificial proof based on the demonstration throughout the speech of the rhetor's goodness, goodwill, and fine moral qualities.[7] The rhetor believed to be a good man (*ethos*)

---

1. There is an ellipsis in v. 20, for 'what is profitable' (τὰ συμφέροντα) is 'what is profitable for salvation'. Ellipsis is a figure of speech in which 'the word omitted may be clearly gathered from the context' (Quint. 9.3.58). Cf. 8.6.21-22 for a similar definition. For further discussion, see Lausberg, *Handbuch*, I, pp. 346-47, §690-91; Martin, *Rhetorik*, p. 300; E.W. Bullinger, *Figures of Speech Used in the Bible* (London: Eyre & Spottiswoode, 1898; repr. Grand Rapids: Baker, 1968), pp. 1-130.
2. Cic. *Inv.* 1.16.23; *Her.* 1.4.7; Quint. 4.1.34.
3. *Her.* 3.6.11-12.
4. Kennedy, *New Testament Interpretation*, p. 133.
5. Ar. *Rhet.* 1.2.1356a.3-4; 1.8.1366a.6; Cic. *De Or.* 2.43.182-84; Quint. 6.2.8-19; Lausberg, *Handbuch*, I, pp. 141-42, §257; Martin, *Rhetorik*, pp. 158-61; G.A. Kennedy, *The Art of Persuasion in Greece* (Princeton: Princeton University Press, 1963), pp. 91-93.
6. Cic. *Or.* 37.128.
7. Ar. *Rhet.* 1.8.1366a.6.

was considered the strongest influence in obtaining goodwill.[1] Paul's ethos is established here by Luke's reference to his long suffering under injustice (v. 19)[2] and being informed by the Holy Spirit of his future circumstances (vv. 22-23).[3] This stress on *ethos* corresponds to the source of the epideictic *exordium* being praise or blame.[4] Praise of Paul naturally increases his *ethos*.

The handbooks give several specific techniques for eliciting audience goodwill using the person of the rhetor.[5] One is to give the impression of struggling against difficulties and misfortunes.[6] Paul does this in his review by describing himself as 'serving the Lord with all humility and with tears and with trials which befell me through the plots of the Jews' (v. 19). This technique employs amplification by accumulation in the listing of the hardships.[7] This technique is prominent in the preview as well: 'Bound in the Spirit, not knowing what shall befall me there; except that the Holy Spirit testifies to me in every city that imprisonment and afflictions await me' (vv. 22-23).

Giving the impression that words are presided over by the gods (or God) is a technique present here in Paul's references to being informed by the Holy Spirit (vv. 22-23).[8] Another technique is to give the impression of having undertaken the case because of a sense of duty, a serious moral consideration, or a weighty and honorable reason.[9] This is what Paul does in v. 24: 'But I do not account my life of any value nor as precious to myself, if only I may accomplish my course and the ministry which I received from the Lord Jesus to testify to the gospel of the grace of God'.[10]

1. Ar. *Rhet.* 1.2.1356a.3-4; 2.1.1378a.5-7; 3.14.1415a.7; Quint. 4.1.7; Aug. *De Doct. Chr.* 4.27.

2. A technique for creating ethos given in Cic. *De Or.* 2.43.184.

3. The Holy Spirit guiding the mission of Paul is a familiar Lukan motif in Acts (13.2; 16.6-10; 19.21; 20.22-23). This guidance of the Holy Spirit concerning Paul's fate in Jerusalem is given specific voice through Christian prophets (21.4), particularly Agabus (21.10-11).

4. Ar. *Rhet.* 3.14.1415a.4.

5. For such techniques, see Cic. *Inv.* 1.16.22; *Part. Or.* 8.28; *Her.* 1.4.8-5.8; Quint. 4.1.7-10, 33; cf. Cic. *De Or.* 2.79.321; Quint. 10.1.48. In epideictic *exordiums*, see *Her.* 3.6.11.

6. Cic. *Inv.* 1.16.22; *Her.* 1.5.8; Quint. 4.1.9.

7. Quint. 8.4.26-27; Long. *Subl.* 12.2; cf. *Her.* 4.40.52-53.

8. Cf. Quint. 10.1.48.

9. Cic. *Part. Or.* 8.28; Quint. 4.1.7.

10. Motif of Paul surrendering himself for the sake of the gospel: 2 Cor. 4.7–5.10; 6.3-10; 12.7-10; Phil. 1.19-26; 2.17; 3.8-11; Col. 1.24. The metaphor of the track

Still yet another technique is to weaken charges of less honorable dealings, a technique which may be working in the disclaimer, 'I did not shrink from declaring to you anything that was profitable' (v. 20). Expressions of joy at the opportunity for self-sacrifice, a favorite motif in rhetorical historiography, are also present.[1]

Topoi characteristic of epideictic that are found here are: an outline of achievements[2] (a most effective emphasis when praising someone);[3] actions worthy as a matter of course;[4] courage in danger, especially when beneficial not just to the person being praised, but to the whole human race;[5] bearing adversity without being crushed;[6] achievement foreshadowed by portents and oracles;[7] and fulfilling an office or ministry.[8] From the perspective of Luke's audience, Paul outlines his achievements with the Ephesians, achievements obtained as a matter of course (vv. 18b-21). The danger he encountered while bringing them the beneficial or profitable gospel is mentioned, clearly from the vantage point of the victor (vv. 19-20). His was an unwavering struggle against trials and plots (vv. 19-20) and his undaunted determination to face imprisonment and afflictions, even to the point of death (vv. 22-24). His ministry was foreshadowed by prophecy (vv. 22-23) and the fulfillment of this ministry is paramount to him (v. 24).

Misrepresentations should also be refuted in the *exordium* of epideictic.[9] Paul may be rebutting the charge that he did not declare everything that was profitable to the Ephesians (v. 20-21). His rebuttal is quite comprehensive, pointing out that his declaration was in both

---

appears in v. 24 where Paul wishes to accomplish his course (δρόμος). The metaphor indicates disciplined struggle toward a goal. For other examples, see Acts 13.25; 1 Cor. 9.24-27; Gal. 2.2; Phil. 2.16; 3.12-14; 2 Tim. 4.7-8.

1. Conzelmann, *Acts*, p. 174.

2. Ar. *Rhet.* 1.9.1367b.33-34. Cf. Cic. *Inv.* 1.25.36 which describes using achievements as *topoi* for supporting propositions in argumentation. The person's deeds, words, and experiences should be discussed in past, present, or future. Here Paul is portrayed as doing just that.

3. Quint. 3.7.15-16.

4. Ar. *Rhet.* 1.9.1367b.32; *Rhet. ad Alex.* 3.1426a.35ff.; 35.1440b.14ff.

5. Ar. *Rhet.* 1.9.1366a–4.1366b.6; Cic. *De Or.* 2.84.343-44; 2.85.346; *Her.* 3.6.10; 3.8.15.

6. Cic. *De Or.* 2.85.346.

7. Cic. *Part. Or.* 21.73.

8. Cic. *De Or.* 2.85.347. Cf. Cic. *Inv.* 1.25.36 which describes having a plan or purpose for doing something as a *topoi* to support a proposition. Paul's plan is clear in v. 24—fulfillment of a divine call.

9. *Rhet. ad Alex.* 35.1440b.5.ff.

major arenas (public and house gatherings) and to both divisions of the civilized world (Jews and Greeks). It even provides a summary of his actual message (vv. 20-21).

The *exordium* also introduces points to be further developed in the *probatio*, the main body of the speech,[1] and reiterated in the *peroratio*, the conclusion of the speech. Of the epideictic *exordium* Aristotle writes, 'the speaker should say at once whatever he likes, give the keynote and then attach the main subject'.[2] Paul's insistence that he 'did not shrink from declaring. . . anything that was profitable' (v. 20) and his intimation that death awaited him (vv. 22-24) are main subjects of the *probatio* (vv. 25-31).

Paul's appeal to the audience's knowledge which begins the *exordium* (v. 18b) recurs in the *probatio* (v. 31, μνημονεύω) and *peroratio* (v. 34, γινώσκω; v. 35, μνημονεύω). The audience's knowledge of how he lived among them (v. 18b) is developed in the *probatio* with regard to preaching the full gospel (vv. 26-27), and in the *peroratio* in reference to how he supported himself and his companions while among the Ephesians (vv. 33-34). The disclaimer to 'not shrink' (ὑποστέλλω) from proclaiming (ἀναγγέλλω) is introduced here in v. 20 and recurs for development in the *probatio* of v. 27. The *topos* of testifying which is associated with this disclaimer (διαμαρτύρομαι, vv. 21, 23, 24) recurs in the *probatio* (μαρτύρομαι, v. 26).[3] The grace of God (χάρις) to which Paul desires to give testimony (v. 24) is prominent in the beginning of the *peroratio* where he commends the audience to the grace of God (v. 32). The *topos* of tears (δάκρυον) introduced in v. 19 recurs in the *probatio* in v. 31 (cf. weeping [κλαυθμός] in the narrative summary in v. 37).

The *exordium* should always attempt to elicit the *pathos* desired from the audience,[4] and this is particularly true of epideictic which

---

1. Cic. *De Or.* 2.80.325; Quint. 4.1.23-27. Cf. Cic. *De Or.* 2.79.320.

2. Ar. *Rhet.* 3.14.1414b.1. See *Rhet. ad Alex.* 35.1440b.5ff. for similar advice.

3. The shift from διαμαρτύρομαι to μαρτύρομαι is an example of paronomasia. It is akin to the type of paronomasia in which there is a change of the preposition with which a verb is compounded (Quint. 9.3.71). For further discussion of paronomasia, see *Her.* 4.21.29–23.32; Quint. 9.3.66-80; Lausberg, *Handbuch*, I, pp. 322-25, §637-39; Martin, *Rhetorik*, pp. 304-305; Bullinger, *Figures*, pp. 307-20.

4. Cic. *De Or.* 2.77.311; *Part. Or.* 8.27. *Pathos* is emotion and, as a means of proof, is arousal of the audience's emotion for or against the matter at hand and those associated with it. For further discussion, see Lausberg, *Handbuch*, I, pp. 140-41, §257; Martin, *Rhetorik*, pp. 158-66; Kennedy, *Persuasion in Greece*, pp. 93-96.

aims at emotion rather than proof.[1] Quintilian advises that it may be necessary to frighten the audience in the *exordium* in order to gain desired objectives.[2] Paul's speaking about his service to them with humility, tears, and trials (v. 19), and the future imprisonment, afflictions, and apparent threat to his life (vv. 22-24) are attempts to elicit *pathos*, the latter of which does so through the fear of Paul's death. Paul's description of his situation as 'I am going to Jerusalem, bound in the Spirit, not knowing what shall befall me there' (v. 22) is remarkably similar to the figure of speech called surrender (ἐπιτροπή) used to evoke pity. This figure occurs 'when we indicate in speaking that we yield and submit the whole matter to another's will'.[3]

The next element of arrangement is the *narratio* which provides the concern for which the rhetor would like the audience to render judgment, and for which the *exordium* has striven to obtain the audience's attention, receptivity, and goodwill.[4] A *narratio* is not necessary in epideictic unless it recounts a deed which is the subject of the rhetoric.[5] No *narratio* is found here and the speech moves immediately into the *probatio*.

c. *The* Probatio (*vv. 25-31*). The *probatio* of the speech is constituted by vv. 25-31. The *probatio* 'is the part of the oration which by marshalling arguments lends credit, authority, and support to our case'.[6] The *probatio* of epideictic rhetoric is not usually formal proofs, but amplification of *topoi* and statements advanced as certain.[7] Brief and frequent amplification is the norm.[8] *Topoi* characteristic of epideictic

---

1. Cic. *Part. Or.* 21.70-71.
2. Quint. 4.1.20-22, 33.
3. *Her.* 4.29.39. Cf. *concessio* in Quint. 9.2.51. For further discussion, see Lausberg, *Handbuch*, I, pp. 425-26, §856; Martin, *Rhetorik*, pp. 280-81; Bullinger, *Figures*, pp. 972-73; cf. pp. 970-71.
4. For full discussion of the *narratio*, see Lausberg, *Handbuch*, I, pp. 163-90, §289-347; Martin, *Rhetorik*, pp. 75-89.
5. Ar. *Rhet.* 3.13.1414a.3; 3.16.1416b.1-3; *Part. Or.* 5.15; *Her.* 3.7.13.
6. Cic. *Inv.* 1.24.34. For similar understandings, see Cic. *Or.* 34.122; *Her.* 1.3.4; cf. Cic. *De Or.* 1.31.143; 2.19.80. For detailed discussions, see Lausberg, *Handbuch*, I, pp. 191-235, §350-426; Martin, *Rhetorik*, pp. 95-137.
7. Ar. *Rhet.* 1.9.1368a.38-40; 2.18.1392a.5; 3.17.1417b.3; *Rhet. ad Alex.* 3; 6.1428a.1ff.; Cic. *Part. Or.* 21.71; Quint. 3.7.1-6.
8. *Her.* 3.8.15.

pertain to what is noble and disgraceful, to virtue and vice.[1] When proof is employed, it is usually ethical or demonstrative (e.g. enthymeme).[2] Exhortation is also common to epideictic.[3]

The *probatio* begins with the transitional phrase 'And now, behold' (καὶ νῦν ἰδού). The figure of speech called *epibole* (ἐπιβολή) is in play, for the opening phrase is repeated from the *exordium* (v. 22).[4] In both occurrences the phrase marks a major transition: from the review to the preview in the *exordium* (v. 22), and from the *exordium* to the *probatio* (v. 24). The phrase fulfills the need to end the *exordium* with a clear transition.[5]

The *probatio* begins, 'And now, behold, I know that all you among whom I have gone preaching the kingdom will see my face no more'. This is a statement considered certain as expected in the *probatio* of an epideictic speech. This statement reiterates the content of vv. 20-21 in the *exordium*, further supporting Paul's contention that he fully preached the gospel to the Ephesians. 'Preaching the kingdom' is a synonymous expression for 'to testify to the gospel of the grace of God' in the previous verse (v. 24). Synonymy is a form of amplification based on repetition,[6] here used as a factor in Paul's self-justification.

This portrayal of Paul's knowledge of his death is an element of the farewell genre and is a tactic for eliciting positive *pathos*. Paul's assurance that he will not see the Ephesian elders apparently comes from prophetic revelation (vv. 22-23) and sounds very much like Paul accepting his fate. One *topos* of epideictic is portents, oracles, and fate.[7] 'Not seeing his face' really stands for never seeing him again, and is thus the figure of thought called emphasis which reveals a deeper meaning than is actually expressed.[8] It is used for amplifica-

---

1. Ar. *Rhet.* 1.9; 2.22.1396a.8; *Rhet. ad Alex.* 3; 35.1440b.14–1441b.29; Cic. *Inv.* 2.59.177; *De Or.* 2.84-85; *Part. Or.* 21-23; *Top.* 23.89; *Her.* 3.6-8; cf. Cic. *De Or.* 2.11.46.

2. Ar. *Rhet.* 3.17.1418a.11–1418b.12; cf. 2.20.1393a.1.

3. Ar. *Rhet.* 1.9.1367b.36–1368a.37; Cic. *Or.* 11.37.

4. ἐπιβολή is the repetition of more than one word at the beginning of successive sentences and is akin to epanaphora. For full discussion, see Lausberg, *Handbuch*, I, pp. 318-20, §629-30; Martin, *Rhetorik*, p. 303; Bullinger, *Figures*, pp. 346-47.

5. Quint. 4.1.76-79.

6. Cic. *Part. Or.* 15.53.

7. *Part. Or.* 21.73.

8. *Her.* 4.53.67; Quint. 8.3.83; 9.2.64; cf. Cic. *Or.* 40.139; Quint. 9.3.67. For further discussion, see *Her.* 4.53.67; Quint. 8.3.83-86; Lausberg, *Handbuch*, I,

tion[1] and to appeal to *pathos*, and recurs in the narrative summary following the speech (v. 38). Luke seems to be presupposing Paul's death.[2]

Verses 26-27 constitute an enthymeme, an incomplete syllogism, a proposition with a single premise.[3] The proposition is v. 26: 'Therefore I testify to you this day that I am innocent of the blood of all of you' (cf. 18.6). The supporting premise is v. 27: 'for I did not shrink from declaring to you the whole counsel of God'. The unstated premise could be stated as: 'There is no blood guilt for the one declaring the whole counsel of God'.

Declaration of innocence is an element of the farewell address.[4] However, the *exordium* already introduced Paul's claim that he did not 'shrink from declaring anything that was profitable' (v. 20). Now what was profitable is described as 'the whole counsel of God'. This previous introduction of the claim and now its defense with an enthymeme is indicative of a refutative stance. It is a suitable foil for the exhortation against false doctrine which follows in vv. 28-30. However, it may also be judicial rhetoric aimed at refuting charges prevalent in Paul's and/or Luke's day. One form of refutation is the enthymeme arguing from the contrary as is the case here.[5] As mentioned in Part 1, it may have been argued that Paul was responsible for the Gnostic doctrine that only the fully initiated possess the whole gospel.

The enthymeme is ornamented with metaphorical language, a common feature of epideictic.[6] The metaphor is based on being guilty of someone's blood or life because proper warning of judgment or danger was not given before they were overcome.[7] Metaphors are used

---

pp. 298-99, §578; pp. 450-53, §905-906; Martin, *Rhetorik*, pp. 254-55; Bullinger, *Figures*, pp. 165-66.

1. Quint. 9.2.3.

2. Conzelmann, *Acts*, p. 174; Haenchen, *Acts,* p. 592.

3. For a detailed discussion of the enthymeme, see Ar. *Rhet.* 1.2.1357a.13-14; 2.22-26; 3.17.1418a.6–1418b.17; *Rhet. ad Alex.* 10; Quint. 5.10.1-3; 5.14.1-4, 24-26.

4. 1 Sam. 12.2-5; *Jub.* 21.2-3; Michel, *Abschiedsrede*, pp. 51-52.

5. Ar. *Rhet.* 2.25.1402a.1–1402b.7.

6. Cic. *Part. Or.* 21.72.

7. Cf. Ezek. 3.16-21 on warning of sin; 33.1-9 on warning of danger. A metaphor is a trope and 'occurs when a word applying to one thing is transferred to another, because the similarity seems to justify this transference' (*Her.* 4.34.45). Cf. Ar. *Poet.* 21.1457b.7 and Quint. 8.6.5 for similar definitions. For further discussion, see Lausberg, *Handbuch*, I, pp. 285-91, §558-64; Martin, *Rhetorik*, pp. 266-

for several purposes, here the purpose of magnifying and embellishing is prominent.[1] The metaphor magnifies the crime Paul is disclaiming so that his contrary conduct appears even more exemplary. It embellishes by bringing to mind several images from warfare and religious sacrifice.

Paul continues with a warning:

> Take heed to yourselves and to all the flock, in which the Holy Spirit has made you overseers, to care for the church of God which he obtained with the blood of his own Son.[2] I know that after my departure fierce wolves will come in among you, not sparing the flock; and from among your own selves will arise men speaking perverse things, to draw away the disciples after them (vv. 28-30).

The warning of false teachers and their doctrine is a standard motif of the farewell genre originally connected with an eschatological outlook.[3] A warning to the audience to be on their guard was also a standard element of Greco-Roman rhetoric and was called *comminatio* (ἀπειλή).[4]

Again, metaphors, common to epideictic, are used. Luke uses traditional metaphors and their positive and negative images to create a general warning about false teachers. Central are the traditional metaphors of the shepherd-sheep for religious overseer and congregation,[5] and of wolves for false teachers.[6] ἄφιξις ('departure') is a

68; A.D. Leeman, *Orationis Ratio: The Stylistic Theories and Practice of the Roman Orators, Historians and Philosophers* (2 vols.; Amsterdam: Adolf M. Hakkert, 1963), I, pp. 126-32; Bullinger, *Figures*, pp. 735-43; G.B. Caird, *The Language and Imagery of the Bible* (Philadelphia: Westminster, 1980), pp. 131-71.

1. Long. *Subl.* 32.5; Demetr. *Eloc.* 2.78; *Her.* 4.34.45; Quint. 8.6.6.

2. Verse 28 presents two difficult, interrelated textual problems. I am adopting the reading 'church of God' (reading θεοῦ rather than κυρίου), and the reading αἵματος τοῦ ἰδίου (rather than ἰδίου αἵματος), understanding ἴδιος in the latter to be a substantive ('with the blood of his own [Jesus]') rather than an adjective ('with his [God's] own blood'). For full discussion, see Bruce Metzger, *A Textual Commentary on the Greek New Testament* (3rd edn; London: United Bible Societies, 1971), pp. 480-81.

3. Mk 13.22; 1 Tim. 4.1-5; 2 Tim. 3.1–4.8; 2 Pet. 2.1–3.18.

4. Ar. *Poet.* 19.1456b.7-9; Cic. *Or.* 40.138.

5. Pss. 23; 100.3; Isa. 40.11; Jer. 13.17; 23.1-4; Ezek. 34; Zech. 10.3; 11.4-17; Lk. 12.32; 15.3-7; Jn 10.1-30; 21.15-17; Heb. 13.20; 1 Pet. 2.25; 5.2-4. See esp. Lövestam, 'Address at Miletus'.

6. *4 Ezra* 5.18; *1 Enoch* 89.13-27; Mt. 7.15; *Did.* 16.3; Ign. *Phld.* 2.2; *2 Clem.* 5.2-4; Justin, *Apol.* 1.16.13; *Dial.* 35.3.

metaphor for death.[1] These metaphors create a vivid mental picture and magnify the message.[2] Paul is a shepherd about to die and leave his sheep unattended, and they may be killed by the fierce wolves that he is keeping at bay while alive. The imagery may magnify the danger posed by the false teachers of Luke's day. The metaphor of the way as the ethical walk of a person in righteousness seems to underlie the phrase 'to draw away the disciples after them'.

Paul caps this prophetic portion of his speech with another warning: 'Therefore be alert, remembering that for three years I did not cease night or day to admonish every one with tears' (v. 31). This warning is a carefully crafted appeal to *pathos*. First, it is by nature another example of a warning about an impending danger, or *comminatio*. This warning to be alert (γρηγορέω) is common to eschatological paraenesis.[3] Also, there is the recurrence of the *topos* of tears from the *exordium* (v. 19). This reference is combined with the figure of emphasis, for 'day and night' is another way of saying 'all the time'. Hyperbole is used, for Paul could not have served day and night with tears.[4] Hyperbole is another form of amplification.[5] There is a trace of refutation here as well, the denial that Paul shrank from declaring all the gospel (cf. vv. 20-21, 26-27).

Regarding the entire *probatio* in epideictic, one *topos* for speaking in censure is to appear to be 'doing so from goodwill, because we think it useful that all men should be apprised of a wickedness and worthlessness without parallel'.[6] This describes Paul's warnings in vv. 28-31. Other *topoi* demonstrate that the subject has the virtue of

---

1. Suggested by Conzelmann, *Acts*, p. 175; Haenchen, *Acts*, p. 593 n. 2.

2. Long. *Subl.* 32.5; Cic. *De Or.* 3.40.160-61; *Her.* 4.34.45.

3. 1 Cor. 16.13; Col. 4.2; 1 Thess. 5.6; cf. 2 Cor 11.12-15; Phil. 3.2 (βλέπετε).

4. Hyperbole is a trope, '. . . a manner of speech exaggerating the truth, whether for the sake of magnifying or minifying something' (*Her.* 4.33.44). Cf. Long. *Subl.* 38.6; Cic. *De Or.* 3.53.203; Quint. 8.6.67 for similar definitions. For further discussion, see Long. *Subl.* 38.1-6; Demetr. *Eloc.* 2.124-27; Quint. 8.6.67-76; Lausberg, *Handbuch*, I, pp. 299-300, §579; pp. 454-55, §909-10; Martin, *Rhetorik*, p. 264; Bullinger, *Figures*, pp. 423-28. This particular hyperbole is common to Pauline (1 Thess. 2.9; 3.10) and Lukan usage (Lk. 2.37; Acts 26.7).

5. Long. *Subl.* 11.2. Cf. Cic. *Part. Or.* 15.53 which espouses the use of exaggerated words for amplification, and Quint. 8.4.29 which notes that hyperbole was once considered a form of amplification.

6. *Her.* 3.6.11.

being kind and beneficent toward others,[1] acts according to moral purpose as a matter of habit,[2] or has acted a particular way for a long time.[3] Paul declared the whole counsel of God to the Ephesians day and night with tears—clearly moral purpose motivated by kindness and done as a matter of habit over a long period of time.

d. *The* Peroratio *(vv. 32-35)*. The *peroratio* or conclusion is composed of vv. 32-35.[4] The *peroratio* has the two main functions and divisions of recapitulating the main points of the *probatio* and, through amplification, arousing emotions according to the speaker's purpose.[5] Epideictic does not require a *peroratio*,[6] but, because amplification occurs throughout the discourse, if a *peroratio* is used, a brief summary is all that is needed.[7]

The *peroratio* begins with the transitional formula, 'And now' (καὶ τὰ νῦν):[8] 'And now I commend you to God and to the word of his grace, which is able to build you up and give you the inheritance among all those who are sanctified' (v. 32; cf. 14.23). Positive *pathos* is mustered by Paul's commendation of the audience to God and his word of grace. The commendation reiterates the *topos* of the word of grace (χάρις) from the end of the *exordium* ('gospel of grace', v. 24). Thus the *exordium* ends and the *peroratio* begins with the same *topos*. The word of grace is personified as a builder able to build up the congregation, and the congregation understood metaphorically as a building underlies the personification.[9] Personification is a form of amplification.[10]

---

1. Ar. *Rhet.* 1.9.1366a.4–1366b.6; 1.9.1366b.17; Cic. *De Or.* 2.11.46; 2.84.343-44; 2.85.346.
2. Ar. *Rhet.* 1.9.1367b.32; *Rhet. ad Alex.* 3.1426a.35ff.
3. *Rhet. ad Alex.* 3.1426a.35ff.
4. This delimitation agrees with Kennedy, *New Testament Interpretation*, p. 133.
5. For full discussion of the *peroratio*, see Ar. *Rhet.* 3.19.1419b.1-6; Cic. *Inv.* 1.52-56; *Or.* 34.122; *Part Or.* 15-17; *Top.* 26.98; *Her.* 2.30-31; Quint. 6.1; Lausberg, *Handbuch*, I, pp. 236-40, §431-42; Martin, *Rhetorik*, pp. 147-66. For a specific treatment of the *peroratio* of epideictic, see *Her.* 3.8.15.
6. Ar. *Rhet.* 3.13.1414a.3.
7. Cic. *Part. Or.* 17.59; *Her.* 3.8.15.
8. Cf. the use of καὶ νῦν within the *exordium* (v. 22) and introducing the *probatio* (v. 25).
9. Cf. 1 Cor. 3.9-15; Eph. 2.19-22; 4.12, 16.
10. Cic. *De Or.* 3.53.205; *Part. Or.* 16.55.

This initial appeal to *pathos* is followed by a carefully constructed recapitulation. It begins with exemplification, a figure of thought, 'the citing of something done or said in the past, along with the definite naming of the doer or author' used to embellish, clarify, and vivify.[1] The example is Paul's own: 'I coveted no one's silver or gold or apparel. You yourselves know that these hands ministered to my necessities, and to those who were with me' (vv. 33-34).[2]

The exemplification is highly amplified. The list of silver, gold, and apparel is an example of amplification by accumulation, a type of amplification already seen in the *exordium* (v. 19). This list may be in an ascending order of value, for the wealth of many orientals was mainly in clothing.[3] Making each successive word or phrase stronger is one type of amplification by accumulation.[4] In any case, the list amplifies that Paul is in no way covetous, being part of the technique of showing a non-grasping, non-covetous disposition as a way of increasing ethos.[5] This portrayal may serve to hold Paul up as an example to the Lukan generation of Christian leaders who may have been taking advantage of pastoral wages.

Verse 34 calls the audience to witness to the truth of Paul's claim. The emphatic position of 'these hands' inherently portrays Paul's statement as accompanied by a rhetorical gesture.[6] This passage is based on Paul's practice of working with his own hands, something he did to avoid burdening his congregations[7] and which gave him a source of boasting.[8] As mentioned previously, Luke may be upholding

1. Her. 4.49.62. See also Bullinger, *Figures*, p. 467. For an important discussion of exemplification, see Benjamin Fiore, *The Function of Personal Example in the Socratic and Pastoral Epistles* (AnBib 105; Rome: Biblical Institute, 1986).

2. In the *peroratio*, one tactic in recapitulation was to 'combine the opposing arguments with yours. . . and after stating your argument, show how you have refuted the argument which has been made against it' (Cic. *Inv.* 1.52.99). Although a disclaimer to fraud is found in at least one farewell address and may merely be a standard *topos* of the farewell genre (1 Sam. 12.3), Paul may be portrayed as weaving a charge of opposition into his *peroratio* in order to refute it in the next verse with reference to his behavior.

3. Haenchen, *Acts*, p. 594 n. 2. See Josh. 7.21; 2 Kgs 5.22-23; 7.8 (same 3 and in the same order); Acts 3.6; Jas 5.2-3.

4. Quint. 8.4.27. Cf. Cic. *Part. Or.* 15.54.

5. Cic. *De Or.* 2.43.182.

6. For a discussion of hand gestures in ancient rhetoric, see Quint. 11.3.85-124.

7. Acts 18.3; 1 Cor. 4.12; 9; 2 Cor. 11.7-11; 12.13; 1 Thess. 2.9; 2 Thess. 3.7-10.

8. 1 Cor. 9.15; 2 Cor. 11.10.

Paul to Christian leaders as a model of those who help themselves and provide for the weak (v. 35).

The exemplification is combined with one type of recapitulation, the proposal of a policy.[1] Paul's proposal of policy is this: 'In all things I have shown you that by so toiling one must help the weak, remembering[2] the words of the Lord Jesus, how he said, "It is more blessed to give than to receive"' (v. 35). In the *probatio* Paul emphasizes that he proclaimed 'all' the counsel of God (v. 27; cf. v. 20). Now Paul is emphasizing that he has exemplified in 'all' he did among them what it means to help the weak. Paul is thus an example in both word and deed. An appeal to imitate is a characteristic *topos* of the *peroratio* of epideictic[3] and farewell addresses.

Paul's example is supported by a maxim of Jesus seemingly unknown to the gospel tradition.[4] Maxims give the speech an ethical quality and a clear moral purpose which increase the speaker's ethos.[5] Maxims should be brief and placed at the end of the sentence,[6] at the end of an element of arrangement[7] (including the *peroratio*),[8] or at the conclusion of an epideictic speech.[9] All three cases are true here.

Several *topoi* common to epideictic rhetoric in general are found in the *peroratio*. These include presenting a past action without argu-

---

1   *Rhet. ad Alex.* 20.1433b.30ff.; 33.1439b.10ff.

2.   The *topos* of 'remembering' (μνημονεύω) occurs at the end of both the *probatio* (v. 31) and the *peroratio* (v. 35).

3.   Burgess, *Epideictic*, p. 126.

4.   There are several theories as to its origin: (1) an authentic saying: Joachim Jeremias, *Unknown Sayings of Jesus* (trans. Reginald H. Fuller; New York: Macmillan, 1957), pp. 77-81; (2) a summary statement of Jesus' teaching on giving: Dupont, *Discours*, pp. 324-31; Lambrecht, 'Farewell-Address', p. 326; and (3) a Christianized Greek maxim: Thucydides 2.97.4; 1 *Clem.* 2.1; Haenchen, *Acts*, pp. 594-95 n. 5; Lüdemann, *Traditions*, pp. 228-29. A maxim is a figure of speech, 'a saying drawn from life, which shows concisely either what happens or ought to happen in life. . .' (*Her.* 4.17.24). Cf. Ar. *Rhet.* 2.21.1394a.2; Quint. 8.5.1-2 for similar definitions. For further discussion, see Ar. *Rhet.* 2.21; *Her.* 4.17.24-25; Quint. 8.5; Lausberg, *Handbuch*, 1.431-34, §872-79; Martin, *Rhetorik*, 122-24, 257-58; Bullinger, *Figures*, 778-803.

5.   Ar. *Rhet.* 2.21.1395b.16.

6.   Quint. 8.5.2. Aristotle states that they can come first or last in a sentence in the *peroratio* (*Rhet.* 2.21.1394b.7). Demetr. *Eloc.* 2.110 states that maxims often come first in a sentence, but can come last.

7.   *Rhet. ad Alex.* 35.1441a.20ff.; 35.1441b.1ff.

8.   Ar. *Rhet.* 2.21.1394b.7.

9.   *Rhet. ad Alex.* 35.1441b.10ff.

ment;[1] emphasizing acts of kindness, goodwill, magnanimity, and generosity done for the sake of others;[2] noting the performance of an action chiefly alone;[3] and upholding actions as consistent according to a moral purpose.[4] Paul presents, but does not defend, his past action of self-support, and notes that it benefited both those who worked with him as well as the weak, he did it alone, and it was consistent with the moral purpose as admonished by Jesus himself.

Cicero's *Part. Or.* 15.52–17.58 lists several forms of amplification that should characterize the *peroratio* in general, and several are exhibited here. These include words used metaphorically,[5] exhortation to hold fast based on *exempla* and important matters advantageous to humankind, showing affection for others (cf. 'commend to God', v. 32), and promoting affection and generosity.[6] Among other things, exhortations in the *peroratio* are listed as having the most effect.[7] The *peroratio* begins with the metaphor of building (v. 32). More importantly, Paul's self-giving, something which is clearly advantageous to others and which shows affection and generosity, is incorporated in an exhortation.

e. *Narrative Summary (vv. 36-38)*. Luke closes this unit with a narrative summary of events which transpired after the speech:

> And when he had spoken thus, he knelt down and prayed with them all. And they all wept and embraced Paul and kissed him, sorrowing most of all because of the word he had spoken, that they should see his face no more. And they brought him to the ship (vv. 36-38).

The narrative summary underscores the role of the speech as a farewell address and indicates Luke's knowledge of the death of Paul, or at least that Paul never visited Ephesus again. The departure is portrayed in typical biblical motifs of embracing, kissing, and weeping.[8] This list of responses constitutes amplification by accumulation

---

1. Cic. *Part. Or.* 21.71.
2. Ar. *Rhet.* 1.9.1366a.3–1366b.13; 1367a.19-20; Cic. *De Or.* 2.11.46; 2.84.343-44; *Her. 3.6.11.*
3. Ar. *Rhet.* 1.9.1368a.38.
4. Ar. *Rhet.* 1.9.1367b.32.
5. 15.53.
6. 16.55-56.
7. 17.58.
8. Gen. 33.4; 45.14-15; 46.29; Tob. 7.6; Lk. 15.20, all upon meeting someone who has been away for a long time.

and adds pathos to the speech. The *topos* of tears recurs from the *exordium* (v. 19) and the *probatio* (v. 31). The expression 'see the face no more' recurs from the introduction of the *probatio* (v. 25) and demonstrates how the narrative summary functions like the *peroratio* in recapitulating the *topoi* of the speech.

Conclusion

The rhetorical analysis of Acts 20.17-38 given above can be outlined as follows:

    I. Historical Preface (vv. 17-18a)
    II. *Exordium* (vv. 18b-24)
        A. Review (vv. 18b-21)
        B. Preview (vv. 22-24) (καὶ νῦν ἰδού)
    III. *Probatio* (vv. 25-31) (καὶ νῦν ἰδού)
        A Statement advanced as certain (v. 25)
        B. Enthymeme (vv. 26-27)
        C. *Comminatio*, a warning to be on guard (vv. 28-30)
        D. *Comminatio* and appeal to *pathos* (v. 31)
    IV. *Peroratio* (vv. 32-35) (καὶ τὰ νῦν)
        A. Appeal to *pathos* (v. 32)
        B. Exemplification (vv. 33-34)
        C. Proposal of policy supported by a maxim (v. 35)
    V. Narrative Summary (vv. 36-38)

This careful structure and interplay of contents indicates that Luke the rhetor has used *prosopopoeia* to create an epideictic encomium and farewell address for Paul as he ends his missionary journey in the East. An element of apologetic for charges against Paul may also be detected, although the primary purpose of the speech, in conjunction with the purposes of epideictic, is exemplification.

PAUL'S PERSUASIVE LANGUAGE IN ROMANS 5

Michael R. Cosby

George Kennedy has done much to acquaint biblical scholars with the tremendous value of rhetorical criticism, but implementation of this methodology remains largely outside the mainstream of biblical commentaries. Although in some circles the significance of the oral dimensions of language in pre-printing press societies has long been recognized,[1] application of research in 'orality' to the study of rhetoric in Pauline letters remains in its infancy. During the past few decades biblical scholars have seriously begun comparing Paul's epistles with the speech structures used in the various forms of ancient rhetoric (deliberative, forensic, and epideictic).[2] Yet there are few studies that elucidate the individual rhetorical techniques he used to make his arguments *sound* persuasive to his listeners.[3]

---

1. For a helpful bibliography of studies pertaining to the oral dimensions of language published by classicists, anthropologists and linguists, see Walter Ong, *Orality and Literacy: The Technologizing of the Word* (New York: Methuen, 1982), pp. 180-95. E.W. Bullinger (*Figures of Speech used in the Bible* [London: Eyre & Spottiswoode, 1898; repr. Grand Rapids: Baker, 1968]) provides a detailed collection of material showing the various uses of rhetorical devices in the Bible. Over the years works like this seemingly exercised little influence on commentaries, although many of the older commentators were quite familiar with ancient rhetoric.

2. For example, Hans Dieter Betz (*Galatians* [Hermeneia; Philadelphia: Fortress, 1979], pp. 14-25) divides Galatians into Epistolary Prescript, *Exordium, Narratio, Propositio, Probatio, Exhortatio,* and Epistolary Postscript or *Conclusio.* Similarly, Wilhelm Wuellner ('Paul's Rhetoric of Argumentation in Romans: An Alternative to the Donfried-Karris Debate over Romans', *CBQ* 38 [1976], pp. 330-51 [repr. in *The Romans Debate*, ed. Karl P. Donfried (Minneapolis: Augsburg, 1977), pp. 152-74]) argues that Romans should be divided into *Exordium, Peroratio, Transitus,* and *Confirmatio.* For other examples, see Duane F. Watson, 'The New Testament and Greco-Roman Rhetoric: A Bibliography', *JETS* 31 (1988), pp. 470-72.

3. See, for example, Duane F. Watson, '1 Corinthians 10.23–11.1 in the Light of Greco-Roman Rhetoric: The Role of Rhetorical Questions', *JBL* 108 (1989), pp. 301-18.

First-century Romans highly valued training in rhetoric, and the great orators who congregated in the Empire's capital city exercised considerable influence on political and social life. Following the rich heritage of their Greek predecessors, these rhetoricians developed persuasive speech into an art form.[1] For the majority of students in the Hellenistic age, rhetoric was the queen of subjects and 'higher education meant taking lessons from the rhetor, learning eloquence from him'.[2]

We do not know the type or extent of rhetorical training that Paul received during his years as a zealous member of the Pharisees, and we know little about the educational background of the members of the church in Rome. We do know, however, that virtually all reading in antiquity was done aloud and that Paul's letters were delivered to assembled believers. The effectiveness of the written word depended largely on how persuasive it sounded in oral presentation. Ancient authors wrote their works to be *heard*, and they paid special attention to the way their words *sounded*. When seeking to persuade an audience, orators considered the way in which they presented their material to be as important as the logical nature of their arguments.[3]

Further investigation into these rhetorical techniques promises to yield deeper insight into Paul's theology. As occasional letters, his epistles largely represent attempts at *persuading* groups of Christians to adopt certain beliefs and behaviors and reject others. Romans is no exception, regardless of one's theory on the composition of this epistle: whether, for example, Romans was Paul's effort to correct a Jew—

---

1. George A. Kennedy (*The Art of Persuasion in Greece* [Princeton: Princeton University Press, 1963], p. 22) observes that 'the world was a rhetorician's world, its ideal an orator; speech became an artistic product to be admired apart from its content or significance'. I am indebted to Dr Kennedy's books for helping to introduce me to the importance of ancient rhetoric for analyzing biblical texts. When I realized that all ancient literature 'was written to be heard, and even when reading to himself a Greek read aloud' (*The Art of Persuasion in Greece*, p. 4), I began to read the rhetorical handbooks from Aristotle through Quintilian. This developing interest in oral techniques of persuasion led quite naturally to books on orality by scholars like Walter Ong.

2. Henri-Irénée Marrou, *A History of Education in Antiquity* (trans. G. Lamb; London: Sheed & Ward, 1956), p. 194. Marrou states that students need not travel far for such education, for 'rhetors were everywhere, in every self-respecting city' (p. 197).

3. George Kennedy, *New Testament Interpretation through Rhetorical Criticism* (Chapel Hill, NC: University of North Carolina Press, 1984), p. 3.

Gentile split in the church at Rome, or his self-introduction to the Roman Christians as a means of eliciting their support of his mission to Spain. Romans is Paul's longest and perhaps most formal theological presentation, and making the letter *sound* persuasive would have been vitally important for the apostle.

Paul's ability to present forcefully a sustained argument is readily apparent in Romans, although his letter is certainly not comparable to the rhetorical artistry of the works of orators such as Isocrates or Cicero, and not on the same level as the Epistle to the Hebrews.[1] Indeed, in his Corinthian correspondence Paul asserts that he refused to use the skills of oratory so that his converts' faith would rest on the power of God and not on persuasive human speech (1 Cor. 2.1-5). In contrast with the 'super-apostles' who boast of their speaking skills, he asserts, 'even if I am unskilled in speaking, I am not in knowledge' (2 Cor. 11.6). Nevertheless, Paul's admission in 2 Cor. 10.9-10 shows something of his reputation for writing effective letters: 'I would not seem to be frightening you with letters. For they say, "His letters are weighty and strong, but his bodily presence is weak, and his speech is of no account"'. Paul's opponents evidently believed that he made up for what he lacked in speaking ability with his 'weighty' letters.

Commentators typically have given some attention to Paul's writing style in Romans, but they have not attributed major exegetical significance to it in their pursuit of the 'weightier' matters of his theological content. For example, in the 1905 ICC, W. Sanday and A.C. Headlam say that Romans

> is characterized by a remarkable energy and vivacity. . . the eloquence is spontaneous, the outcome of strongly moved feeling; there is nothing about it of laboured oratory. The language is rapid, terse, incisive; the argument is conducted by a quick cut and thrust of dialectic; it reminds us of a fencer with his eye always on his antagonist.[2]

In the updated ICC on Romans, C.E.B. Cranfield elaborates on this by stating that

---

1. See C. Spicq, *L'Epître aux Hébreux* (EBib; 2 vols.; Paris: Librairie Lecoffre, 1953), I, pp. 351-78 for analysis of the rhetorical techniques used by the author of Hebrews. See also Michael R. Cosby, *The Rhetorical Composition and Function of Hebrews 11 in Light of Example Lists in Antiquity* (Macon, GA: Mercer University Press, 1988).

2. W. Sanday and A.C. Headlam, *The Epistle to the Romans* (ICC; 10th edn; New York: Scribner's, 1905), p. lv.

there is little, if any, evidence of the concern for literary grace for its own sake which is characteristic of classical Greek prose. John Chrysostom recognized that it was no use looking for the smoothness of Isocrates, the majesty of Demosthenes, the dignity of Thucydides, or the sublimity of Plato in Paul's letters, and admitted Paul's poverty τῇ λέξει and the simplicity and artlessness (ἁπλῆν . . . καὶ ἀφελῆ) of his composition. . . [Yet Romans] provides clear evidence that Paul knew the various figures of speech of the rhetoricians and that it came naturally to him to make use of them from time to time. . . But these things are used by Paul unselfconsciously, not as ends in themselves but as a natural means to the forceful and compelling expression of what he has to say. It is the content that is all-important.[1]

Thus, Cranfield distinguishes between the orators' deliberate artistic use of rhetoric and Paul's efficient use of rhetorical techniques as a means of bolstering his argument.

Cranfield's comments reflect a somewhat typical evaluation of Pauline writing, and this common perception invites elaboration. Although Paul may well have focused more on content than on delivery, he was obviously concerned to deliver his 'all-important' content in ways meant to persuade a particular audience. Understanding more clearly the means by which he communicated his message (whether he chose the means consciously or unconsciously) will enhance our grasp of his material. Rhetoric is the language of persuasion, and rhetorical techniques are intended to evoke specific responses from listeners. Failure to appreciate these facts impoverishes our *hearing* of the message, and we can only hear Paul's word plays and similar techniques by *listening* to the Greek text.

The 'We' Language of Romans 5.1-11

Romans 5 divides nicely into two sections, on the basis of both content and structural distinctions. Verses 1-11 use first person plural forms to describe the common experience of all Christians (e.g. *we* are justified, *we* rejoice, *we* were weak, Christ died for *us, we* were reconciled to God). In this first section Paul shows the results of reconciliation by emphasizing the coming glory and the present hope during affliction. He formulates his language to inspire faithfulness by explaining what his Christian audience can expect in the future based on what they have received in the past. Primarily through vivid use of

---

1. C.E.B. Cranfield, *The Epistles to the Romans* (ICC; 2 vols.; Edinburgh: T. & T. Clark, 1975–79), I, p. 26.

contrast the apostle emphasizes the magnitude of God's gift of justification by stressing that Christians deserve nothing from God— all comes as a glorious gift.

Paul begins Romans 5 with a technique called *transitio*, 'a figure which briefly recalls what has been said, and likewise briefly sets forth what is to follow next' (*Her.* 4.26.35).[1] With well-balanced phrases Paul summarizes the content of Rom. 1.18–4.25 with his comment on justification and sets the agenda for the following argument by introducing the implications of the life lived by faith.

5.1 Δικαιωθέντες οὖν ἐκ πίστεως
  εἰρήνην ἔχομεν πρὸς τὸν θεὸν
    διὰ τοῦ κυρίου ἡμῶν Ἰησοῦ Χριστοῦ,
2   δι' οὗ καὶ τὴν προσαγωγὴν ἐσχήκαμεν τῇ πίστει
    εἰς τὴν χάριν ταύτην ἐν ᾗ ἐστήκαμεν.[2]

5.1 Therefore, having been justified from faith,
  we have peace with God
    through our Lord Jesus Christ
2   through whom also we have access by faith
    into this grace in which we stand.

Paul previously explained in chs. 1–3 that all people desperately need the grace of God expressed through Jesus Christ because all are guilty before God and deserve his wrath. Now in a vivid summary statement of this substantial block of material, he enhances his message by creating a wordplay in 5.2a-b with the repetition of sounds in ἐσχήκαμεν . . . ἐστήκαμεν, and by using the metaphorical imagery of 'standing' in grace.

Paul then redirects his thought from standing in God's grace to boasting in the hope of sharing the glory of God (5.2c). This boasting has an extremely practical purpose: it allows Christians to view the difficult events of life not so much as setbacks but as aids to character building (5.3-5). Such a radical view of justification apart from human effort leads to a reorientation of how to respond to hardships. To

---

1. *Rhetorica ad Herennium* (trans. Harry Caplan; LCL; Cambridge, MA: Harvard University Press, 1954). Similar summaries occur in Rom. 3.23 and 8.1.

2. All Greek quotations are taken from the Nestle-Aland, *Novum Testamentum Graece* (26th edn; Stuttgart: Deutsche Bibelgesellschaft, 1979). Obviously, setting the phrases off in this manner has little to do with the way the original run-together string of all capital letters would have appeared. But in our visually oriented culture, patterning the words like this facilitates hearing some of the verbal cadences. Often it helps us to see what the ancient audience heard.

describe this transformation of thinking, Paul uses the comparative phrase οὐ μόνον δέ, ἀλλὰ καί ('and not only that, but also. . .') to make the transition from the inspirational 'we boast in the hope of the glory of God' (5.2) to the very unusual 'we boast in afflictions' (5.3).[1] Peace with God (5.1) does not mean an easy life at peace in the world.

Instead of merely saying, 'We boast in afflictions because they build character', Paul employs ἐπεζευγμένον, polysyndeton, and *gradatio* to formulate a string of statements that rhetorically builds to a climax.

2c And we boast in [the] hope of the glory of God.
3   And not only that, but also
       we boast in afflictions
       knowing that affliction works patience,
4   and patience [works] character,
       and character [works] hope,
5   and hope does not disappoint.
       because the love of God has been poured into our hearts
       through the Holy Spirit who has been given to us (5.2c-5).

Each of the statements in vv. 4a-5a begins with 'and' (polysyndeton), and both lines in v. 4 rely on the verb κατεργάζεται ('works') at the end of v. 3.

3c εἰδότες ὅτι ἡ θλῖψις ὑπομονὴν κατεργάζεται,
4   ἡ δὲ ὑπομονὴ δοκιμήν,
      ἡ δὲ δοκιμὴ ἐλπίδα.
5   ἡ δὲ ἐλπὶς οὐ καταισχύνει.

Quintilian calls this technique ἐπεζευγμένον and defines it as 'where a number of clauses are all completed by the same verb, which would be required by each singly if they stood alone' (Quint. 9.3.62).[2] The way Paul constructs his sequence of phrases also conforms to what orators call *gradatio*: the speaker repeats what is said in the previous clause and introduces a new part which is then repeated in the next clause (Quint. 9.3.55). *The Rhetorica ad Herennium* 4.25.34 gives the following example: 'The industry of Africanus brought him excellence, his excellence glory, his glory rivals'.[3] Rhetoricians

---

1. The phrase 'And not only that, but also', which connects the two expressions, occurs again in 5.11, and is also followed by an expression of boasting (though the boasting there is 'in God').

2. Quintilian, *Institutio Oratoria* (trans. H.E. Butler; LCL; 4 vols.; Cambridge, MA: Harvard University Press, 1920-22).

3. Quintilian also uses this example in 9.3.56.

considered this technique to be quite artistic and not like normal speech. Quintilian cautions that 'gradation, which the Greeks call *climax*, necessitates a more obvious and less natural application of art and should therefore be more sparingly employed' (Quint. 9.3.54). By using *gradatio*, Paul is not merely focusing on his 'all-important' content; he implements a persuasive tactic of oratory.

After demonstrating why we can 'boast in afflictions' (5.3b) with his *gradatio* in 5.3c-5a,[1] Paul explains why afflictions ultimately build character when he says 'the love of God has been *poured* (ἐκκέχυται) into our hearts through the Holy Spirit who was given to us' (5.5b-c). Quintilian calls such use of language a *trophe*. 'By a *trophe* is meant the artistic alteration of a word or phrase from its proper meaning to another' (Quint. 8.6.1).[2] He explains that metaphor is the most common form of trophe (e.g. 'the crops are thirsty', 8.6.6), and can be purely ornamental (e.g. 'thunderbolts of eloquence', 8.6.7) or used to give expression where literal words do not exist to express what is meant.

By using the verb 'poured' for love in Rom. 5.5, Paul metaphorically moves this word from its natural semantic domain in an effort to increase the vividness of his expression. Although 'to pour out' (ἐκχεῖν) occurs in Acts 2.17-18 (LXX, Joel 3.1-2), 33; 10.45 and Tit. 3.6 to describe the giving of the Holy Spirit, it is doubtful that Paul is merely using a standard form for expressing the gift of the Spirit in Rom. 5.5.[3] As Cranfield points out, ἐκχεῖν is more often used in the LXX for the pouring out of God's wrath (as it is nine times in Revelation). In Sir. 18.11 ἐκχεῖν designates the pouring out of God's mercy, and in Mal. 3.10 it denotes blessing. Paul most likely uses ἐκχεῖν in Rom. 5.5 metaphorically, as a means of indicating the lavish way in which God pours his love through the Spirit into his people.[4] E.W. Bullinger calls the 'pouring out of the Spirit' in Rom. 5.5 an instance of *anthropopatheia* ('the ascribing of human attribute etc., to God').[5]

---

1. Paul also used *gradatio* in Rom. 8.29-30; 10.14-15.

2. Cf. 9.1.2-3, where Quintilian says a trope is the 'transference of expressions from their natural and principal signification to another, with a view to the embellishment of style or, to which they do not properly belong'.

3. For one of the stronger arguments that Paul is using a standard expression for the giving of the Spirit, see James D.G. Dunn, *Romans* (WBC 38A/B; 2 vols.; Dallas: Word, 1988), I, pp. 252-54.

4. Cranfield, *Romans*, I, pp. 262-63.

5. Bullinger, *Figures of Speech*, p. 890.

Paul next moves from his optimistic expression of hope based on the presence of the Spirit to a description of the unworthiness of people to receive God's gracious gift. In Rom. 5.6-8 Paul crafts a rather elaborate antithesis in order to emphasize the radical nature of Christ's death for us. The beginning and end of the antithesis stress the undeserving condition of humanity when Christ gave his life for us. The middle section draws a sharp contrast to Christ's sacrifice by stating that only for a very deserving individual would the normal person dare to die.

6. Ἔτι γὰρ Χριστὸς ὄντων ἡμῶν ἀσθενῶν
    ἔτι κατὰ καιρὸν ὑπὲρ ἀσεβῶν ἀπέθανεν.
7. μόλις γὰρ ὑπὲρ δικαίου τις ἀποθανεῖται·
    ὑπὲρ γὰρ τοῦ ἀγαθοῦ τάχα τις καὶ τολμᾷ ἀποθανεῖν·
8. συνίστησιν δὲ τὴν ἑαυτοῦ ἀγάπην εἰς ἡμᾶς ὁ θεός,
    ὅτι ἔτι ἁμαρτωλῶν ὄντων ἡμῶν Χριστὸς ὑπὲρ ἡμῶν ἀπέθανεν.

Enhancing the construction of the antithesis is the fourfold use of ὑπέρ to introduce types of people, followed each time by a form of the verb ἀποθνήσκω ('die').

For Christ, while we were weak,
at the right time *on behalf of* the ungodly *died.*
For scarcely *on behalf of* a righteous man would someone *die,*
For *on behalf of* a good man perhaps someone might dare *to die.*
But God demonstrates his love unto us
in that while we were sinners, Christ *on behalf of* us *died.*

By stressing how doubtful it is that one person would die for another, even if the other were a very good person, Paul establishes one of his major points. We were weak, ungodly sinners when Christ died for us. This ultimate sacrifice came not because of merit on our part but strictly as an expression of God's grace. By placing side by side these starkly contrasting descriptions of what people might do and what God has done, Paul dramatically increases the impact of his point.

Authors of the rhetorical handbooks highly commend the use of antithesis. Aristotle, for example, explains that antithesis is effective 'because contraries are easily understood and even more so when placed side by side, and also because antithesis resembles a syllogism; for refutation is a bringing together of contraries' (*Rhet.* 3.9.8).[1] The more pungent and to the point the better the antithesis (e.g. 'For some

---

1. Aristotle, *Rhetoric* (trans. J.H. Freese; LCL; Cambridge, MA: Harvard University Press, 1926).

of them perished miserably, others saved themselves disgracefully' [*Rhet.* 3.9.7]).

Quintilian specifies that an antithesis (*contrapositum* or *contentio*) occurs when single words, pairs of words, or sentences are contrasted (Quint. 9.3.81). Rom. 5.6-8 matches admirably these qualifications. Paul appears to have crafted the language of his contrast carefully in order to show the magnitude of God's love for and gracious gift to the sinner.[1] Then he builds on this antithesis by presenting a well-balanced summary that explores the dimensions of God's gracious gift.

Rom. 5.9-10 summarizes the content of 5.1-8, thus providing a brief *transitio*:

> Therefore *how much more*, now that we have been justified by his blood, we will be saved through him from the [coming] wrath. For if while we were *enemies* we were reconciled to God through the *death* of his son, *how much more* now that we are reconciled we will be saved by his *life*.

Beginning with another of his comparative phrases, 'therefore how much more', Paul continues his thought from v. 8 by referring again to Christ's death.[2] He does so, however, not by repeating ἀποθνῄσκω but by using a phrase that means the same, 'by his blood'. This technique, where one word or phrase is substituted for another, is called *metonymy* (Quint. 8.6.23-27). Paul uses it here to emphasize the sacrificial nature of Christ's death which results in justification of the sinner and salvation from God's wrath (5.9).

Verse 10 strengthens Paul's theme of salvation as an undeserved gift by adding the term 'enemies' to his description of people as weak, ungodly sinners in vv. 6, 8. And the repetition of 'how much more' in vv. 9 and 10 (πολλῷ οὖν μᾶλλον . . . πολλῷ μᾶλλον) heightens the emotional content of the message. Paul even implements the form of argumentation known as 'from the lesser to the greater' to increase the persuasive sound of his words.[3] 'If Christ by his death did all of that for us while we were enemies of God, *just think of how much more* his life implies for us now!' This emotional quality of Paul's

1. Bullinger (*Figures of Speech*, p. 696) calls Rom. 5.8 an example of *hyperbaton*, the placing of words out of their normal sequence in a sentence. 'Here the words are out of the natural order to excite our attention. The Greek is: "But commends His own love to us—God". The nominative is put last, and the verb first, to emphasize both.'

2. Rom. 5.9 also harks back to v. 1 through repetition of 'having been justified'.

3. Cf. Aristotle, *Rhet.* 1.2.1358a.21; 1.3.1359a.8-9; 2.18-19; 2.23-24; Cicero, *De Or.* 2.39-40; *Top.* 1.1–23.90; Quint. 5.8.4-5; 5.10.20-99.

words then carries over into v. 11, which begins with οὐ μόνον δέ, ἀλλὰ καί ('And not only that, but also. . .!'), a phrase he previously used to begin v. 3.

Thus, Paul concludes this first section of Romans 5 by asserting that 'we', the former enemies of God, may now boast in God because of the reconciliation received from Christ Jesus the Lord (καυχώμενοι ἐν τῷ θεῷ διὰ τοῦ κυρίου ἡμῶν Ἰησοῦ Χριστοῦ, δι' οὖ νῦν τὴν καταλλαγὴν ἐλάβομεν). This attitude boldly contrasts with the sinful boasting in personal achievement that Paul condemns in 3.27. Weak, ungodly, sinful, enemies of God boast in what they have accomplished to earn their own righteousness. Those who have been justified by faith in Christ boast in what God has accomplished for them.

On that note of confidence in God, Paul moves into the next section of his argument, an intriguing contrast between Christ and Adam. He has made his point in 5.1-11, not by focusing on content alone, but by delivering his message with rhetorical techniques that increase its persuasive sound. There is a degree of oral artistry to his presentation.

Adam and Christ in Romans 5.12-21

The second section, 5.12-21, switches to third person plural forms to speak of the universal human experience of sin and death as a consequence of Adam's sin (e.g. death spread to *all people, all people* sinned, condemnation for *all people*). Here Paul graphically contrasts the effects of Adam's disobedience and Christ's obedience, stringing together a series of five antitheses to establish his point.

Rom. 5.12 begins with διὰ τοῦτο ('therefore'), an obvious refer- ence to preceding material, 'since there is no following clause capable of picking it up'.[1] Because a mere connection with v. 11 makes little sense, the phrase appears to refer either to the summary statement in vv. 9-11 or (more likely) to all of 5.1-11. Thus, Paul uses διὰ τοῦτο as a means of calling to his audience's mind the previous content. Yet the transition is rather abrupt, thereby reducing its rhetorical effec- tiveness. Actually, what seems to tie v. 12 back to v. 11 most effec- tively is the repetition of διά ('through').

    11. διὰ τοῦ κυρίου ἡμῶν Ἰησοῦ Χριστοῦ
       δι' οὖ νῦν τὴν καταλλαγὴν ἐλάβομεν.

---

1. Cranfield, *Romans*, I, p. 271.

12. Διὰ τοῦτο ὥσπερ δι' ἑνὸς ἀνθρώπου
    ἡ ἁμαρτία εἰς τὸν κόσμον εἰσῆλθεν
    καὶ διὰ τῆς ἁμαρτίας ὁ θάνατος,
    καὶ οὕτως εἰς πάντας ἀνθρώπους ὁ θάνατος διῆλθεν,
    ἐφ' ᾧ πάντες ἥμαρτον.

The first three phrases of v. 12 are approximately the same length and form a nicely balanced introductory clause (protasis). Yet the corresponding conclusion to this introduction seems strangely missing. Verse 12d seems to be neither a continuation of nor an apodosis for v. 12a-c. Consequently, many exegetes believe that v. 12 begins a comparison that is not actually completed until v. 18. They surmise that Paul broke off his sentence when he realized that more content needed to be given on the subject; then he completed the thought in v. 18.[1] Verse 18 again speaks of the sin of the one man, begins with ἄρα οὖν ὡς δι' ἑνός ('Consequently, as through one'), and completes the thought with a corresponding οὕτως καὶ δι' ἑνός ('so also through one').

In defense of this position, Paul elsewhere sometimes does break his train of thought to add further material and then return to complete his point.[2] It should also be noted, however, that 5.12d begins with καὶ οὕτως, so it may well complete the thought begun with ὥσπερ in 5.12a. John T. Kirby points out that Paul frequently uses the ὥσπερ/οὕτως form in this section of Romans (5.15, 18, 19, 21; 6.4, 19), and therefore he insists that this construction in 5.12 should not be translated differently from the rest, for that would make it unique in leaving οὕτως implicit.[3]

In light of what he views as the careful construction of the material surrounding v. 12, Kirby objects to viewing Paul's prose here as sloppy. He describes 5.12 as 'an extraordinary instance of isocolon' and goes on to say, 'this sort of attention to details of style, worthy of a veritable Gorgias, does not occur in a passage whose author has carelessly dashed it off without a backward glance'.[4] He argues that

1. Cranfield (*Romans*, I, pp. 272-73) provides an excellent summary of the various positions taken by scholars in interpreting Rom. 5.12.
2. E.g. 1 Cor. 1.14-17 (14.33b-36 may be either a digression or a later insertion). 2 Cor. 6.14–7.1 breaks the train of thought, but may be imported from another letter. Cf. Eph. 3.1, 14; 4.1.
3. John T. Kirby, 'The Syntax of Romans 5.12: A Rhetorical Approach', *NTS* 33 (1987), p. 283.
4. Kirby, 'Syntax of Romans 5.12', pp. 283-84.

ὥσπερ in v. 12 should be translated in the same way as in its other uses in this passage: 'just as through one man [sc. Adam] sin came into the world, and through sin, death, *so too* [sc. through one man, Adam] death came to all men'.[1]

Kirby goes on to say that v. 12 is a rhetorical syllogism, a construction that Aristotle calls an enthymeme:

> If sin entered the world through one man,
> And if death entered through sin,
> Then death spread to all men through one man.[2]

Thus, according to Kirby, Paul opens this second section of Romans 5 by tracing the problem of human sin and mortality back to the sin of Adam. To stress this connection, Paul reverses his normal sequence of οὕτως καί and says καὶ οὕτως, making this an instance of *hyperbaton*. Kirby concludes,

> Had Paul written οὕτως καί here, the emphasis would be on εἰς πάντας ἀνθρώπους, which corresponds not to δι᾽ ἑνὸς ἀνθρώπου but rather to εἰς τὸν κόσμον in the ὥσπερ clause. Following καί as it does, οὕτως here stands for δι᾽ ἑνὸς ἀνθρώπου with a succinctness that avoids clutter.[3]

Kirby's work further reveals the potential benefit of rhetorical analysis for exegesis of difficult passages, since it considers possibilities for interpretation that may lie outside a strictly grammatical approach. The weakness of his argument, however, lies in the fact that he never includes the conclusion of v. 12 in his consideration of its meaning: ἐφ᾽ ᾧ πάντες ἥμαρτον ('because all men sinned').

Rom. 5.12 is not 'an extraordinary instance of isocolon',[4] and Paul's attention to stylistic considerations is not so obviously brilliant as Kirby claims. Verse 12 could just as easily be translated as follows, the logic of viewing it as a complete thought still being maintained: 'wherefore, *as* through one man sin entered into the world, and through sin death (entered), *in the same way* death came to all men because all sinned'. In this reading there is a chiastic structure to the statement:

> Because of Adam sin entered the world and brought death;
> likewise death came to all men because all sinned.

---

1. Kirby, 'Syntax of Romans 5.12', p. 284.
2. Kirby, 'Syntax of Romans 5.12', p. 284.
3. Kirby, 'Syntax of Romans 5.12', p. 286.
4. Kirby, 'Syntax of Romans 5.12', p. 283.

Thus, the blame lies not just on Adam but also on all of his descendants as well; death spread to all because all sinned.

In 5.13-14 Paul develops his explanation of the history of sin and death in the world. He states that sin was indeed rampant in the world prior to the giving of the Law of Moses, but it was not reckoned against people because there was no law. Then, using a metaphor, he describes death as ruling like a monarch from Adam until Moses. Even though people were not deliberately breaking a divine law as Adam had, they still suffered the devastating effects of sin.[1]

Paul's almost absolute distinction between being either under the Law of Moses or being without law seems rather puzzling. He obviously lived within the framework of Roman laws, and one could reasonably assume that his training as a rabbi included instruction concerning pre-Mosaic laws.[2] But all that seems to be preempted as he presents his scheme of history. Within this scheme, Adam and Christ are the two major foci. The Law of Moses plays a relatively minor role in Paul's play.

So universal was the result of Adam's transgression that in 5.14 Paul calls him a type of the 'one to come', namely Christ. In rhetorical terms this is an instance of *antonomasia*, the substitution of a descriptive phrase for a proper name.[3] After drawing this comparison between Adam and Christ, however, Paul immediately begins to contrast these two individuals. In so doing he employs rhetorical tech-

---

1. This seems to reflect the case for universal human guilt that Paul develops in Rom. 1–3. Although Gentiles do not have the Law of God, they are still guilty of sin on the basis of natural revelation and their doing what their consciences tell them not to do. Jews are perhaps more guilty because they break God's law; but whether Jew or Gentile, all stand condemned before God and in need of his grace (3.19-26).

2. W.D. Davies ('Law in First-Century Judaism', *Jewish and Pauline Studies* [Philadelphia: Fortress, 1984], p. 8) lists a number of references to pre-Mosaic laws in Jewish literature. Although most of these are from later rabbinic writings, some are from more ancient sources: Exod. 15.25; *Jub.* 3.10-14, 30-31; 7.20-21. Davies comments, 'These Noachian commandments were placed on all mankind and may roughly be taken to correspond to the Stoic "law of nature". David Daube considers them to signal the recognition on the part of Judaism of the extreme improbability that all nations would ever come to obey the whole law; it resigned itself to this fact by insisting only on a minimum of decency for Gentiles'. Davies goes on to show that Philo calls Abraham an incarnation of the law (νόμος αὐτὸς ὤν καὶ θεσμὸς ἄγραφος).

3. Quint 8.6.29. Quintilian observes that the poets are particularly fond of this device.

niques that show the vastly superior nature of the work of Christ over the universal devastation wrought by Adam's sin.

To assert that God's gift of grace overshadows Adam's trespass, Paul uses an οὐχ ὡς/οὕτως καί ('not as/so also') construction followed by another of his πολλῷ μᾶλλον ('much more') clauses employed previously in 5.9, 10.

> 15. Ἀλλ' οὐχ ὡς τὸ παράπτωμα,
>   οὕτως καὶ τὸ χάρισμα·
>   εἰ γὰρ τῷ τοῦ ἑνὸς παραπτώματι οἱ πολλοὶ ἀπέθανον,
>   πολλῷ μᾶλλον
>   ἡ χάρις τοῦ θεοῦ
>   καὶ ἡ δωρεὰ ἐν χάριτι τῇ τοῦ ἑνὸς ἀνθρώπου Ἰησοῦ Χριστοῦ
>   εἰς τοὺς πολλοὺς ἐπερίσσευσεν.

His expression 'the many' in v. 15c, g is equivalent to 'all men' in v. 12. We may only speculate on whether this is merely a stylistic variation or an echo of the language of Isa. 53.11 ('my servant [shall] make many to be accounted righteous; and he shall bear their iniquities'), or even a rhetorical way of contrasting 'the one' and 'the many'. The rhetorical contrast seems most probable in light of Paul's assertion: 'for if by *the one* transgression *the many* died, *how much more* the grace of God and the gift in grace by *the one* man Jesus Christ abounded unto *the many*'. To increase the impressive sound of the accomplishment of the gracious gift, Paul uses the superlatives 'much more' and 'abounded'. These emotionally laden words increase the persuasive sound of the argument.

In 5.16-17 Paul follows a pattern similar to 5.15, beginning with an οὐχ ὡς phrase (not an οὐχ ὡς/οὕτως construction) followed by a πολλῷ μᾶλλον statement. Again he intends to establish the superiority of Christ's gift of grace over Adam's sin. The motif of the one and the many continues in these verses, initially with a well-formed antithesis in v. 16:

> τὸ μὲν γὰρ κρίμα ἐξ ἑνὸς εἰς κατάκριμα,
> τὸ δὲ χάρισμα ἐκ πολλῶν παραπτωμάτων εἰς δικαίωμα.

> For judgment [came] after one [sin] unto condemnation;
> but grace [came] after many sins unto justification.

Then in v. 17 Paul rehearses the devastating impact of Adam's sin, repeating his metaphor that death *ruled* because of sin (cf. 5.14). This terrible condition is then diminished in importance with Paul's contrast: 'How much more those who have received the abundance of grace and the gift of righteousness will rule in life through the one, Jesus Christ'.

Not only is this construction rather unusual in that the participle λαμβάνοντες ('receiving') in the second part of v. 17 is separated substantially from its article οἱ, but it is also not parallel with v. 17a.

> If by the transgression of the one death ruled through the one, how much more those who receive in life the abundance of grace and the gift of righteousness (οἱ τὴν περισσείαν τῆς χάριτος καὶ τῆς δωρεᾶς τῆς δικαιοσύνης λαμβάνοντες ἐν ζωῇ) will rule through the one, Jesus Christ (5.17).

If the apodosis paralleled the protasis, 'life' in v. 17b would rule even as 'death' ruled in v. 17a. Instead Paul says the Christians rule in life. James D.G. Dunn comments, 'the thought of "life" as exercising rule over believers is evidently inappropriate... The opposite to the coldly final rule of death is the unfettered enjoyment of life—the life of a king.'[1] Paul's language, while effectively communicating his central point, does not exhibit rhetorical sophistication at this stage.

Paul concludes his juxtaposition of Adam and Christ with two beautifully balanced antitheses in 5.18-19. With a minimum of words, v. 18 draws together the content of the preceding verses with tightly formulated phrases in which no verb is expressed. Lines one and three of v. 18 match the structure of lines two and four, succinctly showing the way Christ's righteous action reversed Adam's sinful deed.

> Ἄρα οὖν ὡς δι' ἑνὸς παραπτώματος
>   εἰς πάντας ἀνθρώπους εἰς κατάκριμα,
> οὕτως καὶ δι' ἑνὸς δικαιώματος
>   εἰς πάντας ἀνθρώπους εἰς δικαίωσιν ζωῆς·

> Therefore, as through one transgression
>   all men [entered] into condemnation,
> so also through one act of righteousness
>   all men [entered] into righteousness of life.

Verse 19 further explains v. 18, again employing rhetorical antithesis built on carefully matched statements.

> ὥσπερ γὰρ διὰ τῆς παρακοῆς τοῦ ἑνὸς ἀνθρώπου
>   ἁμαρτωλοὶ κατεστάθησαν οἱ πολλοί,
> οὕτως καὶ διὰ τῆς ὑπακοῆς τοῦ ἑνὸς
>   δίκαιοι κατασταθήσονται οἱ πολλοί.

---

1. Dunn, *Romans*, I, p. 282.

> For as through the disobedience of the one man
>> the many were made to be sinners;
> so also through the obedience of the one
>> the many will be made righteous.

Adam's disobedience caused 'the many' (i.e. everyone except Christ) to be sinners; Christ's obedience will cause 'the many' (i.e. those who believe) to be righteous. Thus, although the antithesis is well formulated, 'the many' in 5.19b is not parallel in meaning to 'the many' in 5.19d.

In v. 20 Paul makes a brief statement about the Mosaic Law, and he does so in a somewhat disparaging way. In light of the extreme degree to which many Jewish teachers exalted the role of the Law, Paul's words are remarkable. The identification of Torah with Wisdom in Proverbs 8 was already accomplished around 180 BC in Sirach. Scribes later began to regard Torah as the blueprint for the cosmos.

> When a king builds a palace, he does not do it himself, but with the help of 'the knowledge of a master builder' (מדעת אומן). And the master builder in turn considers plans and drawings: in just the same way, 'God looked into the Torah' (מביט בתורה) when he created the world.[1]

By Paul's time superlatives for Torah abounded, and there is excellent evidence that many scribes believed that the Law of Moses would not be replaced in the Age to Come, but rather be understood more completely and obeyed more faithfully.[2] Given such belief in the eternity of the Law, Paul's comment in v. 20 should have sounded blasphemous to many Jews: 'the Law sneaked in (παρεισῆλθεν) to increase sin'.

This assertion would prove to be quite confrontational if, as many scholars now believe, Romans 14–15 indicates that some Jewish Christians at Rome were so concerned about obeying Torah that they were judging Gentile Christians for failure to do likewise (e.g. 14.2-3, 5-6, 10, 13-16, 21). For Paul to say that the law *sneaked* in at a later time, and that the net effect was to *increase* sin, surely seemed quite abrasive to many Jewish Christians. But in 5.20-21 Paul can hardly slow down enough to dwell on the topic. Immediately he passes on to assert that, although sin abounded (ἐπλεόνασεν), grace superabounded

---

1. From *b. Sanh.* 67b as cited by Martin Hengel, *Judaism and Hellenism* (2 vols.; trans. J. Bowden; Philadelphia: Fortress, 1974), vol. I, p. 171.
2. See e.g. W.D. Davies, *The Setting of the Sermon on the Mount* (Cambridge: Cambridge University Press, 1964), pp. 139-90.

(ὑπερεπερίσσευσεν). Such graphic language increases the persuasive sound of the argument.

Paul concludes the chapter with one final ὥσπερ/οὕτως καί construction in v. 21: '*as* sin reigned in death, *so also* grace might rule through righteousness unto eternal life through Jesus Christ our Lord'. This last contrast is closely connected to v. 20 through the use of ἵνα, making it an explanation of the previous statement. And so Paul completes his rhetoric of reconciliation in Romans 5 and prepares to deal with the implications of his teaching in Romans 6.

Conclusion

As did all authors of his time, Paul wrote his message to be *heard* by an audience. To *be* persuasive his words needed to *sound* persuasive, and indeed his argument seems to be quite engaging. Although not on a sophisticated enough level to be called eloquent, Paul's 'speech' in Romans 5 reveals attention to detail and rhetorical effectiveness. *Listening* to his words in the Greek text opens up a further avenue by which we may travel in our journey to understand Paul's content.

Since rhetoric is the language of persuasion and Romans is a persuasive document, analyzing Paul's use of rhetorical techniques is an important endeavor. Whether he would have known the technical terms for these techniques or used them consciously or unconsciously does not matter. People lacking formal training in speech frequently use the rhetorical means of expression common in their cultures. However, Paul, the educated Pharisee, the seasoned Christian missionary, the one who wrote weighty letters (2 Cor. 10.9-10), implemented persuasive speech with far more than casual effectiveness.

In the first section of Romans 5, Paul consistently uses first person plural forms to explain the common experience of Christians. Beginning with a *transitio* in v. 1, he summarizes his previous material and introduces that which follows. Paul adorns this transitional statement by creating a word play with the terms ἐσχήκαμεν and ἐστήκαμεν and using the metaphor of 'standing' in grace. Then, to make his assertion about viewing afflictions as character-builders more persuasive, he adorns this comment by combining *epezeygmenon, polysyndeton, gradatio* and metaphor. This artistic formulation substantially enhances Paul's message.

Rom. 5.6-8 emphasizes the magnitude of God's gracious gift through Christ by implementing an *antithesis*, contrasting Christ's death for us (weak, ungodly sinners) with the unusual event of some-one daring to die for a noble person. Verses 9-10 comprise another *transitio* in which Paul uses *metonymy* and a series of emotionally laden words and comparisons to strengthen his point. He concludes this first section with a strong comparative statement that believers, the former enemies of God, may now boast in God, who justified them by faith.

In the second section, vv. 12-21, Paul switches to third person plural forms to describe the universal human experience of sin and death. He begins this section with a statement consisting of a series of clauses of nearly equal length (*isocolon*). The presence of this tech-nique makes it quite possible that, in opposition to the view of most commentators, v. 12 forms a complete statement. It is not an inter-rupted sentence that Paul does not finish until v. 18.

Following v. 12 Paul provides a series of five contrasts in 5.15-19 that employ vividly contrasting words. Verse 20a breaks this string of antitheses with a confrontational sounding assertion that the law *sneaked in* and that its net effect was to *increase sin*. But Paul imme-diately returns to the use of contrast in v. 20b, saying that where sin *abounded*, grace *superabounded*. This leads into one last antithesis in v. 21, which further explains v. 20 by contrasting the rule of sin unto death with that of grace through righteousness unto life.

The net effect of Paul's rhetoric in Romans 5 is to increase substan-tially the impact of his words on his audience. As they listen to the plays on words, as they hear the metaphors, as they are struck by the rapid repetition of a string of striking antitheses, the Roman Christians would find Paul's presentation more persuasive than they would if he had merely provided substantiating data without rhetorical techniques.

THE RHETORICAL FUNCTION
OF NUMERICAL SEQUENCES IN ROMANS

Robert Jewett

Considerable attention has been given to numerical sequences within the Bible, stressing the preference for series of ten, seven, five and three.[1] A coordinated series of terms listed next to each other was called an *enumeratio* in Greco-Roman rhetoric.[2] The discussion of the 'rhetorical use of numbers' in biblical literature by John J. Davis follows the lead of Wolfgang Roth who analyzed the $x/x + 1$ formula as a climactic figure.[3] A classic example of this formula is Amos 1.3, 'for three transgressions of Damascus, yea, for four, I will not turn away the punishment. . .' This figure is often called a 'priamel', as discussed by Bühlmann and Scherer[4] and others.[5] Occasionally the digit is named as in the Amos example, but more frequently 'the rhetorical effect is achieved through a latent number, i.e., certain words or names occur a given number of times, although the actual

1. G.R. Driver, 'Sacred Numbers and Round Figures', *Promise and Fulfillment: Essays Presented to Professor S.H. Hooke in Celebration of his Ninetieth Birthday* (ed. F.F. Bruce; Edinburgh: T. & T. Clark, 1963), pp. 62-90.

2. See Heinrich Lausberg, *Handbuch der literarischen Rhetorik* (2nd edn; 2 vols.; Munich: Hüber, 1973), I, pp. 333-40, §660-74.

3. John J. Davis, *Biblical Numerology* (Grand Rapids: Baker, 1968), pp. 93-102; Wolfgang M.W. Roth, *Numerical Sayings in the Old Testament: A Form-Critical Study* (VTSup 13; Leiden: Brill, 1965); *idem*, 'Ten Commandments, Twelve Apostles and One God', *Explor* 4/2 (1978), pp. 4-11.

4. Walter Bühlmann and Karl Scherer, *Stilfiguren der Bibel: Ein kleines Nachschlagwerk* (BibB 10; Fribourg: Schweizerisches Katholisches Bibelwerk, 1973), pp. 60-62, with additional bibliography listed.

5. Among older items unavailable to me are U. Schmid, *Die Priamel der Werte im Griechischen von Homer bis Paulus* (Wiesbaden, 1964); F. Dornseiff, 'Das altorientalische Priamel', *Antike und Alter Orient: Interpretationen* (ed. F. Dornseiff; 2nd edn; Leipzig: Koehler and Amelang, 1959), pp. 379-93; and W. Kröhling, *Die Priamel als Stilmittel in der griechisch-römischen Dichtung* (Greifswald, 1935).

figure is not specified'.[1] The precedents of such series in the ancient Near East and the parallels in Greco-Roman culture, with its interest in tens, nines, sevens, threes and twos, have been explored.[2] Only at a few incidental points has such discussion touched the debate over Romans. The antithetical quality of the argument of Romans rests on multiple series of twos, of which there are scores of examples.[3] Rengstorf discussed the reference to the 7000 faithful believers in Rom. 11.4[4] and Hauck pointed out the ten forms of demonic power in Rom. 8.38-39,[5] while Dobschütz alluded to the triads in 1.24-26, 2.7-10 and 2.4.[6] No Romans commentary develops or explains the significance of such series, perhaps because there is no example of a numerical saying where the digit is supplied. The question of the rhetorical significance of such series in Romans has understandably not yet been raised.

My interest in this theme emerged in the process of analyzing the rhetorical structure of Romans when a decalogical structure of the argument of the letter came to light.[7] Each of the four proofs in the letter is divided into ten pericopae, which in the case of the first proof (1.18–4.25) are paired into five large pericopae. This macro-structure piqued my interest, so that in the detailed rhetorical analysis of Romans carried out in connection with a commentary project, I began to look for numerical sequences at the micro-structural level and to reflect on their relevance for the argument of the letter. Here is an account of the preliminary results of this investigation, which I hope

---

1. Israel Abrahams, 'Numbers, Typical and Important', *EncJud*, XII, p. 1255.

2. See for instance Eduard Wöfflin ('Zur Zahlensymbolik [mit Probeartikel Septem und Novem]', *Archiv für lateinische Lexikographie* 9 [1896], pp. 333-54) who discusses series of three, seven, nine, and ten in Greco-Roman culture.

3. See the classic study by Ernst von Dobschütz, 'Zwei- und dreigliedrige Formeln: Ein Beitrag zur Vorgeschichte der Trinitätsformel', *JBL* 50 (1931), pp. 117-47; also Jean Nélis, 'Les antithèses littéraires dans les épîtres de Saint Paul', *NRT* 70 (1948), pp. 360-87.

4. Karl Heinrich Rengstorf, 'ἑπτά, κτλ.', *TDNT*, II, pp. 627-35.

5. Friedrich Hauck, 'δέκα', *TDNT*, II, pp. 36-37.

6. E. von Dobschütz, 'Zwei- und dreigliedrige Formeln', pp. 118-19, 123.

7. Jewett, 'Following the Argument of Romans', *WW* 6 (1986), pp. 382-89. Arnold Willer's exploration entitled *Der Römerbrief—eine dekalogische Komposition* (Stuttgart: Calwer, 1981) deals not so much with the rhetorical arrangement of the letter as with the alleged influence of the Ten Commandments on the argument and theology of the letter.

will be aided by colleagues in the fields of rhetoric, classics, and biblical studies.[1]

Series of Tens

While the number ten was prominent in many ancient cultures,[2] probably relating to the number of fingers, it attained a peculiar significance in Hebrew culture because of its association with the commandments, the tithe, and the later requirement of ten males to constitute the quorum for a synagogue service.[3] As Hauck observes, in Judaism 'the number is so fixed in this respect that the word *minjan* (number) may be used for it'.[4] There is a well-known example from Amos 3.3-8 of a denary priamel that is strongly reminiscent of sequences found in Romans:[5]

1. Do two walk together, unless they have made an appointment?
2. Does a lion roar in the forest, when he has no prey?
3. Does a young lion cry out from his den, if he has taken nothing?
4. Does a bird fall in a snare on the earth, when there is no trap for it?
5. Does a snare spring up from the ground, when it has taken nothing?
6. Is a trumpet blown in a city, and the people are not afraid?
7. Does evil befall a city, unless the Lord has done it?
8. Surely the Lord God does nothing, without revealing his secret to his servants the prophets.
9. The lion has roared: who will not fear?
10. The Lord God has spoken; who can but prophesy?

1. Early drafts of this article were read by Wolfgang M.W. Roth, Frank Witt Hughes, and Duane F. Watson, who provided important critical assistance in clarifying the issues and rhetorical categories used in this preliminary study.
2. Schimmel observes, for example, that 'the Pythagoreans regarded ten as the perfect number. . .' (*EncR*, XI, p. 17).
3. See H.A. Brongers, 'Die Zehnzahl in der Bibel und in ihrer Umwelt', *Studia Biblica et Semitica. . . Festschrift T.C. Vriezen* (Wangeningen: Veenman, 1966), pp. 30-45.
4. Hauck, 'δέκα', p. 36; see also S. Krauss, 'Minjan', *Jahresberichte der israelitisch-theologischen Lehranstalt in Wien* 37-39 (1933), pp. 51-74; and H. Hagg, 'Die biblischen Wurzeln des Minjan', *Abraham Unser Vater. . . Festschrift für Otto Michel* (ed. Otto Betz et al.; AGSU 5; Leiden: Brill, 1963), pp. 235-42, cited by Hauck.
5. See Bühlmann and Scherer, *Stilfiguren*, p. 61-62, and the discussion in Roth, *Numerical Sayings*, pp. 8-9, 96-97.

The most prominent example in Romans is the one noted by Hauck, the ten forms of demonic power listed in 8.38-39, which have a similar stylistic symmetry, though on a smaller scale than the example from Amos.

> For I am convinced that
> 1. neither death,
> 2. nor life,
> 3. nor angels,
> 4. nor principalities,
> 5. nor things present,
> 6. nor things to come,
> 7. nor powers,
> 8. nor heights,
> 9. nor depths,
> 10. nor any other creature. . .

This list is clearly marked by epanaphora in the repeated use of 'nor'. The items are paired in an antithetical manner, with an irregularity caused by the insertion of 'powers' that conveys the desire to make the series of 10 end with an inclusive category for which no pairing was available. Rhetorically, the series serves the purpose of amplifying the transcendent power of divine love through an accumulation of forces that were ordinarily thought to be capable of prevailing.[1] This list of ten is reminiscent of the series of evil-doers in 1 Cor. 6.9-10.[2] An almost equally prominent series is found in Rom. 9.4-5 where nine attributes of Israel are listed in a series ending with a classic Jewish doxology to make an artful priamel of ten. Five of the items are connected with καί and the rest with possessive pronouns to create a very graceful series.

> 1. They are the Israelites,
> 2. whose [are] the sonship
> 3. and the glory
> 4. and the covenants
> 5. and the lawgiving
> 6. and the worship
> 7. and the promises,
> 8. whose [are] the patriarchs
> 9. and from whom [came] the Christ according to the flesh,
> 10. who is God over all, blessed for the aeons, amen.

---

1. For a discussion of amplification through accumulation in classical rhetoric, see Lausberg, *Handbuch*, I, pp. 220-22, §400-403.
2. Hauck, 'δέκα', p. 37.

Given the subject matter of a people whose identity was so closely tied with the ten commandments, the tithe, and the ten men required for commencing a synagogue service, the length of this series was likely to have been noticeable.

A third example of a denary series is found in 12.10-13 where five pairs of imperatival expressions serve to elaborate the injunction in 12.9, 'let love be genuine!' Given the subsequent argument that love fulfills the entire law (ch. 13), the length of this series was probably not accidental. It conveys the theme of replacing the Torah-oriented ethic with a new, charismatic ethic based on love.

The last three examples are less easily discernible because they are embedded in larger pericopae rather than appearing in closely connected series. The diatribal exchange of 3.27–4.10 includes ten rhetorical questions. There are ten references to 'sin' in a single pericope of 6.1-14, constituting a thematically significant reduplication. Also, there are ten quotations of Hebrew scripture in the midrashic argument of 9.6-29, five in each of the two successive pericopae that carry out this argument.

Series of Fives

There is a considerably longer list of fivefold series in Romans, a datum that points decisively in the direction of Judaic cultural values as perceived in Paul's time. While series of tens were prominent in Greek culture, a preference taken over to a modest degree in Roman culture as well, series of fives appear to have emerged as more distinctively Jewish because of the association with the five books of the Torah and the later collection of the five 'megillot', the scrolls of Canticles, Ruth, Lamentation, Ecclesiastes, and Esther.[1] While there is little evidence of theological or rhetorical interest in the number five in the Hebrew Scriptures themselves,[2] later Jewish culture including the NT treat it as a favorite digit. Rabbinic Judaism developed the theory of the 'five species' of plants in Israel to which the agricultural regulations of the Torah were to be applied,[3] but the different plants identified in various discussions of this issue suggest a numerical

---

1. See Bruce C. Birch, 'Number', *ISBE*, III, pp. 556-61.

2. Most of the standard articles on biblical numbers pass over 'five' without comment, and there is no article in the *TDNT* on חמש, the Hebrew word for five.

3. See Jehuda Feliks, 'Five Species', *EncJud*, VI, pp. 1332-33.

requirement. The Christian Gospel with closest affinities to Jewish culture evinces a clear interest in this number by referring to the 'five loaves of the five thousand' in the miraculous feeding story (Mt. 16.9) and to the five wise and five foolish maidens and the five talents in Matthew's version of the parables (Mt. 25.1-13, 15-30). These details are hardly coincidental because it has long been recognized that Matthew organizes his Gospel with five teaching discourses in an effort to emulate the five books of the Torah.[1]

The other Gospels refer to sayings of Jesus that reflect first-century Jewish rhetorical preferences: 'five sparrows are sold for two pennies' (Lk. 12.6) and 'in one house there will be five divided, three against two and two against three' (Lk. 12.52). The guest in Jesus' parables says, 'I have bought five yoke of oxen. . . I pray you, have me excused' (Lk. 14.19). The Lazarus story as told by Jesus includes the line, 'for I have five brothers' (Lk. 16.28) while John has Jesus tell the Samaritan woman that she had had 'five husbands' (Jn 4.18). Paul's adherence to this rhetorical preference is evident in 1 Cor. 14.19 where he claims he would 'rather speak five words with my mind. . . than ten thousand words' in glossolalia.

The first example from Romans involves an impressive synthesis of style and content because the subject is Jews who are obedient to the law. In the diatribe concerning observant Jews in 2.17-23, we find three strophes of five lines apiece: in vv. 17-18 there are five examples of Jewish self-identity linked with καί; in vv. 19-20 there are five claims of Jewish superiority in an emphatic series marked by asyndeton, and in vv. 21-23 there are five moralistic injunctions matching the five rhetorical questions concerning the consistency of Jewish principles and performance.

1. [17]But if you call yourself a Jew
2.   and support yourself on the law
3.   and boast in God,
4.   [18]and know the will [of God]
5.   and approve what is important because of being schooled out of the law,

1. [19]and [if you] persuaded yourself that you are a guide of the blind,
2.   a light of those in darkness,
3.   [20]a tutor of the foolish,
4.   a teacher of the immature,
5.   possessing the system of knowledge and of truth in the law—.

---

1. See Reginald H. Fuller, 'Matthew', *HBC*, p. 951.

1a. [21]The one who therefore teaches another,
1b.   do you not teach yourself?
2a.   The one who preaches not to steal,
2b.   are you stealing?
3a.   [22]The one who says not to commit adultery,
3b.   are you adulterous?
4a.   The one who abhors idols,
4b.   do you rob temples?
5a.   [23]The one who boasts in the law,
5b.   do you dishonor God through transgressing
                        the law?

This prominent pentadic structure is strongly evocative of the five books of the Torah, the chief foundation of Jewish piety. The basic issue of adhering to the standards of the Torah is amplified through the accumulation of superiority claims and rhetorical questions. The rhetorical effect of the pentadic structure is ironic and self-condemnatory in that the imaginary interlocutor who boasts in the Torah is shown to fall short of its full demands.

A second series of five is less clearly visible because it consists of pairs of somewhat unbalanced lines that deal with Jewish responsibilities and circumcision of the heart (2.25-29).

1a. [25]For on the one hand circumcision has value if you practice the law.
1b.   But on the other hand if you are a transgressor of the law, your
            circumcision has become uncircumcision.
2a. [26]If therefore the uncircumcise[d one] observes the righteous requirement
            of the law,
2b.   will not his uncircumcision be reckoned as circumcision?
3a. [27]And the one fulfilling the law who is physically uncircumcised
3b.   will judge you who through written letter and circumcision are a
            transgressor of the law.
4a. [28]For [the Jew] is neither the one who is in appearance a Jew,
4b.   nor is [circumcision] that which is in appearance in flesh
            circumcision.
5a. [29]but he is a Jew [who is a Jew] in hiddenness,
5b.   and circumcision is [that] of the heart in spirit rather than letter,
clausula   the praise of which
                is not from humans
                but from God.

The series is artfully brought to a conclusion with the clausula in 2.29c. J.P. Louw has interpreted the structure as five pairs of lines in a ring composition, which is not entirely convincing.[1] But the strophic structure would likely have been discernible to the Greco-Roman hearer of Romans. The tenfold repetition of περιτομή and ἀκροβυστία would also have been noticed, the former being reduplicated six times and the latter four times. The argumentative impact of this discussion of circumcision is related to *expolitio*, the refining of a topic through variation and association with closely related thoughts.[2]

The same kind of noteworthy consistency between subject and style is present in 3.1-9 where there are five dialogical exchanges with Jewish conversation partners. They are as follows:

1.	3.1-2	'Therefore what advantage does the Jew have?'
2.	3.3-4	'So what? If some were unfaithful. . . ?'
3.	3.5-6	'If our wickedness demonstrates. . . ?'
4.	3.7	'But if the truth of God abounds. . . ?'
5.	3.8	'And why. . . should we not do evil. . . ?'

A fourth instance of a pentadic series is found in the midrashic exegesis of 4.1-24, which contains five quotations from the OT, the last being a reiteration of the first. Once again, this stylistic feature is congruent with the argument, which suggests the primacy of faith on the basis of the story of Abraham.

1.	4.3	Gen. 15.6
2.	4.7-8	Ps. 31.1
3.	4.17	Gen. 17.5
4.	4.18c	Gen. 5.5
5.	4.22	Gen. 15.6

There are several other examples of pentadic series in midrashic sections of Romans. In Rom. 9.6-18 there are five supplementary texts cited after the initial text in the extensive midrashic development. In the next pericope, which completes the midrash, there are five more texts cited referring to the 'call' of the faithful, subordinate again to the initial text of Gen. 21.12.[3] In Rom. 10.5-13 there are five scriptural quotations, as also in Rom. 11.1-10. Finally, in the most visible instance of a pentadic series, Paul provides five quotations from the

---

1. J.P. Louw, *A Semantic Discourse Analysis of Romans* (Pretoria: University of Pretoria, 1979), II, p. 55.

2. For the use of *expolitio* in classical rhetoric, see the discussion in Lausberg, *Handbuch*, I, pp. 413-18, §830-42.

3. See William Richard Stegner, 'Romans 9.6-29—A Midrash', *JSNT* 22 (1984), pp. 37-52.

ten commandments in Rom. 13.9. In each of these nine instances, the congruence between subject matter and the choice of a pentadic structure is clear, suggesting a conscious effort on Paul's part to honor Judaic stylistic preferences.

The last three examples appear to be unrelated to the debate concerning Jewish assumptions. In Rom. 5.3-5a there is a fivefold climax with each line taking up motifs from the preceding:

1. [3]not only that, but we also boast in the afflictions,
2.   knowing that the affliction produces endurance,
3.   [4]and endurance confirmation,
4.   and confirmation hope,
5.   [5]and hope does not humiliate. . .

In Rom. 8.24-25 there are five brief lines in which 'hope' or 'to hope' are repeated five times, resulting in an effective paronomasia:

1. [24]For in this *hope* were we saved.
2.   But *hope* that is seen is not *hope*,
3.   for who *hopes* for what he sees?
4.   [25]But if we *hope* in what we do not see,
5.   we wait in patience.

Finally, in Rom. 8.26-27 there are five consecutive lines in which the role of the Spirit is explained, with a threefold reduplication of πνεῦμα:

1. [26]Likewise the *Spirit* also lends assistance in our weakness,
2.   for we do not know how we ought to pray,
3.   but the *Spirit* himself intercedes with unspeakable sighs.
4.   [27]But the one searching the hearts knows what is the mind
            of the *Spirit*.
5.   because he intercedes with respect to God for the sake
            of saints.

Both of these pentadic series in Rom. 8.24-27 appear to be examples of *expolitio*, refining the concepts of hope and spirit through definition, contrast, and association.

Given the prominence of the larger structuring principle of fives and tens in the organization of the pericopae of Romans, this large number of quinary and denary structures appears to signal an effort on Paul's part both to enter into conversation with Jewish partners, and also to legitimize Jewish-Christian culture, which was being discriminated against in the Roman house churches. By using quinary sequences in these last several examples to describe crucial aspects of

Christian life under the Spirit, Paul allows a Judaic stylistic preference to predominate, thus indicating indirectly that the new life does not completely abrogate the Jewish tradition.

Series of Sevens

From the time of the formation of the Hebrew scriptures down through later Jewish history, seven is the most distinctively Jewish number, representing 'totality',[1] 'completeness and perfection'.[2] It was associated with the creation story, the seven-day week, the sabbatical year cycle and the seven-branched Menorah, 'a paramount Jewish symbol, representing light and life eternal'.[3] To a less distinctive degree, this number was valued in Greek culture, reflecting the seven-day periods in the four phases of the moon and later the seven planets.[4] It is the biblical legacy, however, that is reflected in Paul's reference to the 7000 faithful ones who refused homage to Baal during the time of Elijah in Rom. 11.4. The paradigm of seven abominable things that Yahweh hates in Prov. 6.16-19 may well have provided the model for the seven scriptural quotations in the catena of condemnation of Rom. 3.10-18. There is also a close parallel in the seven indictments of CD 5.13-17, which suggests a tradition of sevenfold catenae within Judaism.[5] The catena of condemnations in Romans contains the following seven quotations:

1. Rengstorf, 'ἑπτά', p. 628.

2. Joel F. Drinkard, Jr, 'Numbers', *HBD*, p. 711; Johannes B. Bauer points out some Ugaritic parallels to the biblical symbol of completion in 'Die literarische Form des Heptaemeron', *BZ* 1 (1957), pp. 273-75.

3. Carol L. Meyers, 'Lampstand', *HBD*, p. 546; see also Annamarie Schimmel, *EncR*, XI, p. 16, and Johannes Hehn, *Siebenzahl und Sabbat bei den Babyloniern und im Alten Testament* (Leipziger semitische Studien 2.5; Leipzig: Hinrichs, 1907). Philo provides an extensive discussion of 'the perfecting power of the number 7' in *Op.* 89-130, esp. 103.

4. Rengstorf, 'ἑπτά', p. 627; see also Wöfflin, 'Zur Zahlensymbolik', pp. 342-51; H. Quiring, 'Die "heilige" Siebenzahl und die Entdeckung des Merkur', *Altertum* 4 (1958), pp. 208-14; items unavailable to me are J.H. Graf, *Die Zahl Sieben* (1917), and W.H. Röscher's extensive investigations of series of seven and nine in classical Greece in the *Abhandlungen der königlich-sächsischen Gesellschaft der Wissenschaften, philologisch-historische Klasse* 21.4 (1903); 24.1 (1904), and 24.6 (1906).

5. The thematic parallel was identified by Leander A. Keck, who does not discuss the numerical parallelism in 'The Function of Rom 3.10-18: Observations and Sug-

1.	3.10b	Eccl. 7.20
2.	3.11-12	Ps. 14.1-3
3.	3.13a	Ps. 5.9
4.	3.13b	Ps. 139.4
5.	3.14	Ps. 10.7
6.	3.15-17	Isa. 59.7-8, containing a tricola
7.	3.18	Ps. 35.2, containing the *inclusio* for the catena.

At the end of Romans 8, there are three similarly prominent series of sevens. The first is a sevenfold development ending with a climax on the theme of the glory manifested in Christians. When one eliminates the two theological comments of 8.28c and 29c, the stages of the development are as follows:

1.	The premise in 8.28a: 'those who love God'
2.	The elaboration in 8.28b: 'who are called according to his purpose'
3.	The first synonym of calling in 8.29a: 'those whom he foreknew'
4.	The elaboration in 8.29b: 'he also predestined'
5.	The climax from 'predestined' to 'called' in 8.30a
6.	The climax from 'called' to 'rightwised' in 8.30b
7.	The climax from 'rightwised' to 'glorified' in 8.30c.

In the subsequent verses this rather covert developmental scheme is followed by a much more explicitly visible series of seven rhetorical questions:

1.	8.31a	'What then shall we say. . . ?'
2.	8.31b	'If God be for us, who is against us?'
3.	8.32	'. . . how will he not also grace us. . . ?'
4.	8.33	'Who shall make a charge . . .?'
5.	8.34	'. . . who shall condemn?'
6.	8.35a	'Who shall separate us. . . ?'
7.	8.35b	'Shall affliction. . . ?'

The final question in 8.35b is then divided into seven forms of suffering, each linked 'or' to make an impressive series marked by epanaphora. The series amplifies the theme of Christian suffering through the accumulation of outward forms of tribulation that Paul had experienced:[1]

gestions', *God's Christ and His People: Studies in Honour of Nils Alstrup Dahl* (ed. Jacob Jervell and Wayne A. Meeks; Oslo: Universitetsforlaget, 1977), pp. 148-49.

1. See James D.G. Dunn, *Romans* (WBC 28A/B; 2 vols.; Dallas: Word, 1988), vol. I, p. 505.

1. Shall affliction,
2.   or narrow scrapes,
3.   or persecution,
4.   or famine,
5.   or nakedness,
6.   or peril,
7.   or sword?

An equally impressive series is found in 12.6-8 in the listing of the gifts that mark the Christian community. The first four graces are organized in εἴτε clauses and the last three are in participial clauses beginning with ὁ, resulting in multiple epanaphora:

1. whether prophecy—according to the analogy of faith,
2.   or service—in the serving,
3.   or the teacher—in the teaching,
4.   or the exhorter—in the exhortation,
5. the sharer—with generosity,
6.   the leader—with diligence,
7.   the one showing mercy—with cheer.

The seven types of congregational service and leadership do not appear to be exhaustive, because several other types are listed elsewhere in Paul's letters. The choice of the sacred, rounded number of seven conveys the sense that these examples stand for the wide range of gifts, in which every member of the congregation was thought to participate.

In addition to these clearly visible series, there is reduplication within particular pericopae of Romans. In 6.2-13 there are seven references to 'life' or 'live'. In 6.16-22 there are seven references to 'slave'. And in 9.30–10.4 there are seven references to 'righteousness'.

Only one of these numerical sequences of sevens is patterned directly after a Judaic literary paradigm and has a direct relevance for Gentile-Christian/Jewish-Christian relations. The others may reflect Greco-Roman as well as Judaic stylistic preferences and have no direct relationship to the relationship between such groups. Yet the indirect message of this large number of sevenfold series points to the legitimacy of Judaic preferences, a significant issue in a letter that seeks to overcome the prejudice of a Gentile-Christian majority against a Jewish-Christian minority.

Series of Threes

The prevalence of triads in all of the Pauline letters has been noted by earlier researchers. One thinks immediately of 'faith, hope and love' in 1 Cor. 13.13 and 1 Thess. 1.3-4, 5.8, and the triadic priamel of 1 Cor. 13.8:

> as for prophecy, it will pass away;
> as for tongues, they will cease;
> as for knowledge, it will pass away.

The importance of such series for the OT, with prominent examples such as the Aaronite blessing of Num. 6.24-26 and the threefold 'holy, holy, holy is the Lord of hosts' sung by the seraphim in Isa. 6.3, has been discussed by Usener,[1] Stade,[2] and others.[3] This stylistic figure is found elsewhere in the Greco-Roman world,[4] often with mystical or magical significance,[5] so that the effort to discern a specific cultural implification is pointless. The rhetorical effectiveness of such triads in the Greco-Roman world is indisputable, however, often conveying completeness, perfection, or the superlative in a series.[6]

For Romans, we begin by listing the simple threefold formulations that seem to conform to Paul's style elsewhere.[7] In the following nine examples, for the most part we have nouns linked with καί.

---

1. H. Usener, 'Dreiheit', *Rheinisches Museum für Philologie* 58 (1903), pp. 1-362.

2. B. Stade, 'Die Dreizahl im Alten Testament: Zum Gedächtnis Hermann Useners', *ZAW* 26 (1906), pp. 124-28.

3. Dobschütz, 'Zwei- und dreigliedrige Formeln', pp. 120-41.

4. See Otto Weinreich, 'Trigemination als sakrale Stilform', *Studi e materiali di storia delle religioni* 4 (1928), pp. 198-206; R. Mehrlein, 'Drei', *RAC* 4 (1959), pp. 269-310. I was unable to consult F. Göbel, *Formen und Formeln der epischen Dreiheit in der griechischen Dichtung* (1935).

5. Emory B. Lease, 'The Number Three, Mysterious, Mystic, Magic', *Classical Philologie* 14 (1919), pp. 56-73; he speaks (p. 70) of 'the universality of the use of the mystic number 3' in ancient as well as modern cultures. Dobschütz ('Zwei- und dreigliedrige Formeln', p. 118) mentions well-known Greek sayings related to threefold blessing, luck, unluck, etc.; in fact there are almost 200 Greek terms based in the τρι-stem or prefix according to my count in LSJ.

6. Gerhard Delling, 'τρεῖς, κτλ.', *TDNT*, VIII, p. 217; also W. Deonna, 'Trois, superlatif absolu', *L'Antiquité classique* 23 (1954), pp. 403-28.

7. See Delling, 'τρεῖς', pp. 222-23: 'The triad [of faith, hope and love] is firmly established in Paul. There is no evidence that he borrowed it. . . The triad God–Lord–Spirit is also a fixed one in Paul, though the order varies.'

1.23b	idols 'of birds and animals and serpents'
2.7	The good seek 'glory and honor and immortality'
2.10	The good receive 'glory and honor and peace'
3.4	'. . . the kindness and forbearance and patience' of God
7.12	The law is 'holy and righteous and good'
11.33	'. . . the riches and wisdom and knowledge' of God
12.1	A 'living, holy and acceptable' sacrifice
12.2	The 'good and acceptable and perfect' will of God
14.17	The kingdom of God is 'righteousness and peace and joy'

There are at least eight reduplicative series of threes in Romans, including the repetition of παρέδωκεν in 1.24, 26 and 28; the repetition of 'baptism' in 6.3-4; the triple references to the 'seed' of Abraham in 4.13-18 and 9.7-8; and the impressive paronomastic repetitions of κληρονόμοι and συν—in the climactic series of 8.17:

εἰ δὲ τέκνα, καὶ *κληρονόμοι* ·	1.
κληρονόμοι μὲν θεοῦ,	2.
1. *συγκληρονόμοι* δὲ Χριστοῦ,	3.
2. εἴπερ *συμπάσχομεν*	
3. ἵνα καὶ *συνδοξασθῶμεν*.	

The hymnic conclusion of the third proof is also marked by a triadic structure, with the 'riches and wisdom and knowledge of God' in 11.33 replicated in chiastic order by the three questions with τίς in 11.34-35a.[1] The hymn closes in 11.36 with a prepositional triad with a repetition of αὐτός to elaborate the omnipotence of God.[2] Classical rhetoric used the term *polyptoton* to describe this type of repetition of a term with varied case endings:[3]

Because from him
and through him
and for him
    are all things. . .

The triads in Romans do not appear to have a specific cultural reference, reflecting as they do the stylistic preferences of Jews as well as Greeks. The large number of examples signals, however, an interest on the part of the author to achieve stylistic sonority and completeness.

1. Delling ('τρεῖς', p. 224) observes this chiastic sequence, citing Günther Bornkamm, *Das Ende des Gesetzes* (Munich: Kaiser, 1963), pp. 72-73.
2. See Delling, 'τρεῖς', p. 224.
3. See Lausberg, *Handbuch*, I, pp. 325-29, §640-48; Rom. 11.36 is mentioned in §646.

The Roman audience would have taken pleasure in the rounded rhetoric that Paul so often achieves in this letter.

Series of Sixes

Whether one can speak of formal series of sixes in Romans is debatable because the examples are sparse and ambiguous. In 3.27-31 there are six rhetorical questions in the diatribe, but they are not evenly spaced or parallel in length:

1.	3.27a	'Where then is the boast?'
2.	3.27c	'By what law?'
3.	3.27d	'The [law] of works?'
4.	3.29a	'Or is God belonging to the Jews only?'
5.	3.29b	'Is he not also belonging to the nations?'
6.	3.31a	'Do we abrogate the law. . . ?'

Similarly ambiguous is the series of six citations from the OT in 10.14-21, which may with equal justification be described as two series of three citations. The first three quotes describe the proclamation of the gospel and the last three allude to varying responses thereto.[1]

1.	10.15	Isa. 52.7	'those who preach'
2.	10.16	Isa. 53.1	'what was heard from us'
3.	10.18	Ps. 18.5	'their voice has gone out'
4.	10.19	Deut. 32.21	'jealous of a non-people'
5.	10.20	Isa. 65.1	'found by those who did not seek me'
6.	10.21	Isa. 65.2	'a disobedient and resisting people'

The final example (13.13) is more clearly visible, but it is possibly also a triadic series from the stylistic point of view. The three pairs of evil works are listed in parallel phrases of equal length beginning with μή, producing a triadic epanaphora:

1. not in carousings and drunkennesses,
2. not in affairs and indecencies,
3. not in strife and zealotry. . .

If one were to conclude that these three examples were intentional series of six, the significance would not relate to the Judaic tradition,

---

1. See Otto Michel, *Der Brief an die Römer* (14th edn; Göttingen: Vandenhoeck & Ruprecht, 1978), p. 133.

for which this number had 'little symbolic value'.[1] It also appears that series of six played little role in Greco-Roman rhetoric.

Series of Four

The number four was prominent throughout the Mediterranean world, representing the four cardinal directions, the four winds, the four ages of the world and so forth.[2] In the OT there are references to the four quarters of heaven, the four rivers of paradise, and the four world empires.[3] The Jewish tradition shared the perspective of the Greco-Roman world that four 'signifies completeness and sufficiency'.[4] The effort to create a 'coordinated whole is expressed with particular prominence in the graduated threefold to fourfold sayings in Prov. 30.18-31.[5] Series of four appear in clearly recognizable form in Romans, though their relatively small number indicates a minor role as compared with fives and tens. The first example is in the comprehensive catalogue of evils in 1.29-31, constructed in series of fours with one alteration for rhyming purposes. The first series is marked by homoioteleuton since each word ends with -ια. The second series is marked by parechesis in the predominance of 'o' sounds, ending with a fifth vice that rhymes with the -ια ending. The third series has pairs of associated identifications of evil persons, while the final series is marked again with homoioteleuton in the -ους and -ας word endings and with anaphora in the beginning of each word with the alpha negative:

[29]having been filled with all manner of
1. unrighteousness,
2.   evil,
3.   greed,
4.   badness,

---

1. Israel Abraham, 'Numbers', p. 1257; see also E. Kautzsch, 'Zahlen bei den Hebräern: Zahlensymbolik in der heiligen Schrift', *Realencyklopädie für protestantische Theologie und Kirche*, XXI, p. 605.
2. Horst Balz, 'τέσσαρες, κτλ.', *TDNT*, VIII, pp. 128-29.
3. Balz, 'τέσσαρες', pp. 131-33.
4. Abraham, 'Numbers', p. 1257; see also Kautzsch, 'Zahlen', p. 603.
5. See Roth, *Numerical Sayings*, p. 99, and also 'The Numerical Sequence x/x + 1 in the Old Testament', *VT* 12 (1962), pp. 300-11.

1. full of envy,
2.   murder,
3.   strife,
4.   treachery,
5.   craftiness,
1. whisperers, [30]slanderers,
2.   haters of God, persons of hubris,
3.   egotists, braggarts,
4.   inventors of evil, disobeyors of parents,
1. [31][persons] without understanding,
2.   [persons] without dutifulness,
3.   [persons] without affection,
4.   [persons] without mercy.

The use of the number four to denote comprehensiveness or rounded-ness[1] appears to be congruent with the content of this impressive group of quadruple series. The rhetorical effect is to amplify the picture of the reprobate mind of the human race by the accumulation of vices and evil types. The next example appears relatively late in the letter (10.14-15), opening a pericope with four lines structured as a formal climax and marked by epanaphora in the opening word πῶς ('how?') at the beginning of each line:

1. [14]How therefore might they call upon one in whom they have not believed?
2.   And how shall they believe in one whom they have not heard?
3.   And how might they hear without someone preaching?
4.   [15]And how will they preach if they have not been sent?

A similar quadruple series is found in 13.7 where parallel forms of civic obligation are listed with epanaphora in the identical opening word for each line, τῷ ('to the one') as well as internal reduplication within each line in the repetition of the terms for the four obligations:

1. taxes to whom taxes are due,
2.   custom taxes to whom the custom is due,
3.   fear to whom fear is due,
4.   honor to whom honor is due.

The next example (12.3) features paronomasia again, with an elaborate wordplay based on the stem widely used in philosophical discourse regarding proper self assessment, φρον- ('be minded'):

do not be superminded above what one ought to be minded,
but set your mind on being soberminded. . .

---

1.   Roth, *Numerical Sayings,* p. 131.

The final example is more elaborate, with three series of four admonitions grouped thematically, followed by a final series of four divided two by two. The first twelve items are listed in the admonitions of 12.14-19.

1. [14]Bless the persecutors,
2.   bless and do not curse.
3.   [15]Rejoice with those who rejoice,
4.   weep with those who weep.
1. [16]Be of the same mind toward one another.
2.   Do not set your minds on the heights
3.   but be drawn toward lowly people.
4.   'Never be [wise] minded in yourselves'.
1. [17]Do not pay back evil for evil.
2.   'Take thought for what is good before' all 'persons'.
3.   [18]If possible, so far as you are able,
         be at peace with all persons.
4.   [19]Beloved, do not avenge yourselves,
            but give way to the wrath [of God]. . .

The final series of four admonitions in 12.20-21 is as follows, with the explanatory material that breaks up the series placed in parentheses:

1. [20]But if 'your enemy is hungry, feed him;
2.   if he is thirsty, give him drink;
      (for by doing this you will pile up burning coals upon his head)'.
3. [21]Do not be conquered by the evil
4.   but conquer the evil with the good.

This impressive numerical series based on groupings of four serves as a comprehensive counterpart to the catalogue of evils that appears in ch. 1, conveying the sense that the universal evil of the fallen world is being overcome in the ethic followed by early Christians.

Conclusion

It is premature to suggest that the rhetorical function of all of these numerical series may now be fully grasped. An appropriate starting point, however, is that they appear to reinforce the argument of Romans. If the style of a discourse in classical rhetoric is supposed to be consistent with its content,[1] the large number of series associated with completeness convey the comprehensive argument concerning the

---

1. See *Her*. 1.2.3 and Cic. *Inv*. 1.7.9.

triumph of divine righteousness through the gospel. A large number of the series of threes, fours, and sevens were aimed at comprehensive descriptions of the old life and the new, defined by the rightwising activity of God. In other instances, these series had a decorative, rounding effect that lifts the rhetoric of Romans to a level that would have been satisfying to the hearers in Rome, providing amplification and refinement. The prominent series of fives and tens along with one series of seven appear to reinforce other major goals of the letter. One of these is to interact critically with Jewish theological issues and the other is to lead the Gentile Christian majority to 'welcome' the Jewish Christians into their assemblies, overcoming racial and theological tensions.

There is an ecumenical breadth in the appeal of so many different types of series in this letter, some of which would have resonated more strongly with one cultural group than another. The interest in respecting while transforming cultural distinctions, visible at many points in the argument of Romans, is congruent with this stylistic variety. The desire to communicate effectively with a culturally diverse audience is as clear in the style as in the argument. Finally, the unusual frequency of various numerical series indicates compositional forethought and/or careful editing. As the only Pauline letter addressing an audience that does not know Paul, it appears that he took extraordinary care to create a rhetorically effective vehicle to convey the 'apostolic parousia'. Paul's perception of the importance and sensitivity of this particular mission to Rome manifests itself in these rhetorical details.

THE RHETORIC OF RECONCILIATION:
2 CORINTHIANS 1.1–2.13 AND 7.5–8.24*

Frank Witt Hughes

Partition Theories of the Corinthian Correspondence

One of the most difficult questions faced by NT research is the problem of the early transmission of the letters of St Paul. How did early Christianity come to know the Pauline letters? Or more precisely, which early Churches knew of which Pauline letters? Before attempting to answer these questions, another problem encounters those who would investigate the apostle's writings. What is the relation of the current editions of certain Pauline letters to their original form? Should we assume, for example, that the current form of 2 Corinthians is the original form or the only form which really merits our attention? Or would it be more reasonable to accept some partition theory of 2 Corinthians, such as those proposed by A. Hausrath, G. Bornkamm, W. Schmithals, R. Jewett, or others?[1] The major difficulty

---

*   This paper was presented at the Society of Biblical Literature International Meeting in Heidelberg, on August 11, 1987. I am grateful to colleagues attending that meeting for comments concerning this paper and rhetorical criticism in general.

1. Adolf Hausrath, *Der Vier-Capitel-Brief des Paulus an die Korinther* (Heidelberg: Bassermann, 1870); Günther Bornkamm, 'Die Vorgeschichte des sogenannten Zweiten Korintherbriefes', *Sitzungsberichte der Heidelberger Akademie der Wissenschaften*, philosophisch-historische Classe, 1961; 2. Abhandlung (Heidelberg: Winter, 1961); repr. *Geschichte und Glaube II, Gesammelte Aufsätze IV* (BEvT 53; München: Chr. Kaiser, 1971), pp. 162-94. The classic Meyer-Kommentar of Hans Windisch (*Der zweite Korintherbrief* [MeyerK; 9th edn; Göttingen: Vandenhoeck & Ruprecht, 1924; repr. edn Georg Strecker, 1970]) espoused a partition theory separating chs. 1–9 from 10–13, with 1–7 being separated from 8–9 as well. Rudolf Bultmann (*The Second Letter to the Corinthians* [trans. Roy A. Harrisville; Minneapolis: Augsburg, 1985]; German original: *Der zweite Brief an die Korinther* [ed. Erich Dinkler; MeyerK Sonderband; Göttingen: Vandenhoeck & Ruprecht, 1976]) also assumes a partition theory whereby letter D included 1.1–2.13 and 7.5–8.24, and letter C included ch. 9 as well as chs. 10–13. For an array of thir-

that partition theories pose for those who accept them is that such theories often seem to be quite arbitrary. How does one show that the existence, long ago, of one theoretically reconstructed letter fragment is more plausible than some other theoretical fragment, or, for that matter, than the canonical form of 2 Corinthians?[1]

An assumption of this study is that rhetorical criticism could help to confirm or refute the results of theories of partition or interpolation. Several of the leading ancient rhetorical teachers exhibited a remarkable concern for the coherence of the parts of a speech, expressed especially through teaching about ways to introduce various topics in the *exordium*, argue them in the *probatio*, and recapitulate and embellish them emotionally in the *peroratio*. Hence, this study will proceed by offering a rhetorical analysis of what has been called the 'letter of reconciliation', in an attempt to demonstrate the rhetorical coherence of 2 Cor. 1.1–2.13 and 7.5–8.24. Before that can be done, however, it is necessary to survey various traditions of rhetoric which are in certain ways analogous to what we find in our reconstructed letter.

Traditions of Graeco-Roman Rhetoric

Two handbooks on epideictic rhetoric dating from the late third to early fourth centuries AD are attributed to Menander Rhetor. One of these interesting works lists a speech of consolation, the λόγος παραμυθητικός, as a kind of speech conventionally composed in the *genus* of epideictic rhetoric.[2] A more famous epideictic speech is the

---

teen reconstructed letters of Paul to the Corinthians, see Walter Schmithals, *Die Briefe des Paulus in ihrer ursprünglichen Form* (Zürcher Werkkommentare zur Bibel; Zürich: Theologischer Verlag, 1984), as well as his earlier *Gnosticism in Corinth* (Nashville: Abingdon, 1971).

1. For further discussion of partition theories, see Dieter Georgi, 'Corinthians, Second Letter to the', *IDBSup* (1976), pp. 183-86. For recent evaluations of partition theories and methodological issues, see Victor Paul Furnish, *II Corinthians* (AB 32a; Garden City, NY: Doubleday, 1984), pp. 30-48; Robert Jewett, 'The Redaction of I Corinthians and the Trajectory of the Pauline School', *JAAR Supplement* 46 (1978), pp. 389-444, esp. pp. 391-96, where he discusses Bornkamm's theory in order to apply it analogously to 1 Corinthians. A lengthy history of scholarship on partition theories of 2 Corinthians from 1776 to the 1980s is given by Hans Dieter Betz, *2 Corinthians 8 and 9: A Commentary on Two Administrative Letters of the Apostle Paul* (Hermeneia; Philadelphia: Fortress, 1985), pp. 3-36. Jewett refers to 2 Cor. 1.1–2.13 and 7.5–8.24 as Corinthian Letter G, and I adopt that designation here.

2. *Menander Rhetor* 2.9.

ἐπιτάφιος (funeral oration)[1] which often included consolation and, as Menander Rhetor tells us, may include various kinds of exhortations and prayers.[2] The λόγος παραμυθητικός (consolation speech) itself might include narratives (2.9.414.7), and Menander Rhetor gave as an example a narrative of the destruction of cities and nations (2.9.414.7-8), in which the orator may speak of 'how the change from this life is perhaps to be preferred, since it rids us of troubles, greed, unjust fate' (2.9.414.8-10).

In a Hellenistic handbook of letter-writing attributed to Libanius we learn of the existence of forty-one types of letters, of which the twenty-first is the παραμυθητική, the letter of consolation. In another epistolary handbook attributed to Demetrius there are twenty-one letter types, of which the fifth is the παραμυθητικός. Both epistolary handbooks gave brief examples of the content of a letter of consolation, and Pseudo-Demetrius's example includes a description of how the writer of the letter shares the grief suffered by the addressee, how sufferings are common to all humanity, and how reason will help the sufferer deal with his or her grief.[3]

At about the same time as the development of those two Hellenistic handbooks of letter-writing (heavily influenced by rhetoric as they were), the tradition of Greek rhetoric was being transferred into Latin with some adaptations. An early stage in this transfer is represented by Cicero's famous handbook *De Inventione*. In rhetorical theory (and in most of Cicero's own rhetorical practice) the part of the speech in which one conventionally found appeals to the emotions was the end-

1. For a recent general discussion of epideictic rhetoric, see especially the edition and translation of *Menander Rhetor* by D.A. Russell and N.G. Wilson (Oxford: Clarendon, 1981), pp. xi-xxxiv. On p. xiii they list the following as examples of funeral speeches: the speech of Pericles in Thucydides, *History* 2.34ff., the *Menexenus* of Plato, *Oration* 6 of Hyperides, *Oration* 2 of Lysias, and *Oration* 60 of Demosthenes. On the relation of the funeral speech to early rhetoric, see especially Nicole Loraux, *The Invention of Athens: The Funeral Oration in the Classical City* (trans. Alan Sheridan; Cambridge, MA: Harvard University Press, 1986).

2. Menander Rhetor tells us that advice can be a part of a funeral speech (especially advice to children in place of consultation, 2.11.421.25-26), as well as exhortation to copy the virtues of the deceased, 2.11.421.30-32. The funeral speech may also be 'rounded off with a prayer', 2.11.422.2-5.

3. English translation of Pseudo-Demetrius' example is found in Stanley K. Stowers, *Letter Writing in Greco-Roman Antiquity* (Library of Early Christianity 4; Philadelphia: Westminster, 1986), p. 144; Greek original is in *Demetrii et Libanii qui feruntur Τύποι ἐπιστολικοί et Ἐπιστολιμαίοι Χαρακτῆρες* (ed. Valentinus Weichert; Leipzig: Teubner, 1910), pp. 4-5.

ing of the speech, the *peroratio*. In Cicero's time, there was a conventional understanding that the *peroratio* had two *parts*: the recapitulation (*recapitulatio*) of the points demonstrated in the speech, and the appeal to the emotions (*adfectus*), which was further subdivided in Latin rhetoric into the arousal of emotions against the opponent (*indignatio*) and the arousal of emotions for the orator and his client's case (*conquestio*). In Cicero's youthful handbook *De Inventione* are listed fifteen topics which could be used in *indignatio* and sixteen topics which could be used in *conquestio*. The sixteen commonplaces (*loci communes*) of *conquestio* begin with Cicero's general explanation that such *loci*

> set forth the power of fortune over all men and the weakness of the human race. When such a passage is delivered gravely and sententiously (*graviter et sententiose*), the spirit of man is prepared for pity, for in viewing the misfortune of another he will contemplate his own weakness.[1]

The third such locus is that 'in which each separate phase of misfortune is deplored'; the example Cicero gives is the example of a father's mourning the death of his son, in which all of the past involvements of the father with the son are rather emotionally recounted.[2] The tenth *locus* of *conquestio* is that 'in which one's helplessness and weakness and loneliness are revealed'.[3] Finally the sixteenth *locus* is that 'in which we show that our soul is full of mercy for others, but still is noble, lofty, and patient of misfortune and will be so whatever may befall'.[4]

The traditional topics associated with consolation, as mentioned above, are used in a part of 2 Corinthians, 1.1–2.13 and 7.5–8.24, which has been identified by exegetes as a 'letter of reconciliation'. The situation which we can reconstruct from the several letters to the Corinthians shows that Paul's ἦθος was in deep trouble as a result of his absence from the Corinthian church and the presence of the opponents of Paul. From 2 Cor. 10.10 we learn that the struggle between Paul and his opponents was to no small degree a rhetorical context. That Paul could write persuasive letters and finally (i.e. after 2 Cor.

---

1. Cic. *Inv.* 1.55.106 (English translation by H.M. Hubbell, *Cicero. De inventione, De optimo genere oratorum, Topica* [LCL; Cambridge, MA: Harvard University Press, 1949]).
2. Cic. *Inv.* 1.55.107.
3. Cic. *Inv.* 1.55.109.
4. Cic. *Inv.* 1.56.109.

10–13) win over the Corinthians from the clutches of his eloquent
opponents is no small tribute to the ancient recognition of the power
of his letters, as perhaps the earliest rhetorical critic of Paul, St
Augustine of Hippo, recognized.[1]

The Exordium, 2 Cor. 1.1–11

According to rhetorical theory, we expect, the *exordium* to introduce
the orator and his ἦθος to the audience. The epistolary adaptation of
the *exordium* seems to include what is form-critically identified as the
epistolary prescript and the thanksgiving prayer in Pauline and other
letters. The form of the thanksgiving prayer allows the letter-writer a
golden opportunity to praise the addressees at some length, an opportunity of which Paul usually takes full advantage.[2] This is quite analogous to the traditional function of *captatio benevolentiae* in the *exordium*, as described in several rhetorical handbooks. Exaggeratedly
praising language can be used as part of an appeal to acquire the
goodwill of the audience.

After the epistolary prescript (1.1-2), the thanksgiving prayer (1.3-
11) with its lengthy reasons for thanking God unfolds the subjects of
the letter: affliction and comfort. Affliction (θλῖψις) comes to 'us'
from various sources (Paul will identify these sources in great detail in
his *narrationes* later); consolation comes from God, through 'us'. The
mutuality of Paul's and the Corinthians' suffering of various afflictions
is matched by the mutuality of consolation. No matter what the present
stage of Paul, whether he is 'afflicted' or 'comforted', he refers the
situation to God, Christ, and his ministry to the Corinthians (1.4-6).
Afflictions which Christians suffer can be better borne because of the
knowledge that 'the sufferings of Christ overflow onto us'. Everything
works to the ultimate advantage of the Corinthians, their παράκλησις
from suffering and their ὑπομονή in the midst of sufferings.

Paul uses the motif of his own and Christ's afflictions as a way of
talking about the sufferings experienced by the Corinthians. And he
does this for good reason, since in 2 Cor. 2.4, in a *narratio*, he tells us
of a letter which was deeply painful for him to write, written indeed
'out of much affliction (ἐκ γὰρ πολλῆς θλίψεως) and anxiety of

---

1. Aug. *De Doct. Chr.* 4.12.
2. The notable exception is Galatians in which Paul writes no thanksgiving prayer
and where it would not fit the rhetoric of that letter to do so.

heart, with many tears'. There again he talks around the fact that a major reason why he needs to write a letter of reconciliation was his own sarcastic letter (2 Cor. 10–13) which surely must have caused pain, as Paul can admit only late in the letter (7.8).

As a way of dealing with the paradox of writing a letter of reconciliation necessitated in some measure by his own sarcastic letter, it is no accident that Paul introduces the subject of affliction (θλῖψις) in the context of shared affliction that 'we' experience and indeed, that Christ experienced. The *exordium* of this letter in 1.1-11 is an excellent example of *insinuatio*, the introduction of general subjects in the *exordium* in an indirect manner rather than the direct manner (*principium*),[1] because Paul's strained relationship with the Corinthians would not permit it. The wounded conditions of the audience after their reading and/or hearing the so-called 'letter of tears' is graphically described later in this letter by Paul in 7.9-12. So instead of Paul's writing an 'I told you so' sort of letter after the 'Four-Chapter Letter' had produced its desired effect, Paul's response is similar to that in the sample 'letter of consolation' in Pseudo-Libanius' letter-writing handbook: the writer states that he or she quite strongly *shares* the sufferings of the reader.

Paul perhaps exaggerates in 1.8-10 how terrible his sufferings were: his missionary journey in Asia resulted in Paul's feeling as if he would not live (1.8) and was under a death sentence (1.9). God's response to Paul's sufferings is found in 1.9-10: 'God 'who raises the dead' delivered Paul 'from so deadly a peril' in the past, so that Paul had 'hoped (ἠλπίκαμεν) he will deliver us again'. The *exordium* concludes with an awkwardly worded request for prayer in 1.11, with the apparent purpose that the thanksgiving to God will be increased because more people will be thanking God.

The Partitio, *2 Cor. 1.12-14*

The *partitio*, 1.12-14, gives an enumeration of the subjects which are dealt with in the *probatio*. 2 Cor. 1.12 lists the first subject, which concerns his past behavior, that he had acted 'with holiness (reading the better attested ἁγιότης) and godly sincerity, not by fleshly wisdom but by the grace of God'. The second subject, which concerns the present, is laid out in 1.13-14a, that Paul's teaching by letter is clear

---

1. Cic. *Inv.* 1.15.20.

and understandable. It is, however, related to Paul's claim to sincerity in 1.12; Paul first states that his personal behavior is consistent with his role as an apostle, and secondly he states in 1.13a that his teaching by letter is consistent with what the Corinthians can understand. In 1.13b-14a he gives as an example of his understandable teaching some bit of instruction that they have already understood, possibly the 'letter of tears' about which we hear more in the letter.

The third subject is listed in 1.14b and concerns the future, that is, the eschatological hope. Like the first subject in 1.12, it is stated in terms of a boast: on the Day of the Lord the Corinthians and Paul will be able to boast about each other. These three subjects, encompassing the past, the present, and the future, are precisely what are dealt with in the *probatio* of our reconstructed letter.

The Narratio *and the* Probatio, *2 Cor. 1.15–2.13 and 7.5-13a*

Although ancient rhetorical handbooks customarily provided for a separate section of *narratio* between the *exordium* and the *probatio*, rhetorical theory also allowed the more-or-less standard pattern to be altered in favor of omitting the *narratio* or in favor of inserting pieces of *narratio* within other parts of the oration. Particularly in a political debate (in the genus of deliberative rhetoric), the 'facts' or 'events' that could be dealt with in a *narratio* were often well known to the audience, or had been dealt with by other speakers in the debate, so that no repetition would be desirable.[1] On the other hand, a *narratio* broken up into pieces could also be useful in some circumstances.[2] In the *Rhet. ad Alex.* 1438b.15-25 Pseudo-Aristotle listed two requirements for including a *narratio* within the *exordium*: the oration must be deliberative (cf. 1436a.39-41), and the actions to be narrated must be few in number and well known to the audience. Hence, Pseudo-Aristotle advises that a *narratio* included within other sections of the speech is less an informational 'statement of facts' and more a rehearsal of what was already known—a retelling in a way that would help the orator make as persuasive a case as possible. Quintilian could even say that a *narratio* was a *probatio* 'put forward in a continuous

---

1. According to Aristotle (*Rhet.* 3.16.16) in deliberative rhetoric 'narrative is very rare, because no one can narrate things to come'.

2. Aristotle (*Rhet.* 3.16.1) tells us that in epideictic rhetoric the narrative 'should not be consecutive, but disjointed'.

form'.[1] Hence Graeco-Roman rhetorical theory, as 'speaker-oriented' as some modern rhetoricians find it, certainly did make allowances for various situations in which following the more elementary rules would have resulted in a less persuasive discourse.

When we look for 'facts' in 2 Cor. 1.15–2.13 and 7.5-13a, we find little or nothing that the Corinthians did not already know. They already know the fact that Paul has not recently himself been in Corinth (cf. 1.15-16; 1.23–2.4), although they may be unaware of Paul's apostolic travels to Troas and Macedonia (2.12-13; 7.5-7). They are painfully aware of the fact that Paul sent a 'letter of tears' (2.3-5, 9) to them. They know very well that Titus made a visit after the 'letter of tears' had been received (7.7-13) and the Corinthians had been 'hurt in God's way' (7.9), meaning that this powerful document of epistolary rhetoric had been effective, changing the Corinthians' policy towards their founding apostle. So this letter concerned itself less with 'facts' or 'actions' and more with attitudes towards and reasons for the things that had already happened and were probably common knowledge in the Corinthian church.

Thus the rhetorical structure of 1.15–2.13 and 7.5-13a, in accordance with Greek rhetorical theory, reveals a section of argumentation containing a three-part *probatio*, each part preceded by a short section of *narratio*. Each *narratio* serves to give the historical setting of what is to be argued in the following portion of the *probatio*. All three sections of *narratio* contain material which relates to Paul's travels to Corinth and his relationship with the church there.

The first *narratio*, 1.15-16, tells of Paul's original intention to come to Corinth, within the context of his prospective apostolic mission to Macedonia, and a later return through Corinth in the direction of Judaea. The *probatio* section begins in 1.17a with an *interrogatio*: 'Was I vacillating when I wanted to do this?', to which the understood response would be 'no'. This sentence is a fitting introduction to a proof (1.17-22) which presupposes that Paul's consistency or decisiveness was at issue, exactly what one would expect from the first subject announced in the *partitio* in 1.12, that Paul has behaved 'with holiness and godly sincerity'. The rest of the proof in 1.17b-22 is a demonstration of Paul's blamelessness and sincerity.

---

1. Quint. 4.2.79: *Aut quid inter probationem et narrationem interest, nisi quod narratio est probationis continua propositio, rursus probatio narrationi congruens confirmatio?*

Paul continues with another *interrogatio* in 1.17b, asking rhetorically if his behavior is κατὰ σάρκα, like a person who says 'Yes, Yes', and also 'No, No'. Presumably this interesting question means 'Does Paul say "yes" and "no" at the same time?' Or 'Is Paul insincere?' (cf. the statement in the *partitio* in 1.12). Paul continues with a defense of his sincerity or consistency, by arguing in a sustained way that his oral rhetoric (λόγος) has not been 'yes' and 'no', nor has the gospel he preached (1.19) been 'yes' or 'no', nor has the liturgical 'amen' which has been said in the Corinthian church been 'yes' and 'no'.

Paul further grounds his response to the apparent change of insincerity or inconsistency with a claim to his divine office as apostle: 'God establishes us with you in Christ' (1.21). The result of Paul's apostolic office and mission is the Corinthian congregation itself. 2 Cor. 1.22 concludes this section of *probatio* with an appeal to the experience of the Corinthian church itself. The logic behind this appeal is that if Paul is not a truly sincere representative of God (as he claims in 1.21), then the baptismal 'seal' and the experience of the Holy Spirit in the hearts of the Corinthians at their baptism were not real. All of this section, 1.15-22, argues that Paul had good, honorable intentions to come and make another apostolic visit to the Corinthian church. The sticking point is that he obviously had not done so. This takes us to the next part of the argumentation.

Paul continues with a longer *narratio* in 1.23–2.4, where he demonstrates that it was necessary for him, good intentions and all, to change his travel plans. In 1.23a he calls two witnesses to attest the truth of this statement: first God and second his own soul. Then in 1.23b–2.4 he narrates the specific reasons for the change of plans. Instead of what is argued in 1.17-22 as the reason for his non-visit to Corinth, Paul tells his readers, 'it was out of consideration for you that I did not come to Corinth' (1.23b). He explains in 2.1 why such consideration was needed: he 'decided not to make another painful visit to you (ἐν λύπῃ πρὸς ὑμᾶς ἐλθεῖν)'. Although 2.1 does not specify the antecedent of the phrase ἐν λύπῃ (Paul's or the Corinthians' pain), Paul states in 2.2-3 that his visit while the Corinthians were in error would have been painful for both himself and the Corinthians, so that the pain involved would have been mutual. Then in 2.3 Paul explains why he wrote the sharp letter: he presupposed the Corinthians' knowledge that his joy was also their own joy. The mutuality of pain in 2.1-3a together with the mutuality of joy in 2.3b are fitting consequences to the *exordium* of this letter which states that God comforts 'us' so that 'we can comfort those who are in every affliction' (1.4).

This mutuality is exemplified in 2.4 where Paul concludes this section of *narratio* with his description of the letter which was so rhetorically effective. The letter was clearly sharp, but Paul first says he shared the pain, and then later he says his motive in sending the letter was not to cause pain to the Corinthians, but so that they 'might know my abundant love' for them. So Paul explains his bitter letter by saying the pain was as much his in writing it as the Corinthians' in reading it. Hence, an important part of what the *exordium* does in this letter is to lead up to a non-apologetic, yet sympathetic, explanation of the letter of tears' in 2.4.

The *probatio* in 2.5-11 concerns what was to happen in the congregation as they dealt with the offending Christian brother according to Paul's orders in the 'letter of tears'. Paul's inclusion of this material here gives rise to much speculation about the nature of the offense, and how Paul dealt with it in the 'letter of tears'. Some interpreters, including most recently Victor Paul Furnish, argue against identifying 2 Corinthians 10–13 as the 'letter of tears' even though 2.3-11 deals predominantly with the Christian brother who had committed some sort of offense against Paul.[1] However, the original form of the so-called 'Four-Chapter Letter' could have included a condemnation of the man who had wronged Paul (and then later this specific condemnation was edited out when our canonical 2 Corinthians was put together). And if 'it is easier to think of chs. 10–13 as written in anger rather than sorrow',[2] one should consider the fact that this letter of reconciliation is as persuasive as it is because of the use of the conventional topics of consolation, which prominently included the sharing of pain by the friends of those who had been afflicted with some disaster. I conclude that the 'letter of tears' could very well be the original letter lying behind our edited 2 Corinthians 10–13, because Paul's characterization of that letter in this 'letter of reconciliation' is so consistent with this letter's central use of consolation.

Precisely as a part of consolation, which was dependent on reconciliation between Paul and the Corinthians, which in turn had been dependent on the congregation's fundamentally changing its policy, Paul now orders forgiveness for the offending fellow Christian. The

1. Furnish, *II Corinthians*, p. 37.
2. Furnish, *II Corinthians*, p. 37.

reason Paul gives is one of the standard topics in funeral speeches: how much grief is really appropriate for those who have suffered. Instead of pointing out the fact that the Corinthian church already has acknowledged the guilt of the offending brother (which they know very well), Paul deals with the offender as someone who has suffered a grievous pain. So, since too much grief could 'overwhelm such a man' (2.7), the order is given for forgiveness. In 2.10 the Corinthian congregation is given authority to forgive sins by Paul, and Paul claims this authority ἐν προσώπῳ Χριστοῦ. Further integration of Paul's rhetoric into the cosmic order is provided by the concluding sentence of this *probatio*, where Paul warns that such a man who remained unforgiven could be an easy target for Satan, and 'we are not unaware of his designs'.

The third *narratio* includes 2.12-13 which Bornkamm and others have spliced to 7.5-7. The first part of the *narratio* includes a description of Paul's perhaps otherwise successful mission work, yet Paul shares more of his sorrow in 2.13: in Troas there was for Paul 'no rest for my spirit, for I did not find Titus'. Paul subsequently went to Macedonia. Then, splicing 2.13 to 7.5, we find Paul 'having come to Macedonia', and beautifully parallel to 2.13, we find in 7.5 that Paul had 'no rest for my flesh' as a result of 'fights without, fears within'. This *narratio* thus far has given the setting of Paul's need for consolation by informing the reader of the specifics of Paul's pain. Then in 7.6-7 we read what happens to pain as the result of divine consolation. God 'who consoles the downcast' consoled Paul through the coming of Titus, and in the good news which Titus brought from Corinth, the fact of the Corinthians' 'longing', repentance, and 'zeal' for Paul.

The final *probatio* in 7.8-13 is a further explanation of Paul's motives in sending the 'letter of tears', in the light of its obvious success in changing the Corinthians' policy towards Paul. He earlier told about his 'tears' in writing and sending the letter, yet he can open this proof by saying, 'I do not now regret it' (7.8). Paul never positively says he was sorry for sending the letter, although he says that when he 'saw that the letter had caused you pain, even if only for a time' he 'may have been sorry'. Paul, however, argues that the grief which the Corinthians experienced was 'borne in God's way' (7.10), which caused the Corinthians to demonstrate themselves 'blameless in every particular' (7.11). Thus, Paul again restates his goal in sending the 'letter of tears' in the light of its rhetorical success, its acceptance by the Corinthians: Paul sent the letter, he says, 'so that your eagerness for us might be made clear to you in the sight of God' (7.12).

The Peroratio, 2 Cor. 7.13b-16

The *peroratio* traditionally combined appeals to the emotions with recapitulation of the arguments of the *probatio*. Paul's appeal to the emotions here is not *indignatio* (stirring the readers against a case made by opponents), but rather *conquestio*, the stirring of emotions in favor of the rhetor and what he has argued. Paul has proceeded so far by sharing with his readers his emotional response to events that have happened in the form of three *narrationes*. Here in 7.13b-16, Paul states his joy in terms of his response to the joy of Titus, and he does so in what seems to be quite exaggerated language: 'we rejoiced abundantly at the joy of Titus, because his spirit was refreshed from all of you'. This would perhaps have the rhetorical effect of endearing Paul to the readers. Equally important to the function of the *peroratio* is the fact that it carries out the program of the *exordium* by demonstrating that the consolation flowing from 'the Father of mercies and the God of all comfort' (1.13) through Paul and to the Corinthians, announced at such great length in the *exordium*, really did occur in this case. By the fact that Paul has been consoled at the reconciliation of the Corinthians to him, and the fact that he says so in this letter, the Corinthians can know that the reconciliation with the founding apostle of their church is real, so that they should have no further worries that Paul is going to make another painful visit.

2 Cor. 7.14-16 recapitulates the arguments made by the *narrationes* and *probationes*: the current favorable status of the Corinthians in Paul's eyes, the justification of Paul's boasting to Titus of the Corinthians, the justification of Paul's boasting about Titus to the Corinthians (7.14), the present favorable status of the Corinthians in Titus's eyes (7.15), and a final emotional summary: 'I rejoice because I am completely confident in you' (7.16).

The Exhortation, 2 Cor. 8.1-24

At the end of the letter of reconciliation is an exhortation in 8.1-24 to the Corinthians to give money, which must presuppose that the reconciliation has taken place.[1] We are familiar with other Pauline letters which include emotional *perorationes* recapitulating the *probatio*, and then with an exhortation at the end which is at not such a highly emotional level. Although the conventional rhetorical handbooks do not list 'exhortation' as a separate *pars orationis*, exhortations are found not infrequently at the ends of deliberative and epideictic speeches; most notably at the ends of funeral speeches there are often exhortations to various groups to emulate the virtues of the dead. Exhortations are clearly a standard part of letters. Our task here is not to justify exhortation at the ends of Pauline letters but to describe how it works rhetorically.

The most straightforward way to view the rhetoric of 2 Corinthians 8 is to divide the exhortation into two basic parts. The first part, 8.1-15, is clearly concerned with fundraising. The second part, 8.16-23, is a recommendation of Titus, and the whole exhortation is summed up in 8.24.

The first part of the exhortation, 8.1-15, is based on appeals to two topics standard in deliberative rhetoric, honor and advantage. In the first section, 8.1-9, Paul uses a variety of reasons based on the honor of the Corinthians to ask for their (continued) participation in the offering for the relief of Christians in Judea. First he tells at some length of the generosity of the Macedonians in the midst of their proverbial poverty.[2] Precisely because of the unexpected extent of the Macedonians' financial generosity, they with their 'deep poverty' made an excellent *exemplum* for Paul to use in order to persuade the Corinthians to give to the offering they had begun and that their

---

1. Betz (*2 Corinthians 8 and 9*) argues in favor of 2 Cor. 8 as a separate letter. His proposal concerning the *dispositio* of this chapter seems forced and mechanical; on this point see Stanley K. Stowers's review of Betz's book in *JBL* 106 (1987), pp. 727-30. Although I agree with Betz that the *exemplum* of the Macedonians is used in 2 Cor. 8.1b-5, this fact does not demonstrate that vv. 1-5 are the *exordium* of a separate letter. Since all of Paul's extant integral letters except one include a thanksgiving prayer in the *exordium*, it stands to reason that in a fund-raising letter (whose success depended entirely on the goodwill of the readers) Paul would find a way to praise the Corinthians through a traditional epistolary thanksgiving. I provide what I think is a more straightforward rhetorical analysis of 2 Cor. 8 here, based on the insight that the *exemplum* of the Macedonians, together with the *exemplum* of Christ, functions rhetorically as an appeal to the honor of the Corinthians, as well as the opinion of Jewett and Bultmann that 8.1-24 is the final and integral part of the letter reconstructed with 1.1–2.13 and 7.5-16.

2. See the excursus in Betz, *2 Corinthians 8 and 9*, pp. 49-53.

strained relationship with Paul had quashed. The Macedonians were perhaps poor in a financial sense; yet 'their deep poverty abounded unto the riches of their sincerity'. The Thessalonians did not merely instruct their banker to write a modest check to the church; rather, as the NEB translates it, they 'insistently begged us for the favor of participation in the ministry to the saints' (8.4)!

Paul's language, exaggerated as it is, had a rhetorical purpose. The logic behind the *exemplum* of the poor Macedonians' giving 'according to their means and beyond their means' (8.4) is to make the Corinthians consider their own honor, in having begun an offering and then having terminated it. Yet Paul also tempers his appeal to competitiveness with a theological interpretation of the Macedonians' activity: they 'gave themselves first to the Lord and then, through the will of God, to us', which, in Paul's view, the Corinthians were only barely in the process of doing. Paul maintains that their giving to the offering for the saints depends, not only on their city pride, but on their fundamental reconciliation with Paul and with God. If the Corinthians would be reconciled with both Paul and the one whom Paul represents, then their giving would become not merely a financial matter, but a demonstration of their solidarity with Paul's apostolic ministry and mission. Paul even alludes to the *exordium*'s subject of the 'overflowing' or 'abundance' of pain and consolation (cf. 1.4-5) in connection with the Macedonians: they were experiencing 'much testing of tribulation', yet 'they were abundantly happy' (8.2), happy enough to 'insistently beg' for the privilege of giving for the relief of fellow Christians, obviously unlike the Corinthians.

After the *exemplum* of the poor Macedonians, Paul gives specific reasons for the Corinthians to give money: their own abundance in spiritual things such as faith, λόγος, knowledge, eagerness, and love (8.7; cf. 1 Cor. 1.5). Yet Paul is the sort of master of written λόγος himself that he need not 'order' the Corinthians to give (8.8). As if the *exemplum* of the Macedonians and Paul's reminder of the Corinthians of their own abundance were not convincing enough, Paul concludes the appeal to honor by the ultimate *exemplum*, the example of Christ, who is characterized as having been originally rich, but later having become poor in order to bring blessings to sinners like the Corinthians (8.9).

The other topic standard to deliberative rhetoric is that of advantage, and Paul introduces it quite directly, using the verb form συμφέρει of the rhetorical term σύμφερον in 8.10. Paul argues in 8.10-15 that the Corinthians' giving need not be beyond their means (as indeed the Macedonians' giving was, 8.3), but according to their means, so that there will be equality in the Pauline churches. Paul's goal of equality is indeed a form of advantage, because it would be to the financial disadvantage of the Corinthians to be required to give beyond their means. While Paul specifically says he does not require sacrificial giving (8.13), it is clear that he shows his approval of it, referring to extraordinary generosity as 'the grace of God given among the Macedonian churches' (8.1).

The 'letter of reconciliation' concludes in 8.16-23 with an honorific recommendation of Titus and two unnamed brothers who will receive and apparently guard the collection to which Paul urges giving in 8.1-15.

Conclusions

Since there is a clear thematic unity which is matched by a demonstrable unity of rhetorical structure, it is likely that 1.1–2.13 and 7.5–8.24 are an integral letter. The unity of rhetorical structure includes an *exordium* which announces general themes for the letter which are worked out in specifics through the *partitio* and later a three-part *probatio*, are recapitulated by the *peroratio*, and are worked out as recommendations for specific actions to be taken in the epistolary exhortation.

Generally speaking, it is a deliberative letter, even though it combines with its standard deliberative appeal to advantage and honor the apparently standard epideictic topic of consolation. The fact that Paul can use topics which were advised in rhetorical handbooks for two different *genera* of rhetoric attests to the rhetorical creativity of Paul and the fact that deliberative rhetoric (i.e. political speeches) often combined elements of all three *genera* of rhetoric (dealing with actions in the past, the character of various persons, the honor and advantage of cities and groups, as well as a variety of ways to praise and blame) in order to advise groups of people who were empowered to make significant decisions about their own future. Of course, a person who was still learning rhetoric might very well not mix the *genera* of rhetoric. We know, for example, that in the practice of declamation, there was separate terminology for model speeches in two of the three *genera*. A contrived speech in deliberative rhetoric was called a *suasoria*, and a contrived speech in judicial rhetoric was called a *controversia*. The handbooks tell us that declamation was not done in epideictic rhetoric.[1]

However, if students of oratory had really mastered the training to which the rhetorical handbooks refer (perhaps through the triad of *imitatio*, theory, and practice),[2] they would have internalized the rules to such an extent that they knew the rules, but were not limited by them. Rhetorical theory tells us primarily what rhetorical teachers were interested in, and it is useful because it indicates the range of possibilities. A well-trained rhetor would know these possibilities and would discover and invent even more through actual practice. To analyze the rhetorical strategies of a discourse it is necessary to recognize what an author has received through school tradition and what is the author's own composition.[3] Despite the fact that rhetorical critics differ in their detailed analyses and in their approach to the history of rhetoric, it is clear that an increasing number of scholars are finding 'standard' rhetorical structures in Pauline letters, as well as indications that Paul did not limit himself to precepts drawn from textbooks.

The identification of rhetorical phenomena in this and other NT letters presupposes a renewal of a dialogue between classical and NT scholars. Nothing could be more important, at the end of this essay on 'the rhetoric of reconciliation', than to note the brilliant and enduring contributions of George Kennedy to the current encounter between rhetorical study and the study of early Christian literature.

---

1. On declamation, see especially D.A. Russell, *Greek Declamation* (Cambridge: Cambridge University Press, 1983).

2. *Her.* 1.3: *haec omnia tribus rebus adsequi poterimus: arte, imitatione, exercitatione*; cf. Quint. 3.5.1: *facultas orandi consummatur natura, arte exercitatione, cui partem quartam adiciunt quidem imitationis.*

3. On rhetorical criticism as the identification of an author's rhetorical strategies, see Carl Joachim Classen, *Recht—Rhetorik—Politik: Untersuchungen zu Ciceros rhetorischer Strategie* (Darmstadt: Wissenschaftliche Buchgesellschaft, 1985), esp. pp. 11-12.

PAUL'S DEBT TO THE *DE CORONA* OF DEMOSTHENES: A STUDY OF RHETORICAL TECHNIQUES IN SECOND CORINTHIANS*

Frederick W. Danker

Attention to the position of 2 Corinthians within ancient rhetorical traditions has been on the increase.[1] Since descriptions of the principal developments are readily accessible, I shall confine myself to a relatively neglected area, namely the place of 2 Corinthians in the Hellenic reciprocity system and with special reference to the contributions such inquiry can make to some of the problems associated with chs. 10–13 of that letter.

The reciprocity system as exhibited in those parts of the Mediterranean world that were penetrated by the Greek language is a phenomenon that finds constant expression in classical literature and especially in inscriptions. In 2 Corinthians it plays a dominant role and offers a key for further understanding and theoretical accommodation of various features, including Paul's apparent preoccupation with his own prestige, his insistence on paying his own way, and the tenor of his criticism, not only of his opponents but of his constituency. I do not propose to solve the question of the integrity of 2 Corinthians, but

---

* This essay is a revision of a paper presented at the Society of Biblical Literature International Meeting, Sheffield, England, August 1, 1988. The translations of Greek documents are my own.

1. See e.g. J. Paul Sampley ('Paul, His Opponents in 2 Corinthians 10–13, and the Rhetorical Handbooks', *The Social World of Formative Christianity and Judaism* [ed. Jacob Neusner, Peder Borgen, Ernest S. Frerichs, and Richard Horsley; Philadelphia: Fortress, 1988], pp. 162-77) with reference especially to Cicero's rhetorical instruction. For the secondary literature, consult John T. Fitzgerald, *Cracks in an Earthen Vessel: An Examination of the Catalogues of Hardships in the Corinthian Correspondence* (SBLDS 99; Atlanta: Scholars, 1988).

the data explored in this inquiry may point to other directions for a more informed answer.[1]

As background for the analysis of rhetorical features in chs. 10–13, the first part of this study presents a brief sketch of the reciprocity system in Hellenic culture, with special reference to chs. 1–9. Since no sustained account has ever been made of the light that might be shed on 2 Corinthians through consideration of a complete oration, I have chosen for the second portion of this study a speech by Demosthenes, *On the Crown (De Corona)*, as a heuristic device for the probing of chs. 10–13. This speech is particularly suited for consideration, both for the admiration it enjoyed in antiquity as an oratorical model and for its frequent appeal to Hellenic reciprocity interests.

The Reciprocity System

In the reciprocity system,[2] as popularly understood in Hellenic circles,[3] exceptionally generous individuals or corporate entities are held in high regard.[4] In turn, the grateful recipients express their gratitude in ways that assure the donors of lasting memory.

In Homeric times, warriors were second only to deities in exceptional merit or ἀρετή (hereafter used as a loanword, *aretē*) and through poems such as Homer's they gained immortality.[5] Were it not for the odes of Pindar, the athletes who are enshrined in the latter's verse would have been lost to memory. In honor of Timasarchos of Aigina, Pindar wrote:

---

1. For a convenient summary of the debate, see Victor P. Furnish, *II Corinthians* (AB 32A; Garden City, NY: Doubleday, 1984), pp. 26-54.

2. For a ground-breaking anthropological perspective, see Marcel Mauss, 'Essai sur le don, forme archaïque de l'échange', *L'Année Sociologique*, ns 1 (1923-24), pp. 30-126.

3. For the specific Hellenic perspective, see Frederick W. Danker, *Benefactor: Epigraphic Study of a Graeco-Roman and New Testament Semantic Field* (St. Louis: Clayton, 1982) (hereafter, *Benefactor*).

4. Corporate groups include, e.g., city-states and associations of various types. Danker (*Benefactor*) includes a number of inscriptions which celebrate the accomplishments and generosity of a variety of individuals and corporate entities.

5. On ἀρετή, see Albert Kiefer, *Aretalogische Studien* (Borna/Leipzig: Robert Noske, 1929); Vincenzo Longo, *Aretalogie nel Mondo Greco: I, Epigrafi e Papiri* (Genoa: Istituto di Filologia Classica e Medioevale, 1969); *Benefactor*, p. 318; also the literature cited in Morton Smith, 'Prolegomena to a Discussion of Aretalogies, Divine Men, the Gospels and Jesus', *JBL* 90 (1971), pp. 174-99.

When contests are decided, best anodyne
is festal mirth, charmed forth by songs,
sage daughters of the Muses. To soften
weary limbs, heat not the water,
but bring on the lyre with its meed of praise.
The fame of valor triumphs over time,
when from the caverns of the mind a tongue
blessed by the Graces gives it utterance (*Nemean Odes* 4.1-8).

Sculptors deal with stone, but Pindar carves with words. Statues remain on pedestals, but Pindar's song in honor of an athlete speeds out far beyond the victor's home (*Nemean Odes* 5).

It was only natural that heads of state and those who functioned in the name of states should be rewarded for their services with appropriate recognition. In a decree published between 55 and 59 AD by the inhabitants of Busiris, Egypt, a prefect named Tiberius Claudius Balbillus receives an accolade for distinguished service (εὐεργεσία),[1] and Nero is lauded for his wisdom in dispatching him:

With Good Fortune. Whereas Nero Claudius Caesar Augustus Germanicus Imperator, the Good Divinity of the world, in addition to all the good benefits that he conferred in the past on Egypt has (once again) exercised his most brilliant foresight and sent to us Tiberius Claudius Balbillus as governor; and, owing to the latter's favors and benefactions, Egypt is teeming with all good things and sees the gifts of the Nile increasing annually and now all the more enjoys the equity with which the Nile-God floods the lands; (in view thereof) it was resolved by the inhabitants of Busiris. . . to erect a stone stele. . . [which is to reveal] by its inscribed list of benefits the philanthropy they have enjoyed; and from this recital everyone [will know] what wonderful service

---

1. On the term εὐεργέτης and εὐεργέτις, see the basic presentation by J. Oehler, *et al.*, PW 11 (1907), pp. 978-82; see also *Benefactor*, pp. 323-24 and the literature cited in BAGD, *s.v.* φιλανθρωπία. The term εὐεργέτης and cognates appear throughout classical literature. See e.g. Anna Passoni Dell'Acqua, 'Euergetes', *Aegyptus* 56 (1976), pp. 177-91, with a comparison of Greek and Hebrew terminology. See also Eiliv Skard, *Zwei religiös-politische Begriffe: Euergetes–Concordia* (Avhandlinger. . . Videnskaps-Akademi i Oslo II. Hist.-Filos. Klasse, 1931, no. 2; Oslo: Jacob Dybwad, 1932); Arthur D. Nock, '*Soter* and *Euergetes*', in *The Joy of Study . . . Papers Presented to honor F.C. Grant* (ed. S.E. Johnson, 1951), pp. 127-48; repr. *Essays on Religion and the Ancient World* (2 vols.; Cambridge, MA: Harvard University Press, 1972), II, pp. 720-35. An honorary monument assures immortality (Helmut Häusle, *Das Denkmal als Garant des Nachruhms: Beiträge zur Geschichte und Thematik eines Motivs in lateinischen Inschriften* [Munich: C.H. Beck, 1980]).

(Balbillus) has rendered [to all] of Egypt. Therefore it is appropriate that his godlike favors be inscribed in sacred letters for all time to remember.[1]

A distinctive mark of distinguished figures in the Hellenic world is their ability to endure hazards and perils in behalf of their constituencies in times of crises. Such experiences are frequently referred to with the Greek loanword *peristasis* (περίστασις) meaning 'difficult situation' or 'crisis'.[2]

An inscription found at Dionysopolis, a city near the Black Sea, praises a citizen named Akornion for risking 'life and limb in any crisis (περίστασις) that developed'.[3] Menas, a bureaucrat from Sestos, gained immortality for 'sparing no expense in rendering public service' and 'giving no thought to any hazard (κίνδυνος) that imperils his own interests when he leaves on embassies in behalf of the city'.[4] When Nero went to Greece to treat the Hellenes to his music, he expressed his gratitude to the deities of Hellas for their protection, with the implication that he had endured the perils of the waves in behalf of Hellas, on whom he conferred freedom to an unprecedented degree.[5] In short, Akornion and Nero can be classified as endangered benefactors.[6]

Through Plato's preachments on what constituted true citizenship, a broader base for recognition of merit was developed. Distinguished service begins with knowledge of what constitutes what is really

1. Translation adapted from *Benefactor*, pp. 225-26. Greek text with translation and facsimile, *Egyptian Antiquities* (The Library of Entertaining Knowledge; The British Museum; London: Charles Knight, 1836), II, pp. 376-80; text and other editions, *OGIS* 666.

2. See e.g. Polybius 4.45; 2 Macc. 4.16. For the use of the term in ancient rhetoric, see Fitzgerald, *Cracks*, p. 36; George A. Kennedy, *The Art of Persuasion in Greece* (Princeton: Princeton University Press, 1963), p. 305. On receipt of honor for endurance of hazards, see Aischines, *Against Ktesiphon* 183.

3. *SIG*[3] 762.38; *Benefactor*, no. 12.

4. *Benefactor*, no. 17.

5. *Benefactor*, no. 44.

6. F.W. Danker, 'The Endangered Benefactor in Luke–Acts', *SBL 1981 Seminar Papers* (ed. Kent H. Richards; Chico, CA: Scholars, 1981), pp. 39-48; *Benefactor*, esp. pp. 363-66, 417-27; *Luke* (Proclamation Commentaries; Philadelphia: Fortress, 1976), pp. 37-42. As indicated in these studies, data for the endangered benefactor come from a variety of ancient sources. Robert Hodgson added other sources to the data base, 'Paul the Apostle and First Century Tribulation Lists', *ZNW* 74 (1983), pp. 59-80.

good.[1] One who aids in the cultivation of excellence in others ought to be considered a city's most valued treasure. Thus philosophic theory democratized virtue, and it is not surprising that terms associated with gymnastic competitions came to constitute the metaphors in descriptions of people of extraordinary moral quality. In time, other stock terminology and themes associated with heads of state appear in descriptions of people of much lower status. One of the most common features in ethical presentations is the willingness of candidates for virtue to accept the onerous responsibilities of upright living. Epictetus flung out the challenge (2.19.24-25):

> Show me a person who when sick, when in danger, when dying, when in exile, when in disrepute is content. Show me such a person. By God, I would just like to see a real Stoic! The truth is, you can't show me a person who is shaped like that. Well, then, show me one who is in the process of being shaped, who has taken a move in that direction. Please do me the favor. Don't begrudge such a sight to an old man, who up till now has not seen anything like it.

In the discussion of pain and possible disasters, a participant in dialogue protests, 'But the tyrant will fetter. . .' Before he can finish the sentence, Epictetus interjects, 'What? Your leg?' The other tries again, 'But he will lop off. . .' Epictetus breaks in, 'What? Your neck? But what won't he be able to fetter or lop off? Your moral resolution, of course' (1.18.17). Hence the tradition of Socrates' refusal to save his neck in the face of Athenian reprisal against his moral teaching. On the contrary, said Socrates, he ought to be recognized as Athens' benefactor (Plato, *Apology* 36c). In other words, practitioners of virtue have the status of heads of state, and among their credentials is the ability to endure all kinds of inconveniences and perils.

The implications of this entire socio-politico-cultural development for the understanding of Paul's communication with the Corinthians cannot be ignored. It is one of Paul's boasts that he can move at ease in Jewish and Hellenic cultures (Rom. 1.14). And no other letter of his so demonstrates that adaptability as does 2 Corinthians. Indeed, a basic structural component of his letter is the skill with which Paul maintains contact with his addressees through allusions to the Hellenic reciprocity system. Basic to his rhetorical strategy is the central position that he accords to God through the reciprocity paradigm.

---

1. On the democratization process, cf. Julius Gerlach, *ANHP AΓAΘOΣ* (Munich: Lehmaier, 1932).

The thanksgiving in 1.3-11 sets the tone of the entire letter, with the apostle acknowledging God as the source of all comfort in the midst of trials and tribulations. The fundamental components of reciprocity are performance in behalf of another and acknowledgment by the recipient. Here Paul celebrates the goodness of God and Jesus Christ for comforting him in many perils and for rescuing him from a multitude of hazards. This focus on his perils is designed to direct the Corinthians' attention to what ought to be their own proper evaluation of Paul, who identified himself in 1.1 as a person of exceptional status, namely an apostle of Jesus Christ through the will of God.[1] So lofty is Paul's office as envoy that he muffles it in 3.1–4.1, where he describes some of his interaction with the Corinthians. In this passage he discusses his apostolic activity in the light of Moses' administration of the Sinaitic code. The Corinthians could not fail to interpret the roles of Paul and Moses as superstars under the direction of God, the Supreme Superstar, and Jesus Christ, Great Superstar.[2]

---

1. For the history of research of crisis recitals in 2 Corinthians, see the extensive review in Fitzgerald, *Cracks*, pp. 7-31. Unfortunately, Fitzgerald fails to take account of the influence that Hellenic views of public and private beneficence had on the development of crisis recitals and thereby also underestimates the importance of the stimulating contributions made by Anton Fridrichsen: 'Zum Stil des paulinischen Peristasenkatalogs 2 Cor. 11.23ff.', *Symbolae Osloenses* 7 (1927), pp. 25-29; 'Peristasenkatalog und Res Gestae: Nachtrag zu 2 Cor. 11.23ff.', *Symbolae Osloenses* 8 (1929), pp. 78-82. Fitzgerald also wonders why Hans D. Betz did not engage in a discussion of *peristaseis* in 'Eine Christus-Aretalogie bei Paulus (2 Kor 12, 7-10)', *ZTK* 66 (1969), pp. 288-305; he apparently overlooked Betz's reference to 'Unzahl von Abhandlungen' on the subject (p. 290) and Betz's interest in advancing the discussion to another plateau, namely the broader Hellenic context in which discussion of crisis recital becomes more meaningful. Also overlooked is the fact that in *Benefactor* I had placed crisis recital in a broader Hellenistic context, beyond the schools of philosophy (see esp. pp. 363-66, 471-27).

2. At first sight Lk. 22.24-27 appears to cast a first-century negative vote against the role of benefactors as such, but I have emphasized that the spurious claim made by some politicians, not the legitimacy of the role itself, is challenged in the passage (*Benefactor*, pp. 324, 468, 484 n. 178). As indicated by Danker (*Jesus and the New Age: A Commentary on St. Luke's Gospel* [Philadelphia: Fortress, 1988], p. 349), 'through imitation of the Great Benefactor his followers will be benefactors to the world'. David J. Lull ('The Servant-Benefactor as a Model of Greatness (Luke 22.24-30)', *NovT* 29 [1986], pp. 289-305) expands on the positive affirmation incorporated in the passage. Jesus' rebuke is similar to the advice given by Aischines, *Against Ktesiphon* 247-48: Whatever you do, be on your guard against those who claim title to being public benefactors, but cannot be trusted.

In accordance with his status as envoy of God and Jesus Christ, Paul outlines his credentials: endurance of a variety of hazards, to the very point of death (4.11). Ultimately he must appear before the highest tribunal to undergo audit for his performance as an envoy (5.10).[1] Therefore, just as Balbillus was zealous in earning Egyptian accolades for outstanding services, Paul is 'eager' (φιλοτιμέομαι) to render his service in such a way that he will 'pass audit' in the presence of God (5.9).[2] The term for passing audit is εὐάρεστος,[3] as in the case of a certain Zosimus, who proved himself totally honest in all his financial transactions.[4] Paul's concern apparently dictated his decision to be economically independent in Corinth.

In further support of his claim to be God's envoy (5.20), Paul presents a list of credentials (6.2-10). Some of the items consist of positive virtues, most of which are standard in the Greco-Roman world.[5] The rest refer to perils and hazards that go beyond the recital made earlier in 4.7-18.

After reestablishing his own credentials, Paul celebrates the Corinthians in a veritable explosion of accolades at 7.11:

What concern (σπουδή),[6] what support you gave me (ἀπολογία), what indignation (ἀγανάκτησις), what fear (φόβος), what longing (ἐπιπόθησις),

---

1. The terms πράσσω, ἀγαθόν, and φαῦλον are especially significant. The verb πράσσω connotes public function, and is commonly used for political activity. The adjectives denote contrasting qualities of such activity; so e.g. in *De Corona* 180, Demosthenes boasts that he functioned (ἔπραττον) in a manner becoming a good (ἀγαθός) citizen; *De Corona* 25, 'Who was it that acted (πράσσω) in your behalf and sought the interest (σύμφερον) of the city?'; see also 57. In his speech against Ktesiphon, Aischines paints Demosthenes as one who is of little value (φαῦλος) to the city (*Against Ktesiphon* 168) and then enumerates the qualities of the public-spirited citizen (169-70; cf. 226 and esp. 231). On Paul's sense of responsibility for his ambassadorial assignment, see 2 Cor. 5.20.

2. The verb φιλοτιμέω is commonly used in honorary documents in reference to a passion for public service (*Benefactor*, pp. 328-29).

3. The adverb εὐαρέστως is used in honorary documents to emphasize quality of performance in meeting all requirements; see e.g. *SIG*³ 708.20; 587.10.

4. *Inschriften von Priene* 114.14-15.

5. On the conventional characteristics of vice and virtue lists in the NT, see Hans D. Betz, *Galatians* (Hermeneia; Philadelphia: Fortress, 1979), pp. 281-83; Martin Dibelius and Hans Conzelmann, *The Pastoral Epistles* (Hermeneia; Philadelphia: Fortress, 1972), pp. 50-51.

6. On the noun σπουδή, see *Benefactor*, pp. 320-21.

what zeal (ζῆλος),[1] what vindication (ἐκδίκησις)! In everything you prove yourselves above reproach in the way you handled the matter at hand.

Then he adds, 'I bragged about you to Titus' (7.13-14), and at 9.2 states that he notified the Macedonians of Corinth's enthusiasm (προθυμία).[2]

In effect, Paul gives the Corinthians an opportunity to view themselves within the Hellenic reciprocity structure. They, too, are people of excellence, and the stage is set for the discussion of a delicate matter: the collection for God's people in Jerusalem (chs. 8–9).[3]

The transition at 8.1 is not nearly so abrupt as some commentators have suggested.[4] The particle δέ simply slides the addressees into the next stage of the presentation. 'Now, my brothers and sisters, I want to acquaint you with God's beneficence displayed in the Macedonian assemblies' (8.1). The Corinthians, who bring their cultural traditions to the audition of this epistle would immediately recognize the link of these chapters with what they have been exposed to in chs. 1–7.

Nowhere does Paul spell out the reciprocity system more emphatically than in 8.12-15. And after his correspondents reached the end of ch. 9, they would be pleased to know that the apostle considers them

---

1. In this context ζῆλος indicates enthusiastic support of the apostle. In *SIG*[3] 734.7 the verb ζαλέω (Doric form of ζηλέω) is used in reference to an honorand who was passionately concerned about the interests of the state.

2. On the noun προθυμία (2 Cor. 9.20), see *Benefactor*, p. 321. The semantic field relating to *aretē* is enriched by the term λειτουργία (2 Cor. 9.11); on this technical term relating to public service, see J. Oehler, 'Liturgie', PW 12 (1925), 1871-79; Friedrich Oertel, *Die Liturgie: Studien zur ptolemäischen und kaiserlichen Verwaltung Ägyptens* (Leipzig: Teubner, 1917).

3. See Plutarch, *Moralia* 542b on the importance of praising the audience. On the administrative diction and cultural provenance of 2 Cor. 8–9, see Hans D. Betz, *2 Corinthians 8 and 9* (Hermeneia; Philadelphia: Fortress, 1985); Danker, *Benefactor*, pp. 437-38; *II Corinthians* (Commentary on the New Testament; Minneapolis: Augsburg, 1989), pp. 116-47.

4. For the history of debate concerning the integrity of chs. 8–9, see Betz, *2 Corinthians 8 and 9*, pp. 3-36. Of the three parallel passages cited for the initial 'epistolary phrase' (Gal. 1.11; 1 Cor. 12.3; 15.1), only the last contains the particle δέ. Betz's pronouncement that 'δέ sets the sentence off from the preceding verse' (p. 41 n. 3) begs the question. The discussion of δέ in BDF is inadequate; A.T. Robertson's discussion (*A Grammar of the Greek New Testament in the Light of Historical Research* [4th edn; New York: Doran, 1923], pp. 1183-85) is more linguistically satisfactory. See also BAGD, *s.v.*, 2, where two examples of continuative δέ can readily be added from Thucydides (2.36.1; 2.39.1).

worthy to be classed with the Macedonians as benefactors in their own right.

Paul and Demosthenes

At this point chs. 10–13 round into view. The fact that Paul's boastfulness and invective are the principal features responsible for doubts about the appropriateness of these chapters as a closing section of 2 Corinthians is itself sufficient enticement to examine these features against the backdrop of the reciprocity system exhibited in the first nine chapters. At the same time, the present inquiry requires the control that a document with related content can offer and thus eliminate some of the hazard connected with a random hunt for parallels in a variety of documents.[1]

Because of the swift current of self-praise and invective that runs through it, the *De Corona* is an ideal hunting ground for clues that will help disperse some of the traditional cultural importations that have obscured structural features of the letter.

In the *De Corona*, Demosthenes asserts his right, against denigrating charges made by Aischines, to receive the award of a crown for distinguished merit that he had displayed in behalf of Athens.[2] The very nature of the case demanded that Demosthenes prove his worth to Athens. Moreover, as Aristotle affirmed, an orator's epilogue ought to include, in addition to praise of oneself, blame of the opponent.[3]

---

1. On hazards connected with citation of parallels that fails to take adequate account of cultural factors, see F.W. Danker, *A Century of Greco-Roman Philology, Featuring the American Philological Association and the Society of Biblical Literature* (Atlanta: Scholars, 1988), pp. 161-63.

2. On the preoccupation of orators with the theme of beneficence, see W.P. Clark, 'Private and Public Benefactions in Athenian Litigation', *The Classical Weekly* 23/5 (1929), pp. 33-35. Clark notes that the author of the *Ars Rhetorica ad Alexandrinum* summarizes the types of arguments related to this theme in the orations of Hellenic litigants. On the custom of awarding wreaths (lat. *corona*), see esp. Josepf Köchling, *De coronarum apud antiquos vi atque usu* (Religionsgeschichtliche Versuche und Vorarbeiten 14.2; Giessen: Töpelmann, 1914), and Michael Blech, *Studien zum Kranz bei den Griechen* (Religionsgeschichtliche Versuche und Vorarbeiten 38; Giessen: Töpelmann, 1982); on the thematic formulations used in the inscriptions, see Ernst Nachmanson, 'Zu den Motivformeln der griechischen Ehrenschriften', *Eranos* 11 (1911), pp. 180-96; *Benefactor* (pp. 317-92) discusses the major motifs and their use in NT writings.

3. Ar. *Rhet.* 1419b.

Plutarch echoed the philosopher by writing an essay on the subject.[1] Where Demosthenes' epilogue begins or ends is subject to dispute, for the orator generously celebrates his services to the state throughout the *De Corona*. But near the end of his speech (252), Demosthenes begins to proclaim the script for his own award and at the same time give Aischines the *coup de grâce*.

The intimate connection of boastfulness with the theme of *aretē* and beneficence is a commonplace in the *De Corona*. At one point in his speech, Demosthenes defends his boasting on the ground that, in view of the strenuous services he has rendered to the state, the audience can at least endure (ἀνέχομαι) their recital (160). Implicit is the concern that he expressed in his *exordium*: his listeners must allow for some self-approbation lest they adjudge him incapable of clearing himself of the charges made by Aischines (4). Similarly, Paul asks for patient attention (ἀνέχομαι) to his 'fool's' speech because of his intense commitment to their interests (2 Cor. 11.1-2), and he couples his request with a complaint that the Corinthians gladly put up with (ἀνέχομαι) anyone who proclaims a false gospel (11.3-4). In related vein, Demosthenes chides the Athenians for their tendency to encourage subverters of their own political interest, while putting at risk one of their most loyal supporters (*De Corona* 138).

Demosthenes admits that self-laudation can alienate an audience. In the same breath he therefore promises to engage in the disagreeable task with utmost moderation (4).[2] In keeping with such well-established rhetorical tradition Paul creates a bravura piece out of the theme of reluctant boasting (2 Cor. 10.13–11.1).

A decision on whether 2 Corinthians 10–13 forms the peroration of Paul's letter must await further analysis, but in its present canonical form the letter reveals in these chapters an escalation of the self-attributions recorded in chs. 1–9. Included in Paul's earlier self-inventory was the attribute of 'simplicity' (ἁπλότης, 2 Cor. 1.12), that is, hav-

---

1. 'On Inoffensive Self-praise', Plutarch, *Moralia* 539-47. Self-praise must not be purchased at the expense of another, therefore Plutarch cautions against setting one's foot in another's 'chorus' (540b), a temptation that Paul rejects (2 Cor. 10.12-16; for the carpentry metaphor, cf. Aischines, *Against Ktesiphon* [199-200]).

2. Cf. *De Corona* 110 and 268-69, both with *praeteritio*; 258; 305 (Demosthenes understates his performance so as to forestall begrudging envy); 317; 321. On Demosthenes' rhetorical tactics, see Francis P. Donnelly, *The Oration of Demosthenes* On the Crown: *A Rhetorical Commentary* (New York: Fordham University, 1941).

ing no 'hidden agenda' in one's dealings with others. To charge an orator with manipulation of words to confuse an issue was a common ploy in Greco-Roman jury rooms; Aischines made an issue out of it in his effort to deny Demosthenes the award for public service, and the latter dealt with the charge in *De Corona* 111. Paul further emphasizes that he was honest in his dealings (4.2, 16-18) and not guilty of malfeasance (7.2).[1] On the contrary, we give thought, he wrote, to what is noble (καλός, 8.21).[2] Since public service was high on the Greco-Roman list of entitlement to a crown, Demosthenes took every opportunity in *De Corona* to celebrate his dedication to the state. Similarly, Paul emphasized his service to the new covenant (3.6) and total loyalty to Christ (5.20), whom he proclaims without any attempt at self-aggrandizement (4.5, 7; 5.12). A further mark of a distinguished person was courage, and Paul linked it with a number of other virtues in an extended piece of self-adulation, 6.1-10.

At ch. 10, Paul's boasts begin to take on a stronger defensive cast, with stress on his authority for edifying the Corinthians (10.8).[3] He asserts that he is a man of word and deed (10.11);[4] loyalty is his strong suit (11.1-4); he takes no back seat to the 'superlative' apostles (11.5); is well-informed (11.6); renders his service at no expense (11.7-11); is from the best family stock (11.21-22); displays courage (11.23-27); is filled with empathy (11.28-29); has experienced unusual hazards (1.30-33; 12.1-10); has rendered extraordinary service to the Corinthians (12.11-13); and his primary concern is not personal gain but the interests of the Corinthians (12.14-18). In keeping with the tradition exhibited in the *De Corona*, Paul explicitly states his awareness of the importance of moderation (10.1, 12-18), but at the same time engages in a long series of immoderate boasts, which takes on the guise of moderation through adoption of the fool's role (11.16, 19).

---

1. Cf. Demosthenes, who notes that he did not take advantage of the state, μηδὲν ὑμᾶς ἀδικῶν (125).
2. In Greco-Roman texts relating to exceptional personalities, the adjective καλός ordinarily denotes one who is civic-spirited; the substantive τὸ καλόν, that which contributes to the welfare of the state or community. Paul upbuilds the community.
3. In the semantic field of *aretē* being plowed by Paul, the term οἰκοδομή, used at 2 Cor. 10.8 in the transferred sense of 'edification', would project an image of a generous citizen engaged in public works projects, including the building of baths and temples (see the indexes in *OGIS*, *SIG*[3], and other corpora for numerous occurrences of οἰκοδομή and cognates).
4. On the word-deed pair, see *Benefactor*, pp. 339-43.

In compensation for the necessity of moderation parading his services to the state, Demosthenes states that he is compelled to do so because of the contrary character manifested by his critics (126).[1] Along similar lines, Paul justifies his own boasting (11.16-21; 12.11-13). Thus boastfulness and invective come to constitute the main threads that intertwine in the structural network of the *De Corona* and 2 Corinthians 10–13.

To retain the goodwill of the audience along such a risky rhetorical path one must take the high road. At a climactic state in his oration Demosthenes declaims:

> Citizens who are held in high repute ought not to expect a court that is in session for the common interest to gratify any tendency they might have to indulge themselves in anger or hatred or related feelings, nor should they go before you with such end in mind. Indeed, it were best if such feelings were totally foreign to their disposition; but if that is not possible, they ought to moderate them carefully (πράως καὶ μετρίως). But under what circumstances ought the politician and orator to be vehement? Of course, when the city is in any way imperilled and when the public is faced by adversaries. Such is the obligation of a noble and patriotic citizen (278).

Demosthenes, who earlier states that he was not 'fond of defamation' (126), in this paragraph justifies his invective. The public expects it in the face of their exposure to unprincipled politicians. As noted above, the orator is well aware of the public's predilection for invective as opposed to self-praise (3), but he lays further claim to their goodwill with his adherence to the ideal of 'moderation', while at the same time reinforcing their perception of him as a loyal servant of the state.[2] Paul's reluctant venture into boastful invective is similarly in keeping

---

1. On the importance of response to negative charges, see Plutarch, *Moralia* 540c-d; Christopher Forbes, 'Comparison, Self-Praise and Irony: Paul's Boasting and the Conventions of Hellenistic Rhetoric', *NTS* 32 (1986), pp. 1-30, with references to earlier studies and ancient discussion of ancient rhetorical conventions; Sampley, 'Paul', pp. 169-71.

2. In his conflict with Demosthenes, Aischines (*Against Ktesiphon* 241) had made a point of the fact that self-praise is offensive: 'If we do not even endure the self-praise of good men who are distinguished for many illustrious deeds, is there anyone who could possibly endure the vainglory of one who is a disgrace to our city?' Demosthenes did not ignore the realities (see above, p. 271 n. 2). For the rationale, see Plutarch, *Moralia* 543a-b. For Cicero's viewpoints, see Sampley, 'Paul', pp. 163-65.

with the Hellenic ethos exhibited by Demosthenes and spelled out in the Delphic maxim, γνῶθι σαυτόν.[1]

To strengthen the force of the invective, it is advantageous to heighten one's prestige through comparison of one's own virtues and the baseness of the opponent. Combined with gentle chiding of the audience for being cozened by the opposition, such comparison has powerful persuasive potential. 'You gladly put up with any one who comes proclaiming a message different from the one you first received', upbraids Paul at 11.4. Similarly, Demosthenes takes the Athenians to task for permitting themselves to be deluded by people who serve their own instead of the national interest:

> I could indict Aischines for ten thousand other items, but let it pass. . . . I could point to many other instances in which this fellow was discovered to be lending aid and comfort to our enemies and at the same time libeling me. But you have no accurate recollection of these matters, nor do you display appropriate wrath. Instead, through some bad habit of yours, you have bestowed much authority on one who plots to trip you up and libels one who seeks your best interests, and thereby you trade off your city's welfare for the pleasure and gratification of being entertained by invective. No wonder that it is always safer to hire oneself out in the service of your enemies than to hold public office and loyally serve the state in your behalf (138).

Climaxing a series of sarcastic accolades, in which he declaims how expert his opponents are in trading the safety of the state for cash, Demosthenes upbraids: 'Yes, indeed, Aischines, you, along with your associates, were at the post, racing only thoroughbreds; and I? No match for you (ἐγὼ δ' ἀσθενής), I must confess, but certainly more loyal than you to these' (with a gesture to his fellow-citizens, 320). Paul similarly relates the kinds of behavior championed by his opponents and rounds out his indictment of the Corinthians' passivity in the face of oppressive tactics with the words: 'I hate to say it. We've lacked the spunk for that' (11.21).

To counter other attempts at denigration of his character, Demosthenes chides (159), 'I marvel that you did not forthwith turn your backs on him when first you saw him.[2] Or is it that some dense darkness hides the truth from you?'[3]

---

1. See Hans D. Betz, 'Paul's Apology in II Cor. 10–13 and the Socratic Tradition' (Colloquy 2, The Center for Hermeneutical Studies in Hellenistic and Modern Culture; Berkeley, 1970), p. 15.
2. Cf. Paul in Gal. 1.6.
3. See 2 Cor. 4.4.

This and other examples of rebuke of an audience by the most distinguished orator of Hellas shows that one could safely engage in criticism of the very community whose goodwill was being solicited.[1]

In his essay on self-praise, Plutarch advised that it is appropriate to impress one's auditors, especially if they are imprudent, with one's own qualities. Liberality is certainly among them, but one's opponents might readily interpret it as a cover for self-interest.[2] In the manner of Demosthenes, Paul takes up the canard and comes to grips with the question of his having taken advantage of the Corinthians. 'In fact', Paul counters, 'I pillaged other assemblies. . . to help you out' (11.8).

Reference to lineage with a reputation for distinguished service became a standard feature in Greco-Roman honorary documents.[3] Demosthenes embeds his own superior lineage in an attack on Aischines:

> Consider, if you will, his libelous portrayal of my private life and see for yourselves how simply and fairly I address the matter. If indeed you know me to be the kind of person he alleges—my life among you has been open for all to see—then by all means refrain from hearing another sound from me, even if you must grant that I have earned the highest marks for my public life among you, and forthwith rise up and pronounce your verdict—now! But if I in your judgment and understanding am a far better person than this fellow and can boast a better lineage, and if I and mine are in no way inferior to our general populace—no offence intended—then do not give credence to this man; and this applies to his other assertions, for it is clear that all have been alike contrived by him (10).

In his invective against detractors, Paul similarly calls attention to his enviable lineage (11.22).

Aware that his audience might entertain an image of a clever and manipulative speaker or writer, Demosthenes forestalls the judgment by parrying from two directions. On one front he engages in a bit of self-denigration with a view to casting his opposition in the imagined negative role and on another leaves to the audience a decision concerning his motivation. In either direction, he emerges a winner (110). But persuasion is closely linked with attack, which also offers opportunity

1. See also *De Corona*, 41; 138; cf. 45-46.
2. On liberality as a possible cover for self-interest, see Aischines, *Against Ktesiphon*, 238-40.
3. The rationale is spelled out repeatedly by Pindar, who notes that genetic *aretē* is superior to mere acquired skill; see e.g. *Olympian Odes* 2.86-87; 10.20-21; 11.16-20; *Pythian* 8.44-45; 10.12; *Nemean* 3.40-42.

for negative comparison. Aischines is an expert at exploiting tonality and the resources of rhetoric (280, 308), Demosthenes warns his audience. As for himself, Demosthenes will state things simply and forthrightly (111), and the audience may rest assured that he makes up for the deficiency with loyal service to the state. In the manner of Demosthenes, Paul emphasized the simplicity of his communication (1.12-13) and in his concluding remarks rests his case with the Corinthians (13.6).

Denigration of rhetorical skill, not to speak of accusations about rhetorical tactics, was predictable in ancient assemblies, and it is not surprising that Paul's opponents should engage in some such form of attack.[1] They charge that the apostle writes with a heavy pen, but is himself an amateurish lightweight in personal appearances, deficient in courage (10.10). All smoke, no fire. The criticism is similar to Aischines' repeated charge that Demosthenes lacked the deeds to match his words. In the Greco-Roman world, where deed welded with word denoted an exceptional person,[2] such attack would be interpreted as a telling blow, and Demosthenes declares that he backs off from no one (319). Similarly, Paul assures the Corinthians that he is prepared for anything at Corinth (10.11; 12.21; 13.2-3).[3] In sum, Paul's self-praise is linked with the invective against his opposition in such a manner as to demonstrate his total commitment to the Corinthians' interests.

In reinforcement of his claim to personal integrity, Demosthenes states that his life has been open to scrutiny (111). Paul likewise trusts the Corinthians to make the correct judgment about his own credentials (13.6).

---

1. For Aischines' attack on Demosthenes along these lines, see *Against Ktesiphon* 101, ref. to κόμπος; 142, ἡ τῶν ὀνομάτων σύνθεσιν, masterful phrasing; 152, useless for great deeds, but bold in words; 168, 'fine-sounding words'; 174, Demosthenes is clever δεινός with words; 200, Demosthenes is a word-technician, a rhetorician, not an orator; 210, on tonality; 228-29, Aischines refers to Demosthenes' own charge about mellifluous and disarming rhetoric and his claim to simplicity and sticking to the real issue; 237, Ktesiphon charged with dishonest and bombastic rhetoric in reference to Demosthenes.

2. Cf. *Benefactor*, pp. 339-43.

3. Paul may also be open to the charge of undue timidity or reluctance to improvise (ἀτολμία) that was leveled at Demosthenes. Plutarch (*Demosthenes* 8) states that Demosthenes was said to have lacked extemporaneous ability; see Hartmut Erbse, who calls attention to data that contradict Plutarch, 'Die Bedeutung der Synkrisis in den Parallelbiographien Plutarchs', *Hermes* 84 (1956), pp. 408-409.

To add weight to his credentials, Paul once again recites a catalogue of perils (11.23-29),[1] which have the net effect of establishing his own personal prestige and loyalty to the Corinthians' interests. There was long precedent for this. In the Odyssey (12.209-212), Odysseus calms his comrades when they face the foaming waters of Charybdis:

> No greater peril is this than when the Cyclops hemmed us with mighty force within his cave.
> But thence my merit and my brains wrought our escape.

So also Demosthenes had done: 'I alone of all who addressed you on matters of policy did not in peril's hour abandon my post of loyalty to the state. No, I was there, speaking and writing, in the very midst of terrors, what was to your best interests. . . I shirked no danger and paid no attention to what it cost me personally' (173, 197).

In his speech to the Athenian jury, Demosthenes made capital out of the contrast between his own privileged youth spent in leisure and the early penury of Aischines, who did menial chores (257-58). The point of this comparison is to establish his own superior credentials as a man of *aretē*, that is, a benefactor of exceptional value to the state. Paul cannot take advantage of this ploy in the form used by Demosthenes, for his status as an artisan makes him vulnerable to denigrating criticism, but he cannot avoid the rhetorical summons. Therefore he adopts the maneuver at which he is expert: the turning weakness into strength.[2]

In tune with all his other claims is Paul's boast that he has not taken economic advantage of the Corinthians. He has indeed run the risk of demeaning himself in the eyes of some by engaging in manual labor (1

---

1. See above on *peristasis*.
2. On social status, see Richard L. Rohrbaugh, 'Methodological Considerations in the Debate over the Social Class Status of Early Christians', *JAAR* 52 (1984), pp. 519-46 (lit.). As in many matters, Greco-Romans were ambivalent about hand labor, but sight of this fact is occasionally lost in discussions of 2 Corinthians. The presentation by Furnish (*II Corinthians*, pp. 506-509) of a variety of viewpoints, including especially the detailed study of Roland F. Hock (*The Social Context of Paul's Ministry: Tentmaking and Apostleship* [Philadelphia: Fortress, 1980]) on the subject of Paul's self-support at Corinth should be supplemented by Robert M. Grant's observations (*Early Christianity and Society: Seven Studies* [New York: Harper, 1977]). Grant (p. 66) reminds scholars that Hesiod's *Works and Days* did not survive because Hellenes, including those responsible for transmitting his books to posterity, looked down on labor. Plato's view (*Rep.* 9.590c) indeed set the tone for some philosophers' demeaning of common labor, but there was no consensus (Grant, p. 74).

Cor. 4.12), but he did so out of magnanimous motives (2 Cor. 11.7-11). If there was any thought on the part of Corinthians that they were the patrons and Paul was a client in this matter, the apostle does not hesitate to set the matter straight.[1] Rather, Paul thinks in terms of the far more comprehensive Hellenic model of benefactors. God is the Supreme Benefactor, Jesus is the Great Benefactor. Paul is an envoy of both and his way of life will pass divine audit. As the Corinthians' benefactor, with a record of loyal service, in their behalf, he is entitled to their appreciation. A little thought on their part should make them realize that it is they who have violated the basic cultural code of Hellas, not to speak of their responsibility to God and Jesus Christ.[2] Thus he has taken the steam out of his adversaries' charge. Far from his work being a hindrance to his ability to confer benefits on the public,[3] Paul's method makes it possible for him to confer all the more benefits (11.7).[4]

A person of *aretē* ought to be an example to others.[5] According to Demosthenes, an orator's ultimate purpose is to encourage the popu-

1. On patron–client relationships, see the literature cited by John H. Elliott, 'Patronage and Clientism in Early Christian Society: A Short Reading Guide', *Forum* 3.4 (1987), pp. 39-49; Halvor Moxnes, *The Economy of the Kingdom: Social Conflict and Economic Relations in Luke's Gospel* (Philadelphia: Fortress, 1988), pp. 40-47. It is unfortunate that the narrow term 'patron–client relationship' should have entered the discussion rather than the more comprehensive term 'reciprocity system' of which 'patron–client' more accurately describes an ancient Roman subset. Some of the current application of patron–client theory to Hellenic texts would have caused a shaking of heads in the ancient Greek-speaking world.

2. Hellenes considered ingratitude one of the most heinous of crimes. It would be carrying owls to Athens to cite even 1% of the decrees that contain the phrase: 'so that all may know that our city knows how to render thanks. . .'

3. Demosthenes charges Aischines with the liability of common labor interfering with his ability to confer benefits on the public, *De Corona* 256-75. Some of the snobbishness is connected with the kind of thinking expressed by Ar. *Rhet.* 1367a, about certain types of work being 'tacky'.

4. Appeal to a history of beneficence, whether of oneself or another, is, as Clark ('Private and Public Benefactions', p. 33) observes, a common *topos* in Hellenistic oratory. Pindar's (*Olympian* 4.15) praise of a charioteer named Psaumis for his generous hospitality is typical.

5. On the importance of example by public figures, see Plutarch, *Moralia* 539-40; see also e.g. the accolades accorded Menas of Sestus (*OGIS* 339; trans. *Benefactor*, no. 17). Greco-Roman literature is replete with accounts of exemplary exploits and morality. The secondary literature is also immense, but see e.g. Karl Jost, *Das Beispiel und Vorbild der Vorfahren bei den attischen Rednern und Geschichtsschreibern bis Demosthenes* (Rhetorische Studien 19; Paderborn: Ferdinand Schön-

lace in the direction of harmony, friendship, and a sense of urgency about the things that really matter (246). 'At the very beginning', affirms Demosthenes at the close of the speech, 'I chose a straight and upright path for guiding the fortunes of the state—to cultivate its honor, its power, and its prestige; to augment these and to be a part of them' (322). He concludes with the prayer: 'Grant us who remain a speedy relief from impending fears and a salvation that endures' (324).[1] Similarly, Paul concludes with a plea for unity (12.19-21), and a promise that his detractors will be proved wrong, if they think that he does not have deeds to match his words (13.1-4, echoing 10.10-11). There is subtle humor in this posturing by the apostle. The congregation, of course, will be determined to make Paul's dire projected discipline unnecessary, and Paul will again appear to be 'weak'. But the power of Jesus Christ in them will make it possible for them to function at peak levels of performance (13.5-10). Appropriately, Paul strengthens the plea for unity in vv. 11-12, and reinforces it with a benediction that emphasizes κοινωνία as the distinctive contribution of the Holy Spirit.

The strongest reinforcement is an oath. As Basil Gildersleeve noted, Demosthenes outswears all orators.[2] Paul is less generous with asseveration (11.31; cf. 1.23). Also, the point of his oath in 11.31 is not to affirm something trivial, but to disclaim credit for exceptional cleverness in outwitting the ethnarch of Damascus. On the contrary, God must receive the credit for his escape from a perilous circumstance.

---

ingh, 1936); S. Perlmann, 'The Historical Example, its Use and Importance as Political Propaganda in the Attic Orators', *Scripta Hierosolymitana*, vol. VII: *Studies in History* (ed. A. Fuks and I. Halpern; Jerusalem: Magnes, 1961), pp. 150-66; Heinrich Dörrie, 'Das gute Beispiel—ΚΑΛΟΝ ΥΠΟΔΕΙΓΜΑ: Ein Lehrstück vom politischen Nutzen sakraler Stiftungen in Kommagene und in Rom', *Studien zur Religion und Kultur Kleinasiens*, Festschrift Friedrich K. Dörner (ed. S. Sahin, E. Schwertheim, J. Wagner; Leiden: Brill, 1978), I, pp. 245-62; Klaus Döring, *Exemplum Socratis: Studien zur Sokratesnachwirkung in der kynisch-stoischen Populärphilosophie der frühen Kaiserzeit und im frühen Christentum* (Einzelschrift, *Hermes* 42, Wiesbaden: Steiner, 1979); Alfred Klotz, 'Zur Litteratur der Exempla und zur Epitoma Livii', *Hermes* 44 (1909), pp. 198-214; Henry W. Litchfield, 'National *Exempla Virtutis* in Roman Literature', *HSC* 25 (1914), pp. 1-71; Rudolf Helm, 'Valerius Maximus, Seneca und die "Exemplarsammlung"', *Hermes* 74 (1939), pp. 129-54; A. Lumpe, 'Exemplum', *RAC*, VI (1966), pp. 1229-57 (lit.).

1. 'Enduring salvation' is in dramatic contrast to 'enduring servitude', *De Corona* 204.

2. C.W. Miller (ed.), *Selections from the Brief Mention of Basil Lanneau Gildersleeve* (Baltimore: Johns Hopkins, 1930), p. 124.

Paul's Hellenic public can be counted on to make the correct inference. God delivers a person of exceptional merit or *aretē*.[1]

In conclusion, chs. 10–13 are an appropriate rhetorical climax to Paul's application of the reciprocity paradigm that appears in chs. 1–9. If chs. 10–13 were composed as a separate installment to the Corinthians, the editors responsible for issuing 2 Corinthians in its basic canonical form shared the Hellenic spirit that informed Paul's missionary zeal.

In another sense, 2 Corinthians may be read as a parody of the Greco-Roman epideictic pattern, for it celebrates the superb beneficence of God in Christ and thereby makes all boasting, including that of the apostles, ludicrous.

Ultimately, beneath all Paul's vehemence there breathes the spirit of a loving parent. As Epictetus (3.22.81-82) put it:

> The Cynic has adopted all humanity. The males are his sons and the females his daughters. In such manner he approaches them all, and in such wise he cares for them. Or do you suppose that he reviles every one he meets because he has nothing better to do? Nay, he does it as a father, as a brother, and as the assistant to God, the Father of us all.

---

1. Cf. Nero's boast at Corinth (*SIG*[3] 814.25-26; trans. *Benefactor*, no. 44).

PLACING THE BLAME:
THE PRESENCE OF EPIDEICTIC IN GALATIANS 1 AND 2

James D. Hester

Introduction

In the past I have accepted in the main the identification of Galatians as an apologetic letter cast in the form of a defense, or forensic, speech.[1] While I am satisfied with my identification of 1.11-12 as the *stasis* statement for the letter as a whole and the narrative in particular,[2] it seems to me that the issue of quality underlies the whole letter, not just the narrative. The larger issue is the quality of the relationship Paul had with the Galatians and the values that were the foundation of that relationship. In that sense, the *stasis* gives insight into both the rhetorical and argumentative situations Paul faced and addressed. Moreover, the *stasis* of quality is the *stasis* that is associated with the epideictic genre,[3] a fact which also illuminates the rhetorical situation,[4] and I will make the argument below that Galatians exhibits the features of that genre rather than those of the forensic.

---

1. J.D. Hester, 'The Rhetorical Structure of Galatians 1.11–2.14', *JBL* 103 (1984), pp. 223-33.

2. A helpful review of *stasis* theory is provided by George A. Kennedy, *Greek Rhetoric under Christian Emperors* (Princeton: Princeton University Press, 1983), pp. 73-86. Robert G. Hall ('The Rhetorical Outline of Galatians', *JBL* 106 [1987], p. 285) says that *stasis* 'is a tool for classifying how the defense was related to the accusation'. He argues that by identifying 1.11-12 as the *stasis* statement, I confused 'tool' with form. However, it was my intention that the reader understand that it was in 1.11-12 that the Galatians discovered the basis, or '*stasis*', upon which Paul was going to build the elements of his argument.

3. Ch. Perelman and L. Olbrechts-Tyteca, *The New Rhetoric* (Notre Dame: University of Notre Dame Press, 1969), pp. 47-54.

4. Within the scope of this paper I cannot review the discussions of rhetorical, audience, and argumentative situations. The reader is directed to Lloyd Bitzer, 'The Rhetorical Situation', *PhilR* 1 (1968), pp. 1-4, and subsequent reactions to that article in that journal. The best discussion of audience and argumentative situations can

I had also identified 2.11-14 as a digression (a *digressio* or *egressus*) that should not be understood as part of the narrative but instead as a bridge to the *propositio*, which Betz claims makes up 2.15-21.[1] I now believe that Gal. 2.11-14 is not a digression but a chreia, slightly expanded by Paul, and 2.15-21 the elaboration of the chreia.[2]

In this paper I will attempt to show that the narrative (1.13–2.21) is made up of a self-referent encomium, imbedded in a letter that is primarily epideictic in nature, in which Paul attempts to remind the Galatians of the character of the gospel that was revealed to him and preached by him to them; he is its model and therefore theirs. Moreover, both the chreia and its elaboration, as the final two topics in the encomium, serve to focus the point of the encomium.

Methodological Considerations

1. *Rhetorical Criticism*
Although the rhetorical handbooks spend little if any time discussing the rhetorical nature of letters, the writing of letters in good rhetorical style was a normal part of education in the Hellenistic and Roman world.[3] Letters were to obtain literary qualities by the imitation of oratory, historiography, or philosophical dialogue.[4] By the early middle ages there were handbooks that instructed in the art of letter writing, usually basing the structure of the letter on an evolved form of Ciceronian rhetorical structures.[5] It seems reasonable, therefore, to use some type of rhetorical criticism to analyze Paul's letters. However, before I define what I mean by that term, I must describe

be found in Perelman and Olbrechts-Tyteca, *New Rhetoric*. I see 'rhetorical situation' and 'argumentative situation' as two different situations, the one produced by the exigence, the other constructed by the speaker.

1. Hall ('Rhetorical Outline', p. 285) quite properly challenges my identification of 2.11-14 as a digression; cf. Bernard Lategan, 'Is Paul Defending His Apostleship?', *NTS* 34 (1988), p. 425 n. 1.

2. I have changed my identification of the type of chreia as the 'mixed' type in 'The Use and Influence of Rhetoric in Galatians 2.1-14', *TZ* 42 (1986), pp. 386-408.

3. One of the earlier discussions is found in Demetrius, *On Style* 4.223-35.

4. George A. Kennedy, *New Testament Interpretation through Rhetorical Criticism* (Chapel Hill, NC: University of North Carolina Press, 1984), p. 31.

5. For example, *'Rationes dictandi', Three Medieval Rhetorical Arts* (ed. J.J. Murphy; Berkeley: University of California Press, 1971), pp. 1-25. Also, J.J. Murphy, *Rhetoric in the Middle Ages* (Berkeley: University of California Press, 1974), pp. 194-268.

briefly the concepts of the rhetorical situation and the argumentative situation.

Lloyd Bitzer gave the concept of the rhetorical situation its classic definition:

> Rhetorical situation may be defined as a complex of persons, events, objects, and relations presenting an actual or potential exigence which can be completely or partially removed if discourse, introduced into the situation, can so constrain human decision or action as to bring about the significant modification of the exigence.[1]

Bitzer posits that something occurs to cause the need for discourse or speech. This occurrence he calls the 'exigence'. It is defined as something that needs to be modified; a rhetorical exigence is one which is capable of being modified by means of discourse. The speaker has come out of an audience, the situational audience, in response to the presence of an exigence, with the conviction that the situation can be modified by discourse. If it cannot be, then the situation is not truly rhetorical.

The audience the speaker addresses is the 'actual' audience,[2] in distinction from the 'universal audience' or a 'single interlocutor'.[3] That is, the actual audience can, in part, be defined in time and place, and to it the speaker must be careful to adapt. Furthermore, its presence establishes the contours of the initial argumentative situation. Loosely understood, the argumentative situation is 'the influence of the earlier stages of the discussion on the argumentative possibilities open to the speaker'.[4] It is the argumentative situation that will, for example, determine the selection and order of the topics in the argumentative structure of the discourse. This situation is dynamic. Because to some degree or another any particular audience is a reflection of the universal audience, the speaker must always be aware of the use of arguments meant to convince others than those who are faced in a given situation. In doing this, the speaker tries to bring the

---

1. Bitzer, 'Rhetorical Situation', p. 6.
2. D.M. Hunsaker and C.R. Smith, 'The Nature of Issues', *Western Speech Communications* 40 (1976), pp. 144-55.
3. The terms are used by Perelman and Olbrechts-Tyteca (*New Rhetoric*, p. 30) to refer to the ones who must be convinced or persuaded. They define the audience as, 'the ensemble of those whom the speaker wishes to influence by his argumentation' (p. 19). For them, the actual or particular audience is a subset of the universal audience (p. 35).
4. Perelman and Olbrechts-Tyteca, *New Rhetoric*, p. 491.

audience to a recognition of universal values, tries to bring the audience from where they are in time and place to a more universal world view. As the arguments take effect, he or she must try to predict their effect and judge where the particular audience is along the trajectory from particular to universal. In other words, movement along the trajectory produces new stages in the argumentative situation and new argumentative possibilities open to the speaker, allowing for the introduction of new forms of argumentative discourse. This dynamic underlies the arrangement of speeches and the freedom in speech construction allowed by the rhetoricians.[1]

What, then, is rhetorical criticism? Clearly it is more than identifying and analyzing the functions of rhetorical forms in literature. George Kennedy claims that understanding how rhetoric works is more global than identification of things like genre.[2]

> Rhetorical criticism takes the text as we have it, whether the work of a single author or the product of editing, and looks at it from the point of view of the author's or editor's intent, the unified results, and how it would be perceived by an audience of near contemporaries. . . The ultimate goal of rhetorical analysis, briefly put, is the discovery of the author's intent and how that is transmitted through a text to an audience.[3]

Rhetorical criticism analyzes the historical setting of a particular speaker and audience, the rhetorical situation and the exigence, the argumentative structures and forms the speaker uses to persuade or convince the particular and universal audience, and the development of the argumentative situation along the trajectory of particular to universal.

Paul's response to the rhetorical situations he faced was to write letters, but these situations called for more than ordinary letters. His letters had to function as his rhetorical presence; one finds in them more than epistolary conventions and forms. Therefore, the rhetorical critic must:

1. determine the various rhetorical units in the letters, which might range from the letter itself down to five or six verses;
2. define the situation of the unit, which may be analogous in some instances to identifying the rhetorical exigence for that unit;

---

1. I am dependent on Perelman and Olbrechts-Tyteca (*New Rhetoric*, pp. 11-50) for many of the concepts I have used here.
2. Kennedy, *New Testament Interpretation*, p. 33.
3. Kennedy, *New Testament Interpretation*, pp. 4, 12.

3. identify the arrangement of the material, including stylistic devices;
4. survey the unit and units to evaluate their success in meeting the rhetorical exigence and what its implications might have been for speaker and audience;
5. look for signs that the argumentative situation has shifted and caused Paul to change the trajectory of the argument, thus giving him the opportunity to use different vocabulary, forms, figures, tropes, and other argumentative conventions.[1]

This agenda recognizes that rhetorical analysis is not concerned primarily with questions of style but more importantly with argumentation.[2]

2. *Epistolary Theory*

Traditionally the literary study of Paul's letters begins with an investigation of their form and style. Epistolary conventions are identified, and their purposes are described in general and in the context of a particular letter. Forms characteristic of a particular letter or argumentative style are identified and analyzed. I suppose the bulk of the literary-critical work done on Paul's letters falls into this classification; I hope readers will forgive me for stating the obvious.

Work is also done on placing Paul's letters within certain broad classifications, for example, private letter versus public or official letters.[3] Each of these 'categories' called for a particular style and can be divided into sub-categories of 'familiar and happy' or 'severe and sad'. Studies concerned with analysis of type for purposes of classification attempt to provide analogies or models that could be shown to be illustrative of the Pauline letter type. Recently, Stanley

1. I have adapted these from Kennedy, *New Testament Interpretation*, pp. 33-38. Cf. Elizabeth Schüssler Fiorenza, 'Rhetorical Situations and Historical Reconstruction', *NTS* 33 (1987), pp. 386-403.
2. For important discussions of rhetorical criticism as analysis of argumentation, see Burton Mack, *Rhetoric and the New Testament* (Minneapolis: Augsburg Fortress, 1990); Wilhelm Wuellner, 'Where is Rhetorical Criticism Taking Us?', *CBQ* 49 (1987), pp. 448-63; James L. Kinneavy, *Greek Rhetorical Origins of Christian Faith* (New York: Oxford University Press, 1987).
3. A survey has been done by Nils A. Dahl in 'Paul's Letter to the Galatians', unpublished essay distributed to the SBL Seminar on Paul, 1973, 'I. The Problem of Classification', pp. 2-11. See also Martin Stirewalt, 'Official Letter Writing and the Letter of Paul to the Churches of Galatia', unpublished essay distributed to the SBL Seminar on Paul, 1973.

Stowers has argued not only that the Deissmann legacy of the distinction between 'letter' and 'epistle' (or 'real' and 'non-real') has been difficult to set aside, but equally importantly, that the focus on seeking comparisons in documentary papyri (or 'non-literary' letters) has caused scholars to neglect the larger questions of the 'functions of early Christian letters in their original social and historical contexts'. He makes the observation that examining letters from the trash heaps of Ephesus and Corinth would put us in closer contact with Paul's social world than those from a provincial town in Egypt, which were 'remote from the life of the great centers of Hellenistic culture. . .' He goes on to argue that the distinction between private and public letters, between 'warm, personal, spontaneous, artless, common-private-friendly letters and impersonal, conventional, artificial literary letters' is not very helpful and could be misleading.[1]

Attempts have been made to analyze Paul's letters using one or more of the types that were enumerated by early epistolary theorists. Hans Dieter Betz identified Galatians as the apologetic type, while Nils Dahl has argued that it is ironic.[2] Abraham Malherbe has called 1 Thessalonians paraenetic, one of the 41 types listed by Pseudo-Libanius (4th to 6th century AD).[3] Robert Jewett has called Romans an ambassadorial letter, which is a kind of epideictic literature but not one of the 'types' in the handbooks.[4] Stowers has greatly expanded the use of epistolary theory for analyzing Paul's letters.

Even though epistolary theory was properly part of rhetorical education, it does not occupy a significant place in the extant handbooks. The first significant treatment of it is found in Demetrius, *On Style* 4.223-35. Some of the handbooks on epistolary theory may date from as early as the second century BC, but most come from the third or fourth centuries AD. Two of the most prominent are Pseudo-Demetrius (2nd century BC to 3rd AD and Pseudo-Libanius (sometimes called Proclus, 4th to 6th centuries AD). Demetrius was probably

---

1. Stanley K. Stowers, *Letter Writing in Greco-Roman Antiquity* (Philadelphia: Westminster, 1986), pp. 18-19.

2. Hans Dieter Betz, *Galatians* (Hermeneia; Philadelphia: Fortress, 1979), pp. 14-15; Dahl, 'Paul's Letter to the Galatians', p. 12.

3. Abraham Malherbe, '1 Thessalonians as a Paraenetic Letter', unpublished essay distributed to the SBL Seminar on Paul, 1972. He gives other examples of paraenetic letters in *Moral Exhortation: A Greco-Roman Sourcebook* (Philadelphia: Westminster, 1986), pp. 124-25.

4. Robert Jewett, 'Romans as an Ambassadorial Letter', *Int* 36 (1982), pp. 5-20.

intended for advanced students and devotes some attention to defining a variety of hortatory-type letters. Libanius uses the word 'style' to refer to letter types and lists some 41 of them, thereby producing a refinement of some categories identified by others.[1]

One of the pitfalls to be avoided in using epistolary theory to identify a letter type is the temptation to apply, more or less literally, a description of a type from one of the handbooks. It is widely recognized that such handbooks were for the use of professional letter writers. The models described in them were just that, models to be used as the basis for writing letters suited to the situation. As in the creation of speeches, the letter writer was to keep in mind the complex of things surrounding the sender, receiver, and situation, and shape the letter accordingly. One of the more prominent admonitions of the theorists is that letters, especially to those well known to the sender, should be conversational and relatively brief, not be filled with too many rhetorical devices and periods, and be in a style that was to be natural or 'plain'. If writing to someone of importance or not well known to the sender, the style should be somewhat more 'graceful'.[2]

John White says, 'Epistolary theory was never able to assimilate or control the practice of letter writing. The ancient theorists acknowledged the difference between ideal and practice.'[3] This is almost certainly due to the fact that letters were to be written as though they were one side of a conversation. The letter must be a suitable substitute for one's presence. Given the fact that letter writers could not explain themselves or answer questions that might be raised by their letters, it seems likely that the senders would try to anticipate the impact of what they said and adjust the trajectory of their comments to their construction of the 'audience' response.[4]

In some situations one might expect to find the predominance of one letter type. For example, White suggests that the 'cultivated letter of

1. I am using the texts and translations provided by Malherbe, 'Theorists', pp. 28-39, 62-77.
2. Malherbe, 'Theorists', pp. 16-17, who summarizes teaching on style from the nine theorists he surveyed. See also Kennedy, *Greek Rhetoric under Christian Emperors*, p. 72.
3. John L. White, *Light from Ancient Letters* (FFNT; Philadelphia: Fortress, 1986), p. 190. This observation has been made by many; see e.g. Stowers, *Letter Writing*, pp. 32-35.
4. An interesting early example in a literary letters (as opposed to a papyrus letter) can be found in Isocrates, 'To Dionysius', 2.

friendship' is a letter type that exhibits common formulaic elements in a wide variety of examples.[1] In other situations more than one related type could be used to strengthen the overall rhetorical impact of the letter. This practice of mixing letter types within one letter is permitted by the ancient theorists, but that fact is not often enough acknowledged by modern interpreters.[2]

What is interesting to note in the lists of letter types in the handbooks is the number of styles usually associated with the epideictic genre.[3] Keeping in mind that epideictic is the rhetoric of praise (ἔπαινος) and/or blame (ψόγος)—more will be said about this below—one finds in Demetrius 'blaming' types as follows: blaming, reproachful, rebuking or censorious, admonishing, and vituperative. 'Praising' types include praising, commendatory, and congratulatory. In Libanius one finds four 'blaming' types: blaming, reproaching, reproving, and maligning; and two 'praise' types: commending and praising.[4]

In addition, it is possible to fit letters of exhortation and advice into the epideictic. According to Stowers, this occurs when advice seeks to 'increase adherence to a value or to cultivate a character trait'. Exhortation and advice are the positive side of admonition and rebuke, letter types identified by both Demetrius and Libanius. Admonition is a form of blame intended to encourage change in a person's character while rebuke was a kind of shaming designed to confront the reader with the writer's knowledge of the recipient's deeds with exhortation to change them.[5] Therefore, these types must be seen as epideictic as well.

Without investigating the other types or styles listed by the theorists, one may now ask if it is possible to identify a predominant type for Galatians. I believe Galatians can be categorized as a letter of blame. Stowers identifies the fundamental elements of the letter of blame as: (1) the writer is the recipient's benefactor; (2) the recipient has wronged the benefactor, and (3) the writer attempts to criticize and/or

---

1. White, *Ancient Letters*, p. 191.
2. Stowers (*Letter Writing*, pp. 49-173) illustrates this mixing of types repeatedly in his discussion of 'Types of Letters'.
3. Stowers, *Letter Writing*, pp. 27-28.
4. Stowers (*Letter Writing*, p. 85) claims five types but lists only four, unless he intended to include the ironic. However, he refers to the ironic as 'mock praise'.
5. Stowers, *Letter Writing*, pp. 107, 133.

shame the recipient in such a way that he or she does not destroy their relationship.[1]

These characteristics seem to describe the general situation of Paul and the Galatian churches. It is clear that Paul believes that the Galatians benefitted from his preaching (3.2-5; 4.31–5.1) and that they have wronged him (4.12-20, in which v. 12a is hortatory, but v. 12b is ironic in that it refers to a condition that does not now exist). Now he writes to admonish the Galatians to change their behavior and become like him, restoring what was once a relationship of mutuality. While it is tempting to differentiate between the Galatians and those who were troubling them, it does not appear that Paul assigns blame only or even primarily to the agitators. George Lyons makes a strong case that scholarship has fallen victim to a 'mirror reading' of Galatians in that interpreters identify the presence of opponents and the contour of their arguments by analyzing the statements in which Paul tries to correct some failure in the belief system and/or behavior of the Galatians. Lyons makes the point, quite convincingly I believe, that one cannot talk about opponents of Paul in Galatians, at least not in the sense of some group of outsiders who have come in with 'another gospel' that they claim is the only authentic one.[2] Ultimately the Galatians are to blame for their failure to keep the faith. They have forgotten the reciprocity of the relationship, a reciprocity they once practiced (4.15).

Beyond this general identification, however, there are elements in the letter that suggest that it should be further classified as rebuking or censorious in that it accuses the Galatians of being involved with beliefs and behavior they know to be wrong (1.6-7; 4.8-11, 21; 5.2, 13, 17). It has elements of vituperation (5.2-12) and irony (1.8-9; and 3.1-5, if one allows for sarcasm as a sub-set of irony). Also, there is the presence of paraenetic material (5.16–6.10).[3] However, it seems to me that the overall spirit of the letter is one of reproach, a more particular style or type of blame.

---

1. Stowers, *Letter Writing*, p. 87.

2. George Lyons, *Pauline Autobiography* (SBLDS 73; Atlanta: Scholars, 1985), pp. 76-105.

3. Betz (*Galatians*, p. 22) labeled 5.1–6.10 the *exhortatio* division. He laments the fact that there have been few studies of the 'formal character and function of epistolary paraenesis' (p. 253). His footnotes reference studies of rhetorical handbooks and philosophical letters. See p. 253 nn. 6, 8, 12, 13.

Libanius says that the 'reproach' letter is one in which the recipient is reminded how much he has been benefitted by the sender. Demetrius says, 'it is the reproachful type when we once more reproach, with accusations, someone whom we had earlier benefitted for what he has done'.[1] This is a refinement of the idea of blame. In general, blame as a type allowed the writer to take someone to task for an attitude that threatened to alter the nature of the relationship between the writer and the recipient. Reproach focused that blame on the issue of forgetting the debt of gratitude owed.

The Galatians owed Paul the debt of their freedom in Christ, which they were in the process of giving up. Even though it might be argued that he had been a recipient of their benefactions, their debt to him was greater because he brought them the gospel. In hearing the gospel with faith they received freedom in Christ and life in the Spirit. The gratitude they had shown on an earlier occasion was evidence of their willingness to acknowledge that debt (4.12-15).

The accusations he makes are clear. They are turning to another gospel. This charge is made in the ironic rebuke in 1.6 and in the rhetorical questions in 3.1-5. Almost everything else of which he accuses them—of failing to be reciprocal in their relationship; of practicing works of the law, specifically circumcision; of turning away from freedom in Christ to the slavery of works of the flesh; of selfishness instead of community concern—can be traced to that charge.

Of course, the suggestion that Galatians is a 'blaming' letter of reproach argues against the now classic proposal by Hans Dieter Betz that Galatians is an apologetic letter in the form of a forensic speech. That identification by Betz met with early resistance. I have already noted that Nils A. Dahl, using extensive examples from the common letter tradition, argued that it was an ironic 'rebuke' letter.[2] David Aune in his review of Betz said that the reason Betz had trouble explaining the presence of paraenetic material in an apologetic letter is that Galatians was closer to deliberative speech than forensic, and that in any case it was possible to find a mixture of types in it.[3] Stanley Stowers has stated flatly that there are no apologetic letters in the NT.[4]

---

1. Malherbe, 'Theorists', pp. 30-31, 64-65, 72-73.
2. While the rebuke letter type was known by the theorists. Dahl had to stretch his definition of 'irony' so that it was closer to sarcasm than the classic definition.
3. D.E. Aune, *RelSRev* 7 (1981), pp. 310-28.
4. Stowers, *Letter Writing*, p. 173.

George Lyons has argued that Betz has misunderstood the function of the autobiographical section and therefore cannot use the argument that it is a *narratio* in the sense that that is found in forensic speeches. He also points out that one cannot judge the genre of a speech by its arrangement, a mistake he claims Betz makes, since all three speech types (forensic, deliberative, demonstrative) used more or less the same divisions.[1]

If I am correct in understanding the *stasis* of the letter to be that of quality, both the quality of the gospel and the quality of the relationship between Paul and the Galatians, then the argument can be made that Galatians might be better understood as a reproachful letter aimed at a group of people who once shared a set of commonly held values but, under the influence of some among them, this group has abandoned those values and, by accepting an alternate interpretation of the gospel, has in fact reverted to old values and practices. Paul confronts them with the seriousness of what they have done with his opening rebuke (θαυμάζω ὅτι οὕτως ταχέως μετατίθεσθε) and, having established the issue (*stasis*), launches into an encomiastic narrative to illustrate the legitimacy of his gospel. Its character was so superior to anything the Galatians might have encountered subsequently that he triumphed over his unnamed enemies in Jerusalem and shamed Peter in Antioch. Furthermore, if Galatians is a letter of reproach, then as I have noted above it is mainly epideictic in genre.

Epideictic Type

1. General Definition and Discussion
The epideictic genre, also called the 'demonstrative', 'ceremonial', or 'occasional',[2] was one of the three identified by Aristotle.[3] Its major function was to give praise or to place blame. Its purpose was

---

1. Lyons, *Pauline Autobiography*, pp. 112-19.
2. The standard survey is that of Theodore Burgess, *Epideictic Literature* (Chicago: University of Chicago Press, 1902). A summary is given in Heinrich Lausberg, *Elemente der literarischen Rhetorik* (2 vols.; München; Max Hübner, 1984), I, pp. 18-19. Charles S. Baldwin (*Ancient Rhetoric and Poetic* [New York: Macmillan, 1928], p. 15 n. 14), dissatisfied with most of the usual translations of epideictic (ἐπιδεικτικόν), settles on 'occasional' as best reflecting the use of the genre at ceremonial occasions.
3. *Rhet.* 1.3.3.

educational, urging the honorable, and, while it is often described as being concerned with the present, it is also widely recognized by ancient and modern commentators that it is allied with the deliberative and therefore has an interest in the future behavior of an audience.[1] One can see this quite clearly in the speeches of Isocrates, the *Panegyricus*, for example, or in his hortatory address 'To Demonicus', or in his address to Philip.[2]

Epideictic seems to fall into some disrepute almost from the start because it was associated with a type of rhetorical display that lacked a worthy point of view. The orator seemed comfortable with any side of an issue and was often accused of being more interested in illustrating his skill at creating an elaborate tapestry of verbal ornamentation than in pursuing the truth.[3] It is this aspect of oratory that Plato attacks in *Gorgias*. Forensic oratory, by contrast, became more reputable because it served a practical purpose in the lives of the Greeks and Romans; much of rhetorical education was designed to prepare a person to argue a case successfully. Epideictic was left to the sophists.[4]

Important categories of epideictic speeches included funeral orations and speeches in the praise of a king or very important person. The latter is an important representative of the most characteristic type of epideictic literature, the encomium; we will return to it later. In republican Rome, the most important epideictic type was the funeral oration, but many other forms existed, including panegyrics, marriage and birthday addresses, and even a speech for the arrival of a bride at her new home.[5]

Aristotle said that epideictic was the genre best suited to writing, because its ability to affect the audience depended as much on style as on anything else.[6] It could be read and used on more than one

1. Quint. 3.7.28.
2. Burgess (*Epideictic Literature*, p. 101) says that Isocrates saw the ideal speech as a mixture of epideictic and deliberative. See also George A. Kennedy, *The Art of Persuasion in Greece* (Princeton: Princeton University Press, 1963), pp. 188-90, and Perelman and Olbrechts-Tyteca, *New Rhetoric*, pp. 47-51.
3. Burgess, *Epideictic Literature*, pp. 93-94.
4. George A. Kennedy (*The Art of Rhetoric in the Roman World* [Princeton: Princeton University Press, 1972], p. 641) makes the point that by the third century AD, the attempt of some of the great rhetoricians to prevent oratory from becoming mainly bombastic had not been fully successful, 'for most the appeal of rhetoric was in style and *sententia*'.
5. Kennedy, *Roman World*, pp. 21-22, 428-29, 634-37.
6. *Rhet.* 3.1.7; 3.12.6.

occasion, presumably even read to audiences by someone other than
the author. The inclusion of elementary exercises in epideictic style in
rhetorical education makes it clear that such training was seen to
contribute to judicial eloquence.[1]

The basic arrangement of an epideictic speech followed that of the
other genres:

1. Introduction or *Exordium* or προοίμιον
2. Narrative or *Narratio* or διήγησις
3. Proofs or *Probatio* or πίστις
4. Conclusion or *Peroratio* or ἐπίλογος

According to Aristotle, only two sections of a speech are really
necessary, the narration and the proofs (*Rhet.* 3.13.1, 4). He does say
that the *exordium* in an epideictic speech is the source of praise or
blame (3.14.2), exhortations, dissuasion, and appeals to the hearer
(3.14.4). The purpose of the narrative is moral. Its order 'should not
be consecutive but disjointed' (3.16.1); this is because the speaker was
not involved in the actions being praised but only in recalling them.
Proofs in the epideictic were mainly by amplification.[2] It is suitable
because amplification was a form of praise, consisting of superiority,
'and superiority is one of those things that are noble' (1.9.38-40).

Other sections were optional, with a division of propositions
sometimes appearing before the proofs and a series of refutations
given after the proofs. Digressions were permitted. The presence of
these sections in any given speech was not required, nor was their
order of appearance immutably fixed. The speaker had great freedom
to adapt to the situation of the audience.

Quintilian adopts the overall divisions laid out by Aristotle.
Superficially it would appear that he considered the purpose of the
demonstrative genre to be mainly that of delighting the audience (8.
Pr. 7) by means of any ornamentation suitable to the occasion (8.3.1).
However, in other places he argues that it is impossible to maintain
clear lines of distinction among the genres. 'For we deal with justice
and expediency in panegyric and with honor in deliberation, while you

---

1. E. Patrick Parks, *The Roman Rhetorical Schools as a Preparation for the Courts
under the Early Empire* (Baltimore: Johns Hopkins, 1945), p. 114; Quint. 2.10.12.
Quintilian makes the point that panegyrics have suasory form. Burgess (*Epideictic
Literature*, p. 95) argues that Quintilian was not troubled by moral inconsistencies
found in oratory and yet defended the 'higher' interpretation of epideictic.

2. Burgess (*Epideictic Literature*, p. 105) refers to amplification and comparison.

will rarely find a forensic case, in part of which at any rate, something of those questions just mentioned won't be found' (3.4.16).

His discussion of the arrangement of a speech is based on the model of a forensic speech; therefore, his treatment of the narrative deals with the presentation of the facts of a case (2.4.2).[1] With Aristotle he says that proof consists mainly in amplification (3.7.6). The pattern he lays out for it is not unlike that of the development of an encomium as laid out in the handbooks on elementary exercises (3.7.10-18).

Quintilian's treatment of epideictic illustrates the truth of Burgess's comment that there was no important theoretical development of epideictic oratory from Aristotle to Dionysius of Halicarnassus. What does develop is an abandonment of any focus on rules 'designed to be used by students in actual composition'. Dionysius mentions six varieties of speeches that might be used in praise. By the third century AD, Menander discusses twenty-three.[2] If one compares this development with the evolution of letter types represented by Libanius and Demetrius, it would appear that the epideictic type and style had widespread influence on the literature of the Hellenistic and Roman world.

Perelman and Olbrechts-Tyteca point out that in the ancient world the epideictic genre has nothing to do with the presentation of a debate in which opponents would try to win favorable judgment from an audience.

> The purpose of epidictic [sic] speech is to increase the intensity of adherence to values held in common by the audience and speaker. The epidictic [sic] speech has an important role to play, for without such common values, upon what foundation could deliberative and legal speeches rest?[3]

Because the epideictic is concerned with recognizing values, the speaker's aim is often to gain and enhance adherence to those values. He is asking them, at least implicitly, to decide for that which is beautiful or good or true over their opposites, and because these values are usually of a universal nature, the speaker becomes an educator.[4]

---

1. I can find no separate discussion in Quintilian of narrative in an epideictic speech. Cf. Ar. *Rhet.* 3.16.2.
2. Burgess, *Epideictic Literature*, pp. 106-107.
3. *New Rhetoric*, pp. 47-49.
4. *New Rhetoric*, pp. 51-53.

It is important to note that, because the speaker does not need to defend a set of values as much as increase adherence to those already accepted, epideictic discourse is not designed to change value systems. Furthermore, because speaker and audience share value systems, they also share the rhetorical situation. The speaker is part of the audience; he is not an outsider, nor an opponent, but one who responds to the exigence of an occasion for promoting the community's value system no matter how that occasion arises.

A few NT scholars claim a wider presence for the epideictic genre in Paul. In addition to his identification of Romans as ambassadorial, Jewett has undertaken a careful analysis of 1 Thessalonians, creating an outline of its epideictic style.[1] Wilhelm Wuellner has long championed the identification of 1 Corinthians as epideictic, using as important arguing points the function of rhetorical questions and the digressions in that letter. He has also argued for the epideictic as the genre of Romans.[2] But others, even while acknowledging the presence of certain features of the epideictic—the presence of paraenetic material, praising and blaming motifs, etc.—prefer to see many of Paul's letters, including Galatians, as deliberative.[3]

Aside from the epideictic features we have already identified in Galatians, perhaps the most important epideictic feature is found early in the letter in the narrative section, to which we turn now.

2. *The Encomium*

According to Burgess, 'no single term represents the aim and scope of epideictic literature so completely as the word ἐγκώμιον'.[4] While the word encomium can be synonymous with epideictic literature as a

---

1. Robert Jewett, *The Thessalonian Correspondence* (Philadelphia: Fortress, 1986), pp. 71-78.

2. See his discussion of 1 Corinthians in 'Paul as Pastor', *L'Apôtre Paul* (ed. A. Vanhoye; BETL 73; Leuven: Leuven University Press, 1986), pp. 49-77; 'Paul's Rhetoric of Argumentation in Romans', *CBQ* 38 (1976), pp. 330-51; repr. *The Romans Debate* (ed. K. Donfried; Philadelphia: Fortress, 1977), pp. 152-75.

3. This is the somewhat astonishing conclusion that Lyons (*Pauline Autobiography*, pp. 173-74) reaches after admitting that the epideictic is a 'prominent feature' of Galatians but not its 'overarching genre'! George Kennedy (*New Testament Interpretation*, p. 145) has also placed 1 Corinthians squarely in the deliberative camp, as have Robert Hall ('Rhetorical Outline', pp. 277ff.) and Joop Smit ('The Letter of Paul to the Galatians: A Deliberative Speech', *NTS* 35 [1989], pp. 1-26).

4. In what follows I will be summarizing relevant points from Burgess, *Epideictic Literature*, pp. 113-31.

whole, it can also be a subordinate feature in other forms. In general, it is a statement praising the good qualities of a person or thing and can refer to a style or point of view, or a composition produced as a result of involvement in one of the elementary exercises.

The authors of handbooks on elementary exercises provide details on the rules of how one composes an encomium. Hermogenes, Aphthonius, and Menander, for example, outline more or less the same topics for an encomium of a person.[1] They were to be developed in the following order:

1. Prologue προοίμιον
2. Race and Origins γένος, γένεσις
3. Education ἀναστροφή
4. Achievements πράξεις
5. Comparison σύγκρισις
6. Epilogue ἐπίλογος

The essential features of these major topics were:

1. προοίμιον: a statement which indicates the importance of the person or thing being praised, often with reference to the fact that the speaker feels inadequate to the task.
2. γένος and γένεσις: a reference to the ancestry and origins of the one being praised, and a reference to the circumstances of the person's birth, especially to any noteworthy fact or event associated with it.
3. ἀνατροφή: a review of the circumstances of the person's youth, particularly those that give an early indication of character. An important sub-category of this division was ἐπιτηδεύματα: deeds that illustrate choice guided by character.
4. πράξεις: activities or achievements, which illustrate the person's virtues.
5. σύγκρισις: comparison with others to highlight character. This was also one of the elementary exercises.
6. ἐπίλογος: a recapitulation and appeal to others to imitate virtues of the one being praised. The contents of the epilogue are dependent on the subject and circumstances just as in the προοίμιον.

---

1. Translations for the elementary exercises of Hermogenes can be found in Baldwin, *Medieval Rhetoric*, pp. 23-38; and for Aphthonius in Ray Nadeau, 'The Progymnasmata of Aphthonius', *Speech Monographs* 19 (1952), pp. 265-85.

There were sub-categories associated with race, education and activities, but the presence of any topic was to be determined in part by the circumstances of the speech setting and the audience situation.[1]

With this review completed, we can bring together the evidence for epideictic features in Galatians 1–2.

Epideictic in Galatians 1 and 2

When describing the *exordium* in Galatians, Hans Dieter Betz notes that it has the character of epideictic because of Paul's expressions of disapproval of the Galatian's activities.[2] Letters with this feature can be classified as letters of reproach, one of the epideictic types. The *stasis* of quality clearly represents the epideictic. We may now turn to the narrative because it has been widely identified as an autobiographical statement of facts more likely to be found in forensic literature than in panegyrics or funeral orations.

The *stasis* statement (1.11-12) should be seen as the προοίμιον to the encomium.[3] γνωρίζω (v. 11) indicates the beginning of a

1. Baldwin (*Medieval Rhetoric*, p. 31 n. 60) compares in translation the encomiastic topics of Aphthonius and Menander.

2. *Galatians*, p. 45 n. 16. He cites Ar. *Rhet.* 3.14.2, 4. The θαυμάζω period is a feature of epideictic address; note, for example, Isocrates, who, in 'To Dionysius', 9, exhorts Dionysius not to be amazed that Isocrates is trying to defend Greece and give counsel in the same letter. More to the point, Nils Dahl ('Letter to the Galatians', in an appendix) lists thirteen papyrus letters and two letters from Cicero in which there are both expressions of astonishment and references to negligence on the part of the recipient as reasons for the letter writer's disapproval. John White (*Ancient Letters*, pp. 208-10, esp. n. 95) remarks that expressions of astonishment tend to occur in earlier sections of papyrus letters, typically in the letter opening, when the sender, usually a superior, expresses dismay at the failure of the recipient to accomplish some assigned task. Other references can be found on pp. 237-38 ('Index of Letter Writing').

3. In a section entitled 'The Form and Structure of Paul's Autobiographical Narrative', George Lyons (*Pauline Autobiography*), says that the autobiography proper starts with 1.13, and the reference to Paul's former life in Judaism (ἠκούσατε γὰρ τὴν ἐμὴν ἀναστροφήν). The use of ἀναστροφήν is associated with an emphasis on one's *ethos* and suggests that 'the following autobiographical remarks should be understood as in the philosophical lives to be more interested in ethics than history' (pp. 132-33). Before Lyons creates his outline for the narrative, he shows that autobiography can be apologetic or encomiastic. He rejects the notion that Paul faces 'opponents' in Galatia, arguing that a forensic understanding of the rhetorical situation is based on a 'mirror reading' of the text (see esp. ch. 2, 'Existing Approaches'). This means that the narrative is not apologetic *per se*, but functions

disclosure statement.[1] Such statements often opened the body of the letter[2] and their presence signals a division point. In 1.11-12, the subject is Paul's gospel, the unusual feature of which is the fact that it was given not naturally through human agency, but, if you will, supernaturally, through revelation. Its importance derives from the fact that it revealed Jesus Christ to Paul.

Despite the occurrence of ἀναστροφή in 1.13, the content of vv. 13-14 suggests the presence of a γένος/γένεσις topic. The reference to Paul's life in Judaism and zeal for the traditions that he inherited have more to do with origins than the circumstances of his youth. Paul's 'birth' comes at his conversion. His life in Judaism exists in a past as distant as though it had been another life. His use of ἀναστροφή obliges his reader to see that former life as γένος.

If we understand Paul's 'real' birth as his conversion and calling (1.15), it means that the essential feature of the ἀναστροφή topic is found in 1.15-17. As noted above, one of the sub-categories of that topic is ἐπιτηδεύματα. What deed was guided by his character? The 'youthful' Paul did not seek an authoritative source to interpret his revelation nor did he go to Jerusalem, but instead he went to Gentile territory! (Gal. 1.16-17).

The 'chief' topic in the encomium was πράξεις.[3] In describing the activities or achievements of the one being praised, it was important to illustrate the underlying principles and moral purposes producing these achievements. This attempt can be seen in 1.18-24. Three years after his conversion, Paul went to Jerusalem for fifteen days of conversations with Cephas and James, and then on to Syria and Cilicia. The testimony in Judea concerning his change of character caused the churches to glorify God despite the facts that they had never seen him and that he seemed to prefer Gentile contact over Judean. Clearly this contact did not weaken the impact of his _ethos_.

---

instead to portray Paul as 'an ideal representative of the gospel' or as 'a paradigm of the gospel of Christian freedom, which he seeks to persuade his readers to reaffirm in the face of the threat presented by the troublemakers' (pp. 170-71). I agree with Lyons's understanding of the function of the narrative, but not with his reconstruction of its divisions or his identification of the genre of Galatians.

1. T.Y. Mullins, 'Disclosure: A Literary Form in the New Testament', _NovT_ 7 (1964), pp. 45-50.

2. White, _Ancient Letters_, p. 207; 'The Structural Analysis of Philemon', unpublished paper distributed to the SBL Seminar on Paul, 1970, p. 22. See also his 'Introductory Formula in the Body of the Pauline Letter', _JBL_ 90 (1971), pp. 91-97.

3. Burgess, _Epideictic Literature_, p. 123.

The comparison of character (σύγκρισις) 'is regarded as the most important division but in application it is left to circumstances and the judgment of the writer'.[1] There were two distinct kinds, minor and general, the latter allowing for a fuller comparison to be made. Lyons says that the chief comparison is between Cephas and Paul in 2.11-21,[2] but he seems to overlook the nature of the meeting in Jerusalem and the comparison Paul makes in reporting that incident between himself, the 'false brethren', and the 'pillars'. The presence of two different temporal particles, ἔπειτα in 2.1, and ὅτε δέ in 2.11, do signal two different incidents unrelated to one another in time, but there is no inherent reason to see ὅτε δέ as the sign for a new division. Therefore, the σύγκρισις topic is found in 2.1-14.

The relationship between the two incidents lies in the fact that they both illustrate Paul's character in defense of his gospel, the value system derived from it, and his defense of the character of the gospel itself. In the first incident, Paul went up to Jerusalem in defense of his gospel (2.1),[3] and his character and that of his gospel are compared with that of the false brethren and pillar apostles. In the second, both are compared to Cephas.

Quite obviously that leaves 2.15-21 as the ἐπίλογος. Admittedly this is a somewhat lengthy epilogue, but its length can be accounted for by the fact that it is also a chreia elaboration. The elaboration and encomium are completed by the epilogue for the elaboration, 'I do not nullify the grace of God, for if righteousness were through the law, then Christ died to no purpose' (v. 21).

Chreia Elaboration[4]

With the introduction of the Antioch episode at 2.11, there is a shift in the trajectory of the argumentative situation. The comparison topic in 2.1-10 had demonstrated the superiority of the character of Paul's gospel over that of the false brethren who may have confronted Paul with a demand that Titus be circumcised. It also confirmed the

---

1. Burgess, *Epideictic Literature*, p. 125.
2. *Pauline Autobiography*, pp. 134-35.
3. See my article ('The Use and Influence of Rhetoric', p. 397) for my exegesis of κατὰ ἀποκάλυψιν.
4. I acknowledge the helpful criticisms made by members of the NT Graduate Seminar of the Claremont Graduate School who provided useful information in response to an earlier version of this paper.

reputation he enjoyed in Judea fourteen years earlier; Paul was preaching the gospel, a gospel that needed nothing added to it by those of repute (οἱ δοκοῦντες στῦλοι εἶναι). These 'pillar' apostles acknowledged the character of Paul's gospel, the gospel to the uncircumcised, by giving Paul the right hand of fellowship. The shift in the argumentative trajectory is signaled by the return to the ὅτε δέ formula first encountered in 1.15, at the beginning of the ἀναστροφή topic. Having demonstrated the superiority of the character of his gospel in Jerusalem, he turns to an incident in Gentile territory and, therefore, to an audience situation more nearly like that of the Galatians, who had also changed their behavior on account of the presence of some disruptive influence. It is a situation more analogous than that of Jerusalem and therefore allows Paul to focus on the essential value question.

The shift is also signaled by the presence of an expanded chreia,[1] followed in 2.15-21 by an elaboration of that chreia. The anecdote in 2.11-14 fits the general description of a sayings chreia.[2] The chreia has been expanded slightly by Paul. He tells the circumstances surrounding Peter's behavior and then reports his reaction. Verses 11-12a outline the exigence for the unit. In v. 12b, he repeats the ὅτε δέ formula and moves into the chreia proper. Without its context, it states:

> When I saw that they were not straightforward in accordance with the truth of the gospel, I said to Cephas in front of everyone, 'If you, though a Jew, live like a Gentile and not like a Jew, how can you compel the Gentiles to live like Jews?'

It is important to note here that the issue is not over the nature of faith but over the nature of life that is lived in faith. The function of the rhetorical question is to focus on the values commonly held by Paul and the Galatians and particularly on the value of life lived under the values established by the gospel of the uncircumcised. It seems

1. Burton Mack ('Decoding the Scripture: Philo and the Rules of Rhetoric', *Nourished in Peace* [ed. F.E. Greenspahn *et al.*; Chico, CA: Scholars, 1984], p. 87) notes that Theon taught that a brief chreia can be expanded. See Ronald Hock and Edward O'Neil, *The Chreia in Ancient Rhetoric*, vol. I, *The Progymnasmata* (Atlanta: Scholars, 1986), p. 101. This volume provides translations of examples of chreia and elaboration patterns as described in Theon, Quintilian, Hermogenes, Aphthonius, and others.

2. Hock and O'Neil, *The Progymnasmata*, pp. 28-29. Hock (pp. 27-28) tells us that Theon identified two sub-classes of sayings chreiai. One of those, the ἀποφαντικόν, includes a sub-class introduced by participles of seeing.

likely that Paul and the Galatians agreed on the basis of the Christian life, justification, but disagreed sharply on the conduct of Christian life, which Paul insists is characterized by freedom; not license, but freedom (5.1ff.). The appearance of the concept of justification in 2.15-21 is a function of the chreia elaboration and its use in that elaboration derived from the argumentative situation.

Through to 2.10 the argumentative situation has been dominated by the willingness of the Galatians to consider the ethos of Paul's gospel weaker than that of the 'other' gospel. The encomiastic topics have addressed that situation. The reference to the collection is the culmination of those proofs of character. The chreia itself sets the comparison with a person of acknowledged reputation, somehow known to the Galatians even by his Jewish name.[1] The failure of 'Cephas' to behave sincerely is challenged by Paul, and implicitly that is also a challenge to the Galatians. Now the argumentative situation lies with Paul. He can show that their ethos is weak (e.g. 4.19). It is the function of the chreia elaboration to establish the theological foundation of that demonstration.

The elaboration (ἐργασία, *tractatio*) pattern laid out by the author of the *Rhetorica ad Herennium* is among the oldest ones extant. It is for a maxim and is as follows: theme, paraphrase, argument from the contrary, argument by comparison, argument by example, and conclusion.[2] This pattern may have been adapted by others and used for the chreia by later authors. The elaboration pattern developed by Hermogenes is: praise for the subject of the chreia, paraphrase,

---

1. It is interesting to see Paul use the interchange of 'Cephas' and 'Peter' to send a subtle signal of association and dissociation with James and his *ethos*. In 1.18-19 Paul sees only James and Cephas. In 2.9, James, Cephas and John are the reputed pillars. In 2.11-12, Cephas reacts to men from James, and Paul addresses Cephas as he might during his first visit to Jerusalem. Contrast that with 'Peter' who is paralleled with Paul in 2.7-8. It is a subtle rhetorical device to suggest the honorable and the dishonorable.

2. *Her.* 4.44.57. For full discussions of chreia and chreia elaboration in the progymnasmata of Theon, Hermogenes and Aphthonius, see Burton Mack, 'Anecdotes and Arguments: The Chreia in Antiquity and Christianity' (Institute for Antiquity and Christianity Occasional Papers, 10, 1987); also, Burton Mack and Vernon Robbins, 'Elaboration of the Chreia in the Hellenistic School', *Patterns of Persuasion in the Gospels* (Sonoma, CA: Polebridge, 1989), pp. 31-68. I am using the categories, with some editing, shown in the notes of the Loeb Classical Library edition (trans. Henry Caplan; Cambridge, MA: Harvard University Press, 1954), pp. 370-74. The notes show rationale statements for both the chreia and the paraphrase. Caplan has not been followed in his identification of this pattern as pertaining to that of a chreia.

rationale, statement from the opposite, statement from analogy, statement from example, statement from authority (which can include a quotation), and conclusion or exhortation.

Gal. 2.15-21 seems to fit the elaboration pattern of the *Rhetorica ad Herennium*.[1] There is no statement of praise for the subject of the chreia. That is understandable in light of the fact that the one who is doing the elaboration is the subject of the chreia and that it stands as part of an encomiastic narrative. The function of the praise topic was to establish the *ethos* of the subject, and that had already been done. Furthermore, while self-praise was allowed in speeches, it was expected that it would be modest in its scope and appropriate to the situation.[2]

The first unit of the elaboration we encounter, 2.15-16a, is the paraphrase:[3] 'We who are Jews by birth and not sinners from [the] Gentiles know that a human being is not justified by works of the law but only through faith in Christ Jesus'.[4] While this contrast set out by Paul between Jews and Gentiles has social and historical roots, it is also sarcastic and serves to embarrass those who would claim some spiritual priority based on birthrights. Note that Paul has already shifted the grounds of the issue; he has forced the Galatians to deal with the heart of the matter, justification by faith. Any attempt to insist on works of the law within the life of faith—the apparent issue at Antioch—is not representing the true life of faith that is based on justification by faith—the real issue at Antioch.

The rationale or explanation follows in 2.16b-d: 'So we also have come to believe in Christ Jesus, in order that we might be justified by faith in Christ and not by works of the law, since it is not by works of the law that all flesh will be justified'. The verb πιστεύω is in the aorist here, and I want to stress the *Aktionsart* of the tense in this

1. Edward O'Neil, director of the Chreia Project at the Institute for Antiquity and Christianity, said in a speech at the Institute that he had yet to discover a formal chreia elaboration pattern outside of the handbooks. In his judgments, elaboration was an exercise in building skills which was not intended to have practical application. It seems to me that his observation fits in the general classification with those who point out the amount of latitude a speaker had in using rhetorical elements in his speech.

2. Lyons, *Pauline Autobiography*, pp. 53-59.

3. In most places in what follows I am using the translation provided by Betz in his commentary. I find it often illustrates the elaboration pattern most clearly.

4. Mack ('Decoding the Scripture', p. 95) says that the chreia should be 'restated in the form of an assertion that can be argued'. That is clearly what Paul has done here.

context. The act of believing was accomplished in the past and is the foundation upon which a life of faith built on justification by faith cannot now be had through works of the law.

If the full syntax of vv. 15-16 is observed, it might be possible to translate the passage as follows:

> We ourselves are Jews by nature and not sinners from the Gentiles; but, knowing that a man is not justified out of works of the law but instead through faith in Jesus Christ, we ourselves also believed in Christ Jesus in order that we might be justified by faith in Christ and not by works of the law.

This translation illustrates the integral relationship between the paraphrase and the rationale. By maintaining the force of the participle εἰδότες in v. 16a as a dependent clause, it is possible to find a chiastic pattern in v. 16:

A   not justified by works of the law
B   through faith in Christ
C   we have believed
B′   justified by faith
A′   no one justified by works of the law

Seen this way, relationship between the paraphrase and the rationale is further demonstrated formally.

The contrast or argument from the contrary in 2.17 expands the idea further: 'If, however, we who are seeking to be justified in Christ are also found to be sinners, is Christ then a servant (minister) of sin? This can never be!'[1] This series of propositions[2] poses the issue of life in Christ in a new way. Those who do seek the nature of life in Christ through the law might as well be judged sinners under the terms of the law, thus ironically becoming what they claimed the Gentiles to be. To put it differently, the fault for sin lies in the sinner, not with Christ! Anyone seeking to be justified, presumably by works of the law, cannot, by definition, be in Christ. Seeking to be justified is evidence

1. I pass over any detailed discussion of the exegetical difficulties posed by this verse. A criticism of Betz's interpretation/translation of it can be found in Lyons, *Pauline Autobiography*, pp. 93-94. Among other things, Lyons is concerned about Betz's translation of εὑρέθημεν. He points out that it is aorist and therefore points to the past. He fails to note that it is passive and therefore denotes punctiliar action more than time of action.

2. Betz, *Galatians*, pp. 119-20. His argument here is conditioned by his assumption that Paul is countering his opponents. Obviously I prefer to see these series of statements as making the argument from the contrary.

of the absence of the state or condition or life of righteousness. Christ is not part of unrighteousness and therefore cannot possibly (μὴ γένοιτο) be a minister of sin.

Comparatively, in 2.18, only those who return to what they had given up can be called transgressors: 'For if I establish again what I have dissolved, I set myself up as a transgressor'.[1] The use of the first person singular here does not necessarily refer to Paul, but more probably to the one who is a Jew 'by nature' and who has been the subject of the argument since 2.15. The use of γάρ here suggests the presence of an enthymeme. Christ cannot be a minister of sin if 'I', seeking to be justified, revert to the old value systems, i.e. the works of the law. Within the context of faith, the only way one can live legitimately is through faith in Jesus Christ.

The subject changes in 2.19, with the introduction of ἐγώ. In 2.19 and 20, Paul uses himself as an example of one who leads the true life of faith because he has died to the law.[2] Paul is not guilty of sinful behavior, for he has kept the faith! Christian life is enabled in dying and rising with Christ and is a life founded in faith. Typically the appeal to an example was to an authoritative figure, or to one to whom honor was due. Here Paul uses himself as one well known to the Galatians and authoritative by way of the life he leads and the gospel he has preached among them. (Note the return to that example in the *pathos* section of Gal. 4.12-20.) No secular authority could provide the same worthy example, and only Paul can provide the example that takes advantage of the ethos established by the comparison of character described in 2.1-14. Furthermore, by using the metaphor of 'Christ lives in me', he is also appealing to the authority of Christ.

Verse 21 serves as the conclusion or epilogue for both the chreia elaboration and the encomium, or, said differently, the epilogue for the chreia elaboration serves also as the concluding summary of the

1. The comparison or analogy usually contains reference to everyday life; the closest allusion we have to that here is Paul's use of οἰκοδομῶ, 'build up (again)'.

2. Betz (*Galatians*, p. 121) says that Paul uses himself as the 'prototypical example of what happens to all Pauline Christians', but then relates the use of ἐγώ to v. 18. I disagree. I think Paul means to shift from the 'I' who was a Jew by nature to the 'I' who died and was raised in Christ, continuing the association and dissociation pattern of Paul's gospel/another gospel, Jerusalem/Gentile territory, James and Cephas/Peter and Paul, false brethren/right hand of fellowship, Jews by nature/born in Christ, and works of the law/justification by faith. Unfortunately a full discussion of that pattern and its significance for the argumentation in Galatians must wait for another forum.

thesis of the epilogue for the encomium. The thesis is restated on two levels. On the one hand, Paul returns to the episode at Antioch and reminds the Galatians what truly happened there: 'I do not nullify the grace of God'; by implication the behavior of Cephas and by analogy that of the Galatians does nullify God's grace. On the other hand, he restates the theological issue underlying the question of how one is able to live justly within the context of the grace of God. One comes to life in Christ, one is justified through faith; if not, the grace of God has been nullified and Christ's death is purposeless.

The Function of the Chreia

It is important to recognize that the narrative section is fashioned as an encomium because of the ability of the encomium to express character, and for its usefulness in fulfilling the argumentative purpose of character contrast.[1] Moreover, the chreia allows Paul to shift the trajectory of blame exactly at 2.14. Normally one would expect encomiastic narrative to be carried out in the third person. Obviously that cannot be the case in this narrative. Paul as narrator is also participant in the events and situations he describes. From the point of view of the Galatians, they are observers watching the imitation of the events being carried through. However, for effective mimesis to occur (that is, for the Galatians to become again what Paul is, to imitate him once more) Paul has to change the situation of his audience from observer to participant. That is the function of the chreia in 2.14.

As long as Paul is narrating the demonstration of the power of the gospel to change character, the audience can avoid the argumentative situation; they can see and hear, but not understand. When the chreia is read,[2] however, nothing is being demonstrated. As discourse, it can be

---

1. See Christopher Forbes's discussion ('Comparison, Self-Praise and Irony: Paul's Boasting and the Conventions of Hellenistic Rhetoric', *NTS* 32 [1986], pp. 1-30) of the use of 'comparison' as a means of amplification in an encomium.

2. Scholars tend to ignore or discount the fact that much of what was written in the ancient world was to be read aloud. Publication could consist of reading something out loud in the marketplace after posting a notice that such was your intention. Cicero, among others, understood the letter to function in most situations as one side of a conversation. It was common for letters to be read aloud, even by lone recipients who read in a low voice to themselves. Augustine tells us that he was taken aback by the sight of Ambrose reading without speaking the words (*Confessions* 6.3). Because letter composition was a part of rhetorical education and was viewed as a kind of sub-category of oratory, it is important to remember that the text of the letter

heard as though addressed to them. That is its power. Although the narrative suggests that Peter or those associated with withdrawal from table-fellowship at Antioch are the intended hearers of the chreia, the chreia is not narrative; it is discourse. It asks the question of the Galatians, 'How can you compel Gentiles to live like Jews?'

Once spoken, the chreia sets the stage for further discourse, the elaboration, in which Paul can use the inclusive 'we' to imply the condition and behavior of Peter, Barnabas, the Antiocheans, himself and the Galatians; and the inclusive 'I', as the one whose character should be imitated. The Galatian reader/ hearers are drawn into a new argumentative situation in which they are charged, in the implied contrast with Paul, with misrepresenting the gospel, building up the things that have been torn down, forgetting the fact that they have been crucified with Christ. Given this new situation, Paul can confront them directly with the rhetorical questions of 3.1-4, and enter into the task in 3.5–6.9 of amplifying why they are to blame and what they must do to correct that situation. Finally, in 6.17, he can lay claim to the highest status of all, provide an almost perfect model to be imitated, the position of one who bears τὰ στίγματα τοῦ Ἰησοῦ.

The Results of the Analysis

An outline based on this analysis looks like this:

Encomium   1.11–2.21

προοίμιον	1.11-12
γένος	1.13-14
ἀναστροφή	1.15-17
πράξεις	1.18-24
σύγκρισις	2.1-14
	Chreia 2.14

Ἐπίλογος for the Encomium and the Chreia Elaboration Pattern

Paraphrase	2.15-16a
Rationale	2.16b-d
Contrast	2.17
Comparison	2.18
Example	2.19-20
Epilogue	2.21

served to provide a basis for speech. For an excellent explanation of this phenomenon and what it means for NT study, see Paul J. Achtemeier, '*Omne verbum sonat:* The New Testament and the Oral Environment of Late Western Antiquity', *JBL* 109 (1990), pp. 3-27.

Conclusion

In order to create a shift in the argumentative situation so that blame can be placed on the Galatians for their failure to maintain the values they had learned as a result of Paul's preaching of the gospel, Paul had to express his disapproval in the *exordium* (1.6-10) of their reported negligence in keeping the faith. He also had to remind them (γνωρίζω γὰρ ὑμῖν) in his *stasis* statement (1.11-12) of the origins of the values of the gospel revelation, a revelation so powerful that it changed his character (1.13-14), just as it did theirs when they heard it from him (3.2-4; 4.8-20). Because Paul's gospel was the origin of the value system they shared, he writes an encomiastic self-referent narrative (1.13–2.14) intended to illustrate the life of one who lives by those values. It also functions as the source for understanding what it means for the Galatians when Paul exhorts them to 'become as I am' (4.12, γίνεσθε ὡς ἐγώ). They are to be proclaimers of justification by faith for Jews and Gentiles alike in the face of any opposition, even that of other Christians. The device he uses to bring the Galatians into a new argumentative situation, where they are not outsiders to the debate concerning the nature of the practice of faith but directly involved in it, is the chreia, for, when it is read, narrative shifts to discourse and all that follows is intended for them.

By the end of the encomium, the groundwork has been laid for placing the blame for the situation in the churches directly on the Galatians. It seems likely that Paul had been characterized by some as a sophist; the narrative has shown that he was not. The rhetorical questions that open ch. 3 not only recall values/truths once held in common by both Paul and the Galatians, but also demonstrate that *they* have been guilty of sophistry; they have adjusted their beliefs and practices under the influence of traditions and teachings that were not based on the gospel revealed to and by Paul.

In consequence of these observations, it would appear that chs. 1–2 of Galatians are a fairly carefully crafted epideictic discourse, laying the foundation for a more direct discussion of the values commonly held by Paul and the Galatians, but being neglected by the Galatians as a result of some in their midst arguing for other value systems that Paul chose to call 'another gospel'.

HISTORICAL INFERENCE AND RHETORICAL EFFECT:
ANOTHER LOOK AT GALATIANS 1 AND 2

Robert G. Hall

The recent re-issue of the masterful book by John Knox, *Chapters in a Life of Paul*, highlights the importance of his work for Pauline studies. Knox re-aligned the burden of proof for studying Paul's life:

> We can justly say that a fact only suggested in the letters has a status which even the most unequivocal statement of Acts, if not otherwise supported, cannot confer. We may, with proper caution, use Acts to supplement the autobiographical data of the letters, but never to correct them.[1]

Gerd Lüdemann and Robert Jewett have followed Knox in basing their influential studies of Pauline chronology on the letters of Paul, according a prime position to Galatians 1 and 2.[2] Since ancient historians enjoyed greater freedom than their modern counterparts in rearranging events and speeches, students of Paul's life have reasonably decided to treat Acts, their other major source, with reserve.[3]

Results of several recent studies pose implicit questions for Knox and other interpreters who base historical reconstruction primarily on the Pauline letters. Jack T. Sanders compares Gal. 1.11-12 with 1 Cor. 15.1-3 and concludes that since 'Paul forces certain events in his own past to support a particular theological point, . . . one cannot simply pose the alternative, either Acts or Galatians, and then prefer Paul as having firsthand historical knowledge of his own life'.[4] Edvin Larsson

---

1. John Knox, *Chapters in a Life of Paul* (Macon, GA: Mercer University Press, 1987), p. 19.

2. See Robert Jewett, *A Chronology of Paul's Life* (Philadelphia: Fortress, 1979) and Gerd Lüdemann, *Paul, Apostle to the Gentiles: Studies in Chronology* (Philadelphia: Fortress, 1984).

3. Knox frequently argues that assertions in Acts are most suspect when they illustrate themes Luke emphasizes. See Knox, *Life*, pp. 12-16, 26, 35, 48-51.

4. Jack T. Sanders, 'Paul's "Autobiographical" Statements in Galatians 1–2', *JBL* 85 (1966), pp. 338-39.

argues that Paul gives historical data only to make a point with his readers.[1] George Lyons notes that ancient autobiographers (influenced by ancient rhetoricians) sought not to recount events accurately but to persuade, and concludes that historians should determine the function of Paul's autobiographical statements before assigning historical value to them.[2] Such conclusions suggest that it is time to re-evaluate the burden of proof for studies of Paul's life. Can we still follow Knox in systematically preferring Paul's reminiscences to the stories in Acts? Can Galatians 1 and 2 ground Pauline chronology by establishing how frequently Paul visited Jerusalem?[3] I will seek to answer these questions by redirecting Lyons's rhetorical line of inquiry: if Paul writes Galatians under the influence of ancient rhetorical practice,[4] then instructions ancient rhetoricians offer for composing narrations may help modern students assess the value of historical data from Galatians 1 and 2. I will argue that ancient rhetorical practice gave Paul license to use historical events as freely as he wished, showing that Paul employed this historical license to make his point, and that, therefore, historians of Paul's life are on scarcely firmer footing in Galatians than they are in Acts. Finally I will employ rhetorical principles to show how much historians can infer from Galatians 1 and 2 about the frequency of Paul's visits to Jerusalem.

1. Edvin Larsson, 'Die paulinischen Schriften als Quellen zur Geschichte des Urchristentums', *ST* 37 (1983), pp. 33-53.
2. George Lyons, *Pauline Autobiography: Toward a New Understanding* (SBLDS 73; Atlanta: Scholars, 1985), pp. 29-33, 60-73.
3. Knox, *Life*, pp. 31-42.
4. Many interpreters find rhetorical influence on Galatians and consider 1.13–2.21 (approximately) a narration in the technical, rhetorical sense. See H.D. Betz, *Galatians: A Commentary on Paul's Letter to the Churches in Galatia* (Hermeneia; Philadelphia: Fortress, 1979); 'The Literary Composition and Function of Paul's Letter to the Galatians', *NTS* 21 (1975), pp. 353-79; James D. Hester, 'The Rhetorical Structure of Galatians 1.11-14', *JBL* 103 (1984), pp. 223-33; *idem*, 'The Use and Influence of Rhetoric in Galatians 2.1-14', *TZ* 42 (1986), pp. 386-408; George A. Kennedy, *New Testament Interpretation through Rhetorical Criticism* (Chapel Hill, NC: University of North Carolina Press, 1984), pp. 144-52; Robert G. Hall, 'The Rhetorical Outline for Galatians: A Reconsideration', *JBL* 106 (1987), pp. 277-87; François Vouga, 'Zur rhetorischen Gattung des Galaterbriefes', *ZNW* 79 (1988), pp. 291-92; Eric Dubuis, 'Paul et la narration soi en Galates 1 et 2', *La narration. Quand le récit devient communication* (ed. P. Bühler and J.-F. Habermacher; Lieux Théologiques 12; Geneva: Fonds des Publications de l'Université de Neuchâtel, 1988), pp. 163-73; Joop Smit, 'The Letter of Paul to the Galatians: A Deliberative Speech', *NTS* 35 (1989), pp. 1-26.

Hellenistic Rhetoric and Historical Accuracy

Ancient rhetoricians studied the art of persuasion. Since orators have always found storytelling one of the most gripping and effective means of persuasion, rhetoricians eagerly investigated the best ways of recounting past events and recommended that most speeches contain a narration or recital of events. A study of the rhetoricians shows how far they were ready to go in preferring rhetorical effect to historical accuracy.

Quintilian defines 'narration' as 'the persuasive exposition of that which either has been done, or is supposed to have been done' (Quint. 4.2.31).[1] The goal of a narration is not to instruct but to persuade (Quint. 4.2.21). The author of the *Rhetorica ad Herennium* offers a similar definition, 'The Narration or Statement of Facts sets forth events that have occurred or might have occurred' (*Her.* 1.3.4; cf. Cic. *Inv.* 1.19.27),[2] and classifies three types of narrations according to their purposes: those that turn facts to one's advantage; those that win belief, incriminate one's adversary or set the stage for something; and those *progymnasmata* composed for practice (*Her.* 1.8.12; cf. Cic. *Inv.* 1.19.27). For both authors, narrations are written not to instruct readers or hearers in what happened but to convince them; persuasion is the goal.[3] From their perspective a speaker or author is entirely justified in making up events as well as recasting them.

Quintilian, who considers narrative his specialty,[4] ties narrations closely to proof: narration is proof in continuous form (Quint. 4.2.79). Since the narration prepares for the proofs presented later in the work, speakers must compose narrations after they compose their proofs (Quint. 3.9.7) and carefully contour the recital of events to hint at the proofs to follow (Quint. 4.2.54-55); the best hints cannot be recognized as such without careful study of a written speech (Quint. 4.2.57). So intimately tied to proof are good narrations that an artfully

---

1. Unless otherwise noted, quotations of Quintilian are from the English translations of *Institutio Oratoria* by H.E. Butler (LCL; 4 vols.; Cambridge, MA: Harvard University Press, 1920–22).

2. English quotations from *Rhetorica ad Herennium* stem from the translation of H. Caplin (LCL; Cambridge, MA: Harvard University Press, 1954).

3. Compare Cicero's definition of rhetoric. 'The function of eloquence seems to be to persuade an audience, the end is to persuade by speech' (*Inv.* 1.5.6). Quotations from *De Inventione* follow the translation of H.M. Hubbell (LCL; Cambridge, MA: Harvard University Press, 1949).

4. See Quint. 4.2.86.

composed digression can conclude the narration and begin the proof (Quint. 4.3.5).[1] Again authors of narrations write not to pass on what happened; they should unapologetically form historical examples to make a point. Quintilian here suggests that speakers carefully color their accounts to ensure that the hearer (or reader) anticipates the argument to come. Readers will be more easily persuaded by a proof they think they have thought up themselves.

Narrations should be concise so that the hearers can remember the points made. Speakers should cut out everything which weakens the argument to follow as well as what neither weakens nor strengthens it (*Her.* 1.9.14). A speaker should cut out everything which when removed neither hampers the activity of the judge nor harms his or her own case (Quint. 4.2.40). 'We should discard from our facts and our words those that are not necessary to be said, leaving only those the omission of which would make our meaning obscure' (*Rhet. ad Alex.* 30.1438a.38-40).[2] The orator should omit improbable events even when they are true (*Rhet. ad Alex.* 30.1438b.1-5). Authors should say nothing but what is likely to win belief (Quint. 4.2.35). 'One must refrain no less from an excess of superfluous facts than from an excess of words' (Cic. *Inv.* 1.20.28). Since speakers should select events to rehearse without regard to what is historically significant but only considering what will best induce the audience to embrace the desired conclusion, historians should never expect a complete account in a narration.

Speakers should craft their narrations to be plausible: those facts crucial to the argument should appear natural and obvious. The narrator will achieve this by telling the story to supply motives for the crucial actions and developing the characters of the actors so that we expect them to act as they do (Quint. 4.2.52; *Her.* 1.9.16; cf. *Rhet. ad Alex.* 30.1438b.1-5). Rhetoricians must exert themselves to make narratives plausible as strenuously when they are true as when they are fictitious (Quint. 4.2.34; *Her.* 1.9.16). The orator must labor to make the interpretation in the narration obvious and self-evident whether narrating truths or fabrications (Quint. 4.2.63-64). For the rhetorician plausibility is more important than factuality.

1. Although probably not a digression, Paul's speech to Peter (Gal. 2.17-21) intimately ties narration to proof. This speech simultaneously concludes the narration and introduces the proof.

2. Quotations of *Rhetorica ad Alexandrum* are taken from the translation of H. Rackham (LCL; Cambridge, MA: Harvard University Press, 1965).

Although clarity demands presentation in the order of actual or probable sequence (*Her.* 1.9.15; *Rhet. ad Alex.* 31.1438b.19-23; Cic. *Inv.* 1.20.29), speakers should order the recital of events to their own advantage (Quint. 4.2.83-84).[1] Narratives can be continuous or divided into sections, following the actual or an artificial order of events (Quint. 2.13.5). In a rhetorical composition little can be deduced from the order in which events are told.[2]

Narrations persuade by charm as well as by content. 'The statement of facts should be characterized by passages which will charm and excite admiration of expectation, and marked by unexpected turns, conversations between persons and appeals to every kind of emotion' (Quint. 4.2.107; cf. Cic. *Inv.* 1.19.27). Quintilian refers to the storyteller's art; once again facts are subsidiary to persuasion: the orator is sovereign over the facts to make them yield the desired effect. Needless to say, suspense, *pathos*, and conversations are not inherent in the historical data but are crafted by the author of a narration. Authors can handle the 'facts' sovereignly to elicit these effects.

The previous recommendations suffice when the facts support the speaker's case; advice to narrators who face recalcitrant historical facts illustrates how thoroughly the goal of persuasion dominates rhetorical theory. The orator must treat facts which tell against the case in the most advantageous way: facts should be denied, added, altered or omitted according to what is most persuasive (Quint. 4.2.67).[3] Those too widely known must be admitted, but the orator should labor to extenuate them, countering the odium by ascribing acceptable motives for them, calling vices by the name of virtues,[4] and inciting pity. When properly handled, even a frank confession can move the audience to tears (Quint. 4.2.76-77). In a good cause, one should narrate fabrications:

---

1. Quintilian expressly differs from other rhetoricians at this point. No rule should stand except the requirement that everything should contribute to the best possible rhetorical effect.

2. Lüdemann (*Apostle to the Gentiles*, pp. 57-59, 75-77) applies this to Gal. 2.11-21 when trying to establish that Paul's rebuke of Peter in Antioch precedes the Jerusalem Council.

3. See also Cicero, 'The speaker must bend everything to the advantage of his case, by passing over all things that make against it which can be passed over, by touching lightly on what must be mentioned and by telling his own story carefully and clearly' (*Inv.* 1.21.30).

4. Luxury becomes generosity; avarice, economy; carelessness, simplicity (Quint. 4.2.77).

> We must take care, first that our fiction is within the bounds of possibility, secondly that it is consistent with the persons, dates and places involved and thirdly that it presents a character and sequence that are not beyond belief: if possible it should be connected with something that is admittedly true and should be supported by some argument that forms part of the actual case. . . Above all we must see that we do not contradict ourselves, a slip which is far from rare on the part of spinners of fiction. . . (Quint. 4.2.89-90).

Speakers must carefully invent what evidence cannot contradict: they can impute words and actions to those who are dead, to those in sympathy with themselves, and to their enemies, since no one will believe when their enemy denies his supposed actions (Quint. 4.2.93). Since ordinarily some facts can tell in the speaker's favor, orators should labor to strengthen these by arrangement and argument, but should weaken contrary facts by showing why the audience should not believe them (Quint. 4.2.101-102). When discussing measures to make narrations plausible, the author of the *Rhetorica ad Herennium* offers the following advice to those who compose false narrations: 'If the matter is fictitious, these measures will have to be observed all the more scrupulously. Fabrication must be circumspect in those matters in which official documents or some person's unimpeachable guaranty will prove to have played a role' (1.9.16; see Quint. 4.2.34). Although teachers of rhetoric regularly assume that orators will fabricate facts for their narrations, Quintilian discusses the practice more freely than the others. Rhetoricians were sensitive to the charge that they could 'make the worse appear the better cause'; Quintilian can talk freely because he has carefully prepared the reader for this discussion. Earlier he argued at length that one who aspired to be a good orator had first to become a good human being.[1] In the context of Quintilian's *magnum opus*, advice to recount false and falsely coloured events shares in Quintilian's high moral tone. A disciple of Quintilian would assume that a narration of fabrications would on occasion not only be expedient but also be the right thing to do.

In the ancient world, then, writers of narrations ruled sovereignly over the historical data at their disposal. They omitted, altered, rearranged, or fabricated events for maximum effect. Even when truthful,

---

1. See especially Quint. 2.15-16. Quintilian defines rhetoric as follows: 'the definition which best suits its real character is that which makes rhetoric the science of speaking well. For this definition includes all the virtues of oratory and the character of the orator as well, since no man can speak well who is not good himself' (2.15.34).

they contoured their accounts so that events suggested proofs to be advanced later, cut out any events not essential to their argument, and attributed motives to their characters to make plausible their interpretation of events. They told events in chronological order or did not do so as suited their purpose. They invented conversations, inserted unexpected twists of plot and developed suspense to enhance the interest of the audience. Implications for the modern historian are clear: narrations do employ historical data when the truth is the most effective means of persuasion, but they cheerfully bend or even invent history to make whatever points they wish. Historians must use these narrations with caution. Modern students of Pauline chronology should assume *a priori* that the historical account in the narration in Galatians is just as suspect, perhaps more suspect, than the account in Acts.

Galatians and Historical Inference

Study of the rhetoricians undercuts the presumption that Paul is the best source for details of his life by drawing a sharp distinction between what Paul knows and what he tells. Of course Paul knows more of what he did than any other source, but how much of what he knows does he tell? To what extent does he follow rhetorical principles to color or reinterpret events he recounts? These questions can at best be answered only on a case by case basis. We will consider two sample cases. The first shows how far Paul was willing to go in reinterpreting the past; the second shows how one can apply rhetorical criticism to a historical question: does Paul recount all of his journeys to Jerusalem in Galatians 1 and 2?

1. *Pauline Reinterpretation*

Jack T. Sanders points to a well-known contradiction between Galatians and 1 Corinthians:[1]

> For I would have you know, brethren, that the gospel which was preached by me is not man's gospel. For I did not receive it from man, nor was I taught it, but it came through a revelation of Jesus Christ (Gal. 1.11-12; RSV).

> For I would have you know, brethren, that the gospel which I preached to you, which you received. . . I delivered to you. . . what I also received, that Christ died. . . (1 Cor. 15.1, 3; my translation).

---

1. See Sanders, '"Autobiographical" Statements', pp. 335-43.

Sanders concludes that Paul allows the exigencies of argument and situation to draw him into a discrepancy.[1] Galatians 1.13–2.10 is 'historically relative and therefore unreliable as a source for reconstructing either the sequence of events in Paul's life or the objective historical details related to the "apostolic council"'.[2] Although Sanders may reach a more negative inference than his evidence will support, Paul's cavalier handling of the 'facts' should sober any historian. Ancient rhetoricians, however, would applaud Paul for thoroughly reinterpreting the past to further the argument in each letter. The juxtaposition of these two passages well illustrates the extent to which Paul appropriates the ancient rhetorical attitude toward historical events. Paul is a child of his age; the tension discovered between the passage from Galatians and that from 1 Corinthians would neither embarrass Paul nor offend his first readers. Historians must expect Paul to employ far-reaching rhetorical coloration elsewhere in the narrative as well.

2. Rhetorical Criticism and Historical Inference: The Jerusalem Journeys

Crucial to Knox's chronology is his contention that Paul made only three journeys to Jerusalem after his conversion or call. He argues from the narration in Galatians that Paul visited Jerusalem only once before the Jerusalem Council:

> We may hope for general agreement that when Paul "went up again to Jerusalem" after "fourteen years" (Gal. 2.1), he was making only his second visit. His whole purpose in this passage in Galatians requires that he be accurate on this point. That he is being careful in his statement appears not only in its definiteness but also in the oath he takes to its truth (1.20). Occasionally it is suggested that he may have been mistaken; perhaps he was forgetting a trip or two. But this suggestion is rarely made, and never with much conviction. Paul would hardly have made an error so egregious or one that would have laid him so open to opponents who apparently were representing his relations with Jerusalem in somewhat the same way as Luke–Acts later represents them. No, it can be known, as surely as such facts can ever be known, that when he went up to Jerusalem 'fourteen years later', he had been only once before since his conversion.[3]

Assuming that Gal. 1.10–2.21 is a narration, can we support Knox's conclusion? Immediately we run into difficulty, for, in the interest of

1. Sanders, '"Autobiographical" Statements', p. 339.
2. Sanders, '"Autobiographical" Statements', p. 340.
3. Knox, *Life*, p. 36.

brevity, authors of narrations were to leave out anything that did not directly advance their case. Had Paul gone up to Jerusalem frequently, but found only two of the visits necessary to make his point, he would mention only two. From boyhood he would have been trained to submerge concerns for completeness or accuracy in the interest of persuasion.[1] Initially then, we could expect Paul to enumerate his journeys only if his argument required him to do so.

Does Paul's subject require him to mention every journey he took to Jerusalem? Knox tries to show that Paul must recount all of his journeys to Jerusalem since he must counter his opponents' claim that he is dependent on the authorities there: the narration is Paul's defense against their accusations. To show his independence, Paul asserts that he has visited Jerusalem only twice in seventeen years.[2]

But if Paul seeks to prove his independence in the narration, he certainly goes about it oddly. To demonstrate his autonomy, one would expect Paul plainly to deny his dependence on Jerusalem authorities and to recount events which prove his independence. But, although Paul affirms that he did not receive his gospel from the authorities in Jerusalem, he never declares his independence from them. In fact, he implies his dependence: on the second journey he goes up to lay his gospel before those in Jerusalem lest he had run in vain (Gal. 2.2). If Paul wants to prove his independence from Jerusalem, he should never have alleged that motive for the visit. Rhetoricians specifically urge the inventing of motives to further one's point, but on Knox's supposition the motive Paul supplies tells against the case Paul tries to argue! If Knox correctly interprets the narration, Paul should allege a different motive: that he went up to correct those in Jerusalem who wanted Gentile Christians to be circumcised or the like. Oddly enough, the motive asserted in Acts can accommodate Knox's interpretation better than the motive Paul gives in Galatians.[3]

---

1. Quintilian assumed that teachers of literature began teaching pupils to give narrations and urged that a teacher of rhetoric be employed even at this early age (Quint. 2.1.8-13). Hence young pupils would have practiced reciting events as persuasively as possible.

2. Knox's position is a time-honored one, supported by distinguished interpreters including the two most widely read commentators in English. See Ernest De Witt Burton, *A Critical and Exegetical Commentary on the Epistle to the Galatians* (ICC; Edinburgh: T. & T. Clark, 1920), pp. liv-lvi; Betz, *Galatians*, pp. 72-73, 88.

3. In Acts, 'men from Judea' irritated Paul by troubling Gentiles about circumcision. Paul and Barnabas 'were appointed to go up to Jerusalem to the apostles and the elders about this question' (RSV).

The narrative in Galatians does not attempt to prove that Paul is independent of Jerusalem.[1]

The same conclusion follows from a rhetorical analysis of the place of the narration in the argument of Galatians. Narrations were to prepare for the proofs to follow. If Paul needed to show his independence from the Jerusalem apostles, one would expect an argument for his independence in the proof (3.1–6.10), but none appears. Instead in the proof Paul argues that God's recent act in Christ places Jews and Gentiles in a new sphere of God's activity; they should stand fast in the new sphere and not return to the old. Jews and Gentiles alike formerly lived in the old sphere: they were 'in this present evil age' (1.4); they were enslaved under the law, the στοιχεῖα or the 'beings not gods' (4.1-11); they were enslaved children of the Gentile slave woman Hagar who represented the earthly Jerusalem and Mt Sinai (4.21–5.1); they lived by the flesh (3.1-6; 5.16-26). But now they have been transferred in Christ to the new sphere: they live in the new creation (6.15); they are freed from the Law and the στοιχεῖα (4.1-11); they are free children of the free Hebrew woman Sarah who represented Mt Zion and the heavenly Jerusalem; they are living by the Spirit (3.1-6; 5.16-26); they are the real children of Abraham (3.1-29); therefore they should stand fast in the freedom with which Christ set them free (5.1).[2] These arguments, and others like them, support the purpose expressed in the letter as a whole. Paul begins by requiring the Galatians to choose between his gospel and his opponents' 'gospel' (1.6-9), which Paul later interprets as a choice between the new sphere and the old. He ends the letter by laying the alternatives before them once more (6.11-16). Since Paul never seeks to establish independence from Jerusalem in the proof, never asserts his independence in the narration and actually alleges a motive which assumes his dependence, Paul probably does not seek to establish his autonomy in the narration in Galatians. Knox's rationale for holding that Paul must recount all his journeys to Jerusalem breaks down.

To decide whether Paul's argument required him to mention every visit he made to Jerusalem, we must understand how the narration functions in the letter. How does the narration prepare for the argu-

---

1. For further argument against the 'dependence hypothesis' see Lyons, *Autobiography*, pp. 83-91 and the literature cited there.

2. My use of 'two spheres' is analogous to J.L. Martyn's apocalyptic antinomies: 'Apocalyptic Antinomies in Paul's Letter to the Galatians', *NTS* 31 (1985), pp. 410-24.

ments in the proof? How does it act as a 'continuous proof' supporting the central contention of the letter that the Galatians should cling
to Paul and his gospel and repudiate the agitators and their false
gospel?[1] At the beginning of the narration Paul mentions two points he
wishes his recital of events to illustrate: he seeks not to please human
beings but God (1.10); he received his gospel not from human beings
but from God (1.11-12). The second of these two points grounds the
message Paul will explain later in Galatians: Paul has this message
directly from God. The first shows how the Galatians should act: like
Paul, they should seek not to please humans but God; they should stand
fast in the message from God as Paul did even should Peter himself
withstand them.

Events in the narration well support these two contentions. Paul
recites incidents to demonstrate that this gospel comes from God and
not human beings: He received it by revelation (1.13-17). He could not
have derived his gospel from the apostles in Jerusalem for he gets to
know Peter and makes the acquaintance of James for the first time
after already obeying the revelation for three years. He could not have
derived it from the Judean churches, for, even before they knew him,
they rejoiced that he was preaching the gospel he had sought to destroy
(1.16-24). His gospel has stood the test of time and passed the test for
prophecy:[2] after fourteen years he submitted it to the elders in
Jerusalem and they found no need to add anything to what Paul habit-
ually said (2.1-10). Paul, on the basis of this acknowledged revelation,
can rebuke even Peter. Paul's gospel, including his exposition of it in
Galatians, is reliable; it comes from God; the Galatians should listen to
it.

Paul also shows by his own actions that he has never sought to please
human beings and implies that the Galatians should act as he has.[3]
Though zealous for the Law, Paul throws that zeal aside and immediately goes to the Gentiles in obedience to the revealed gospel. He does
not please human beings but stands against anyone—false brothers
(1.4-5), Barnabas and all the other Jews in Antioch, and even Peter—

---

1. Hall, 'Rhetorical Outline', p. 287.
2. See 1 Cor. 14.29, 1 Thess. 5.21, and J.D.G. Dunn, 'The Relationship
between Paul and Jerusalem according to Galatians 1 and 2', *NTS* 28 (1982),
p. 468.
3. B.R. Gaventa ('Galatians 1 and 2: Autobiography as Paradigm', *NovT* 28
[1986], pp. 309-26) correctly points out that Paul wants the Galatians to imitate his
actions. See also Lyons, *Autobiography*, p. 171.

who acts or speaks inconsistently with respect to the gospel. The Galatians have a similar opportunity to 'stand fast in their liberty' and repudiate 'false brothers'; the narration implicitly calls them to do so.

Hence, the narration, consonant with the rest of the letter, argues that the Galatians should stand with Paul squarely upon the gospel God revealed and, like Paul, repudiate those who judaize. Features of the narration can be explained without hypothesizing extensive replies to opponents' charges.[1] Only the practice of 'mirror reading', critiqued effectively by Lyons,[2] justifies reading the narration as a defense. Rhetorical practice and the flow of argument in Galatians effectively encourage a hortatory rather than an apologetic interpretation for the narration.[3]

Study of ancient views of the narration as an oratorical and literary form lead us to expect that Paul would omit all journeys to Jerusalem he might have made except those required by his argument. Nothing in Paul's argument outlined above requires him to have enumerated every visit. He can argue that his gospel comes from God and illustrate how to listen to God rather than human beings without recounting every stay in Jerusalem. Therefore, we cannot follow Knox in concluding from Galatians that Paul visited Jerusalem only twice between his 'conversion' and the writing of Galatians. Perhaps we may deduce that Paul had not visited Christian leaders in Jerusalem before the third year, since he hastens to mention that, of the apostles, only Peter and James as yet knew him. That the Judean churches did not know him shows he knew few other Christians there as well, but had Paul visited some friend in Jerusalem even within the three years, sound rhetorical practice would have required him to omit that visit from the narration since mentioning it would not strengthen his case. After the three-year visit, nothing in the argument requires Paul to mention other journeys he might have taken to Jerusalem. Of course nothing in

---

1. I do not intend to deny that Paul throws out 'digs' at the agitators but only to affirm that replies to his opponents do not provide the main structure for his argument in the narration.

2. Lyons, *Autobiography*, pp. 75-121.

3. A growing number of interpreters have seen Galatians as hortatory rather than apologetic. See Kennedy, *New Testament Interpretation*, pp. 144-52; Hall, 'Rhetorical Outline'; Vouga, 'Rhetorische Gattung'; Smit, 'Galatians: A Deliberative Speech'. J.D. Hester, using modern as well as ancient categories, argues in this book that Galatians is epideictic, but agrees with the hortative purpose of the letter. Betz (*Galatians*, pp. 14-25) had argued for interpreting Galatians as an 'apologetic letter'.

the narration enables us to conclude that Paul did travel to Jerusalem on other occasions. When interpreted as an integral part of the argument in the letter, the narration offers no data about any visits to Jerusalem except the two specifically mentioned.[1] The narration in Galatians does not provide data adequate to construct a sequence for Paul's life. Does this conclusion mean historians should immediately adopt Luke's outline for Paul's life? Of course not. It only illustrates the principle that historians must weigh the letters of Paul as carefully as they weigh Acts.

Conclusion

Since ancient rhetoricians urged writers of narrations to re-interpret history in the interest of persuasion and since Paul structures his narration according to the rhetorical principles accepted in his age, Galatians is not an ideal historical source. The historical strictures that apply to Acts apply likewise to Paul. Neither merely reports facts; both use history to make theological points. Therefore neither source deserves markedly to outrank the other. The burden of proof Knox assumes should be allowed to shift. Writing 'chapters for a life of Paul' requires careful assessment of data from Acts and Paul as well as from other relevant sources.

---

1. The oath (Gal. 1.20), on which Knox relies, at most confirms everything Paul says (of course, it affirms nothing about what he does not say) and may confirm no more than that, of the apostles, Paul saw only Peter and James.

THE RHETORICAL FUNCTION OF COMMERCIAL LANGUAGE
IN PAUL'S LETTER TO PHILEMON (VERSE 18)

Clarice J. Martin

> As persuader, the rhetorician seeks not just to affect but to affect with a view
> to establishing consensus in the face of possible demur and opposition. Suc-
> cess has only one meaning and one measure to him: bringing the audience's
> viewpoint into alignment with his own.[1]

Meir Sternberg's cogent description of the aim of the rhetorician is
especially relevant to the investigation of the function of commercial
language in v. 18 of Paul's letter to Philemon. Two terms in v. 18,
ὀφείλει ('he owes'), and ἐλλόγα ('charge. . . to my account'), were
familiar terms in Greco-Roman and early Jewish business, commercial, and legal transactions in the Common Era.[2]

In fact, 'commercial language', as Wayne A. Meeks calls it, is used
in the Pauline letters directly to describe aspects of the relationship
between the apostle and local congregations, and metaphorically to
make theological statements.[3] The language of commercial partnership

---

1. Meir Sternberg, *The Poetics of Biblical Narrative: Ideological Literature and the
Drama of Reading* (Bloomington: Indiana University Press, 1985), p. 482.

2. In Greco-Roman usage, ὀφείλω means 'to owe someone something', usually
money. The phrase ὀφείλω τινί means 'I have debts with someone'. The term
ὀφείλειν, 'to owe', is used five times in the MT and ten times in the Apocrypha. It is
rare in the LXX. In NT usage the term is used figuratively of one who is a debtor to
God (Mt. 6.12; Lk. 11.4). The term is used literally in Phlm 18, but Heb. 5.3
employs the word as a legal term. For a full discussion of the history of the range of
meanings and usage in Greco-Roman antiquity and the NT, see Friedrich Hauck,
'ὀφείλω, κτλ', *TDNT*, V, pp. 559-66.

The Greek term ἐλλογέω, 'to charge to someone's account', is the regular form of
the verb. Forms such as ἐλλόγα (Phlm 18), and ἐλλογᾶται (Rom. 5.13) reflect the
confusion of the inflectional types -εῖν and -ᾶν. Cf. BAGD, p. 252; BDF, p. 45,
§90. See also Herbert Preisker, 'ἐλλογέω', *TDNT*, II, pp. 516-17 for a list of other
occurrences of the term in Greco-Roman usage.

3. Wayne A. Meeks, *The First Urban Christians: The Social World of the Apostle
Paul* (New Haven: Yale University Press, 1983), pp. 66-67.

is heard in the reference to 'gain and loss' in Phil. 3.7-8, and in the 'receipt' that Paul returns to the Philippian Christians for their gift (4.15-19). The proverb that Paul quotes in 2 Cor. 12.14b contains explicit pecuniary allusions: 'Children ought not to save up for their parents, but the parents for their children'. Col. 2.14 speaks of Christ 'canceling the note that was against us'. In these places in the NT at least, the *ethos* suggested is one where artisans, merchants, and persons with some economic assets[1] (however modest) were possibly the 'rule' instead of the 'exception'.

If the Apostle Paul seeks to accomplish any objective in his impassioned epistolary discourse to Philemon, it is to bring Philemon's viewpoint—to use Sternberg's words—'into alignment' with his own regarding a new status for Onesimus. This essay explores the ways in which Paul masterfully employs the art of rhetoric (τέχνη ῥητορική) in his use of commercial language in v. 18 to accomplish precisely this aim.

Rhetorical Artistry in Philemon

In 1978, F. Forrester Church observed that even if interpreters have generally acceded that Philemon was a 'well-crafted and carefully woven' Pauline letter, the consensus that the letter 'owed nothing to the graces of rhetoric' was held for decades.[2] Church's own essay on rhetorical structure and design in Philemon represents an important contribution among the still sparse ranks of rhetorical studies of the letter.[3] Certainly, Church's essay has demonstrated that former assessments of the letter's negligible rhetorical character are no longer tenable.

Church argues convincingly that Paul utilizes the genre of deliberative rhetoric to achieve his hortatory purpose. Among the three major forms of rhetoric, judicial (also known as legal or forensic rhetoric), epideictic (panegyric or ceremonial), and deliberative, it is deliberative rhetoric, with its emphasis on effecting the expedient (or inexpe-

---

1. Meeks, *First Urban Christians*, pp. 66-67.
2. F. Forrester Church, 'Rhetorical Structure and Design in Paul's Letter to Philemon', *HTR* 71 (1978), p. 18.
3. Cf. P.L. Couchoud, 'Le style rythmé dans l'Épitre de Saint Paul à Philemon', *RHR* 96 (1927), pp. 129-46; J. White, *The Structural Analysis of Philemon. A Point of Departure in the Formal Analysis of the Pauline Letter* (SBLASP; Missoula, MT: Scholars, 1971), pp. 1-47.

dient) and the advantageous (or disadvantageous) in future time, that best serves the objective of the narrative discourse.[1]

Whether hortatory or dissuasive, deliberative rhetoric may be used both by those who seek to give advice in private and those who speak in the assembly.[2] The speaker may narrate past events, but these events are recalled only to enable the hearers to take better counsel about future action.[3]

Deliberative oratory has a tripartite division. The first part is the *exordium* (προοίμιον), the 'preamble' or beginning of the speech wherein one seeks to 'excite or remove prejudice, and magnify or minimize the importance of the subject'.[4] The second part of deliberative oratory is the main body or proof (πίστις). It is here that the speaker employs the three proofs (or internal modes of persuasion): *ethos* (appeals to one's authority and good character), *pathos* (a rousing or stirring emotional appeal to the heart), and *logos* (inductive and deductive argument, including the ideas, structure, and logic of a speech evaluated in terms of their persuasive force).[5]

It is the 'conclusion' or peroration (ἐπίλογος) which concerns us in particular in this essay. The deliberative speech concludes with a peroration, a 'finishing off' of one's plea.[6] Aristotle cites a fourfold function of the peroration: (1) disposing the hearer favorably toward oneself and unfavorably toward an adversary, (2) amplification or depreciation, (3) exciting the emotions of the hearer—evoking pity, anger, emulation, etc., and (4) recapitulation.[7] Herein the speaker places the 'finishing touches' and a summary statement of the proofs.

1. White, 'Structural Analysis', p. 19. For a discussion of the three kinds of rhetoric, cf. Ar. *Rhet.* 1.3.3-4; 3.17.10; George A. Kennedy, *The Art of Rhetoric in the Roman World, 300 BC–AD 300* (Princeton: Princeton University Press, 1972), pp. 3-23.

2. Ar. *Rhet.* 1.3.3-4.

3. Ar. *Rhet.* 3.16.11.

4. Ar. *Rhet.* 1.1.9; 3.14.1.

5. Ar. *Rhet.* 1.2.3; Quint. 3.8.12; 6.2.9-12. The descriptions of the particular function of *logos* are provided by George A. Kennedy, *New Testament Interpretation through Rhetorical Criticism* (Chapel Hill: University of North Carolina Press, 1984), p. 49; Burton L. Mack, *Rhetoric and the New Testament* (Guides to Biblical Scholarship; Minneapolis: Fortress, 1990), p. 36. Cf. Friedrich Solmsen, 'Aristotle and Cicero on "the Orator's Playing upon the Feelings"', *Classical Philology* 33 (1938), pp. 390-404.

6. Edward P.J. Corbett, *Classical Rhetoric for the Modern Student* (2nd edn; New York: Oxford University Press, 1971), p. 328.

7. *Rhet.* 3.19.1-6.

Quintilian treats the peroration under two headings, the *enumeratio* (a summary of the facts),[1] and the *adfectus* (evoking the appropriate emotional response in the audience).[2] Quintilian argues that the peroration provides an opportunity for the orator to 'display the full strength of his case before the eyes of the judge':

> On the other hand in the peroration we have to consider what the feelings of the judge will be when he retires to consider his verdict, for we shall have no further opportunity to say anything and cannot any longer reserve arguments to be produced later. It is therefore the duty of both parties to seek to win the judge's goodwill and to divert it from their opponent, as also to excite or assuage his emotions.[3]

In the *Rhetorica ad Herennium*, 'Cicero' divides what he calls the 'conclusions' (*conclusiones*) of a speech into three parts: summing up, amplification, and appeal to pity.[4] While 'conclusions' can be used in four places in a speech (the direct opening, after the statement of facts, after the strongest argument, or in the actual conclusion of the speech), the speaker should be certain to employ the vocal organs in such a way as to secure a 'sustained flow' (*continens vox*), for this form of delivery is beneficial to the voice and stirs the hearer most vigorously at the conclusion of the entire discourse (*Quid? haec eadem nonne animum vehementissime calefacit auditoris in totius conclusione causae?*).[5]

Epistolary Structure and Rhetorical Strategy

John L. White has observed that the Apostle Paul may be the Christian leader who was responsible for first introducing Christian elements into the epistolary genre and for adapting the then existing epistolary conventions to express the particular interests of the earliest Christian communities.[6] Functioning as a substitute for Paul's presence, the

---

1. 6.1.1. The Greeks call this repetition of the facts ἀνακεφαλαίωσις. This enumeration refreshes the memory of the hearer or audience.

2. 6.1.1, 36.

3. Quintilian, *Institutio Oratoria* (trans. H.E. Butler; LCL; 4 vols.; Cambridge, MA: Harvard University Press, 1976–80), 6.1.10-11.

4. *Her.* 2.30.47. 'Cicero' identifies six parts of a discourse: the Introduction, Statement of Facts, Division, Proof, Refutation, and Conclusion (*Her.* 1.3.4).

5. 'Cicero', *Rhetorica ad Herennium* (trans. Harry Caplan; LCL; Cambridge, MA: Harvard University Press, 1981), 2.30.47; 3.12.22.

6. *Light from Ancient Letters* (FFNT; Philadelphia: Fortress, 1986), p. 19.

letters became an appropriate 'surrogate' medium by which Paul could address the congregations as God's representative.[1] While the Christian letters differed from ordinary Greek letters in many respects, the Pauline letters nevertheless reflect Paul's familiarity with recognizable epistolary conventions[2] (an opening, body, and closing) and rhetorical techniques reminiscent of oral argumentation.[3]

Traditionally, Paul's letter to Philemon is divided into four major sections, appended by greetings. Eduard Lohse identifies the major divisions as introductory greetings (vv. 1-3, thanksgiving (vv. 4-7), the main body or principal part of the letter (vv. 8-20), and a conclusion (vv. 21-25).[4] John Knox, who wrote one of the few extant monographs on Philemon in the first third of the twentieth century, assigned the same division to the letter.[5]

This essay follows Church's structural and rhetorical division of the letter. Thus, after the introduction (vv. 1-3), the following divisions are indicated:[6]

1. The *Exordium* (vv. 4-7)
2. The Main Body, or Proof (vv. 8-16)
3. The Peroration (vv. 17-22)
4. Final Greetings (vv. 23-25)

---

1. White, *Ancient Letters*, p. 19.
2. White, *Ancient Letters*, pp. 19-20, 218-20. Cf. Paul Schubert, 'The Form and Function of the Pauline Letters', *JR* 19 (1939), pp. 365-77; Abraham J. Malherbe, *Ancient Epistolary Theorists* (SBLSBS 19; Atlanta: Scholars, 1988); John L. White, 'Ancient Greek Letters', *Greco-Roman Literature and the New Testament: Selected Forms and Genres* (ed. David E. Aune; SBLSBS 21; Atlanta: Scholars, 1988), pp. 85-105; U. Wickert, 'Der Philemonbrief—Privatbrief oder apostolisches Schreiben?', *ZNW* 52 (1961), pp. 230-38.
3. White, *Ancient Letters*, p. 19. The growing number of works on rhetorical criticism and the Pauline writings are too numerous to list here, but cf. Robin Scroggs, 'Paul as Rhetorician: Two Homilies in Romans 1–11', *Jews, Greeks, and Christians: Essays in honor of W.D. Davies* (ed. R. Hamerton-Kelly and R. Scroggs; Leiden: Brill, 1976), pp. 271-320; and the bibliography in Burton L. Mack, *Rhetoric and the New Testament*, pp. 103-10.
4. *Colossians and Philemon* (Hermeneia; Philadelphia: Fortress, 1971), p. 187.
5. *Philemon Among the Letters of Paul. A New View of Its Place and Importance* (Chicago: University of Chicago Press, 1935), pp. 4-5. Although Knox's allusion to the address and thanksgiving sections are more clearly delineated than that of the body and the conclusion.
6. 'Rhetorical Structure', pp. 21-31.

While the rhetorical function of the commercial terms in Phlm 18 is the chief concern of this essay, a few preliminary comments about the rhetorical character of the letter as a whole are appropriate here. Particular attention is given to the *exordium* and the main body or proofs.

As noted above, the *exordium*, located at the beginning of the speech, represents the first major division of deliberative rhetoric. It is here that the speaker seeks to 'excite or remove prejudice, and magnify or minimize' the importance of the subject.[1] Paul seeks to 'remove prejudice' from Philemon even as he seeks to 'mollify'[2] him with regard to the offense of Onesimus' 'displacement from'[3] Philemon. Paul accomplishes this mollification by employing at least a twofold strategy in vv. 4-7. First, Paul praises Philemon, reestablishing goodwill between them (vv. 4-5). Second, he highlights particular exemplary qualities which Philemon exhibits, and to which he will appeal to advance his case (vv. 5-7) in the main body of the letter.[4] These qualities include love (τῇ ἀγάπῃ σου), and the ability to refresh others (ὅτι τὰ σπλάγχνα τῶν ἁγίων ἀναπέπαυται διὰ σοῦ). In short, 'Paul strives to secure Philemon's favor, by introducing the motifs of "love", "good", "partnership", etc., in such a way that they redound to Philemon's credit'.[5]

In the main body or proof of the letter (vv. 8-16) Paul uses *ethos* (a reference to good character) and *pathos* (a stirring, emotional appeal to the heart) to advance the argument. Ulrich Wickert has illustrated what is, in actuality, a very balanced appeal to the two proofs (πίστεις):[6]

vv. 8, 9a	vv. 9b, 10a
Accordingly, though I am	—I, Paul, *an ambassador,*
bold enough in Christ to	*and now a prisoner*
command you to do	*also for Christ Jesus—*
what is required,	*I appeal to you* for my

---

1. Ar. *Rhet.* 1.1.9; 3.14.1.

2. Church, 'Rhetorical Structure', p. 22.

3. This phrase is used for reasons which will become clear in the discussion of the peroration. This writer is trying to avoid explicit reference to the popular assumptions of many interpreters that Onesimus either 'ran away' or was a thief or scoundrel. He *could* have run away, he *may have* taken something, but these data are never stated clearly in the letter.

4. Church, 'Rhetorical Structure', p. 22. Church cites a threefold strategy here.

5. Church, 'Rhetorical Structure', p. 24.

6. 'Der Philemonbrief', p. 235. All English translations of the Bible in this essay are taken from the RSV unless indicated otherwise.

> *yet for love's sake*   child, Onesimus. . . (italics mine)
> *I prefer to appeal*
> *to you*. . . (italics mine)

Verses 11-14 highlight Paul's tremendous appreciation and love for the slave Onesimus. Onesimus is not only 'useful' (εὔχρηστον) to Paul, he is profitable to Philemon (v. 11).[1] In v. 12 Paul describes Onesimus as his 'very heart' (τὰ ἐμὰ σπλάγχνα), a deeply affective and emotionally evocative phrase, and one which provides a perfect illustration of an appeal to *pathos*. Paul employs the very touching and personal term, σπλάγχνα three times in the letter: in the *exordium* (v. 7), the main body or proof (v. 12), and in the peroration of the letter (v. 20).

Onesimus would have been of inestimable value to Paul in the apostle's imprisonment, serving Paul on Philemon's behalf (v. 13), but Paul preferred to send him back, wanting to do nothing without Philemon's consent (v. 14). The appeal to Philemon's goodness is an appeal to the motive of honor (*honestas*).[2]

> Not only is Onesimus Paul's son, begotten in his bonds (v. 11), but his very heart, that is, his very self. . . He doesn't substitute himself for Onesimus: He embodies himself in him. Then Philemon too is bound by this relationship. Onesimus' service to Paul has been rendered in Philemon's stead (ὑπὲρ σοῦ). Moreover, by sending Onesimus back to Philemon, Paul will lose that service. Thus, it is at some cost to himself that Paul commends by his own actions the quality of selfless love he wishes to instil in Philemon. With considerable persuasive force, he now has established grounds for mutual reciprocity between Philemon, Onesimus, and himself, a reciprocity based upon service in the Lord.[3]

---

1. Paul's play on words with reference to Onesimus' 'usefulness' and 'uselessness' is well known. The reader is invited to consult critical commentaries on Philemon for a discussion of the creative repartee.

2. Church, 'Rhetorical Structure', p. 27. Cicero describes honor as one of two aspects of Advantage in political deliberation. The other aspect is security: 'The Honourable (*honesta*) is divided into the Right and the Praiseworthy. The Right is that which is done in accord with Virtue and Duty. Subheads under the Right are Wisdom, Justice, Courage, and Temperance. . . The Praiseworthy is what produces an honourable remembrance, at the time of the event and afterwards. . . When therefore a thing is shown to be right, we shall show that it is also praiseworthy, whether in the opinion of qualified persons, . . . or of certain allies, or all our fellow citizens, or foreign nations, or our descendants' (*Her.* 3.2.3; 3.3.7).

3. Church, 'Rhetorical Structure', p. 27.

Verses 15-16 contain an implicit allusion to the work of providence in the circumstances surrounding Paul's appeal:

> Perhaps this is why he was parted from you for a while, that you might have him back for ever, no longer as a slave but more than a slave, as a beloved brother, especially to me but how much more to you, both in the flesh and in the Lord.

The passive of ἐχωρίσθη (v. 15) de-emphasizes the particular reason for Onesimus' absence from Philemon's household. Many commentators assume that Onesimus was a runaway slave, even though the warrant for that assumption is not specified explicitly within the text.[1] What is clearer here, however, is Paul's inference that God may have used Paul as an instrument for a higher end:[2] to establish a new relationship, a new standing, for Onesimus. He will henceforth be brought into 'a new society' in which all are fully brothers and sisters in the Lord.[3] The reception of Onesimus as a brother, then, would represent the completion of God's design.[4]

---

1. Cf. R.C.H. Lenski (*The Interpretation of St. Paul's Epistles to the Colossians, to the Thessalonians, to Timothy, to Titus and to Philemon* [Minneapolis: Lutheran Book Concern, 1937; repr. Augsburg, 1961], p. 966 on v. 15: 'The slave ran away, which fact, of course, rightly angered Philemon. Now he comes back.' Ralph P. Martin (*Colossians and Philemon* [NCB; Grand Rapids: Eerdmans, 1973], pp. 165-66) observes of v. 15: 'In a letter so full of nuances and hidden meanings it may well be believed that Paul's expressions are carefully contrived. His giving providential aspect to such a sordid business as a slave's misdemeanour and escape is a case in point.'

2. Lenski, *Philemon*, p. 965.

3. Martin, *Colossians and Philemon*, p. 166. But Martin (p. 166) does not understand Onesimus' 'new relationship' to include full legal emancipation: 'Onesimus' new standing as a Christian is all-important, since this brings him into a new society in which all men are brothers; he will still be a slave in the flesh, as a man, but he will gain new dignity as Philemon's equal in the Lord, as a fellow Christian'. This interpretation of v. 16 has many adherents; cf. Lohse, *Colossians and Philemon*, p. 203; G.B. Caird, *Paul's Letters from Prison* (New Clarendon Bible; Oxford: Clarendon, 1976), p. 222; S.S. Bartchy, *First-Century Slavery and the Interpretation of 1 Corinthians 7.21* (SBLDS 11; Missoula, MT: Scholars, 1971). The widely held view that v. 16 *can refer only to a new relationship of 'spiritual equality'* between Onesimus and Philemon is, in this writer's view, very problematic. The subject will be addressed in a forthcoming monograph on Philemon.

4. Church, 'Rhetorical Structure', p. 28.

Philemon 18: Res Adjudicata *or Rhetorical Capitulation?*

As noted above, the peroration is that final major category of delib-erative speech in which the speaker attempts to reinforce and recapitu-late the arguments and appeals in the *exordium* and the main body (or proofs) of the letter with maximum effect upon the hearer.[1] Elements of the fourfold Aristotelian scheme of (1) disposing the hearer favor-ably toward oneself, (2) amplification, (3) exciting the emotions of the hearer, and (4) recapitulation,[2] may be identified in the peroration of Paul's letter to Philemon.

The peroration is found in vv. 17-20, where, beginning with v. 17, Paul makes his request to Philemon on behalf of Onesimus most explicit. It is only at this point that Paul makes his request that Phile-mon receive Onesimus as he would Paul himself:[3]

So if you consider me your partner,
receive him as you would receive me.

The Greek connective οὖν suggests a return to the main theme of the letter, to the carefully cultivated and personal appeals in the proofs which have up to this point in the speech laid the groundwork for his request. The introductory conditional clause εἰ οὖν με ἔχεις κοινωνόν represents an intensification of the appeal at the outset of the perora-tion, functioning to dispose Philemon favorably toward Paul by reminding Philemon of the special partnership that they share. The Greek word κοινωνός refers to those who share 'common interests, common feelings, common work'.[4] The reminder of their partnership, then, serves to elicit loyalty (*fidelitas*) and goodwill (*studium*), and provides a motive for Philemon to respond to the stated request.

In v. 18, Paul amplifies the now accumulated force of the argument even more as he ingeniously employs the rhetorical device of 'anticipation' to remove any remaining hindrances or possible objec-tions to his petition. Amplifying his argument, he promises to repay

1. Quint. 6.1.10-11.
2. Ar. *Rhet.* 3.19.1-6.
3. Lohse, *Colossians and Philemon*, p. 203.
4. J.B. Lightfoot, *The Epistles of St. Paul. The First Roman Captivity. Epistle to the Colossians. Epistle to Philemon* (London: Macmillan, 1875), p. 409. On the possible similarities between consensual *societas* (a prevalent partnership contract of Roman law) and the Pauline writings, see J. Paul Sampley, *Pauline Partnership in Christ: Christian Community and Commitment in Light of Roman Law* (Philadelphia: Fortress, 1980).

330   *Persuasive Artistry*

Philemon for any loss that he may have suffered with regard to Onesimus:

> If [εἰ δέ] he has wronged you at all [τι ἠδίκησέν σε], or owes you anything [ἢ ὀφείλει], charge that to my account [τοῦτο ἐμοὶ ἐλλόγα].

Anaximenes enjoins the use of anticipation. Anticipation is a rhetorical strategy in which the rhetor 'anticipates the objections' that can be advanced against his or her arguments, and then 'sweeps them aside', thus minimizing the possibility that the other party may find grounds to deny the stated request.[1] By offering to defray any financial loss which Philemon may have suffered, Paul may have removed the last remaining obstacle or hindrance in Philemon's favorable reception of Onesimus.

Traditionally, many exegetes have understood Phlm 18, and particularly the imperatival phrase τοῦτο ἐλλόγα ('charge that to my account'), to function as a *res adjudicata*, a reference to a legal case whose outcome is already decided.[2] That is, interpreters have concluded that since Paul alludes *at all* to the possibility that some remuneration may be forthcoming to Philemon, that Onesimus *was necessarily a thief, robber, and impious scoundrel* whose action as a runaway slave had occasioned great pecuniary loss to Philemon. For these interpreters Onesimus' egregiously criminal character is an incontestable fact—a 'closed case'. A few examples of this long-held view are appropriate here.

As early as the nineteenth century at least, interpreters have concluded that Onesimus absconded with economic or material possessions belonging to his master. After all, ὀφείλει and ἐλλόγα are both technical, commercial terms regularly employed in business transactions and this commercial sense is implied in v. 18.[3] J.B. Lightfoot describes Onesimus' conduct, as he believes it may have developed in the circumstances surrounding his departure, with a highly censorious tone:

---

1. *Rhet. ad Alex.* 36. See also Church, 'Rhetorical Structure', p. 29.
2. J.A. Crook alludes to the matter of 'decided cases' in *Law and Life of Rome 90 BC–AD 212* (Aspects of Greek and Roman Life; Ithaca, NY: Cornell University Press, 1967), p. 27, but see esp. a discussion of the term by Gaius, the second-century jurist, in Gaius, *Elements of Roman Law* (trans. Edward Poste; Oxford: Clarendon, 1890), pp. 420-21.
3. See Hauck, 'ὀφείλω', pp. 559-66, and Preisker, 'ἐλλόγεω', pp. 516-17.

Onesimus represented the least respectable type of the least respectable class in the social scale. He was regarded by philosophers as a 'live chattel', a 'live implement'. He had done what a chattel or an implement might be expected to do, if endued with life and intelligence. . . He had declined to entertain any responsibilities. There was absolutely nothing to recommend him. . . he had confirmed the popular estate of his class. . . He was a thief and a runaway.[1]

Another nineteenth-century commentator, Heinrich A.W. Meyer, is also convinced that Paul alludes to the specific crime of theft in v. 18: 'the slave had probably been guilty, not merely in general of a fault in service which injured his master. . . but in reality. . . of purloining or of embezzlement, which Paul here knows how to indicate euphemistically'.[2] Meyer is convinced that the wrong is 'hinted in'[3] Paul's use of both ὀφείλει and ἠδίκησεν.

H.C.G. Moule, writing in the twentieth century, observes that the supposition that Onesimus is a thief is 'probable' in his imaginary depiction of Onesimus' return to Philemon's household: 'Here are two parties face to face with each other; one is an injured master, the other a slave, a fugitive, and probably also once a thief'.[4]

G.H.P. Thompson suggests that regional peculiarities may have enhanced the probability of Onesimus' culpability:

Slaves of that area [Colossae] had a notoriously bad reputation. Onesimus had lived up to it. He had run away, robbing his master in the process (verse 18, 'And if he has done you any wrong or is in your debt. . .').[5]

Among more recent commentators, G.B. Caird robs the conditional clause in the protasis of v. 18 of its conditional or contingent character altogether. He delineates Onesimus' offense with great specificity in his interpretation of v. 18:

1. Lightfoot, *Colossians and Philemon*, pp. 377-78, and also p. 409, where Lightfoot comments on the εἰ δέ τι in v. 18: 'The case is stated hypothetically but the words doubtless describe the actual offense of Onesimus. He had done his master some injury, probably had robbed him; and he fled to escape punishment.'
2. *The Epistle to the Ephesians and Philemon* (Edinburgh: T. & T. Clark, 1880), p. 378.
3. Meyer, *Ephesians and Philemon*, p. 378.
4. *Colossians and Philemon Studies: Lessons in Holiness and Faith* (London: Fleming H. Revell, 1893), p. 285.
5. *The Letters of Paul to the Ephesians, to Colossians, and to Philemon* (Cambridge: Cambridge University Press, 1967), p. 178. See also p. 177 for Thompson's discussion of Philemon's conversion.

The sentence is hypothetical only in form. Paul knows very well that Onesimus has *wronged* his master and owes him a considerable sum of money. He
must have helped himself to at least enough to pay his way to Rome.[1]

Peter Stuhlmacher precludes the possibility of a rhetorical intent in
Paul's conditional statement in v. 18, concluding that Onesimus
absconded with something (a matter which, for him, is also confirmed
by v. 19):

> In einer Doppelformulierung stellt der Apostel fest, er wolle selbst für den
> Schaden, den Philemon durch Onesimus erlitten hat, aufkommen. Die
> doppelte Wendung εἰ δέ τι ἠδίκησέν σε ἢ ὀφείλει scheint darauf hinzu-
> deuten, daβ Onesimus seinen Herrn bei seiner Flucht nicht nur um sich
> selbst, sondern auch noch dadurch geschädigt hat, daβ er bei seiner Flucht
> Geld (?) entwendete. Für den Arbeitsausfall und jene gestohlene Summe will
> Paul aufkommen. Dies ist, wie der folgende Vers zeigt, keineswegs nur
> rhetorisch gemeint.[2]

The view that Paul's use of commercial terminology *confirms*
Onesimus' status as a runaway and a thief must be re-examined. The
matter should be reconsidered on both syntactical[3] and rhetorical
grounds.

First, in most of the aforementioned interpretations of v. 18, the
conditional character of εἰ δέ τι ἠδίκησεν is minimized or deemed to
be of negligible consequence.[4] But in fact, one cannot deduce from the
commercial terminology in the conditional protasis alone that a crime
has occurred.

Verse 18 is a simple conditional sentence, with εἰ and the indicative
(here, there is a double indicative with ὀφείλει and ἐλλόγα) in the
protasis, and the indicative, but also any other form of the simple sentence appropriate to the thought (present, perfect, imperfect, aorist,
pluperfect, or imperative) in the apodosis.[5] In this case, the verb in the

---

1. *Paul's Letters from Prison*, pp. 222-23 (his emphasis).
2. *Der Brief an Philemon* (EKKNT; Zürich: Benziger Verlag, 1975), p. 49.
3. Syntax is an aspect of grammar which deals with 'the relationship and use of
words and larger elements in a sentence'; it always involves interpretation. James A.
Brooks and Carlton L. Winbery, *Syntax of New Testament Greek* (Washington:
University Press of America, 1979), p. 1.
4. Many other examples could be cited.
5. Herbert W. Smyth, *Greek Grammar* (Cambridge, MA: Harvard University
Press, 1980), pp. 516-17. The chart on p. 516 illustrates the forms appropriate to
the present and past tenses. The imperative in the apodosis of the simple condition is
not listed as a regular possibility in the chart, but although it occurs less frequently, it
is still used (see pp. 534-36). See also on this point Maximilian Zerwick, *Biblical*

apodosis is the imperative ἐλλόγα. 'Simple present or past conditions simply *state* a supposition with no implication as to its reality or probability.'[1] When speaking of the supposition in the protasis of the simple conditional sentence, 'there is nothing implied as to whether or not this fact usually exists'.[2]

The situation described in the protasis of v. 18 should not be presumed to have occurred *sine dubio*; that is, we cannot say with *certainty* that Onesimus harmed or injured (ἠδίκησεν) Philemon, or that he owes him anything (ὀφείλει). This type of condition should be taken at face value without any insinuations or implications. 'The context, of course, must determine the actual situation,[3] and Paul does not provide sufficient specificity about the circumstances surrounding Onesimus' separation from Philemon (ἐχωρίσθη, v. 15) to indict him conclusively as a thief or a scoundrel.

In simple conditions, the reality of the condition is assumed, that is, the condition is considered a 'real case', but '*with emphasis on the reality of the assumption (not of what is being assumed)*'.[4] The reality of the condition does not mean that the speaker has regarded the condition as fulfilled, '*indeed, the opposite may be the case*'; it is treated, however, as a concrete case.[5] Robertson and Davis have observed of the simple conditional sentence that 'some of the grammars have erred in the failure to distinguish clearly between the *statement* and the *reality*'.[6] Similarly, Zerwick notes of this tendency:

> It is an astonishing fact that even scholars sometimes overlook what has just been said and seem to forget that εἰ, even in a 'real' condition, still means 'if' and not 'because' or the like.[7]

Greek (Scripta Pontificii Instituti Biblici 114; Rome: Biblical Institute Press, 1963), p. 102 §303; Brooks and Winbery, *Syntax*, p. 163. Cf. Mk 4.23; Lk. 4.3; Gal. 5.18.

1. Smyth, *Greek Grammar*, p. 516.

2. H.E. Dana and Julius R. Mantey, *A Manual Grammar of the Greek New Testament* (Toronto: Macmillan, 1957), p. 287. This is, however, another form of the simple conditional sentence which is called the 'contrary to fact condition', and which uses εἰ in the protasis, and ἄν (usually) in the apodosis (p. 289).

3. A.T. Robertson and W. Hersey Davis, *A New Short Grammar of the Greek Testament* (10th edn; Grand Rapids: Baker, 1979), p. 350.

4. James A. Hewitt, *New Testament Greek. A Beginning and Intermediate Grammar* (Peabody, MA: Hendrickson, 1986), p. 33.

5. Zerwick, *Biblical Greek*, p. 103 §306 (my emphasis).

6. Robertson and Davis, *Grammar*, p. 350 (their emphasis).

7. Zerwick, *Biblical Greek*, p. 104 §308.

If a syntactical analysis of the contingent character of v. 18 should prompt interpreters to consider that Paul is not stating conclusively (*certus ac definitus*) that Onesimus had actually robbed Philemon, a rhetorical analysis of v. 18 shows that Paul uses commercial language to achieve a quintessential aim of the peroration: a final and august presentation of the case or appeal in such a way as to bring the audience's [Philemon's] viewpoint into alignment with that of the speaker [his own].[1]

When the commercial terminology in v. 18, ὀφείλει and ἐλλόγα, are examined with reference to their possible rhetorical force only, that is, if it is assumed that Paul refers to possible injury or economic loss by Philemon *merely for the sake of argument* (and not as a subtle allusion to actual injury or loss), then the function of these terms in the peroration can be appreciated as providing a kind of 'capstone' to Paul's argument on behalf of Onesimus.

That a conditional sentence can exhibit a primarily rhetorical intent has been shown by Robertson and Davis:

> In Matt. 12.27 εἰ ἐγὼ ἐν Βεελζεβοὺλ ἐκβάλλω τὰ δαιμόνια *if I by Beelzeboul cast out the demons,* Jesus *assumes* as true the charge of the Pharisees against him, *but merely for the sake of argument.* The conclusion is a crushing reply οἱ υἱοὶ ὑμῶν ἐν τίνι ἐκβάλλουσιν; *Your sons by whom do they cast them out?* They claimed to have this power. It is the *argumentum ad hominem.* Then in verse 28 Jesus gives the truth by this same first class condition: εἰ δὲ ἐν πνεύματι θεοῦ ἐγὼ ἐκβάλλω τὰ δαιμόνια *but if by the Spirit of God I cast out the demons,* which Jesus again *assumes* to be true. The conclusion is not a rhetorical question as above, but an obvious logical result (ἄρα ἔφθασεν ἐφ᾽ ὑμᾶς ἡ βασιλεία τοῦ θεοῦ *then is come to you the kingdom of God . . .* These two examples illustrate well the first-class condition.[2]

Following the first example of Robertson and Davis, then, it is plausible that v. 18 may exhibit a fully rhetorical intent, that is, Paul's commercial allusions are *merely for the sake of argument.* The task, then, is to assess the function of the commercial terminology in the peroration.

As noted above, Paul ingeniously employs the rhetorical device of anticipation in v. 18 to remove any possible objections to his petition. He doubtless stirs the emotions of Philemon in his emphatic and

---

1. Sternberg, *Poetics of Biblical Narrative*, p. 482.
2. Robertson and Davis, *Grammar*, pp. 350-51 (their emphasis except the words 'but merely for the sake of argument', which this writer has emphasized).

poignant declaration that he will defray all costs pertaining to any financial loss that Philemon may have suffered. The imperatival force of ἐλλόγα highlights the heightened and intensive force of Paul's plea at this point in the peroration, and underscores as well the depth and breadth of his love for and commitment to the one whom he had earlier called 'my child' (τοῦ ἐμοῦ τέκνου, v. 10) and 'my very heart' (τὰ ἐμὰ σπλάγχνα, v. 12). Paul has already fully identified with Onesimus (v. 17), and now he is willing to invest any resources at his disposal to secure Onesimus' well-being. 'This wonderfully gracious offer to assume the financial obligation of Onesimus is an altogether astonishing statement. We can only speculate how Paul came to have such warm feelings toward him.'[1]

Aristotle, Quintilian, and Cicero all describe as essential the task of stirring the emotions of the hearer in favor of one's appeal in the peroration. Aristotle cites as appropriate in the 'epilogue' or peroration the evocation of 'pity' 'when the nature and importance of the facts are clear'.[2] Quintilian argues that appeals to the emotions are necessary in the peroration, and 'the appeal which will convey most weight is the appeal to pity'.[3] Cicero uses the phrase 'Appeal to Pity' as a major subheading for the conclusion of the speech.[4] There are several ways in which the speaker may arouse pity:

> We shall stir Pity in our hearers by recalling the vicissitudes of fortune. . . by entreating those whose pity we seek to win, and by submitting ourselves to their mercy; by revealing what will befall our parents, children, and other kinsmen through our disgrace, and at the same time showing that *we grieve not because of our own straits but because of their anxiety and misery; by disclosing the kindness, humanity, and sympathy we have dispensed to others. . .* [5]

Paul's willingness to place his economic resources fully at Philemon's disposal on behalf of Onesimus represents a powerful and moving 'appeal to pity' and an example of the true nature of sacrificial Christian love on behalf of others. Paul's willingness to have 'charged

---

1. Arthur A. Rupprecht, 'Philemon', *Ephesians, Philippians, Colossians, 1, 2 Thessalonians, 1, 2 Timothy, Titus, Philemon* (ed. Frank E. Gaebelian; Expositor's Bible Commentary; 12 vols.; Grand Rapids: Zondervan, 1978), XI, p. 262.

2. Ar. *Rhet*. 3.19.3.

3. Quint. 6.1.1, 7, 23.

4. *Her*. 2.30.1.

5. *Her*. 2.31.50 (my emphasis).

to his account' any debts that Onesimus may have incurred corroborates his earnest concern for his 'kinsman' Onesimus.

Paul's stated readiness to share his economic resources[1] shows the boundless character of his concern for Philemon. The commercial allusions function, then, as a quintessential illustration of the fact that Paul would utilize all resources at his disposal to prevent possible economic barriers, or any hindrances from forestalling the full granting of his request. Philemon is now free to act in full obedience to Paul's request, for Paul's rhetorical offer of a 'promissory note', a kind of *cheirographon* (Col. 4.18), an autographed 'I.O.U.', has fully opened the door for Philemon's full cooperation.[2]

It is *possible* that Onesimus was a runaway slave, but that is not stated in any definitive sense. There are a number of other reasons which could account for his presence with Paul: he could have been sent to Paul by Philemon for a particular purpose, and decided to remain with Paul. John Knox questions whether Philemon had sent Onesimus to Paul with some message or gift for Paul or one of Paul's companions in prison.[3] Was he simply overdue in his absence from Colossae on Philemon's business?[4]

There are several problems with the runaway-slave hypothesis. The letter indicates that Onesimus *was away* from the household, but it does not state that he *ran away*. Second, as Sara C. Winter has shown, a study of the thanksgiving of the letter does not fit the runaway-slave hypothesis. The thanksgiving in vv. 4-7 exhibits the form of a Pauline thanksgiving precisely, and yet it nowhere identifies the epistolary situation or theme as in any way related to a presumed flight by the slave Onesimus.

> From the thanksgiving's apparent failure to mention Onesimus' arrival with Paul, given that the main body of the letter is a request concerning Onesimus, one must either posit a previous letter (or communication) or conclude that the recipient knew that Onesimus was with Paul.[5]

1. According to Acts 24.26, Felix detained Paul with the hope that Paul could purchase his own freedom. Were significant financial resources available to Paul? (cf. Acts 28.30).

2. C.F.D. Moule, *The Epistles of Paul the Apostle to the Colossians and to Philemon* (Cambridge Greek New Testament; Cambridge: Cambridge University Press, 1957), p. 148.

3. John Knox, *Philemon*, p. 1. Cf. Col. 4.10; Phlm 23.

4. Martin, *Colossians and Philemon*, p. 167.

5. 'Paul's Letter to Philemon', *NTS* 33 (1987), pp. 2-3.

It is also questionable whether Paul's location would have been recognized as a place of asylum (as many commentators propose).[1]

The question whether Onesimus ran away or actually owed Philemon anything will continue to be debated among interpreters. It is important to note, however, that the rhetorical function of the commercial language not only serves to 'clinch' Paul's appeal on behalf of Onesimus in v. 18 of the peroration, but the language of personal indebtedness also 'brings Philemon's story line to a climax' in v. 19.[2] It provides the *coup de maître* fully and finally to remove any remaining objections to the granting of Paul's request.

Paul reminds the addressee, Philemon, that he is also indebted to Paul. In actuality, whereas Paul *may* owe Philemon money, Philemon owes Paul far more:

> I, Paul, write this with my own hand, I will repay it [ἀποτίσω]—to say nothing of your owing me [προσοφείλεις] even your own self.

In actuality, Philemon is himself a 'metaphorical debtor'. Now that he has canceled Onesimus' (possible) literal debt, Paul 'calls in' Philemon's debt to him. 'The mode of Philemon's repayment of his debt is important because it is linked to the source of his indebtedness to Paul, namely, Philemon's own conversion, for which his indebtedness is a metaphor, and by which he became a brother to Paul (cf. vv. 7, 20).'[3] The rhetorical function of the commercial language in v. 18 of Philemon, then, achieves much more than merely providing a stylistic flourish to Paul's appeal, or euphemistically understating a promise to reimburse Philemon for actual debts incurred. The commercial language in the peroration has enabled Paul skillfully and masterfully to formulate a convincing and practicable case for conforming (realigning) Philemon's will to his own.

---

1. Winter, 'Philemon', p. 2. See also Lohse, *Colossians and Philemon*, p. 187 n. 5; and Thomas Wiedemann, *Greek and Roman Slavery* (Baltimore: Johns Hopkins, 1981), pp. 195-97. It is certain that one who harbored a slave or sold him or her away without the owner's permission was subject to a financial penalty. See Alan Watson, *Roman Slave Law* (Baltimore: Johns Hopkins, 1987), pp. 49-50, 59-60, 64; Wolfgang Schrage, *The Ethics of the New Testament* (trans. David E. Green; Philadelphia: Fortress, 1982), pp. 234-35.

2. Norman R. Petersen, *Rediscovering Paul: Philemon and the Sociology of Paul's Narrative World* (Philadelphia: Fortress, 1985), p. 74.

3. Petersen, *Rediscovering Paul*, pp. 75-76 (his emphasis).

ISOCRATES AND CONTEMPORARY HERMENEUTICS

Stephen Mark Pogoloff

There is no institution devised by man which the power of speech has not helped us to establish. . . . This faculty. . . which we use in persuading others when we speak in public, we employ when we deliberate in our own thoughts. . . . None of the things which are done with intelligence take place without the help of speech.[1]

Language is the universal medium in which understanding itself is realized . . . All understanding is interpretation, and all interpretation takes place in the medium of a language. . . . Thus the hermeneutical phenomenon proves to be a special case of the general relationship between thinking and speaking, the mysterious intimacy of which is bound up with the way in which speech is contained, in a hidden way, in thinking.[2]

So wrote Isocrates nearly 2500 years ago, and H.-G. Gadamer less than thirty. Despite this distance in time, as well as the gulf created by the Enlightenment, Gadamer's hermeneutics indicate a renewed interest in rhetoric. This interest both fuels and is fueled by radical changes in hermeneutical theory. As C. Perelman notes, the recovery of rhetoric as a theory of persuasive discourse

is not always called rhetoric. Sometimes it may be called hermeneutics. Hermeneutics is another kind of rhetoric because you do not go from the speaker to the audience, but from the text written to the audience, and back to the author or to the background, and so on. But it is another way of doing more or less similar things. The idea of looking for meaning is done now through the rhetorical method.[3]

1. Isocrates, *Nicocles or the Cyprians* (trans. George Norlin; LCL; Cambridge, MA: Harvard University Press, 1966), pp. 6-9.

2. H.-G. Gadamer, *Truth and Method* (New York: Crossroad, 1984), pp. 350-51.

3. C. Perelman, 'Address at Ohio State University', *Practical Reasoning in Human Affairs: Studies in Honor of Chaim Perelman* (ed. J.L. Golden and J.J. Pilotta; Dordrecht: D. Reidel, 1986), p. 11.

Gadamer himself explicitly describes his dependence upon classical rhetoric: 'Where else should theoretical reflection on the art of understanding turn than to rhetoric?. . . The rhetorical and hermeneutical aspects of human linguisticality interpenetrate each other at every point.'[1]

One place we see the congruence of rhetorical and hermeneutical interests is in the NT exegetical techniques proposed by G.A. Kennedy.[2] He begins by offering us the possibility of 'reading the Bible as it would be read by an early Christian', ultimately aiming to discover 'the author's intent and. . . how that is transmitted through a text to an audience'.[3] Virtually all the research inspired by Kennedy's book attempts to fulfill this promise of adding yet one more historical critical 'tool'.

I agree that we can better understand the rhetoric of the early Christians when we read it within the communicative conventions of their age. But once we imaginatively enter the rhetorical world of Hellenistic society, we discover that Kennedy's initial claims for rhetoric are too modest. We discover not only communicative conventions, but a world-view in which speech was valued, used, and understood in ways that profoundly affected the proclamation and understanding of the gospel. Moreover, we find a culture which treated its own words in a way which might seem bizarre to modern positivist historical critics, but a way which bears remarkable similarities to NT hermeneutics in the wake of Heidegger, Wittgenstein, and Gadamer.[4] Gadamer in particular has spawned

1. H.-G. Gadamer, 'Rhetoric, Hermeneutics, and the Critique of Ideology', trans. Jerry Dibble, *The Hermeneutics Reader* (ed. K. Mueller-Vollmer; New York: Continuum, 1989), pp. 278-80; Gadamer, *Truth and Method*, pp. 18-23. The role of rhetoric in Gadamer's hermeneutics is brilliantly analyzed by K. Dockhorn, 'Hans-Georg Gadamer's *Truth and Method*', trans. and ed. Marvin Brown, *PhilR* 13 (1980), pp. 160-80.

2. G.A. Kennedy, *New Testament Interpretation through Rhetorical Criticism* (Chapel Hill, NC: University of North Carolina Press, 1984).

3. Kennedy, *New Testament Interpretation*, pp. 5, 12.

4. For good summaries, see A.C. Thiselton, *The Two Horizons: New Testament Hermeneutics and Philosophical Description with Special Reference to Heidegger, Bultmann, Gadamer, and Wittgenstein* (Grand Rapids: Eerdmans, 1980); R.E. Palmer, *Hermeneutics: Interpretation Theory in Schleiermacher, Dilthey, Heidegger, and Gadamer* (Evanston, IL: Northwestern University Press, 1969); for a superb synthesis, see D. Tracy, *Plurality and Ambiguity* (San Francisco: Harper & Row, 1987).

a new way of thinking about art, history, literature, and language, a way so at variance with the modern as to suggest terms like 'postmodern' thinking. . . Modern 'epistemology' represents a search for foundations, but 'hermeneutics' recognizes the finitude of human knowledge and searches for 'edifying' knowledge.[1]

This 'anti-foundational' argument, Fish writes, 'has been made in a variety of ways and in a variety of disciplines. Obviously it is not an isolated argument; in fact, today one could say that it is the *going* argument.' And in this argument, we find rhetoric re-established as the queen of the disciplines. Indeed, another word for

anti-foundationalism *is* rhetoric, and one could say without too much exaggeration that modern anti-foundationalism is old sophism writ analytic. The rehabilitation by anti-foundationalism of the claims of situation, history, politics, and convention in opposition to the more commonly successful claims of logic, brute fact empiricism, the natural, and the necessary marks one more chapter in the long history of the quarrel between philosophy and rhetoric.[2]

This radical shift is noted by Kennedy:

Twentieth-century thought as seen in some of its most original philosophers, writers, and artists, as well as at the frontiers of theoretical science, points toward a conclusion that mankind cannot know reality. . . At most, it is argued, we can know structures, words, and formulae perhaps representative of reality.

In line with these changes, 'the methods of historical criticism, form criticism, structuralism, and other methods have, at least for many readers, seemed to move us further away from a sense of certainty about what actually happened in the formation of Christianity'.[3] We might add that many readers despair not so much of the certainty as of the *relevance* of historical criticism, that is, its ability to enable meaningful readings. Rhetoric *cannot* remedy the historical-critical problem, for it 'cannot describe the historical Jesus or identify Matthew or John. . . But it *does study a verbal reality*.'[4]

1. R.E. Palmer, Review of J.C. Weinsheimer's *Gadamer's Hermeneutics: A Reading of Truth and Method, PhilR* 20 (1987), p. 135.
2. S.E. Fish, *Doing What Comes Naturally: Change, Rhetoric, and the Practice of Theory in Literary and Legal Studies* (Durham, NC: Duke University Press, 1989), pp. 345-47.
3. Kennedy, *New Testament Interpretation*, p. 157.
4. Kennedy, *New Testament Interpretation*, p. 159 (my emphasis).

If that is true, then rhetorical criticism may begin as another tool to attempt to discover 'the author's intent' (i.e. an objectively determined historical author rather than an imaginatively constructed implied author); but it quickly deconstructs its own narrowly historical endeavor to become the ruling paradigm for all interpretation.[1] Such interpretation will not seek the truth in some alternative meta-discourse (e.g. historicism, existentialism, sociologism), but will seek to find meaning by bringing our discourses into conversation with the rhetoric of the text. Rather than replacing one discourse with another, rhetorical criticism should aim to extend the hermeneutical circle toward the side of authorship by enriching our socio-linguistic imaginations.[2]

πίστις *or* ἐπιστήμη?

Isocrates wrote of the central role of language in human affairs in the context of criticism from Plato. Many scholars described this criticism as part of an unyielding confrontation between rhetoric and philosophy,[3] but this oversimplifies the debate. Even Plato had to admit that philosophy is a rhetorical endeavor, for the philosopher 'plants and sows in a fitting soul intelligent words which are not fruitless, but yield seed from which there spring up in other minds other words capable of continuing the process for ever'.[4] And today, philosophy has become the hotbed of hermeneutical discussion, a discussion that increasingly takes for granted the radical socio-linguisticality of understanding.[5]

1. On rhetorical criticism as paradigm, see E. Schüssler Fiorenza, 'Rhetorical Situation and Historical Reconstruction in 1 Corinthians', *NTS* 33 (1987), pp. 386-403; *The Book of Revelation: Justice and Judgement* (Philadelphia: Fortress, 1985).

2. On the role of imagination in understanding, see Dockhorn, p. 164; P. Ricœur, *The Rule of Metaphor* (trans. R. Czerny with K. McGloughlin and J. Costello; Toronto: Toronto University Press, 1977), p. 244; Tracy, *Plurality and Ambiguity*, pp. 45-46; W. Wuellner, 'Where is Rhetorical Criticism Taking Us?', *CBQ* 49 (1987), pp. 462-63.

3. E.g. S. Ijsselling, *Rhetoric and Philosophy in Conflict: An Historical Survey* (trans. Paul Dunphy; The Hague: Martinus Nijhoff, 1976), pp. 15-23.

4. Plato, *Phaedrus* (trans. Harold North Fowler; LCL; Cambridge, MA: Harvard University Press, 1914), 276e-277a.

5. 'Philosophy died so that rhetoric could be born. For many modern philosophers this means philosophy delivered and now parents rhetoric following the unfruitful labors of the epistemological paradigm' (J. Sutton, 'The Death of Rhetoric and its Rebirth in Philosophy', *Rhetorica* 4 [1986], p. 203).

But these discussions are far broader than philosophy. What philosophy discusses in general, we find applied to law, Bible, literature, in fact to anything that might be construed as 'text'. Our world is inescapably rhetorical or hermeneutical. This is true for writers, since 'the author cannot choose to avoid rhetoric; he can choose only the kind of rhetoric he will employ'.[1] It is equally true of readers, for 'to understand at all is to interpret'.[2]

The rhetoricians recognized the fundamental insight recovered in contemporary hermeneutics: words do far more than merely encapsulate prelinguistic ideas. Rather than this instrumental view of language, rhetoric views speech as shaped by and in turn shaping the situation, and thus as highly social. The rhetoricians were interested in performative language,[3] in speech acts: what language *does* and how it does it. This means that the rhetor, aiming for persuasive end rather than disembodied content, must take into account such audience-oriented factors as possible perceptions of his character or inferences of his style, or his audience's psychological or social profile. Thus, rhetorical speech is not just a mechanical act of putting labels on concepts. Instead, it is an activity in which a speaker attempts to shape social realities with speech itself shaped by of social realities (while these realities are themselves shaped by other speech). Further, since the rhetors claimed that virtually all speech is rhetorical, the same is true for all speech and all realities.

Just as classical rhetoric insisted that words and meanings cannot be divorced from situations and communities, so too does contemporary hermeneutics. Often these insights are carried to extremes, as in those brands of reader-response criticism or deconstruction which narrow the situation to that of a particular reader in an arbitrary time and place. But just as rhetoric recognized that speakers are tied to audiences and their situations, so many hermeneutical theorists recognize that readers are tied to authors and their situations. Although readers have only indirect, subjective access to authors and their situations, such imaginative reconstructions are nevertheless important for understanding.

---

1. W.C. Booth, *The Rhetoric of Fiction* (2nd edn; Chicago: University of Chicago Press, 1983), p. 83.

2. Tracy, *Plurality and Ambiguity*, p. 9.

3. The notion of performative language entered hermeneutical discussion through J.C. Austin, *How to Do Things with Words* (Oxford: Clarendon, 1962).

For example, 'situation' is important to Gadamer primarily as 'hermeneutical situation', that is, the situation of the interpreter within the stream of 'effective history' (the history of the effects of tradition). For this reason, many interpret him to mean that attempts at historical reconstruction are not important for interpretation. However, since, for Gadamer, conversation is the model for all hermeneutics, and conversation requires listeners to be in dialogue with speakers, he recognizes that historical reconstruction is helpful. He only wants to warn us of two things and celebrate one other. He warns us, first, that pretense to objectivity guarantees misunderstanding; and second, that historical reconstruction, while helpful, is no more than a means or phase toward the end of understanding. Further, rather than viewing temporal distance as a problem to be overcome, he celebrates its hermeneutical fruitfulness through the creative and filtering processes of tradition.[1]

Similarly, Fish emphasizes the communal nature of interpretation. Only the illusion of 'free-floating and individualistic' authors and readers or 'free-standing and self-declaring texts' move theorists to the 'extremes' of 'the objectivity of meanings that are "just there" and the subjectivity of meanings that have been "made up" by an unconstrained agent'. Rather, readers cannot avoid constructing the situation and intention of the author.

> One cannot understand an utterance without *at the same time* hearing or reading it as the utterance of someone with more or less specific concerns, interests, and desires, someone with an intention. . . This, of course, does not mean that intention anchors interpretation in the sense that it stands outside and guides the process; intention like anything else is an interpretive fact; that is, it must be construed; it is just that it is impossible *not* to construe it.[2]

The insight that meanings are socially constructed has just begun to affect NT criticism. In fact, for much of the history of Christianity, theology has been viewed as an epistemological, not a rhetorical exercise. According to Richard Bell, this is still true even in the philosophy of religion:

> A close monitoring of standard course texts, journal articles, and various colloquia offered in the philosophy of religion reveals that the majority of literature and discussion still focus on questions of rational justification of religious claims, concern for proof and evidence, and the limits of 'epistemic creden-

---

1. Gadamer, *Truth and Method*, pp. 267-74.
2. Fish, *Doing What Comes Naturally*, p. 100.

tials'. The concerns are derived from the earlier, more empirically oriented discussions—it is as if the field of philosophy of religion, and consequently some theology, has not really caught up with the rest of philosophy.[1]

If the philosophy of religion has not caught up with the rest of philosophy, then we should not be surprised that NT criticism still operates largely with the assumptions of 19th-century historiography. Yet, as shown by the increasing number of rhetorical-critical studies like those published in this volume, the NT documents themselves testify to the rhetorical wellsprings of theology. Christianity first developed not in isolated, esoteric discussions between teacher and pupil about universal eternal truths, but in the public speeches of evangelists which were provoked and constrained by the rhetorical situations[2] of their authors. As Wuellner notes, 'Rhetoric. . . has been and remains . . . religion's closest ally'.[3] Christianity was and is among the public things which cannot take place without the help of speech.

Of course epistemology, when viewed through the same rhetorical lens, is itself a rhetorical or hermeneutical enterprise. For we experience no reality other than that of our models, symbols, and metaphors. Thus, even when we assert our most axiomatic views of reality, we are involved in community-based, persuasive, interpretive activity.[4]

---

1. R.H. Bell, 'Introduction: Culture, Morality, and Religious Belief', *The Grammar of the Heart: New Essays in Moral Philosophy and Theology* (ed. R.H. Bell; San Francisco: Harper & Row, 1988), p. 12. See also the forthcoming dissertation 'Faithful Persuasion' by D. Cunningham (Duke University) which was unavailable to me but commended by my colleague A.K.M. Adam as concentrating on the rhetorical issues raised here.

2. The concept of the rhetorical situation, as proposed by L.F. Bitzer, 'The Rhetorical Situation, *PhilR* 1 (1968), pp. 1-14, is commended by Kennedy (*New Testament Interpretation*, pp. 34-36). The debate provoked by Bitzer's article itself reflects the difficulty in equating verbal and objective realities. See R.E. Vatz, 'The Myth of the Rhetorical Situation', *PhilR* 6 (1973), pp. 154-61; J.H. Patton, 'Causation and Creativity in Rhetorical Situations: Distinctions and Implications', *QJS* 65 (1979), pp. 36-55; S. Consigny, 'Rhetoric and Its Situations', *PhilR* (1974), pp. 175-85; A.B. Miller, 'Rhetorical Exigence', *PhilR* 5 (1972), pp. 111-18; A. Brinton, 'Situation in the Theory of Rhetoric', *PhilR* 14 (1981), pp. 234-48; P.K. Tomkins, J.H. Patton, L.F. Bitzer, 'Tomkins on Patton and Bitzer; Patton on Tompkins; Bitzer on Tomkins (and Patton)', *QJS* 66 (1980), pp. 85-93.

3. Wuellner, 'Rhetorical Criticism', p. 449.

4. E. Grassi, *Rhetoric as Philosophy: The Humanist Tradition* (trans. J.M. Krois and A. Azodi; University Park: Pennsylvania State University Press, 1980), pp. 37-39; J.L. Bineham, 'The Cartesian Anxiety in Epistemic Rhetoric: An Assessment of the Literature', *PhilR* 23 (1990), pp. 43-62.

Human knowledge. . . is embodied, communal, finite, discursive. . .
Former claims for a value-free technology and a history-free science have
collapsed. The hermeneutical character of science has now been strongly
affirmed. Even in science, we must interpret in order to understand.[1]

Once we see epistemology in this sense, it is reborn as theology's
debating partner. No longer does epistemology view theology as the
dogmatic, pseudo-scientific, or 'blind faith' competitor of empiricism
and reason, but as one of the many rhetorical activities of various
communities which compete for varying degrees of persuasiveness and
community assent. Reborn in this sense, epistemology loses the traditional division between fact and value, knowledge and opinion, reason
and faith. As G. Ebeling wrote, 'hermeneutic now takes the place of
the classical epistemological theory, and indeed. . . fundamental onto-
logy appears as hermeneutic'.[2]

But philosophy has generally opposed rhetoric, partly because the
latter was concerned with opinion (δόξα or πίστις) rather than knowledge (ἐπιστήμη).[3] This was one of Plato's criticisms of rhetoric, and
his pithy comments became *topoi* for many philosophers with less
appreciation for the subtleties of his dialogues. 'But philosophy was
never in a position either to destroy rhetoric or to absorb it. . .
Philosophical discourse is itself just one discourse among others.'[4]

Plato exalted philosophical knowledge over rhetorical belief, yet
admitted that philosophy is rhetorical. He could hold these two views
together by means of his mystical view of language. Philosophical dialogue, contingently shaped to the needs of the philosopher's soul,
prompts the philosopher to remember the purely rational truths his
soul had forgotten when it fell into bodily existence.[5] Thus, the dia-
lectical search for truth necessarily involved rhetorical activity, but its
end was the prelinguistic idea.

Later philosophers, particularly the Stoics, did not share this mystical understanding of language, and could envision a role for rhetoric

---

1. Tracy, *Plurality and Ambiguity*, pp. 27, 33.
2. G. Ebeling, 'Word of God and Hermeneutic', *The New Hermeneutic* (ed. J.M.
Robinson and J.B. Cobb, Jr; New Frontiers in Theology 2; New York: Harper &
Row, 1964), p. 92.
3. For the history of this debate, see Ijsselling, *Rhetoric and Philosophy in
Conflict*; Grassi, *Rhetoric as Philosophy*; Fish, *Doing What Comes Naturally*,
pp. 471-502.
4. Ricœur, *Rule*, pp. 10-11.
5. Pl. *Phdr*. 249.

only as the packaging for philosophically achieved truth. Thus, Epictetus viewed rhetoric as a tool for philosophy to teach and learn moral principles. But if elevated beyond this instrumental role, it becomes a trap. Employing Platonic *topoi*, Epictetus complains, 'this faculty of speech and of the adornment of language, if it really is a separate faculty, what else does it do, when discourse arises about some topic, but ornament and compose the words, as hairdressers do the hair?'[1]

The Stoics, according to Cicero, rejected the hermeneutical and rhetorical priority of colloquial, socially determined language only to end up with an attempt to establish the kind of technical, private language later declared meaningless by Wittgenstein.[2] Cicero complains that the Stoic's style of discourse is

> quite impossible to employ in public speaking; for the Stoics hold a different view of good and bad from all their fellow-citizens or rather from all other nations, and give a different meaning to 'honour', 'disgrace', 'reward', 'punishment'—whether correctly or otherwise does not concern us now, but if we were to adopt their terminology, we should never be able to express our meaning intelligibly about anything.[3]

Without Plato's mystical understanding of dialectic, the Stoics could not maintain even his proximate embodiment of truth in language. On the other hand, a small number of philosophers held truth and language together by abandoning Plato's hierarchy of truth over belief. Arcesilaus and Carneades led the Middle and New Academies of the 3rd and 2nd centuries BC into a skeptical attitude toward the truth. In place of certainty about the truth, they asserted that one can only have belief according to the relative probability of an assertion.[4] Carneades

---

1. Epictetus, *The Discourses as Reported by Arrian, The Manual, and Fragments* (trans. W.A. Oldfather; LCL; London: Heinemann, 1926), 2.23.

2. L. Wittgenstein, *Philosophical Investigations* (trans. G.E.M. Anscombe; 3rd edn; New York: Macmillan, 1958), secs. 199, 202, 243, 256, 257, *passim*.

3. Cicero, *De Oratore* (trans. E.W. Sutton; LCL; 2 vols.; London: Heinemann, 1942), 3.18.66; Cf. Tracy (*Plurality and Ambiguity*, p. 16) on the impossibility of private language: 'Anyone who uses a language bears the preunderstandings, partly conscious, more often preconscious, of the traditions of that language. The Enlightenment belief in a purely autonomous consciousness has been. . . torn apart. . . Autonomy is a mirrored mask that ripped away, reveals Narcissus peering at an indecipherable code, believing all the while that he has at last found his true self.'

4. E. Brehier, *The History of Philosophy: The Hellenistic and Roman Age* (trans. W. Baskin; Chicago: University of Chicago Press, 1965), pp. 116-24; J.L. Kinneavy, *Greek Rhetorical Origins of Christian Faith: An Inquiry* (Oxford: Oxford

argued both sides of a question 'with great force and rhetorical skill'[1] to search out which side was most probable, that is, persuasive.

The affinities with rhetoric are apparent, so it is not surprising that Carneades deeply impressed Cicero, who searched for ways to fulfill the Platonic and Isocratean vision of the philosopher-rhetor. A philosophy which emphasized opinion was bound to appeal to him, for the truth the rhetoricians sought was always practical and always, in the final analysis, a matter of opinion: the best course for a government to take; the guilt or innocence of an accused person; equitable punishments or settlements of disputes; or whether to confer honor or shame on a member of the community. Communities could not defer decisions on such matters until they achieved certainty; they had to proceed on the basis of what seemed most persuasive. But this practical role of rhetoric excluded for Cicero any possibility of epistemological foundations. 'Any form of dogmatism was repugnant to one whose training had taught him that Truth, in philosophy as in the courts, is not easily discovered.'[2] The rhetoricians were so successful in establishing πίστις over ἐπιστήμη as the source of social truths that rhetoric became the arbiter and purveyor of Greco-Roman culture (παιδεία).

πίστις: *Civic and Apocalyptic*

Into this world stepped the early Christian preachers and pastors who gave us the documents of the NT. Their own words entered the market-place of words which competed to persuade, found, and shape communities. Throughout the NT are scattered references to this persuasive purpose of evangelistic speech: 'How are they to believe in him of whom they have never heard? And how are they to hear without a preacher?. . . Faith comes from what is heard, and what is heard comes by the preaching of Christ' (Rom. 10.14b-17, RSV). 'It is no longer because of your words [speech] that we believe, for we have heard for ourselves' (Jn 4.42). 'Knowing the fear of the Lord, we per-

University Press, 1987), pp. 40-41; *The Oxford Classical Dictionary* (ed. N.G.L. Hammond and H.H. Scullard; 2nd edn; Oxford: Clarendon, 1970), pp. 95, 206-207.

1. *Oxford Classical Dictionary*, p. 207.
2. E.E. Sikes, 'Literature in the Age of Cicero', *The Cambridge Ancient History* (ed. S.A. Cook, F.E. Adcock, and M.P. Charlesworth; New York: Macmillan, 1932), IX, p. 761.

suade men' (2 Cor. 5.11). 'He expounded the matter to them. . .trying to convince them about Jesus. . . And some were convinced by what he said, while others disbelieved' (Acts 28.17-24).

Thus, the words of the evangelists were not just any words, but words which aimed to achieve a specific purpose: to engender and nurture faith. In one sense, this was nothing new, since the words of God's messengers had often been understood as words with a purpose. Purposeful words are rhetorical, for rhetoric is 'that quality in discourse by which a speaker or writer seeks to accomplish his purposes'.[1] The prophetic word, then, is the ultimate rhetorical speech, since God's word was believed never to fail in accomplishing its purpose.[2]

However, something new was at stake in the purpose of Christian speech: conversion. The role of rhetoric in this new relationship of faith and language has been brought to our attention by J. Kinneavy.[3] He points out that no one has ever found the source of the NT's concept of 'belief', which it frequently adds to the Hebrew scriptures' sense of πίστις as 'faithfulness'. He argues that this additional concept comes from Hellenistic culture, primarily from rhetoric. He points out that NT scholars have doubted any Greek origin for a positive notion of belief because they are familiar only with the Platonic tradition of exalting knowledge over belief. But this tradition does not reflect the full picture of Hellenistic society. As pointed out above, even some philosophers valued belief over the impossibility of secure knowledge. But even more among rhetoricians and the dominant rhetorical culture, we find a high value placed upon belief. In fact, rhetoricians and Christians used the same word for belief: πίστις meant both 'a belief' and 'a persuasion', the counterparts of πίστεις, the rhetorical 'means of persuasion'.

Kinneavy, like Kennedy, recognizes that the Hebrew texts are just as rhetorical as those of the NT; the difference lies in the former's lack of any concept of their own persuasive techniques. Thus, faith, in the Hebrew scriptures, is a matter of relationship, of trust and obedience, not of persuasion and belief. This contrasts with conceptions of faith in Philo and Josephus, who add to the Hebraic concept of faithfulness the

---

1. Kennedy, *New Testament Interpretation*, p. 3.
2. Isa. 55.11. Ordinary human speech, however, could only be viewed as purposeful in the negative sense criticized by Plato's Socrates: making the worse case appear the better: Isa. 29.21; 32.7; 59.4, 13b-15a.
3. Kinneavy, *Greek Rhetorical Origins*.

element of assent due to verbal argument. This same addition Kinneavy also finds common in the NT texts. Thus, he concludes, Judaism in a Hellenistic culture easily combined two concepts: Hebraic faithfulness and Hellenistic belief produced by the persuasiveness of speech. This Hellenistic-Jewish understanding then became normative in the NT.

However, like most other arguments which seek to link Christianity to Hellenistic culture by direct conceptual dependence, Kinneavy's argument falls short. The differences in conceptions are just as illuminating as the similarities. Kinneavy stresses that the recipient of persuasive discourse freely assents to knowledge of the subject matter if he or she believes that this assent is to his or her good. To some extent, this aspect of Hellenistic rhetoric overlaps that of faith in the NT, but often the understanding is radically different. 'Free assent' hardly accords with 'it depends not upon man's will. . . he hardens the heart of whomever he wills' (Rom. 9.15, 18). Nor does 'knowledge of the subject matter' accord with 'no one comprehends the thoughts of God except the Spirit of God'. Nor does the 'good' of the recipient accord with, 'he died for all, that those who live might live no longer for themselves' (2 Cor. 5.15). NT texts generally see faith as a result of God's will: 'No one can say "Jesus is Lord" except by the Holy Spirit' (1 Cor. 12.3b). Only secondly, because of God's love and grace, do people choose, understand, and ultimately or even proximately benefit. Understanding, choice, and benefit are the foundations of happy civic life, but faith sees the end of the πόλις in the apocalyptic act of God in Jesus Christ.

So Kinneavy's conceptual argument fails; nevertheless I am persuaded that Christian proclamation and resultant belief are best understood in the context of Hellenistic rhetoric. Though Christianity did not simply borrow the rhetorical concept of πίστις, it did use the concept as a metaphor. In other words, although the first Christian preachers, teachers, and pastors never *equated* their situation to that of the rhetors, they could not escape *analogies* between the two.[1] Both

---

1. As Tracy (*Plurality and Ambiguity*, pp. 20-21) points out, such difference in similarity is the source of most understanding: 'To recognize possibility is to sense some similarity to what we have already experienced or understood. But similarity here must be described as similarity-in-difference, that is, analogy. . . Otherness and difference rarely become sameness or even similarity. Otherness and difference can become, however, genuine possibility: the as other, the as different becomes the as possible. Thus we find ourselves discovering similarities-in-difference, that is,

they and the rhetors employed verbal πίστεις to provoke πίστις, but one was civic, the other apocalyptic.

Also unlike rhetors, but parallel to Hebrew prophets, the NT writers believed they had been entrusted with a revelation and a commission to witness to that revelation. 'That which was from the beginning... which we have heard, which we have looked upon and touched with our hands... we proclaim to you' (1 Jn 1.3). 'I did not receive the gospel I preach from man, nor was I taught it, but it came through a revelation of Jesus Christ' (Gal. 1.11). Even their own words they considered not their own but God's (Mk 10.20; Acts 6.7; 19.20; 1 Cor. 2.13; 1 Thess. 2.13).

Thus, the NT writers tended to see the source, authority, and aim of their speech as prophetic or apocalyptic, not civic.[1] But just as their rhetorical situation differed from that of civic rhetors, it differed from that of the prophets in two important respects. First, their preaching quickly became directed primarily toward people outside the traditional community of faith (i.e. Gentiles rather than Jews). Second, both those recipients and the speaker lived in a socio-linguistic world shaped by the conscious rhetoric of Hellenism. The first difference meant that proclamation aimed to provoke conversion before

---

analogies.' Cf. Gadamer (*Truth and Method*, pp. 388-89), who points out that language does not understand through direct conceptual relationships, but through similarity and metaphor: 'The universality of genus and the classificatory formation of concepts are far removed from the linguistic consciousness... If a person transfers an expression from one thing to the other, he has in mind something that is common to both of them, but this need not be in any sense generic universality. He is following, rather, his widening experience, which sees similarities... It is the genius of linguistic consciousness to be able to give expression to these similarities. This is its fundamental metaphorical nature, and it is important to see that it is the prejudice of a theory of logic that is alien to language if the metaphorical use of a word is regarded as not its real sense.' Cf. P. Ricœur (*Interpretation Theory: Discourse and the Surplus of Meaning* [Fort Worth: Texas Christian University Press, 1976], pp. 51-53) on similarity as difference in metaphor: 'A metaphor... is in effect, a calculated error, which brings together things that do not go together and by means of this apparent misunderstanding it causes a new hitherto unnoticed relation of meaning to spring up between the terms that previous systems of classification had ignored or not allowed... There are no live metaphors in a dictionary... A metaphor tells us something new about reality.' On the necessity for language to be broken to speak the truth, see S.M. Halloran ('Language and the Absurd', *PhilR* 6 [1974], pp. 97-108) who also points to metaphor as the paradigm of this deconstructive process.

1. Kennedy, *New Testament Interpretation*, pp. 6-8.

faithfulness. The second difference meant that the preachers' desires to provoke this πίστις were incarnated in Hellenistic rhetoric.

These two aspects of the evangelists' situation produced a new constraint for their rhetoric, a constraint which is resurrected in contemporary hermeneutical discussions. As part of a self-consciously rhetorical culture, the NT texts implicitly and often explicitly partake of the recognition that human realities occur in linguistic worlds. Just as philosophy could not escape the dominance of rhetoric, neither could the writers of the NT. Christian proclamation is thus subsumed to rhetoric. It strives not to establish itself vis-à-vis rational or empirical knowledge, but to discover and shape a linguistic world while simultaneously seeking to transcend that world. Its point of departure is not epistemology, but rhetoric.

By the same token, a hermeneutically conscious reader cannot treat biblical texts as somehow separate from the universal hermeneutics of texts. As K. Froehlich put it,

> God has the same problem with human language we all have. This is the price of incarnation. . . Language always involves a speaker and a listener. The process of reception, language as it is *heard*, must be part of the investigation . . . The entire web of human relationships and their key role in the perception of reality plays into the interpretation of language.[1]

Thus, most contemporary hermeneutics share in the '"linguistic revolution" of the twentieth century, from Saussure and Wittgenstein to contemporary literary theory'. The 'hallmark' of this revolution 'is the recognition that meaning is not simply something "expressed" or "reflected" in language. . . It is not as though we had meanings, or experiences, which we then proceed to cloak with words.'[2] Rather, 'we understand in and through the languages available to us'.[3] 'What this suggests, moreover, is that our experience as individuals is social to its roots; for there can be no such thing as private language, and to imagine a language is to imagine a whole form of social life.'[4]

---

1. K. Froehlich, 'Biblical Hermeneutics on the Move', *A Guide to Contemporary Hermeneutics: Major Trends in Biblical Interpretation* (ed. D.K. McKim; Grand Rapids: Eerdmans, 1986), p. 177.
2. T. Eagleton, *Literary Theory: An Introduction* (Minneapolis: University of Minnesota Press, 1983), p. 60.
3. Tracy, *Plurality and Ambiguity*, p. 48.
4. Eagleton, *Literary Theory*, p. 60.

Communis Sensus

This social and linguistic nature of meaning is implicit in everything the rhetoricians taught. If one wants the community to reach some view, one cannot address that community in any language. Rather, the orator must meet his audience in a shared communal language. Thus, even diction must follow common usage, for 'usage is the surest pilot in speaking, and we should treat language as currency minted with the public stamp'.[1] This is the kind of insight given us by the linguistic theory of Saussure: the signifier is an arbitrary convention of societies; only within the conventions can *communi*-cation take place. Like modern linguistic theory, Quintilian had little use for etymology, since current usage, not past history, communicates in a given community: 'Archaic words must be used sparingly and must not. . . be drawn from the remote past. . . What a faulty thing is speech, whose prime virtue is clearness, if it requires an interpreter to make its meaning plain!'[2] 'The very cardinal sin', according to Cicero, 'is to depart from the language of everyday life, and the usage approved by the sense of the community (*communis sensus*)'.[3]

In classical rhetoric and modern linguistics, then, the speaker's choice of language is constrained by the linguistic world of the audience. The same is true not only of diction, but of all levels of signification, from words to genres. One prominent place the communal (common sense) nature of understanding appears is the idea of topics as developed by Aristotle in his *Topica* and applied in his *Rhetorica* and in the theories of later rhetoricians. As distinct from his *Prior* and *Posterior Analytics* which employed the syllogism to move from one necessary truth to another, the *Topica* sought 'to discover a method by which we shall be able to reason from generally accepted opinions'. The role of community is immediately apparent, since 'generally

---

1. Quintilian, *Institutio Oratoria* (trans. H.E. Butler; LCL; 4 vols.; London: Heinemann, 1920–22), 1.6.3; he goes on to qualify this comment (1.6.44) to mean the usage not of the majority but of the best educated. This is typical of Quintilian and much rhetorical tradition, which saw itself as safeguarding the sense not of the whole community but of the elite. To Quintilian, if usage were determined by the majority, 'we shall have a very dangerous rule affecting not merely style but life as well, a far more serious matter'. Thus, he recognized, but did not criticize, the ideological nature of rhetoric.

2. Quint. 1.6.41.

3. Cicero, *De Or.*, 1.3.12; affirmed by Quint. 8.25.

accepted opinions. . . are those which commend themselves to all or to the majority or to the wise'.[1]

Such appeal to opinion might seem to doom us to circular reasoning since 'we shall be dealing with people on the basis of their own opinions', but Aristotle is confident that a systematic method to eliminate self-contradiction from opinion will lead to practical knowledge. Such a method he calls dialectic, emphasizing its communal, conversational nature. In fact, he recognizes that even scientific demonstration is ultimately based on opinion rather than knowledge. Dialectic (as opposed to scientific demonstration)

> is useful in connection with the ultimate bases of each science; for it is impossible to discuss them at all on the basis of the principles peculiar to the science in question, since the principles are primary in relation to everything else, and it is necessary to deal with them through the generally accepted opinions on each point.[2]

This same ultimate primacy of rhetoric or hermeneutic over science is noted by K.-O. Apel:

> A scientist cannot *by* himself explain something *for* himself alone. In order even to know 'what' he is to explain, he must already have come to an understanding with others on the matter. As C.S. Pierce recognized, a semiotic community of interpretation always corresponds to the community of experimentation of natural scientists. Now, such an agreement on the intersubjective level can never be replaced by a procedure of objective science, precisely because it is a condition of the possibility of objective science.[3]

Aristotle sees a close relationship between dialectic and rhetoric (the difference seems to be primarily dialogue between two philosophers versus oration to an often uneducated audience). Thus, he repeatedly appeals to the *Topica* in his *Rhetorica*. For example, the rhetorician must be able to appeal to topics relevant to the audience's perception

---

1. Aristotle, *Topica* (trans. E.S. Forster; LCL; Cambridge, MA: Harvard University Press, 1960), 1.1.

2. Ar. *Top.* 1.2.

3. K.-O. Apel, 'Scientists, Hermeneutics, Critique of Ideology: An Outline of a Theory of Science from an Epistemological-Anthropological Point of View', trans. L.G. DeMichiel, pp. 330-31; similarly, J. Habermas, 'On Hermeneutics' Claim to Universality', p. 299; both in *The Hermeneutics Reader* (ed. K. Mueller-Vollmer; New York: Continuum, 1989). This insight is usually attributed to T.S. Kuhn, *The Structure of Scientific Revolutions* (Chicago: Chicago University Press, 1970).

of the case at hand.[1] If these topics are merely general, they will not be persuasive; they must touch specific beliefs about the case.[2] These topics are then formed into enthymemes. Enthymemes reason from the topics in loose ways by assuming rather than stating any premises which would sound self-evident; thus the world-view shared by the speaker and audience is taken for granted.[3]

Aristotle's insights into topical arguments were among his more influential contributions to the development of rhetorical theory. They were developed by Hermagoras into *stasis* theory, which became a fixture for most judicial rhetoric.[4] In this specialized form, lawyers could easily deduce on what generally believed basis (fact, definition, quality, or jurisdiction) they could invent and arrange their case. Thus, these topics connected the particular case to the *communis sensus* gathered in law, precedent, and general notions of equity.

The rhetoricians often distinguished between general topics, like status, and special ones which applied only to particular situations. The general ones sometimes troubled them because they seemed too abstracted from specific situations; yet special ones could be too rigid to reflect accurately the subtleties of immediate situations. Thus, experienced rhetors moved beyond the prescriptions of technical manuals, flexibly adapting their speech to specific situations.[5] This lesson of experience, even as it shows the weakness of topics, underlines their aim: to abstract, categorize, and fine tune, as would any casuistry, a communal understanding of real-life situations. That casuistries are by nature abstract or rigid or both does not detract from their basic ability to describe recurrent features of the common life of communities. But only by transcending their abstraction or rigidity does one reach the communal realities at hand.[6]

1. Aristotle, *The 'Art' of Rhetoric* (trans. John Henry Freese; LCL; London: Heinemann, 1926), 1.2.21-22; 2.22.10, 23.

2. Ar. *Rhet*. 2.22.11.

3. See also Quint. 5.14.14. Quintilian, who prefers the term *epicheireme*, emphasizes that its topics generally deal with the credible, rather than the true.

4. G.A. Kennedy, *Classical Rhetoric and Its Christian and Secular Traditions from Ancient to Modern Times* (Chapel Hill, NC: University of North Carolina Press, 1980), pp. 82-83.

5. Quint. 2.12.2.

6. That topics can be used non-stereotypically is T.Y. Mullins's point in 'Topos as a New Testament Form', *JBL* 99 (1980), pp. 541-47, against D.G. Bradley, 'The *Topos* as a Form in the Pauline Paraenesis', *JBL* 72 (1953), pp. 238-41.

Paul employed *topoi* in a typically Hellenistic manner, couching 'his message in the language of his hearers in order to insure a good reception for that message'.[1] So too, notes Mullins, do the letters of James, 1 Peter, and 1 John, and the Synoptic Gospels.[2] In each case, the *topos* supplied possible answers to typical communal questions, answers which the speaker shapes to the particular situation.

> What the *Topos* supplied was a set of conditions which measured the adequacy of the answers which the user made to common questions. . . Its function, therefore, was to assure the speaker or writer that he had given the kind of answer to the question which his audience would be most likely to accept as valid.[3]

The conventional nature of communication is underlined in those hermeneutical theories which follow Heidegger, since something is always understood in terms of something else. 'Only where word has already taken place can word take place. Only where there is already previous understanding can understanding take place.'[4] As Richard Palmer puts it, 'since communication is a dialogical relation, there is assumed at the outset a community of meaning shared by the speaker and the hearer'.[5]

This general hermeneutical point is just as relevant to understanding kerygmatic texts as any other. This is observed by Thielicke: 'God . . . wants us to turn to him spontaneously. We can do this, however, only if we are vanquished or inwardly persuaded by the claim of the message. . . The question is now relevant what points of contact the message finds in our prior understanding.'[6]

Rhetoric and New Communities

Since audience expectations shape rhetoric, the change in audience from Jewish to Gentile forced the NT writers to change language worlds. But incarnating the Christian message in the language of non-

---

1. Bradley, *'Topos'*, p. 238.
2. Mullins, *'Topos'*, p. 544.
3. Mullins, *'Topos'*, pp. 546-47.
4. Ebeling, 'Word of God and Hermeneutic', p. 96.
5. Palmer, *Hermeneutics*, p. 7.
6. H. Thielicke, *The Relation of Theology to Modern Thought-Forms, The Evangelical Faith*, I (Grand Rapids: Eerdmans, 1974), pp. 38-39.

Christian culture is fraught with danger, since content and form always co-inhere.[1]

Precisely this problem can be read in 1 Corinthians, where Paul employs words common in non-Christian use, such as σοφία and λόγος. But the discourse of 1 Corinthians forces the reader to interpret these words in senses unfamiliar to Hellenistic culture. Never could the Corinthians, without the intrusion of Paul's discourse, imagine how wisdom, the highest achievement of culture, could be weak and foolish; nor how weakness and foolishness (what is culturally despised) could be wise. In the conversation of which we hear one side, Paul is appalled at the Corinthians' interpretations of his language as justifying boastful, divisive behavior. Yet these interpretations were quite natural to Hellenistic usage; they had taken his persuasive speech as the human power of a cultured, wise, rhetorician, rather than as the mysterious power of God.[2]

Such misunderstandings Paul might have attempted to avoid by using terms foreign to Gentiles. Perhaps this is why John used 'rabbi' rather than 'teacher', aiming to ensure that Jesus would be perceived as a Jewish religious spokesman rather than a Hellenistic philosopher. But foreign terms still must be interpreted in language familiar to the *communis sensus* ('rabbi, which when translated [μεθερμηνευόμενον] means teacher' [Jn 1.38]). Instead, Paul attempted to overcome this problem, according to Robert Funk's hermeneutical analysis,[3] by beginning with the community sense and then 'deforming it, using words which originally implied power and syntactically relating them to the weakness of the cross'. Thus, the contrast of wisdom of word and word of the cross is 'a contrast between two words, two languages'.[4] It might be more accurate to say the words changed their meaning in a new 'language game' (Wittgenstein); or that they provoked new meaning through metaphor, juxtaposing two incompatible

1. On form and content, see Grassi, *Rhetoric as Philosophy*, pp. 26-27; C. Perelman, *The New Rhetoric and the Humanities: Essays on Rhetoric and Its Applications* (Boston: D. Reidel, 1979), pp. 28, 45; J. Kovesi, *Moral Notions* (London: Routledge & Kegan Paul, 1967), pp. 23-25; Tracy, *Plurality and Ambiguity*, pp. 42-43; Cic. *De Or.* 3.5.19, 24.

2. See my dissertation, 'Logos and Sophia: The Rhetorical Situation of 1 Corinthians 1–4 in the Light of Greco-Roman Rhetoric', Duke University 1990.

3. R.W. Funk, *Language, Hermeneutic, and the Word of God* (New York: Harper & Row, 1966), p. 296.

4. Funk, *Language*, p. 275.

terms (foolish—wisdom, wise—foolishness, strong—weakness).[1] In any case, the question for Paul, as Funk puts it, was 'whether the God of Jesus Christ was being given a presence in language'.[2]

Paul's word, then, could only be heard if the *communis sensus* changed. The rhetors understood their speech not just as shaped by the *communis sensus*, but as shaping that very sense. Isocrates' claim that rhetoric is the source of all civilization became a commonplace for rhetoric's apologists.[3]

> The persuasion that Isocrates invokes is no mere technique; rather, she is
> . . . the source of law, art, politics—in short, those activities that are constitutive of the fully human life. . . Persuasion is the very way of coming to the 'truth' of an action. In this more fundamental sense, persuasion is the political disposition upon which life in the *polis* is grounded.[4]

When language changes attitudes and shapes communities, it is not just referential, but rhetorical and performative. Such language is sometimes called a 'language event' by contemporary hermeneutical theorists, meaning that it has heuristic power to offer to its audience a possible new world springing from the old one. If that new world is embraced, its new language can become the language of a new community, with its own *communis sensus*. Paul explicitly describes such a situation: 'the word of the cross is folly to those who are perishing, but to us who are being saved it is the power of God' (1 Cor. 1.18).

So, in one sense, the first Christian preachers, like other orators, could communicate only insofar as they could speak within the previously established world of their audience. But if they stopped there, they would have been no more than just another group of civic orators. Instead, they claimed that while their rhetoric began with human

---

1. Ricœur, *Interpretation Theory*, p. 50; cf. Quint. 8.2.4-6: when no word exists, 'abuse or catachresis of words becomes necessary, while metaphor, also, which is the supreme ornament of oratory, applies words to things with which they have strictly no connection. Consequently propriety must be tested by the touchstone of understanding [*intellectus*], not of the ear.'

2. Funk, *Language*, p. 276.

3. E.g. Quint. 2.26.9: 'Never in my opinion would the founders of cities have induced their unsettled multitudes to form communities had they not moved them by the magic of their eloquence'. Cf. Cicero, *De Inventione* (trans. H.M. Hubbell; LCL; Cambridge, MA: Harvard University Press, 1949), 1.2.

4. F.I. Kane, 'Peithō and the *Polis*', *PhilR* 19 (1986), pp. 100, 117. Kane's distinction between rhetoric as τέχνη versus rhetoric as constitutive of human life parallels my distinction between rhetorical criticism as historical-critical tool versus paradigm for understanding.

words it did not end there: 'We also thank God constantly for this, that when you received the word of God which you heard from us, you accepted it not as the word of men but as what it really is, the word of God, which is at work in you believers' (1 Thess. 2.13). The old words had become new speech to a new community about a new world.

Community and Canon

Once having been formed, communities frequently maintain their communal language, world-view, and identity (i.e. their culture) by means of a canon of approved texts. For the rhetors, this was the fairly stable collection prescribed for study in primary and secondary education. This study was not mere schoolboy exercise, but the foundation of παιδεία (education or culture).[1] These texts included a wide variety of literature, comprised not only speeches of great orators but also poetry, drama, history, and philosophy; for in the liberal educational model designed by Isocrates, a rhetor could only have full integrity and be fully persuasive if he worked within the received humanistic tradition.

This emphasis on canon and tradition is a fixture in traditional Christian hermeneutics, particularly of more Catholic varieties, but it also appears prominently in the hermeneutics of Gadamer.[2] Gadamer argues that the prejudices we receive from our tradition are potential bearers of truth. The tradition need not be arbitrary nor contrary to reason; rather, prior generations have chosen to preserve and develop it. These traditions come to us primarily through language, which gives us a certain way of being in the world. Thus, the horizons of our world are not simply subjective, but given to us by an inter-subjective vision carried in language, the 'effective history' of conversations and texts. Moreover, our horizons are not static; rather, they can be changed by conversing, by translating, and by interpreting texts, since the horizons of other people, cultures, and times are related to, yet

---

1. A. Louth (*Discerning the Mystery: An Essay on the Nature of Theology* [Oxford: Clarendon, 1983], p. 42) appears quite correct in equating Gadamer's idea of *Bildung* with the Greek notion of παιδεία.

2. Gadamer, *Truth and Method*, pp. 241-58. On the parallels between Gadamer and Catholic tradition, see Louth, *Discerning the Mystery*, esp. pp. 107-109; Dockhorn ('Gadamer's *Truth and Method*', pp. 164-66) points to the role of rhetorical affects in reformation hermeneutics, especially Luther.

alien from our own. If we are to understand them, we must attempt to enter those alien worlds. But since we can never leave our own world, we can only seek to understand by allowing our horizons to 'fuse' with theirs. Particularly important among the texts are those which our tradition deems classical, for they offer horizons which have been repeatedly understood and affirmed, and are thus both authoritative and the source of our most productive prejudices.

The NT texts can be understood in this framework of communal world maintained within tradition, canon, and authority. The meanings of the texts are not to be found just in their original rhetorical situations (as seen through ours), but in their 'effective history' in shaping the world of Christians through the centuries (and much of the secular world as well) and, in turn, our own world. This parallels the insights of canonical criticism, which asks us to move away from the historicism of seeing the earliest strata as the locus of meaning toward finding the meaning in the whole movement of the text into the canon of the Christian community.[1]

This is expressed in a rhetorical way by the exponents of the New Hermeneutic (Fuchs and Ebeling), when they insist that the meaning of the text is found only when what was once preaching becomes that again as the community continually reappropriates it. 'The norm of our interpretation is preaching. The text is interpreted when God is proclaimed!'[2] That is, what is rhetorically effective in one situation is not necessarily effective in another. To us, a Pharisee has become synonymous with a hypocrite, but to the original hearers, he was a righteous man. The rhetorical truth of a parable like 'The Pharisee and the Publican' is lost unless the text is translated into our new rhetorical situation. Our preaching should thus translate the texts so they can again become language events, giving us a world and establishing our community.

Situations and Worlds

The NT texts, then, record for us the rhetoric of particular situations, rhetoric which aimed to draw the original readers deeper into realities

---

1. E.g. B.S. Childs, *The New Testament as Canon: An Introduction* (Philadelphia: Fortress, 1984).
2. E. Fuchs, 'The New Testament and the Hermeneutical Problem', *The New Hermeneutic* (ed. J.M. Robinson and J.B. Cobb, Jr; New Frontiers in Theology 2; New York: Harper & Row, 1964), p. 141.

which both intersected and transcended their everyday experience. The specificity of particular situations is of utmost importance to both rhetoric and hermeneutics. This situational nature of rhetorical speech constitutes the primary problem for NT hermeneutics as well as, paradoxically, the primary source of understanding. It is the primary problem because the NT texts were written not for us but for communities of Christians whose worlds are foreign to us in time, place, language, and culture. Yet it is also the primary source of understanding because, as Ricœur puts it, we are liberated from a situation and gain a world.[1] That is, when texts continue to speak to us, they do so not within the historicism of their original situations, nor within the limited reference of our own situations; rather, they speak of a possible way of being in the world, that is, faith. As Gadamer would put it, our horizons have fused with those of the text.

The importance of situation is emphasized by Gadamer, who points out that incarnation of meaning in language event is particularly congenial to Christian theology: 'The meaning of the word cannot be detached from the event of proclamation. Rather, its eventual character is part of the meaning itself.'[2] J.C. Weinsheimer expands on Gadamer's thought:

> The Platonic and Pythagorean idea of embodiment. . . is quite distinct from incarnation and implies a different theory of language as its analogue. In embodiment, the soul maintains an identity separate from the body. . . The relation of soul and body is something like that between content and form, or the thing in itself and its appearance. The content can take on any number of forms but it is not itself any one of them. . . In incarnation, by contrast, the Word becomes flesh. . . Spirit is not lessened but instead realized by its incarnation. The advent, moreover, is an event which, like all historical events, is unique; and thus in contrast to the ideality of the disembodied logos, the Christian doctrine of the incarnate Verbum insists on the reality of history. In the event of incarnation the word is uttered, spoken, and thereby realized.[3]

Thus, Christianity has a peculiar affinity with rhetoric, which notes the same analogy of body and soul to form and content. Cicero condemns the half-educated (by which he apparently means philosophers) who

---

1. Ricœur, *Interpretation Theory*, pp. 36-37.
2. Gadamer, *Truth and Method*, pp. 386-87; for the dialectic between God's word and human words, see also Ebeling, 'Word of God and Hermeneutic', p. 106.
3. J.C. Weinsheimer, *Gadamer's Hermeneutics: A Reading of Truth and Method* (New Haven: Yale University Press, 1985), pp. 233-34.

'separate words from thoughts as one might sever body from soul—
and neither process can take place without disaster'.[1]

These rhetorical and hermeneutical insights have relocated the purpose of reading the NT texts. No longer can the texts be seen as
depositories of universal propositional truths, so that our task is to
strip away the linguistic packaging to obtain the real content. No
longer can the original sense be the sole locus of meaning, for meanings are born in living conversation among communities. No longer
can the locus be the individual reader's response couched in existential
language. No longer can we have faith in programs of 'scientific' exegesis, which idealize scientific discourse as the norm of our linguisticality. Even in this, the modern approach has overlooked the fundamental rhetorical nature of science's own discourse (i.e. the construction of metaphors for what is essentially unknowable), treating scientific language instead as a one-to-one correspondence between labels
and realities.

Ironically, this was still true of Bultmann's hermeneutic, even
though he brought so much of Heidegger's hermeneutical insight into
NT exegesis. His dualism of a scientific world view on the one hand
and individualist existentialism on the other led him to dissatisfaction
with the crudity of what he took to be the misplaced scientific
(objectivizing) language of the text which necessitated its removal and
restatement as a prelinguistic existential decision. As Funk notes,
Bultmann's interpretation 'cannot. . . be brought into relation to the
specific existence of a given period or individual. . . The existentialist
analysis converts the particular into an abstraction, thereby cutting it
out of its historical nexus.'[2]

The specificity of the rhetorical situation, then, is not dissolved by
hermeneutics, but emphasized. We must first enter the alien world of
the text if we are to be liberated from our situations and gain a world.
The meaning is no longer bound to the original situation, but becomes
meaningful to us only when the horizons of our language world
stretch to touch or even fuse with those of the text's first home.

We can read of the young congregation in Corinth as it struggled
with divisiveness, and, when we incarnate our understanding in Paul's

---

1. Cicero, *De Or.* 3.5.19, 24.
2. R.W. Funk, 'The Hermeneutical Problem and Historical Criticism', *The New
Hermeneutic* (ed. J.M. Robinson and J.B. Cobb; New Frontiers in Theology 2; New
York: Harper & Row, 1964), p. 191.

rhetoric, see our own competition for esteem as the destructive opposite of Christ's suffering love. We can read of the righteousness of the Pharisees and their conflict with Jesus over the Sabbath and find language for our own dynamics of guilt, projection, self-justification, power, and liberation. We can read of kings and their relative impotence in the face of spiritual powers, and understand our sense of powerlessness over apocalyptic battles incarnated in genocide, planetary poisoning and mutual assured destruction, versus human movements of love and hope. These texts addressed the everyday world of the first century and forged a new world, a world charged with a God and his Son, with light and darkness, death and resurrection. Though much of that everyday world has vanished, our own everyday world can fuse with the new one, just as it has for Christian congregations throughout the centuries.

LIST OF CONTRIBUTORS

C. Clifton Black
Perkins School of Theology, Southern Methodist University, Dallas, Texas

Michael R. Cosby
Warner Pacific College, Portland, Oregon

Frederick W. Danker
Lutheran School of Theology at Chicago, Chicago, Illinois (Emeritus)

Yehoshua Gitay
Bornblum Judaic Studies, Memphis State University, Memphis, Tennessee

Rollin Grams
Nairobi Evangelical Graduate School of Theology, Nairobi, Kenya

Robert G. Hall
Hampden-Sydney College, Hampden-Sydney, Virginia

James D. Hester
University of Redlands, Redlands, California

Frank Witt Hughes
LaSalle University, Philadelphia, Pennsylvania

Robert Jewett
Garrett-Evangelical Theological Seminary, Evanston, Illinois

John R. Levison
North Park College, Chicago, Illinois

Clarice Martin
Princeton Theological Seminary, Princeton, New Jersey

Stephen Mark Pogoloff
Duke University, Durham, North Carolina

Vernon K. Robbins
Emory University, Atlanta, Georgia

Frank Thielman
Beeson Divinity School, Samford University, Birmingham, Alabama

Richard B. Vinson
Averett College, Danville, Virginia

Duane F. Watson
Malone College, Canton, Ohio

Wilhelm Wuellner
Pacific School of Religion, Berkeley, California

INDEXES

INDEX OF BIBLICAL REFERENCES

I. OLD TESTAMENT

INDEX OF ANCIENT AUTHORS

INDEX OF MODERN AUTHORS

JOURNAL FOR THE STUDY OF THE NEW TESTAMENT

Supplement Series